# THE EUROPEAN UNION'S NON-MEMBERS

The European Union (EU) is a supranational organization, whose reach and influence extends well beyond its member states, especially to the many states that have signed various forms of association agreement with it.

This book asks whether qualifying states who have eschewed EU membership experience negative effects on their legal and political self-governing abilities, or whether they manage their independence with few such effects. It explores the idea that the closer the affiliation a non-member state has with the EU, the more susceptible to hegemony the relationship appears to be. In addition, the book provides an overview of the total range of agreements the EU has with non-member states.

This text will be of key interest to scholars and students of EU/European studies, Scandinavian studies, European and comparative politics, international relations, and democratization studies.

**Erik O. Eriksen** is Professor in Political Science and Director of ARENA Centre for European Studies at the University of Oslo, Norway.

**John Erik Fossum** is Professor in Political Science at ARENA Centre for European Studies at the University of Oslo, Norway.

# Routledge studies on democratising Europe

Edited by Erik O. Eriksen and John Erik Fossum
*ARENA, University of Oslo*

**Routledge Studies on Democratising Europe** focuses on the prospects for a citizens' Europe by analysing the kind of order that is emerging in Europe. The books in the series take stock of the EU as an entity that has progressed beyond intergovernmentalism and consider how to account for this process and what makes it democratic. The emphasis is on citizenship, constitution-making, public sphere, enlargement, common foreign and security policy, and Europe society.

1. **Developing a Constitution for Europe**
   *Edited by Erik O. Eriksen, John Erik Fossum and Agustín José Menéndez*

2. **Making the European Polity**
   Reflexive integration in the EU
   *Edited by Erik O. Eriksen*

3. **Questioning EU Enlargement**
   *Edited by Helen Sjursen*

4. **The European Union and the Public Sphere**
   A communicative space in the making?
   *Edited by John Erik Fossum and Philip Schlesinger*

5. **Law, Democracy and Solidarity in a Post-national Union**
   The unsettled political order of Europe
   *Edited by Erik O. Eriksen, Christian Joerges and Florian Rödl*

6. **The New Politics of European Civil Society**
   *Edited by Ulrike Liebert and Hans-Jörg Trenz*

7. **Rethinking Democracy and the European Union**
   *Edited by Erik O. Eriksen and John Erik Fossum*

8. **The Politicization of Europe**
   Contesting the constitution in the mass media
   *Paul Statham and Hans-Jörg Trenz*

9. **Democratic Decision-making in the EU**
   Technocracy in disguise?
   *Anne Elizabeth Stie*

10. **States of Democracy**
    Gender and politics in the European Union
    *Edited by Yvonne Galligan*

11. **The European Union's Non-Members**
    Independence under hegemony?
    *Edited by Erik O. Eriksen and John Erik Fossum*

# THE EUROPEAN UNION'S NON-MEMBERS

Independence under hegemony?

*Edited by*
*Erik O. Eriksen and*
*John Erik Fossum*

LONDON AND NEW YORK

First published 2015
by Routledge
2 Park Square, Milton Park, Abingdon, Oxon OX14 4RN

and by Routledge
711 Third Avenue, New York, NY 10017

*Routledge is an imprint of the Taylor & Francis Group, an informa business*

© 2015 selection and editorial material, Erik O. Eriksen and John Erik Fossum; individual chapters, the contributors

The right of Erik O. Eriksen and John Erik Fossum to be identified as the authors of the editorial material, and of the authors for their individual chapters, has been asserted in accordance with sections 77 and 78 of the Copyright, Designs and Patents Act 1988.

All rights reserved. No part of this book may be reprinted or reproduced or utilised in any form or by any electronic, mechanical, or other means, now known or hereafter invented, including photocopying and recording, or in any information storage or retrieval system, without permission in writing from the publishers.

*Trademark notice*: Product or corporate names may be trademarks or registered trademarks, and are used only for identification and explanation without intent to infringe.

*British Library Cataloguing-in-Publication Data*
A catalogue record for this book is available from the British Library

*Library of Congress Cataloging-in-Publication Data*
A catalog record for this book has been requested

ISBN: 978-1-138-80751-8 (hbk)
ISBN: 978-1-138-92245-7 (pbk)
ISBN: 978-1-315-75103-0 (ebk)

Typeset in Bembo
by Apex CoVantage, LLC

# CONTENTS

| | |
|---|---|
| *List of tables and figures* | *vii* |
| *Notes on contributors* | *ix* |
| *Acknowledgements* | *xiii* |
| *Preface* | *xv* |

| | | |
|---|---|---|
| 1 | Introduction: Asymmetry and the problem of dominance<br>*Erik O. Eriksen and John Erik Fossum* | 1 |

**PART I**
**Forms of association without membership**      **15**

| | | |
|---|---|---|
| 2 | The European Union's different neighbourhood models<br>*Sieglinde Gstöhl* | 17 |
| 3 | The Swiss way: The nature of Switzerland's relationship with the EU<br>*Sandra Lavenex and René Schwok* | 36 |
| 4 | Switzerland: Bilateralism's polarising consequences in a very particular/ist democracy<br>*Joachim Blatter* | 52 |

## PART II
## Welcomed, inside, but still unwilling: Two EEA countries assessed          75

5  Despoiling Norwegian democracy          77
   *Erik O. Eriksen*

6  The EEA and the case law of the CJEU: Incorporation without participation?          102
   *Halvard Haukeland Fredriksen*

7  Iceland: A reluctant European          118
   *Baldur Thorhallsson*

8  Norway's constitutional acrobatics under the EEA Agreement          137
   *Eirik Holmøyvik*

9  Representation under hegemony? On Norway's relationship to the EU          153
   *John Erik Fossum*

10 National administrative sovereignty: Under pressure          173
   *Morten Egeberg and Jarle Trondal*

11 Reinforcing executive dominance: Norway and the EU's foreign and security policy          189
   *Helene Sjursen*

## PART III
## Sovereignty under hegemony          209

12 The United Kingdom, a once and future(?) non-member state          211
   *Christopher Lord*

13 Hegemony by association          230
   *Erik O. Eriksen and John Erik Fossum*

*Index*          *243*

# TABLES AND FIGURES

**Tables**

| | | |
|---|---|---|
| 10.1 | Percentage of Norwegian civil servants who say that the following bodies are important when it comes to influencing the agency's application of EU legislation | 181 |
| 10.2 | Percentage of Norwegian agency officials who say that the ministry is important when it comes to influencing the agency's application of EU legislation | 182 |
| 10.3 | Percentage of top leaders in Norwegian agencies who report about the relations that their own agency has with EU agencies, the European Commission and 'sister agencies' in other countries | 182 |
| 11.1 | Norway's agreements with the EU in the domain of foreign and security policy | 194 |

**Figures**

| | | |
|---|---|---|
| 10.1 | Number of employees in the European Commission | 177 |
| 10.2 | Number of EU agencies | 179 |

# NOTES ON CONTRIBUTORS

**Joachim Blatter** is Professor of Political Science at the University of Lucerne. His main fields of interests are conceptualizations and long-term transformations of governance and democracy. His current focus is on migration and its impact on national, transnational and cosmopolitan citizenship. Recent publications include 'Horizontalföderalismus und Schweizer Demokratie', *Swiss Political Science Review* (2010); 'Dual Citizenship and Theories of Democracy', *Citizenship Studies* (2011); and 'Conceptualizing and Evaluating (New) Forms of Citizenship between Nationalism and Cosmopolitanism' (co-authored with Andrea Schlenker), *Democratization* (2014).

**Morten Egeberg** is Professor of Public Policy and Administration at the Department of Political Science and ARENA Centre for European Studies, University of Oslo. His main fields of interest include the European Commission, EU agencies, national executives and the relationship between the EU level and national administration. His recent publications include 'The European Commission: From Agent to Political Institution', *Public Administration* (2014); 'A Not So Technocratic Executive?' (co-authored with Åse Gornitzka and Jarle Trondal), *West European Politics* (2014); and 'The Quest for Order: Unravelling the Relationship between the European Commission and European Union Agencies' (co-authored with Jarle Trondal and Nina Vestlund), *Journal of European Public Policy* (2015).

**Erik O. Eriksen** is Director and Professor of Political Science at ARENA Centre for European Studies, University of Oslo. His main fields of interest are political theory, democratic governance, public policy and European integration. Recent publications include *The Unfinished Democratization of Europe* (2009), *Rethinking Democracy and the European Union* (co-edited with John Erik Fossum, 2012), *Det* *norske paradoks* [*The Norwegian Paradox*] (co-edited with John Erik Fossum, 2014) and *The Normativity of the European Union/Die Normativität der Europäischen Union* (2014).

**John Erik Fossum** is Professor of Political Science at ARENA Centre for European Studies, University of Oslo. His main fields of interests include political theory, democracy and constitutionalism in the EU and Canada, Europeanisation and transformation of the nation state. Recent publications include *The Constitution's Gift: A Constitutional Theory for a Democratic European Union* (co-authored with Agustín José Menéndez, 2011), *Practices of Interparliamentary Coordination in International Politics* (co-edited with Ben Crum, 2013) and *Det norske paradoks* [*The Norwegian Paradox*] (co-edited with Erik O. Eriksen, 2014).

**Sieglinde Gstöhl** is Professor and Director of EU International Relations and Diplomacy Studies and at the College of Europe in Bruges. Her main fields of interests are EU external relations (particularly EU trade policy, European Neighbourhood Policy, EU external representation and EU diplomacy), theories of international relations, and global governance. Recent publications include *European Union Diplomacy* (co-edited with Dieter Mahncke, 2012), *The Neighbours of the EU's Neighbours: Diplomatic and Geopolitical Dimensions beyond the European Neighbourhood Policy* (co-edited with Erwan Lannon, 2014), and *The European Union's Broader Neighbourhood: Challenges and Opportunities for Cooperation beyond the European Neighbourhood Policy* (co-edited with Erwan Lannon, 2015).

**Halvard Haukeland Fredriksen** is Professor of Law at the University of Bergen and an associate of the Bergen Centre for Competition Law and Economics (BECCLE). His main field of interest is EU/EEA law, in particular the interface between European and national law. Recent publications include 'Bridging the Widening Gap between the EU Treaties and the Agreement on the European Economic Area', *European Law Journal* (2012); 'State Liability in EU and EEA Law: The Same or Different?', *European Law Review* (2013); and 'The Troubled Relationship between the Supreme Court of Norway and the EFTA Court – Recent Developments', in P.-C. Müller-Graff and O. Mestad (eds) *The Rising Complexity of European Law* (2014).

**Eirik Holmøyvik** is Professor of Law at the University of Bergen. His main fields of interests are constitutional law and legal history. Recent publications include *Maktfordeling og 1814* [Division of Power and 1814] (2012), *Tolkingar av Grunnlova* [Interpretations of the Constitution] (ed., 2013) and *Writing Democracy: The Norwegian Constitution 1814–2014* (co-edited with Karen Gammelgaard, 2014).

**Sandra Lavenex** is Professor of European and International Politics at the University of Geneva. Her main fields of interests include the external effects of European integration, EU and international democracy promotion, international migration policy and power shifts in global economic regulation. Recent publications include *Democracy in the Age of Globalization and Mediatization* (co-authored with Hanspeter Kriesi, Daniel Bochsler, Jörg Matthes, Marc Bühlmann and Frank Esser, 2012) and 'Demoi-cracy in the European Union: Principles, Institutions, Policies' (co-authored with Francis Cheneval and Frank Schimmelfennig), *Journal of European Public Policy* (2014).

**Christopher Lord** is Professor of Political Science at ARENA Centre for European Studies, University of Oslo. His main fields of interests include the study of democracy, legitimacy and the European Union. Recent publications include 'The EU's Many Representative Modes: Colliding? Cohering?' (co-authored with Johannes Pollak), *Journal of European Public Policy* (2010), *Multilayered Representation in the European Union* (co-edited with Tatjana Evas and Ulrike Liebert) (2012), and 'The Legitimacy of Co-Decision', *Journal of European Public Policy* (2013).

**René Schwok** is Professor at the Global Studies Institute and Department of Political Science and International Relations at the University of Geneva. He is Director of the Master Programme in European Studies and holder of Jean Monnet Chair in Political Science. His main fields of interests are European Union politics, external relations of the EU, and international relations of Switzerland. Recent publications include *Switzerland – European Union: And Impossible Membership?* (2009), *Die Schweizer Aussenpolitik nach Ende des Kalten Kriegs* (2014) and *L'Union européenne favorise-t-elle la paix?* (2015).

**Helene Sjursen** is Professor of Political Science at ARENA Centre for European Studies, University of Oslo. Her fields of interests are the EU as an international actor, the EU's foreign and security policy, and EU enlargement. Recent publications include 'Norge og EU – rett og politikk' [Norway and the EU – Law and Politics] (co-edited with John Erik Fossum), *Nytt Norsk Tidsskrift* (2008); *The EU's Common Foreign and Security Policy: The Quest for Democracy* (2012); and 'A Certain Sense of Europe? Defining the EU through Enlargement', *European Societies* (2012).

**Baldur Thorhallsson** is Professor of Political Science and Jean Monnet Chair in European Studies at the Faculty of Political Science, and Programme and Research Director at the Centre for Small State Studies at the University of Iceland. His main fields of interests are small state studies, European integration and Iceland's domestic and foreign policy. Recent publications include 'Iceland's Economic Crash and Integration Takeoff: An End to European Union Scepticism?' (co-authored with Christian Rebhan), *Scandinavian Political Studies* (2011); 'Financial Crises in Iceland and Ireland' (co-authored with Peadar Kirby), *Journal of Common Market Studies* (2012); and 'The Icelandic Economic Collapse: How to Overcome Constraints Associated With Smallness?' *European Political Science* (2013).

**Jarle Trondal** is Professor of Public Administration at the University of Agder and at ARENA Centre for European Studies, University of Oslo. His main fields of interests include public administration, the EU as a political system, administrative integration and transformation, the EU/EEA and Norway, the European Commission, and EU committee governance. Recent publications include *An Emergent European Executive Order* (2010), 'The Rise of European Administrative Space: Lessons Learned' (co-authored with B. Guy Peters), *Journal of European Public Policy* (2013), and *The Palgrave Handbook of the European Administrative System* (co-edited with Michael W. Bauer, 2015).

# ACKNOWLEDGEMENTS

Every book is a collective effort. In preparing this book we have benefitted a lot from our colleagues at ARENA and from the many good colleagues that make up our vital research networks across Europe. This book is part of the ARENA-led Eurodiv project, which is funded under the Norwegian Research Council's Europe in Transition programme. Some of the chapters in the book emanate from the book *Det Norske Paradoks* [The Norwegian Paradox] (Universitetsforlaget 2014) which we co-edited, and was one of the publications under the project 'The Norwegian Constitution in a Changing European Context'.

We are very grateful for the administrative support we have obtained from the ARENA administrative staff. Amidst numerous pressing obligations they, in particular Marit Eldholm and Veronica Thun, have guided the process of turning a collection of papers into a coherent manuscript. We would also like to thank the doctoral students at ARENA who have contributed with invaluable support in the critical final stage of this process.

*Erik O. Eriksen and John Erik Fossum*
*Oslo, December 2014*

# PREFACE

Europe is differentially integrated. Most European countries are members of the European Union (EU), those that are not are associated through a complex tapestry of arrangements of different density. The EU is also highly differentiated. Not all EU members are members of the Eurozone, and some are not part of Schengen. Whether there is a Europe of *different speeds* or a Europe of permanent *concentric circles* is not settled. The Eurozone crisis raised possibilities of the euro area breaking up, or of several countries leaving the euro area. At least one member state (the UK) has floated the idea of renegotiating its relationship with the EU. The EU was differentiated before the crisis struck, but a Europe of differentiated arrangements was not considered a defining trait of the system as the exemptions that states had obtained were conceived of as temporary. Hence, integration was seen as a 'one-way street', albeit at different speeds. The crisis has brought up the prospect that states may come to occupy *permanently* different roles and *statuses* and that this is a recognised and defining feature of the EU. What would that entail for the idea of a united and democratic Europe? Can the idea of a Europe of concentric circles, a Europe of permanent differentiation be sustained in democratic terms, or does it lead to hegemony where the core dominates the rest? Can states have differentiated membership status in the same Union and yet preserve sovereignty and self-rule, or will such a situation engender domination?

In order to shed light on these issues this book addresses the relations between the European Union and its associated non-members. There are two main categories of non-members: those that want to be members but do not (yet) qualify and those that qualify but are not willing to join. The main focus of this book is on this latter group of states that have developed ever closer relations with the EU. Their experiences contain important lessons for the ongoing debate on what kind of relationship states can have without being dominated. What do the conditions for the EU's associated non-members tell us about the prospects for democracy in a differentiated Europe?

The book's title, *The European Union's non-members: Independence under hegemony?* suggests that non-EU members' relationship may entail loss of independence and have worrying implications. Are the people in the associated member states able to govern themselves through law and politics, or are they subject to alien rule? The question is motivated by the fact that these states are closely associated to a constantly changing and integrating entity over which they have no formal say. They may find not only that they relinquish sovereignty but also that this is not recompensed through co-determination. The question we discuss is whether the upshot of this is the loss of independence under hegemony and dominance. The assumption we work from is that in contemporary Europe the associated non-members, in effect, experience some form of submission, whose effects could resemble living under hegemony. The apparent paradox of this condition being particularly relevant to those non-member states that are most closely affiliated with the EU is given particular emphasis. For them there is lawmaking without representation. An interesting point is that this effect is likely not to be experienced under full membership. That there may be a direct relationship between magnitude of affiliation and experience of hegemony is important to establish.

# 1

# INTRODUCTION

## Asymmetry and the problem of dominance

*Erik O. Eriksen and John Erik Fossum*

The European Union's motto is 'united in diversity', which has a deep historical resonance. Europe throughout the centuries has seen a constant tension between unity and diversity, between uniformity and differentiation. The post-war emergence of the European Union gives a distinct twist to this story. This process of integration must navigate and (re)direct the underlying centripetal and centrifugal forces; it cannot on its own completely reshape them. The trend has long been cast as one towards further integration, which is inevitable and the telos of Europe. That story has tended to downplay the important interplay between integration and differentiation that marks contemporary Europe.

The European Union (EU) has slowly grown from a geographically delimited Western European 'club' of six members based on a rather narrow remit of action to an almost continent-wide union of 28 member states whose realm of action is wide-encompassing, indeed. Membership in the EU is voluntary, but states that are interested in becoming members must comply with a set of entrance requirements. Any member state may also choose to leave the Union, and there are explicit provisions in place to regulate how exit is to take place.[1] But most European countries want to be members and no state has as yet left the Union.

A general assumption is that the EU is an *international organisation*, viz., an organisation made up of states whose main purpose is to serve the interests and concerns of the member states. Membership is voluntary as is the relinquishment of sovereignty. So the EU may be seen as belonging in the category of international organisations. In today's world that state-centric view is increasingly questioned as international organisations take on and exercise functions that exceed well beyond this orthodox view. The European Union is the most explicit site in which this argument is contested. Formally speaking, the EU is an international organisation because the states are the masters of the treaties, but whether the EU at all should be placed in the (extended) category of international organisation is hotly debated.

Simply put, at issue is whether the EU is a means of consolidating and aiding the existing system of states, or whether the EU epitomises a broader process of transformation, where the European system of states is profoundly transformed under the weight of European integration.

Today's EU is clearly more than what we generally associate with an international organisation. Many depict it as a transnational organisation in order to distance it from both an international organisation and a state. The EU is a system of constitutionally regulated binding interstate cooperation where states *and citizens* co-decide issues of common concern. Member states pool and share sovereignty in a set of common institutions. A distinguishing and distinctive feature is that EU law enjoys direct effect and supremacy in those areas where the EU has been granted competence from the member states.

The exceptional precepts of EU law pertaining to supremacy and direct effect are but some of the aspects of the EU that serve to underline that the Union has strong effects on the member states. These effects are shown in the ability to pursue a steady increase in EU membership, a process that is *coupled with* an ever-deeper EU penetration into the affairs of the member states. This penetration does not stop at the EU's boundaries and is also found – with depth depending on the form of association – in the many arrangements that the EU has formed with non-members. These association arrangements effectively extend EU norms and regulations far beyond the EU's boundaries. The issue that concerns this book is whether, to what extent and how the EU affects (affiliated) non-member states across Europe (and beyond).

More specifically, what happens to states that are close to the *gravitational centre* but are not members of the EU? With proximity to the gravitational centre we refer to the extent to which EU norms and rules effectively apply on a non-member's territory as well, despite it formally not being a member of the EU. The closer a non-member state is to the gravitational centre, the more encompassing – in terms of breadth and depth – its incorporation in the EU is.

There are two main categories of affiliated non-member states: (a) those that qualify for membership but have either declined membership or failed to apply for it and (b) those that do not qualify but seek as close a relationship to the EU as possible (preferably through becoming member states). Do such non-member states experience negative effects on their national systems of democratic governing from their affiliations with the EU, are they able to sustain their independence with few such effects or do effects vary with form of affiliation?

The main focus of this book is on the former group of states that qualify for EU membership, but have not taken it up and have instead entered into binding cooperation with the EU through different forms of agreements or through a distinct category of 'associated non-membership'. Within this group of states there are two main types of affiliation: (a) the multilateral, or two-pillar, system that ties the states in the European Economic Area (EEA)[2] to the EU (Norway, Iceland and Lichtenstein) and (b) the system of bilateral sectorial agreements that Switzerland has established with the EU.[3]

The assumption is that the closer the affiliation a non-member state has to the EU, the more susceptible to hegemony the relationship will be. The book's title, *The European Union's non-members: Independence under hegemony?*, was chosen precisely to underline what is at stake here. To what extent is that the case? Is it something that marks a state's EU relations whether these are regulated through a *multilateral agreement* such as the EEA (here discussed in relation to the cases of Iceland and Norway) or through a set of sectorial *bilateral agreements* (with Switzerland as the sole case)?

## A danger of hegemonic dominance

The basic problem of the relationship between the EU and its associated members is that of asymmetry and arbitrary power, viz., *dominance*, which is rule without justification. Dominance occurs when the citizens are subjected to others' will; to arbitrary power. Such rule is undemocratic because it does not appropriately track the interests, views or wills of the citizens (Richardson 2002). Dominance is illicit because of the dominators' capacity to interfere in zones of freedom (Pettit 1999). It is thus referred to as a kind of unfreedom that people experience when they are in the power of others, a form of suppression that can in principle be eliminated by those who have installed it. It is a kind of unfreedom that carries 'the whiff of illicitness' (Shapiro 2012: 308). Democratic forms of rule are antithetic to dominance as they put the citizens on an equal footing and assign the citizens the rights to enforce their will, also against the will of the power holders. Even if it is easy to associate domination with hierarchy, it is, clearly, not synonymous with hierarchy.[4] As we discuss in Chapter 13, hierarchies amount to dominance when those affected are excluded from participating in decision-making. Rather absence of hierarchy can be a source of dominance, as unchecked power then likely prevails. In such settings decisions are typically made in opaque and unpredictable ways; there are no proper procedures to challenge and there is no explicit authority to hold to account. Dominance may therefore occur in principally different institutional configurations that range from anarchy to hierarchy. People are more vulnerable to domination in settings where their basic interests are seriously affected.

In international affairs the dominator is a hegemon – a hegemonic state – that wields power over subordinate states. The EU may take the form of a hegemon that autocratically rules the associated states because of the way its affairs with the associated non-members are arranged. The EU is not in itself a hegemon, but the way the relationship is organised pits it over and against the associated states. The EU makes laws – its rules – not via the threat of might or by direct military force but by the manner in which it makes the associated members receivers not makers of the law. The countries have to adopt the better part of the EU's *aquis communitaire* and the ongoing legislation in order to have access to the internal market or to the Schengen agreement. But because the arrangement is voluntary, and the EU wants the associated countries to be members, it is not a hegemonic relationship by intent. Rather, the EU has taken the shape and function of a hegemon unintendedly.

It is hegemony created by complex interdependence and the European integration process.

Hegemony is undemocratic, and dominance is 'unconstitutional'. Therefore, the book's focus is on the constitutional-democratic implications of the changing nature of state sovereignty in contemporary Europe. The emphasis is on clarifying what these changes entail for democratic self-rule in EU-affiliated non-member states. This examination is important for at least four reasons.

First is that it provides a comprehensive assessment of the implications for the states under consideration, including discerning similarities and differences between them. Is it so that different forms of formal association have different effects?

Second, when viewed from the perspective of the EU these forms of non-membership affiliation are cases of horizontal differentiation (Leuffen et al. 2013). In that sense the book sheds added light on the constitutional-democratic implications of differentiated integration, paying particular heed to the effects this has on the states rather than the institutions at the EU level, which is typically the focus in studies of differentiated integration.

Third is that the book pays specific attention to EU member states that seek to renegotiate their status with the EU (such as the UK). In addition to paying explicit attention to the UK debate, two additional points about this book's relevance to that debate need to be mentioned. One is that a member state that seeks to renegotiate its relationship to the EU would still normally belong to the category of states that qualify for membership but for various reasons does not want to be a full member. In that sense it will belong in the same category of states as the ones that form the core of this book. The other point is that the investigation that is undertaken in this book covers *the entire range of ways* in which states that qualify for EU membership have organised their relations with the EU. These association forms will very likely figure in subsequent discussions about an exited state's relations with the EU. How easily transferable the findings will be is of course a matter of conjecture. The UK is a major European state and a global player, whereas this book focuses on small states. The analysis provided here does nevertheless give us some sense of the wiggle room for states that seek close association without EU membership. That ties up with the broader issue of how firmly the EU holds on to legal unity and uniformity across its policy areas versus how accepting it is of opt-outs, special arrangements and differentiation in general.

Fourth, and finally, the main theoretical aim of the book is to analyse the changing conditions for state sovereignty and its implications for constitutional democracy in today's Europe. Can individual states within the EU's remit retain their sovereignty and democracy, or is EU membership the only way to regain some control over the agenda?

In the following section we provide a brief overview of the basic tenets of modern constitutionalism – not only why there is a promise of democratic self-rule but also why there is disagreement concerning what it takes to realise it. Thereafter, we spell out in further detail the nature of the European challenge, with particular emphasis on how it affects the core tenets of democratic constitutionalism. Based on the examinations in these two sections we identify a set of evaluation criteria – core components of constitutional democracy – that will be of direct relevance to the assessment of the cases. In the subsequent section, we provide a brief overview of the two main forms of affiliation in order to clarify the nature and density of these – how binding and committing they are. The final section outlines the contents of the book.

## Democratic constitutionalism

It is a widely held assumption that in the modern constitutional democratic state there is congruence between state and popular sovereignty in the sense that the people governs itself through the institutions of the state and that those self-same institutions ensure the continuity and integrity of the democratic people. The core components of this by now dominant constitutional doctrine or even constitutional orthodoxy are basic rights that ensure citizens' autonomy, a division of powers (legislative, executive and judiciary) and popular sovereignty. Constitutional orthodoxy is based on the notion of the constitution as constitutive of the national community. Constitutions define nation states and nation states give rise to and sustain constitutions. Democracy is equated with the rule of a given – nationally defined – people or democratic *demos*.

This notion is challenged in a world marked by increased mutual interdependence and the development of a comprehensive body of international law. Institutional arrangements such as the Council of Europe (which spawned the European Convention on Human Rights and the European Court of Human Rights) and the EU – both of which operate beyond the territorially delimited national community exercise political influence with constitutional implications. They – the EU in particular – constrain and condition the domestic exercise of law and they curtail state sovereignty. Today it is widely held that a state is truly sovereign only if it upholds human rights. Accordingly, many argue that constitutional orthodoxy is at a historical crossroads, or might even be in the process of being undermined. European integration and globalisation more generally, sceptics contend, mutually reinforce each other so as to undermine state sovereignty and democratic self-governing.

From a national perspective it appears that the problem of increased mutual interdependence can be avoided only if a state avoids being bound by the European integration process. If that is not possible, the second best option is to enter into only those forms of binding collaboration that do not have negative constitutional implications. Those are the considerations that motivate the forms of non-membership association that such states as Iceland, Norway and Switzerland (and principalities such as Liechtenstein) have chosen to regulate their relations with the EU.

These association arrangements, however, also engender problems and challenges. From an interest-based perspective, going solo becomes deer when others choose cooperation and integration. Going alone easily becomes a suboptimal strategy when it comes to handling mutual interdependence. There are consequences related to being seen as free riding on others' endeavours to solve collective action problems. There is an element of moral hazard – the act of taking a risk when other people stand to pay any damage – which may affect the standing and perception of affiliated non-members and that may be detrimental to solving their problems in the long run. What is also important to note is that a nation state approach is not necessarily in synch with democratic constitutionalism itself. The term for constitution in German is *Verfassung*, a pact made up of its authors. The modern idea of constitution is that it depicts a horizontal association of citizens whose rules are authored by those subjected to it. This is reflected in modern constitutions as they contain a set of universal principles, such as individual freedom, legal equality, tolerance, freedom of conscience and expression – principles that apply to all persons regardless of membership in a nation state. They are not simply based on the will of one single people or the citizens' arbitrary preferences but claim to be based on universally applicable principles of reason. In other words, the law is not based on power or national identity – on pre-political essentials – but on principles that all will be able to subscribe to as members of a legal community. Constitutional democracy with its principles of legal certainty, predictability and popular participation are intended to ensure a just, dignity-protecting and reason-based system of governing. We therefore find the same principles pertaining to the citizens' equal and free rights, legal certainty, and participation rights in all modern (Western) constitutions. The fact that they are also present in human rights declarations serves as a clear reminder that democratic constitutionalism is meant not only to protect the integrity of a territorially based people, but also to protect citizens' rights and dignity *in general*.

Constitutions always develop in an international context. They develop in political contexts that are made up of states and international conventions and organisations. In overall terms, it is not 'the people' as a collective mythological entity that legitimates the modern constitution but a self-legislating political community. In other words, it is not the notion of ethnic or national homogeneity – *Volksgemeinschaft* – that forms the basis for modern constitutional thought but the citizens' self-governing through law and politics as we are well familiar with from the philosophical tradition notably reflected in the works of Rousseau and Kant.

It follows from this that nationally enclosed democracy can only be realised if there are options for citizens to launch complaints to external bodies or agencies against rights violations. Human rights are universal and refer to humanity as such – they are correct according to the free will of autonomous persons – and they can, when positivised, be enforced by courts. When not sanctioned by proper democratic institutions such rights enforcement implies *juridification*. Democracy on its part refers to a particular community of legal consociates who come together to make binding collective decisions. Democracy depends on particular states with very different political cultures, which are geared towards self-maintenance: the primary responsibility of the decision makers is their own constituency at the potential detriment of individual rights and the interests of other states. Hence, democracies may be *illiberal* (Eriksen 2009: 102ff.).

Every 'people' can thus err and get it wrong and needs correctives, majoritarian decisions can violate the rights and integrity of individuals and minorities, and national constitutional – higher law – is not always capable of holding back 'a people' that is enraged and politically mobilized. Supranational bodies are needed to prevent nation states from violating citizens' rights, to prevent that a state violates the rights of other states and to prevent its policies from having negative effects on others (without due compensation). But supranational bodies must also be subject to democratic oversight and control. Supranational legal protection in the shape of court-driven juridification will be a problem as long as there is no supranational democracy, because the citizens are subject to rules and laws that they have not participated in making. Because of globalisation and complex interdependence a world citizenship might be required.

Where does the EU figure in this picture? In what sense and to what extent does the Union that is neither a fledgling nation state nor an international organisation relate to the global-legal transformations?

## *The European challenge*

A central question that has long been discussed in the European context is whether the European integration process is steeped in and capable of drawing on the core principles of democratic constitutionalism. The question is: Insofar as the EU is a constitutional construct *of some kind* (as is clearly implied in the notions of supremacy and direct effect), to what extent is it informed by and capable of propounding the norms and principles embedded in democratic constitutionalism?

There are two main positions on this question in the European debate. On one hand, we find the proponents of the so-called *no demos* thesis which asserts that a European constitution must be steeped in a European people (Etzioni 2013; Grimm 1995, 2004; Miller 1995). They underline that there is no European people; furthermore, the EU is not an organisation that will prove capable of establishing or bringing into existence a European people. Thus, it follows that the very notion of a European Constitution is a utopian dream.

On the other hand, there is a broad range of what we may label European constitutionalists who all assert that it is possible to establish or bring about a European constitution but disagree deeply on what it will look like.[5] It is important to underline that this discussion takes as its point of departure the core tenets of democratic constitutionalism. It is an attempt to establish how much and in what sense the core tenets that underpin contemporary constitutional orthodoxy are already embedded in and can be further developed in the context of the EU. In that sense it is also important to note that the EU explicitly subscribes to these principles. Consider Article 2 in the Treaty of the European Union (TEU), which states that

> [t]he Union is founded on the values of respect for human dignity, freedom, democracy, equality, the rule of law and respect for human rights, including the rights of persons belonging to minorities. These values are common to

the Member States in a society in which pluralism, non-discrimination, tolerance, justice, solidarity and equality between women and men prevail.[6]

European constitutionalists are concerned less with the principles and more with the organisational form that these principles can and ought to be embedded in. Or, to put it differently, how far present-day EU is from realising these principles and in what direction it has to move in order to approximate them.

A core question that animates the entire European debate then is who is and should be the guarantor of the core principles of democratic constitutionalism in Europe? Europeans are clearly divided as to whether that should be the EU's member states or whether it should be the EU itself. Those that stress the role of the EU member states must demonstrate that the EU is an organisation that enables the member states to uphold these principles or that the EU is capable of upholding the principles either at the behest of the member states or in direct collaboration with them. Those that assert that the EU should uphold and embed these principles in its own constitutional construct must demonstrate that the Union is an organisation that is fit for doing so and further that the EU is in its actions capable of ensuring the citizens' freedom and equality. These different positions entail a broad range of underlying conceptions of the EU qua polity: a state-in-the-making; a transnational system of governance and, hence, an alternative to the state form; or a stepping stone towards some form of global institutionalisation of world citizenship.

We thus see that the European constitutional debate is a site where national, transnational, federal and cosmopolitan visions compete and claim normative and practical preponderance. There is wide disagreement as to what type of entity the EU *is* and what it can become. Some of the uncertainty pertaining to the EU's constitutional nature relates to the fact that EU law is formally based in a set of treaties. A treaty is a contract between states and forms the basis for international organisations. As noted earlier, if the EU had been nothing more than an international or intergovernmental organisation, then it would not seriously affect the members' autonomy and sovereignty. Under such a circumstance affiliated non-members would not find their sovereignty threatened by EU integration.

When we look more closely at the issue of sovereignty in an EU context, the most commonly used term to depict this is the notion of *pooling of sovereignty*, which shifts the practical meaning of sovereignty from an onus on *self*-determination to a stronger onus on *co*-determination. Such a reading of the EU clearly alters the equation for affiliated non-members because they will have to contend with how this process of pooling of sovereignty shapes and conditions the EU's core precepts of supremacy and direct effect, among others.

Furthermore, the EU's distinct form of pooling of sovereignty is closely related to the historical development of a distinct form of EU constitutionalism, which from the onset was authorised by the member states, through specific constitutional provisions that authorised integration with constitutional implications. Five of the EU's six original members contained such provisions which authorised constitutional integration. This conditional constitutional license was premised on EU compliance with the core constitutional principles common to the member states (Fossum and Menéndez 2011). It enabled the development of an EU based in a material constitution and anchored in a political system with legislative, executive and judicial powers.

The present crisis of the Eurozone has raised serious questions as to the EU system's compliance with core constitutional tenets, and the EU's ability to continue the gradual process of supranational democratisation. But the important point to note is that the discussion of the effects of the crisis must start from the recognition of the constitutional development that has already taken place. In constitutional terms it is thus not a matter of establishing an EU constitution; it is a matter of ensuring that the material constitution that the multilevel EU already has established will actually comply with constitutional democratic norms and principles.

What are then the basic components of constitutional democracy that the assessment in this book should be based on? As already noted we cannot simply pin constitutional democracy on nationally based popular rule; we need a standard of evaluation that does not confine democracy to the nation state context. Nevertheless, it is also obvious that at the base of democracy we find the notion of collective self-governing; that is, it is about citizens' ability to govern themselves through law and politics. The key free-standing principles we pin this on are *autonomy* and *accountability*. With autonomy is meant that the addressees of the law should also be able to understand themselves as the authors of the law, directly or through elected representatives.

Autonomy, which is the basic democratic principle, has two components: on one hand, rules pertaining to popular authorisation – including elections and electability. On the other, autonomy pertains to authoritative institutions that are capable of making binding decisions and distributing resources. The latter refers to political action capability – social control and rational calculation. Do citizens through their institutions control relevant action parameters? Are they capable of influencing the conditions for goal realisation? The basic evaluation parameters pertain to citizens' ability to consider themselves as co-authors of the laws and rules to which they are subject, coupled with citizens' abilities to exercise influence. Accountability is about both making an account and holding to account. It is about 'a justificatory process that rests on a reason-giving practice, wherein the decision makers can be held responsible to the citizenry, and where, in the last resort, it is possible, to *dismiss*, incompetent rulers' (Eriksen 2009: 36).

Democracy thus requires, on one hand, a political public sphere where opinion formation can take place. This requires a legal rights-based infrastructure to ensure that the process is protected from undue incursions by powerful groups and actors. Democracy also requires procedures to sanction non-compliance and to prevent bad forms of governing. Elections therefore matter for both reasons. The basic evaluation parameter here is to what extent citizens are able to hold the decision makers to account, to demand explanations and justifications for those decisions that are made and, finally, to have recourse to procedurally acceptable means to sanction these.

These criteria are not tied to the nation state as a political form but to a set of overlapping arrangements ensuring public and private autonomy. These are the division of powers principle with its tripartite division of state power and functions (legislative, executive and judicial); the institutionalisation of the public sphere as a state-free locus of criticism and authorisation of power exercise; and the principle of legality which constrains political power and renders it predictable, neutral and based on equal treatment.

We use these standards of evaluation to discern if citizens in closely affiliated non–member states have seen their political autonomy weakened. How capable are they of controlling their political agendas and how capable are they of influencing decision-making in the relevant realms? Is citizens' ability to hold decision makers accountable weakened or increased, and what is the scope of informed debate and criticism?

## Forms of association

The observations on the EU's constitutional nature and status are important to keep in mind when considering the different forms of non-membership affiliation. The fact that these forms of affiliation tie states to a constitutional construct matters. The EU's constitutional nature has consequences for the self-determination and sovereignty of the affiliated states. But forms of affiliation differ and so may the impact of the EU. An important issue is to establish the nature and magnitude of constitutional democratic impact. As part of that we need to establish whether the effects are roughly similar across forms of affiliation or whether they vary significantly from one form of affiliation to another. This latter question is pertinent because the forms of affiliation are at least on paper very different. As noted above, there are two main forms of affiliation for states that qualify for EU membership but have chosen not to accept it. The first is the EEA Agreement, which in effect is a way of incorporating non-members into the EU's internal market.

### Multilateralism: The EEA Agreement

The EEA Agreement came into effect in 1994, and was intended to include the remainder of the European Free Trade Association (EFTA)[7] states in the EU's internal market. Today the EEA encompasses 31 states: the 28 EU member states and the three EFTA states Iceland, Liechtenstein, and Norway. When the EEA Agreement took effect in 1994,[8] the three latter states that presently make up the EFTA portion of the EEA had to incorporate all relevant EU legislation that was in effect at the time the agreement was signed. That is because the EEA Agreement is intended to ensure legal homogeneity within the entire 31-member EEA. Precisely because of this onus on legal homogeneity the EEA Agreement is a dynamic agreement: new relevant EU legislation is incorporated in the agreement in an ongoing manner albeit subject to specific decision procedures. The EEA Agreement ensures free movement of persons, goods and services and capital in the entire EEA. That in turn also entails expansion into related flanking areas, such as for example environmental and social affairs. An open market in goods and services requires low-threshold access and passage. That is one of the reasons why Iceland and Norway, the two main EEA–EFTA states, have also signed Schengen association agreements which in effect locates them within the EU's external borders and systems of border controls. Norway has signed a number of additional parallel agreements with the EU, including agreements on asylum and police cooperation (Dublin I and II) and on foreign and security policy – Norwegian troops are at the disposal of the EU's battle groups.

As the various chapters of this book will show, the EEA Agreement is a very comprehensive agreement, no doubt the most comprehensive international agreement that both Iceland and Norway has ever entered into. It comes with its own *supranational institutional arrangement*, a court and a surveillance body (EFTA Surveillance Authority [ESA]). The agreement is dynamic, both in depth and breadth terms: new relevant legislation is included in an ongoing manner and the agreement is expanded territorially in line with every expansion in EU membership. It has been characterised as a 'semi-colonial' setting (Tovias 2006). Is the Swiss arrangement less comprehensive, and less semi-colonial?

## *Sectorial bilateralism: Switzerland*

Switzerland is a member of EFTA, but the Swiss people turned down membership in the EEA in a referendum in December 1992. Switzerland's relationship to the EU is instead based on two bilateral agreements. Bilateral I which entered into force in 2002 and Bilateral II which was signed in 2004 and is gradually being implemented since then. Swiss authorities have also since the late 1980s operated with the doctrine of 'autonomer Nachvollzug', which refers to autonomous adaptation and represents a policy of voluntary alignment with the EU. This doctrine 'stipulates that each new piece of legislation is evaluated with respect to its compatibility with EU norms' (Lavenex 2009: 552). In a similar manner Alfred Tovias notes that 'Switzerland has had an EC reflex for more than a decade now and tries to shadow EU moves autonomously. Because this process is invisible and silent, it is frequently but wrongly ignored' (Tovias 2006: 215).

The unique Swiss form of sectorial bilateralism is less comprehensive than the EEA Agreement. There is no set of supranational arrangements that regulate this. Thus, the Swiss affiliation is less hierarchical than is the case with the EEA, but it has also been claimed that this comes with the cost of greater uncertainty associated with the Swiss arrangement (Vahl and Grolimund 2006). In contrast to the dynamic EEA Agreement the Swiss arrangement is held to be a static system which therefore leaves Swiss authorities with more autonomy and control than is the case with the EEA countries. In a comprehensive study Marius Vahl and Nina Grolimund (2006: 3) dispute that and instead argue that 'the relationship between Switzerland and the EU is highly dynamic'. The scope for Swiss influence is also questionable.

These brief observations of the two main forms of association underline that we need to look at practice, not simply formality when assessing their constitutional democratic implications. Swiss official rhetoric highlights Swiss autonomy and ability to influence the relationship, whereas in practice

> EU–Swiss relations follow the general pattern in the EU's relations with small neighbouring countries: the EU is the policy maker and the associate is the policy taker. Access to the EU market and to EU programmes and agencies takes place on the EU's terms.
>
> (Vahl and Grolimund 2006: 2)

The chapters in the book shed added light on the nature of these two forms of association: how similar and different they are, what they entail for sovereignty and what their constitutional-democratic implications are.

## The contents of the book

The main question this book asks is whether those states that qualify for EU membership but have not taken it up and have instead entered into binding cooperation with the EU through different forms of agreements also experience constitutional and democratic effects from their affiliations with the EU or whether they are able to sustain their independence with few such effects.

To address this question of constitutional democratic effects the book's first part provides a survey of all forms of association with the EU. This is undertaken in order to get a better sense of how much these arrangements vary, including how they vary between those states that have been approved as potential EU members and those that have not. The basic assumption is that precisely because they are considered by the EU to qualify as members, constraints on inclusion first and foremost rest with these states and not with the EU. Chapter 2 provides a broad survey of all the relevant forms of association, whereas Chapters 3 and 4 provide a more in-depth overview of the Swiss case and its form of sectorial bilateral relationship with the EU.

In the second part the main focus is on the two main EEA countries, Norway and Iceland. Here the findings from the Swiss case are compared to the Norwegian and Icelandic cases, as the two main instances of close association without membership (Liechtenstein is the third but is considerably smaller). Particular emphasis is placed on Norway for several reasons. One is that Norway is the most closely associated non-member there is and is especially suitable for in-depth exploration of the hegemony hypothesis presented earlier. Norway is the largest of the EEA countries and has declined membership in the EU. It is nonetheless closely affiliated with the EU through the European Economic Agreement (EEA), Schengen and a host of other arrangements, including defence cooperation. Norway has been less hit by the Eurozone crisis than probably any other European country; thus there is little sense of need or urgency for EU membership. Another reason for placing particular emphasis on Norway is that its status as a member of the EEA has figured centrally in the UK debate as a possible alternative to EU membership for the UK precisely because the EEA Agreement effectively gives a state membership in the EU's single market. As noted, the EEA Agreement is dynamic and is based on the precept of *legal uniformity*, thus ensuring equal conditions for all economic actors.

The third part of the book is devoted to the discussion of the main findings – the constitutional democratic implications of non-membership. Those findings are considered in relation to the UK and how it understands and debates its relationship with the EU. How does the UK debate address the question of sovereignty? What lessons from non-members figure centrally in the UK debate? How does the UK – a former imperial power – consider democracy and sovereignty in the contemporary world? The final chapter picks up on the issues that were presented in this chapter and that have been discussed in the different parts. It identifies the broader implications for sovereignty and democratic governing in contemporary Europe in which the EU by default becomes a hegemon vis-á-vis associated non-members.

The book helps the reader to get a clear sense of the factual basis of the different alternatives to EU membership that have been bandied about in the UK debate, through relating the UK debate to the findings from the Norwegian, Icelandic and Swiss cases. The book will also consider what sense there is for the UK to draw on these two cases, given the important differences between, on one hand, the UK and, on the other, Norway, Iceland and Switzerland.

The main scientific contribution of the book is to establish how state sovereignty and the conditions for democratic governing are affected by being a closely associated non-member of the EU. The European integration process reconfigures sovereignty in Europe. Through not only 'pooling of sovereignty' but also sharing sovereignty, states and peoples find themselves part of a system that places strong emphasis on co-decision and co-determination. The states' autonomy is accordingly reduced. National self-determination and independence are in the process of being substituted by *co-determination* and joint control.

This book analyses the disquieting effects on states that are closely associated to such a constantly changing and integrating entity, an entity over which they have no formal say and where they find not only that they lose sovereignty but also that this is not recompensed through co-determination. The question we discuss is whether the upshot of this is dominance and the loss of independence under hegemony. An interesting point is that this effect is likely not to be experienced under full membership (the most crisis-inflicted debtor states possibly excepted).

## Notes

1 Article 50(1) TEU states that '[a]ny Member State may decide to withdraw from the Union in accordance with its own constitutional requirements'.
2 European Economic Area (EEA). Available at http://www.efta.int/eea, last accessed 17 December 2014.
3 Politique européenne de la Suisse. Available at http://www.europa.admin.ch/themen/00500/index.html?lang=en, last accessed 17 December 2014.

4 Hence, domination is not Herrschaft in Max Weber's sense, even though this is the English translation of it, see Weber (1921/1978: 53).
5 A small selection would include key academics such as Armin von Bogdandy, Grainna de Burca, Damian Chalmers, Jürgen Habermas, Daniel Halberstam, Matthias Kumm, Neil MacCormick, Miguel Maduro, Ingo Pernice, Jo Shaw, Neil Walker and Joseph Weiler. They differ in how they conceive of the EU but share a constitutional reading of the EU. Eriksen et al. (2004) provides a collection of contributions to illustrate the breadth of this debate. In Eriksen (2014) and Fossum and Menéndez (2011) detailed accounts are provided to show where the editors of this book stand in this comprehensive and very sophisticated debate. See also Eriksen and Fossum (2012).
6 Consolidated version of the Treaty on European Union, *Official Journal of the European Union*, C 326, 26 October 2012.
7 EFTA was established in 1960. Today the organisation has four members: Iceland, Liechtenstein, Norway and Switzerland. Three of these countries are members of the EEA but not Switzerland. For more information, see http://www.efta.int/about-efta/the-efta-states, last accessed 30 December 2014.
8 Note that Liechtenstein's membership of the EEA entered into force 1 May 1995.

## References

Eriksen, E.O. (2009) *The Unfinished Democratization of Europe*, Oxford: Oxford University Press.
—— (2014) *The Normativity of the European Union*, Houndsmills: Palgrave Macmillan.
Eriksen, E.O. and Fossum, J.E. (eds) (2012) *Rethinking Democracy and the European Union*, London: Routledge.
Eriksen, E.O., Fossum, J.E. and Menéndez, A.J. (eds) (2004) *Developing a Constitution for Europe*, London: Routledge.
Etzioni, A. (2013) 'The EU: The Communitarian Deficit', *European Societies*, 15(3): 312–330.
Fossum, J.E. and Menéndez, A.J. (2011) *The Constitution's Gift – A Constitutional Theory for a Democratic European Union*, Boulder, CO: Rowman and Littlefield.
Grimm, D. (1995) 'Does Europe Need a Constitution?', *European Law Journal*, 1(3): 282–302.
—— (2004) 'Treaty or Constitution: The Legal Basis of the European Union after Maastricht', in E.O. Eriksen, J.E. Fossum and A.J. Menéndez (eds) *Developing a Constitution for Europe*. Abingdon: Routledge.
Lavenex, S. (2009) 'Switzerland's Flexible Integration in the EU: A Conceptual Framework', *Swiss Political Science Review*, 15(4): 547–575.
Leuffen, D., Rittberger, B. and Schimmelfennig, F. (2013) *Differentiated Integration: Explaining Variance in the European Union*, Basingstoke: Palgrave Macmillan.
Miller, D. (1995) *On Nationality*, Oxford: Oxford University Press.
Pettit, P. (1999) *Republicanism: Theory of Freedom and Government*, Oxford: Oxford University Press.
Richardson, H. (2002) *Democratic Autonomy*, Oxford: Oxford University Press.
Shapiro, I. (2012) 'On Non Domination', *University of Toronto Law Journal*, 62(3): 293–336.
Tovias, A. (2006). 'Exploring the "Pros" and "Cons" of Swiss and Norwegian Models of Relations with the European Union: What Can Israel Learn from the Experiences of These Two Countries?', *Cooperation and Conflict*, 41(2): 203–222.
Vahl, M. and Grolimund, N. (2006) *Integration without Membership: Switzerland's Bilateral Agreements with the European Union*, Brussels: Centre for European Policy Studies.
Weber, M. (1921/1978) *Economy and Society: An Outline of Interpretative Sociology* [reprint], Berkeley: University of California Press.

# PART I
# Forms of association without membership

# 2
# THE EUROPEAN UNION'S DIFFERENT NEIGHBOURHOOD MODELS

*Sieglinde Gstöhl*

**Introduction: The neighbours' stake in the internal market**

The European Union (EU) has different policy models in place for integrating neighbouring countries which would, in principle, be eligible for membership. This book differentiates between those states that do not (yet) qualify for EU membership, on one hand, and those that qualify but have decided not to join the EU, on the other. Nevertheless, most of the EU's neighbouring countries have been developing 'a stake' in the EU's internal market, be it as an alternative or as a 'stepping stone' towards EU membership. This chapter provides an overview of the forms of affiliations that the EU has developed with these countries.

Those countries that qualify for EU membership but have chosen not to opt for it have organised their relations with the EU along two main routes: a multilateral one and a bilateral one. The first is exemplified by the multilateral agreement on the European Economic Area (EEA). In 1989 Commission President Jacques Delors (1989: 17–18) offered the seven countries of the European Free Trade Association (EFTA), which feared disadvantages as a result of the completion of the EU's internal market, to look for 'a new, more structured partnership with common decision-making and administrative institutions', extending the internal market to EFTA on the basis of 'two pillars', the European Community (EC) and a strengthened EFTA. However, the final institutional set-up of the EEA with its 'participatory deficit' was a source of frustration for the EFTA countries (Gstöhl 1994). In 1995, Austria, Finland and Sweden joined the EU, while Norway, for the second time, failed to accede because of a negative referendum. Switzerland suspended its application after the failure to ratify the EEA Agreement in 1992. This has left Iceland, Norway and Liechtenstein as EEA EFTA states.

Subsequently, Switzerland built up its 'stake' in the internal market step by step by concluding bilateral sectoral agreements in addition to its 1972 free trade agreement (FTA) with the EC. This bilateral approach has come to stand as the second route of integration with the EU. Although this policy has in substance been approaching the contents of the EEA Agreement, it lacks an overarching structure, and 'there is less institutionalised political dialogue between the EU and Switzerland than between the EU and most other third countries' (Vahl and Grolimund 2006: 112).

A different approach was taken by Andorra, San Marino and Turkey which in the 1990s entered the EU's customs union based on bilateral agreements. They acquired 'a stake' in the internal market in exchange for the implementation of the relevant *acquis*. Since 1963 Turkey holds an association agreement with the EU and opened accession negotiations in 2005, whereas Andorra and San Marino have concluded additional bilateral cooperation and monetary agreements with the EU and in recent years called for deeper relations. Although the three countries share a customs union with the EU, they encounter, compared to the EFTA countries, still many obstacles to a free movement of persons, goods and services.

In 2004 the enlarged EU offered its Eastern and Southern Mediterranean neighbours in the framework of the newly launched European Neighbourhood Policy (ENP) enhanced preferential trade relations, increased financial and technical assistance and 'the prospect of a stake in the EU Internal Market based on legislative and regulatory approximation, the participation in a number of EU programmes and improved interconnection and physical links with the EU' (European Commission 2004: 14). Commission president Romano Prodi (2002: 6) was much more cautious than Delors had been 13 years earlier, when proposing a framework for the ENP 'in which we could ultimately share everything but institutions'. Based on the two core principles of conditionality and differentiation, '[t]he ambition and the pace of development of the EU's relationship with each partner country will depend on its degree of commitment to common values, as well as its will and capacity to implement agreed priorities' (European Commission 2004: 8).

This chapter examines these different models of deep economic integration between the EU and neighbouring countries, including current discussions about their likely future development. As stated in the introduction to this volume, the book aims to assess whether, to what extent and how the EU affects affiliated non-members across Europe and beyond. It is particularly interested in those states which qualify for EU membership but have instead sought for alternative forms of association with the Union. This chapter thus asks to what extent such affiliations lead to challenges of democracy and legitimacy by comparing the range of such neighbourhood models, their main differences and similarities, and some of the dilemmas and trade-offs involved for the EU and the affiliated neighbours.

The term *deep integration* was coined by Robert Z. Lawrence (1996: xviii, 17) as 'behind-the-border' integration such as common standards or competition rules, in contrast to 'shallow integration' which focuses on the removal of border barriers such as tariffs and quotas. In the context of EU external relations, deep economic integration entails legal approximation or the adoption of parts of the *acquis communautaire*. This externalisation of the *acquis* requires a unilateral adaptation of the third country, be it through an institutionalised process or through voluntary action. As shown elsewhere, the export of internal market norms is most far-reaching in the EU's neighbourhood (Gstöhl 2008). Sandra Lavenex (2011) distinguishes several concentric circles of 'EU external governance' in terms of an extension of the EU's regulatory and organisational boundaries to its neighbours. As the notion of concentric circles implies, the intensity of *acquis* export tends to diminish with the growing distance to the EU.

In this chapter, I show that affiliations of deep economic integration with the EU currently take several forms, ranging from narrow, bilateral, static models to broad, multilateral, dynamic models. On the whole, it can be argued that the broader, the more institutionalised and *acquis*-based the relationship between the Union and a third country, the more likely it constitutes a deep and dynamic form of cooperation. Such a cooperation, which covers many 'behind-the-border' issues and closely follows the evolution of the *acquis*, may raise legitimacy concerns in the partner country. EU neighbours are affected by EU decisions but are not represented in their making. This poses a problem in particular for the more dynamic relationships which require an almost 'automatic' alignment with the evolving *acquis*, thus leaving little room for parliamentary control. Conversely, the narrower, the less institutionalised and *acquis*-based the relationship, the more likely it constitutes a shallow, loose and static form of cooperation that should not provoke many worries about its democratic quality or legitimacy.

While the externalisation of its internal market may constitute an instrument of influence for the EU, for third countries such a 'norm import' may raise legitimacy concerns. Yet, the cooperation and compliance of third countries is at least partly secured by their reading of EU rules as being legitimate. Thomas M. Franck (1988: 706) defines legitimacy as that quality of a rule 'which derives from a perception on the part of those to whom it is addressed that it has come into being in accordance with right process'. Even if the affiliations have deficiencies in input legitimacy ('government for the people'), they may in some policy areas deliver output legitimacy ('government for the people') through effective problem solving (Scharpf 1999). Anand Menon and Stephen Weatherill (2002) argue that the EU institutions may also contribute to input legitimacy compared to nation states by taking into account interests (such as consumers or foreign exporters) that are often affected by decisions but are excluded or underrepresented on the national level. With regard to the external dimension of the internal market, the input legitimacy is obviously very low given the non-members' lack of influence in the EU decision-making process, but to a certain extent 'the realisation of a more efficient market for Europe offers itself as a factor of output legitimation that can be taken as a justification for an apparent absence of orthodox input legitimacy' (Menon and Weatherill 2002: 120). The question then is under what conditions economic (and political) gains, in particular in areas which surpass the governments' problem-solving capacity, may justify an alignment with the *acquis* – and whether a membership perspective is on hand, as in the long term, output legitimacy might not be sufficient to balance a deficit of input legitimacy. Any deep economic integration with the EU needs to address in a satisfactory manner the substantive and participatory gaps created by a close affiliation.

The main challenges related to the neighbourhood models can, in particular, be captured in the dichotomies of uniformity versus fragmentation and homogeneity versus sovereignty. The problems manifest themselves differently for the EU than for the affiliated states: the EU's concerns are not only with ensuring uniformity and market homogeneity, but it also seeks to accommodate non-members and therefore faces coordination and fragmentation challenges. The third countries are torn between market access, political co-decision and the threats of exclusion and marginalisation.

The next section analyses the existing neighbourhood models and their possible future development. Based on this overview, the subsequent section identifies some challenges of affiliation before conclusions are drawn based on the findings.

## Neighbourhood models of deep economic integration

This section presents six neighbourhood models which vary in both the substance of the internal market which they cover and their degree of institutionalisation:[1] the EEA, Switzerland's bilateral approach, Turkey's customs union, the position of the European small-sized countries, the ENP and sectoral multilateralism such as the Energy Community Treaty. The pre-accession model – including the 'pre-pre-accession' model of the Stabilization and Association Process launched in 1999 for the countries of South Eastern Europe – is not considered here as a separate model because it has been designed to prepare for EU membership.

The structure of the policy models can be bi- or multilateral, based on a single pillar or two-pillar system, and the *acquis* import can be static with regard to a given number of norms identified at the time of an agreement or (partly) dynamic in terms of an incorporation of future *acquis* as well. The mechanisms through which the EU promotes an externalisation of its rules may rely on legal obligations, on incentives (attempting to induce the partners to embark on certain policies out of material self-interest) or on socialisation and persuasion (aiming at a change of the partners' preferences through interaction and dialogue). Hence, third countries may accept EU norms either because they have to (legal obligation), because they want to (for instance in order to obtain the rewards that come with the 'policy import' or to avoid the costs of non-compliance) or because they view these EU norms as appropriate and legitimate (Börzel and Risse 2012: 5–10). These mechanisms can be observed in varying combinations and to varying degrees in the EU's relations with its neighbouring countries.

The EEA has become an important reference point in the debate on neighbourhood models. Already in 2002 Commission president Prodi (2002: 7) suggested that it was 'worth seeing what we could learn from the way the EEA was set up and then using this experience as a model for integrated relations with our neighbours'. In 2003, the European Commission (2003: 10, 15) proclaimed that with the ENP 'all the neighbouring countries should be offered the prospect of a stake in the EU's Internal Market and further integration and liberalisation to promote the free movement of – persons, goods, services and capital (four freedoms)'; the long-term goal being 'to move towards an arrangement whereby the Union's relations with the neighbouring countries ultimately resemble the close political and economic links currently enjoyed with the European Economic Area'. The Eastern Partnership, the ENP's Eastern dimension, also envisages that 'the EU and its partners may reflect on a broader regional trade approach establishing a Neighbourhood Economic Community, taking inspiration from the European Economic Area where appropriate' (European Commission 2008: 10).

Moreover, in view of enlargement (respectively membership) fatigue and Euroscepticism, the EEA has in recent years been discussed as an option for other countries such as Turkey (Gylfason and Wijkman 2010), the United Kingdom (Van Randwyck 2011), the small-sized European countries (European Commission 2012a) or Serbia.[2] Also the Swiss government regularly includes the EEA in its integration policy reviews. According to Art. 128 in the EEA Agreement, the Swiss Confederation may at any time apply to become a contracting party.

## *The EEA: Broad, multilateral, dynamic two-pillar model*

The EEA between the EU and the EFTA countries Norway, Iceland and Liechtenstein, established in 1994, covers the free movement of goods, services, capital and persons and competition rules as well as horizontal and flanking policies. It constitutes 'the most prominent case of acquis export outside the enlargement paradigm' (Magen 2007: 377). Excluded are the EU's external relations, the common agricultural, fisheries and transport policies, budget contributions and regional policy and taxation as well as economic and monetary policy.

The EEA constitutes a complex two-pillar system with 'quasi-supranational' features that attempts to reconcile the principles of internal market homogeneity and decision-making autonomy, with the result that EFTA lacks a real right of co-decision (Van Stiphout 2007). The EC retains the exclusive right to initiative, but it consults EFTA experts for the preparation of relevant new acts. The main discussions take place within the EEA Joint Committee in the so-called decision-shaping phase after the EC transmitted its proposals to the EU Council and the European Parliament as well as to the EEA EFTA states. The EEA Joint Committee decides by consensus as closely as possible in time to the adoption of the rules in the EU in order to allow for a simultaneous application of the *acquis*. On the EFTA side, enforcement is carried out by the EFTA Surveillance Authority and the EFTA Court. It includes infringement procedures and advisory opinions delivered upon request of national courts in EEA EFTA countries. In case of an opt-out, the EFTA countries, which need to 'speak with one voice', face the threat of a suspension of related parts of the agreement. This has so far not yet happened.

From 2010 to 2013 a comprehensive review of the EEA took place (European Commission 2012b; Official Norwegian Report [NOU] 2012:2; Pelkmans and Böhler 2013). In general, the reviews confirmed that, despite shortcomings, the EEA has overall been functioning in a satisfactory manner. However, as the contributions in Erik O. Eriksen and John Erik Fossum (2014) underline, for Norway there are serious democratic and constitutional problems associated with the EEA. By contrast, very small countries such as Liechtenstein have traditionally taken a more pragmatic approach to issues of sovereignty. For them, European integration may in fact help counterbalance their strong bilateral dependence on a bigger neighbour and thus serve as a means to strengthen their sovereign statehood (Frommelt and Gstöhl 2011: 12, 20, 28).

Since the EEA Agreement was signed in 1992 the EU has gone through significant changes, including several treaty revisions. However, the EEA Agreement itself has, despite the annual incorporation of more than 300 new EU acts, remained largely unchanged. According to the European Commission (2012b), allowing the scope of the EEA Agreement to develop alongside with the development of the EU would have offered the EEA EFTA countries an 'alternative EU membership-status on an *à la carte* basis'. The Court of Justice of the European Union (CJEU) and the EFTA Court have to some extent bridged the gap through their case law (Fredriksen 2012), but there have been unavoidable controversies on the actual scope and depth of the EEA Agreement, in particular with regard to the selection of EU acts as 'EEA relevant' by the EEA Joint Committee. Moreover, the EEA internal market legislation 'is often blurred with other policies that fall outside the scope of the EEA Agreement' (Tobler et al. 2010: 7). There is a grey zone between what is internal market legislation in a strict sense, and the EU increasingly adopts packages instead of individual acts. The creeping extension of the reach of the EEA Agreement does not go hand in hand with the participation of the EEA EFTA states in the relevant decision-shaping process. In addition, several EU acts vest the European Commission or EU agencies with the competence to assess the compliance of member states or introduce new forms of governance, which does not fit easily with the two-pillar structure of the EEA. As a result, the incorporation of new EU acts into the EEA Agreement has required an increasing number of adaptations to legal acts by the EEA Joint Committee. Such adaptations lead to delays in the implementation and risk weakening the homogeneity of EEA law (Frommelt and Gstöhl 2011: 48–49). The EEA EFTA states are not represented in the Council of Ministers or in the European Parliament. Hence, by strengthening the role of the European Parliament (and of national parliaments) the Lisbon Treaty has further increased the 'participatory deficit' on the EFTA side. At the discretion of the rotating EU presidency, the EEA EFTA ministers have sometimes been invited to informal EU ministerial meetings or conferences relevant to the internal market.

Finally, EEA EFTA member Iceland has been negotiating its accession to the EU since 2010. Its EU membership would raise serious questions about the functioning of the EEA as it would only leave Norway and Liechtenstein in the EFTA pillar. However, in May 2013 the new Icelandic government announced a halt to the accession talks until Icelanders vote in a referendum within the next four years on whether they want membership negotiations to continue.[3]

All these factors have raised the question of revising the EEA Agreement after two decades. The European Commission (2012b) *inter alia* suggested considering a more comprehensive approach by bringing some of the more than 70 existing bilateral agreements under the EEA, adding judicial cooperation (for instance human trafficking) to the EEA Agreement, exploring the possibility of updating and simplifying some of the procedures with regard to the technical functioning of the agreement and opening up for more members such as Switzerland, Andorra, Monaco and San Marino.

In future, the EEA is likely to remain a multilateral, dynamic two-pillar model if its membership is not shrinking. An 'EEA 2.0' may have a broader scope or wider membership, but any renegotiation risks opening a 'Pandora's box' of demands on both sides. Moreover, as joining the EEA means first joining EFTA, the EFTA countries would have to unanimously agree.

## *EU–Switzerland: Broad, bilateral, static, sectoral model*

EFTA member Switzerland opted out of the EEA through a referendum in 1992, which also led to a 'freezing' of the EU membership bid it had launched in the same year. Instead, the country pursued a pragmatic bilateral approach, building mainly on its 1972 FTA with the European Communities (Schwok 2009). In two package deals in 1999 and 2004 it concluded 16 new sectoral agreements with the EU (free movement of persons, technical barriers to trade, public procurement, civil aviation, overland transport, agriculture, research, Schengen and Dublin association, taxation of savings, fight against fraud, processed agricultural products, environment, statistics, media, education and pensions). Most of these 'bilaterals' are based on the notion of equivalence of laws between the two parties. However, Switzerland accepts the *acquis* in the area of air transport (where the European Commission and the CJEU have competences in surveillance and arbitration in specified areas) and in the Schengen and Dublin association agreements, where new *acquis* requires approval from the Swiss legislature (but in case of a refusal, the agreement could be terminated) and Swiss representatives participate without a vote in the relevant committees and working groups. While the bilateral approach has been expanding sector by sector, it lacks an overarching structure to deal with the around 20 main agreements, most of which are on a technical level run by a consensus-based joint committee, and more than 100 secondary agreements. Additional agreements were concluded *inter alia* on Switzerland's cooperation with Europol (2004), Eurojust (2008) and the European Defence Agency (2012), on education (2010), and on cooperation between competition authorities (2013). Besides, negotiations are still underway on electricity, agriculture, food and product security, public health, navigation by satellite and emissions trading.

For the Swiss Federal Council (2010) bilateral agreements are still the most suitable instrument. However, the Council of the European Union insisted on the limits of such a static, sectoral approach and on finding a solution for the horizontal, institutional issues:

> Due to a lack of efficient arrangements for the take-over of new EU acquis including ECJ case-law, and for ensuring the supervision and enforcement of

the existing agreements, this approach does not ensure the necessary homogeneity in the parts of the internal market and of the EU policies in which Switzerland participates.

(Council of the European Union 2010: para. 42)

In June 2012, the Swiss Federal Council (2012) submitted a number of institutional proposals to the EU: it accepted the overall objective of homogeneity, to negotiate based on the relevant *acquis* and to incorporate future developments of this *acquis*, provided that such incorporation was not automatic and that Switzerland could in turn participate in the decision-shaping process – like in the EEA. If, exceptionally, Switzerland was not able to incorporate new *acquis* (for example due to a negative referendum), the EU could take appropriate compensatory measures, the proportionality of which could be submitted to an arbitration body. Finally, still in line with the EEA model, a two-pillar approach was suggested, whereby each party would retain responsibility for ensuring the application and interpretation of the common rules on its territory. However, such an independent national Swiss Surveillance Authority was not acceptable to the EU (Barroso 2012).

In 2013, a joint non-paper was elaborated that outlined the possible options: the EFTA Surveillance Authority and the EFTA Court monitor and enforce the bilateral agreements, the EU and Switzerland establish in Switzerland new joint bodies for the surveillance of the functioning of the agreements on Swiss territory or the CJEU interprets the EU *acquis* that Switzerland has adopted or will adopt. The third option was chosen by both sides as a basis for future negotiations. For the Council of the European Union (2012: para. 33), 'this institutional framework should present a level of legal certainty and independence equivalent to the mechanisms created under the EEA Agreement'.

Overall, if EU–Swiss relations change in this direction, they are bound to turn into a bilateral dynamic, sectoral model with an umbrella agreement, including a one-pillar solution.

### *EU–Turkey: Narrow, bilateral, partly dynamic customs union model*

Turkey is already since 1963 associated with the EU, and in 2005 accession negotiations were opened. Turkey's customs union with the EU, established in 1996, allows all industrial goods and processed agricultural products that comply with EU norms to circulate freely. The European Commission informally consults Turkish experts when drafting new relevant *acquis* and further consultations may take place in the Joint Committee. To some extent, this mechanism has been taken from the EEA, but 'the flaws in the EEA provisions have been compounded by the failure to adjust them to reflect Turkey's involvement in the EC's trade policy' (Peers 1996: 423).

Turkey adopted the common external tariff and the *acquis* in the area of technical barriers to trade, and it aligns its legislation in other essential internal market areas, notably competition policy and protection of intellectual property rights. Moreover, in order to ensure the proper functioning of the customs union, provisions which are identical in substance to the corresponding provisions of the EU Treaty should be interpreted in conformity with the relevant case law. The Association Council tries to find a solution to any conflict and may unanimously decide to submit a dispute to the CJEU, another court or an arbitration tribunal.

The customs union binds Turkey to the EU's common commercial policy without offering it proper means of influencing that policy, and the EU's FTAs have opened up third markets for EU exports but not for Turkish exports (despite granting FTA partners access to the Turkish market). While such an arrangement 'was initially accepted by Turkish policymakers as a transitional measure to be eliminated with Turkey's EU accession' (Ülgen 2012: 9), it is now increasingly put in question.

If EU membership will no longer be the agreed medium-term goal, building a 'customs union 2.0' becomes more important. For instance, the EU could systematically insert a 'Turkey clause' in new trade agreements to encourage its trade partners to negotiate similar agreements with Turkey. There have also been suggestions that the EU should hold consultations with Turkey on trade agreements or include a Turkish representative as observer in its Trade Policy Committee (Ülgen 2012: 21). The customs union could also be deepened to include new areas such as trade in services and agriculture. Finally, other aspects of the internal market that go beyond the customs union could be added to a 2.0 version.

## *The European small-sized countries: Narrow, bilateral, static absorption model*

The European small-sized countries other than Liechtenstein – Andorra, San Marino and Monaco – also maintain close relations with the EU which have developed from an indirect integration based on historical relations with neighbouring EU member states to direct agreements with the EU (Friese 2011). Like Turkey, they are part of the EU's customs union (while the Vatican is not). Whereas Andorra and San Marino have concluded bilateral cooperation and customs union agreements with the EU, Monaco continues to rely on its special relationship with France. Unlike Turkey, the three very small countries have no participatory rights in the EU's decision-making process but still have to implement the relevant *acquis*. They have also concluded bilateral monetary agreements which allow them to use the Euro and grant exclusive competence to the CJEU. Hence, their limited relations with the EU can be characterised as an absorption model.

The EU promises in its declaration on Art. 8 in the Treaty of the European Union (TEU), which deals with the EU's neighbouring countries, to 'take into account the particular situation of small-sized countries which maintain specific relations of proximity with it'. All three countries have in recent years expressed the wish to enhance their relations with the EU because they still face obstacles to internal market access. Andorra and San Marino have shown an interest in joining the EEA. However, the EFTA states have so far been very sceptical towards accepting the small-sized states, which have little diversified economic structures, into their organisation (Gahr Støre 2011; Swiss Federal Council 2010: 27). In addition,

San Marino had in 2002 and 2007 – without success – approached the EU presidency to discuss the possibility of submitting its candidature for EU membership (Frommelt and Gstöhl 2011: 53). In October 2013 a referendum in San Marino proposing to open accession talks with the EU was rejected because of low voter turnout.[4]

For the future, the European Commission (2012a) suggested exploring a multilateral framework association agreement with the three states or their accession to the EEA, but it did not retain alternative options such as bilateral sectoral agreements or EU membership. A framework association would entail special governance arrangements for the small-sized states' consultation ('decision-shaping') and for the monitoring and enforcement of the *acquis* (European Commission 2012a: 17). Unlike the EEA, it would, however, not constitute a two-pillar system. The monitoring and enforcement of the relevant *acquis* would have to be carried out by the EU institutions, the corresponding EEA EFTA institutions or 'an equivalent supra-national authority' (European Commission 2012a).

## *The ENP: Narrow, bilateral, static hub-and-spoke model*

The ENP's legal bases are the bilateral Euro-Mediterranean Association Agreements and the Partnership and Cooperation Agreements with the transition countries to the East, respectively, that were concluded throughout the 1990s. The latter are being replaced by association agreements as well. The agreements encourage the approximation of legislation to the *acquis*; tailor-made bilateral action plans define the jointly agreed but non-binding political and economic reform priorities for the next few years; and the EU supports the implementation process with technical and financial assistance. Monitoring is carried out in the relevant joint bodies, and the European Commission and the European External Action Service regularly prepare progress reports. The ENP originally worked mainly with incentives, such as financial aid and preferential market access, and instruments based on persuasion such as policy dialogues or twinning and targeted expert assistance.

In a further step, the bilateral association agreements are to comprise deep and comprehensive free trade areas (DCFTAs) which are being negotiated with ENP countries that are members of the World Trade Organization and whose economies are ready to sustain the effects of far-reaching liberalisation. The DCFTAs cover substantially all trade in goods and services as well as 'behind-the-border' issues, such as technical, sanitary and phytosanitary standards; competition policy; industrial policy; research cooperation; intellectual property rights; trade facilitation measures; company law; public procurement; and financial services. They require the partners' capacity to approximate to and selectively take over the EU *acquis*. The association agreements with Ukraine, Moldova and Georgia, signed in June 2014, contain several different legislative approximation mechanisms with varying degrees of obligation and various procedures to amend the incorporated rules. Also the dispute settlement varies across sectors from consultation, arbitration or mediation to rulings by the CJEU (Van der Loo et al. 2014: 14–22). In particular, the countries commit to incorporate the relevant *acquis* regarding technical barriers to trade and certain services. The Association Council monitors the application of the agreement and serves as forum to discuss new relevant legislation. The DCFTAs do not *per se* aim at the creation of a homogenous and dynamic legal space but are instead based on far-reaching market access conditionality, which links additional access to the EU's internal market to the progress in implementation. They entail 'a move from the soft law approach based on persuasion and assistance to a comprehensive, binding and detailed legal framework structuring relations between the EU and its Eastern neighbours' (Delcour and Wolczuk 2013: 190). Unlike for the Mediterranean ENP countries, a future perspective of EU membership is not excluded for the Eastern partners.

In 2006 the European Commission (2006: 5) introduced the longer-term vision of a Neighbourhood Economic Community (NEC) with the application of shared regulatory frameworks and improved market access for goods and services. A future NEC would build on the full implementation of the action plans and of the DCFTAs and on increased intra-regional integration between the ENP partners themselves. The ENP economies would have to be able to withstand the competitive pressures of the internal market, to adopt the relevant *acquis* and to implement it. Finally, an institutional framework would have to be explored: 'Any change from the bilateral/regional "hub-and-spokes" approach to a broader regional approach would need to be supported with appropriate structures, including the possibility to let partners have a voice in policy-shaping' (European Commission 2007: 8).

The NEC could take the form of an enhanced bilateral 'hub-and-spoke model 2.0', combining a partly dynamic free trade area with limited collective decision-making capacity, or it could acquire a multilateral dimension. The ENP countries are encouraged to establish a network of FTAs among themselves. So far, however, progress on intra-regional integration has been slow, *inter alia* due to regional conflicts and a low level of trade complementarity. Moreover, in late 2013 the Armenian government's announcement of its intention to join the customs union established in 2010 by Russia, Belarus and Kazakhstan and the decision of the Ukrainian government to suspend the signature of its association agreement and DCFTA with the EU, which led to the 'Euromaidan' protests and a change of government in Kiev, clearly demonstrated that the countries of the Eastern Partnership are facing two 'centres of gravity': the EU and Russia. The launch of the Eurasian Economic Union 'means that the EU is no longer the only actor promoting deep economic integration premised on regulatory convergence in the post-Soviet space' (Delcour and Wolczuk 2013: 180).

## *The Energy Community Treaty: Narrow, partly dynamic, sectoral multilateralism*

Steven Blockmans and Bart Van Vooren (2012) put forward 'legally binding sectoral multilateralism' aiming at treaty-based legal integration in selected areas between the EU and (able and willing) neighbours and between the latter themselves. Examples for potential open regional building blocks are the Energy Community Treaty, which entered into force in 2006 and extends the EU's internal market for electricity and gas to South Eastern Europe, Moldova and Ukraine (with Armenia, Georgia, Norway and Turkey as observers); the European Common Aviation Area with the Western Balkans, Iceland and Norway (with the possibility of ENP countries joining) signed in 2006; and the forthcoming Transport Community Treaty with South Eastern Europe. Unlike the current ENP or Swiss model, this sectoral integration is based on multilateral agreements. Besides the extension of the internal market, these communities also aim at closer cooperation between the participating countries themselves.

In the Energy Community the members agreed to adopt the relevant *acquis* on energy, environment, competition and renewables (Petrov 2012). With regard to the post-signature evolution of the *acquis*, the Energy Community Treaty stipulates a right but not an obligation to follow the *acquis*. It does not have the same binding effect as the provisions on homogeneity in the EEA Agreement. The Community may take measures on a proposal from the European Commission to implement amendments in line with the evolution of relevant *acquis*, if necessary with adaptations. Moreover, it must interpret the provisions in conformity with EU case law, yet there is no judicial authority to assist national courts.

In sum, a general shift can be discerned across the EU's neighbours towards broader, more dynamic models of deep integration. While the EEA, the most far-reaching model, might be modernised but will remain a two-pillar model, the Swiss sectoral bilateralism is set to acquire an institutional umbrella agreement, and the future of the Turkish customs union is open, depending on the fate of the accession negotiations. The 'absorption model' of the small-sized countries might develop into a multilateral framework association, while the ENP's bilateral 'hub-and-spoke' model is, in the long run, supposed to progress towards a (multilateralised) NEC inspired by the EEA.

## Challenges faced by the neighbourhood models

Based on the preceding analysis, two major challenges can be identified. From the perspective of the EU, the 'uniformity versus fragmentation' challenge describes the dilemma that the classic Community method of uniform integration does not apply to external relations and that more flexibility for third countries allows for tailor-made integration but at the price of complex arrangements. The proliferation of integration schemes, which carry the risk that third countries fail to follow changes in the *acquis* or its uniform interpretation, may therefore lead to a fragmentation of the EU legal space (Łazowski 2008: 1444–1445). This may not only affect the coherence of the legal regime, but in some cases also the rights of individuals. Furthermore, the 'more for more' approach to the ENP presented by the European Commission and the High Representative (2011: 2) promises 'a much higher level of differentiation allowing each partner country to develop its links with the EU as far as its own aspirations, needs and capacities allow'. Against the background of searching for deeper integration yet greater flexibility in function of a country's merit and political will, the question arises how the increasing differentiation can be reconciled with an economic community that aspires to share in a 'common' market with a measure of joint decision-making (Gstöhl 2014). Marise Cremona argued already at the time of the EEA's creation that

> [t]he most effective way of protecting the integrity and autonomy of the Community legal order, while responding effectively to the changing patterns of relationship within Europe, may be to accept the need for varied forms of membership.
> (Cremona 1994: 525)

Instead of constructing ever more forms of association that partly externalise the *acquis* and require novel institutional solutions, she considered admitting different levels of commitment within Union membership.

From the perspective of the affiliated neighbours, the 'homogeneity versus sovereignty' challenge refers to the dilemma that third countries face in case of a deep integration with the internal market. Safeguarding market homogeneity implies a measure of supranational surveillance, enforcement and dynamic adaptation to the *acquis*, which encroaches upon national sovereignty due to the lack of participation in the relevant EU decision-making processes. Already in 1987 the European Commission had made clear that EU–EFTA relations should be governed by three basic principles: the priority of the Community's internal integration, the preservation of its decision-making autonomy and the maintenance of a balance of benefits and obligations (De Clercq 1987). In other words, any deep integration with third countries must be in conformity with EU rules and not interfere with EU decision-making procedures. Likewise, the CJEU had in its Opinion 1/91 objected to the structure and competences of a proposed joint EEA Court of Justice, composed of EFTA and CJEU judges, on the ground that its legally binding interpretations could adversely affect the autonomy and exclusive jurisdiction of the CJEU. This opinion is likely to play a role whenever the CJEU assesses the need to safeguard the autonomy of the Community legal order with regard to international agreements (Baudenbacher 2007). The EEA negotiations showed that real joint institutions and decision-making procedures with the EU are not possible (Gstöhl 1994). As Lawrence (1996: 108) already stated, '[d]eeper regional arrangements mean sharing sovereignty'.

Adam Łazowski (2008: 1433) argues that 'enhanced multilateralism and bilateralism as models of integration without membership [...] are acceptable, providing they meet three benchmark criteria: they must secure the effectiveness, efficiency and enforcement of *acquis communautaire*'. He claims that the EEA is currently the only such model meeting these requirements (Łazowski 2008: 1434). Any association with the EU's internal market, such as an NEC, needs to find a mechanism through which third countries keep up with the evolution of the *acquis* and for the uniform enforcement and application of the rules. It produces a fundamental trade-off between the benefits resulting from the adoption of the *acquis* and the lack of participation in the decision-making process. In other words, a balance has to be struck between input and output legitimacy. The legal-institutional issues involved are '(i) the dynamic adaptation of the agreement to the evolving *acquis*; (ii) the homogeneous interpretation of the agreements; (iii) independent surveillance and judicial enforcement; (iv) and dispute settlement' (European Commission 2012a: 18). In the EEA these challenges have been solved by an elaborate two-pillar system which, at the time of its creation, still counted 12 EU member states on one side and 7 EFTA countries on the other. The Council of the European Union underlined that Switzerland's bilateral approach of concluding more and more sectoral agreements had reached its limits and needed to be reconsidered in the absence of a horizontal institutional framework:

> Any further development of the complex system of agreements would put at stake the homogeneity of the Internal Market and increase legal insecurity as well as make it more difficult to manage such an extensive and heterogeneous system of agreements.
> 
> (Council of the European Union 2012: 5–6)

Finally, the question whether third countries should and could join the EEA has been raised by the EU and interested candidates. However, a simple enlargement of the EEA by countries other than Switzerland is not likely to meet with much enthusiasm from the EFTA countries. The ENP and the small-sized countries are politically and economically heterogeneous, and they (currently) lack the necessary institutional and administrative capacities or political will to meet the requirements of an EEA membership. The EEA is also not an optimal model for big countries such as Turkey or the UK. The non-participation in EU decision-making would constitute a much larger price to pay for them because as EU members they would have many votes and seats. Moreover, adding big members to the EEA would risk politicisation (Pelkmans and Böhler 2013: 114). Also, Ulf Sverdrup (2011: 132) argues that 'there are geographical, institutional and political factors that reduce the exportability of the EEA, or at least significantly limit the range of countries that the EEA could successfully be exported to'.

## Conclusion: No stake in decision-making?

In this chapter, I examined the different models of deep economic integration that the EU maintains with neighbouring countries that are not (yet) able or willing to join. The EU's neighbourhood relations range from narrow, bilateral, static models to broad, multilateral, dynamic models.

The EEA offers the EFTA countries at least a say in the decision-shaping phase of new legislation as well as own surveillance and enforcement mechanisms and – if they wanted to – the possibility to join the EU. According to the EFTA

Secretariat (2009: 7), the decision shaping provides 'legitimacy to an inherently asymmetric process whereby the EEA EFTA states adopt legislation which has been decided without their participation'. Yet, the EU decision makers cannot be held accountable by third-country nationals; they can only vote their own national representatives out of office. For Switzerland, three of its many bilateral agreements are directly based on an adoption of the *acquis*, but the cumulative effect of all treaties might nonetheless raise concerns of sovereignty and democracy. Stephan Kux and Ulf Sverdrup (2000: 64) conclude with regard to both Switzerland and the EEA member Norway that 'the process they are involved in remains formally intergovernmental, but the effects they experience are supranational'. Turkey has not much influence in Brussels either, even with regard to economic and trade issues:

> The Customs Union is thus undemocratic insofar as Turkey had to cede important parts of its national sovereignty without being represented in the EU's political decision-making mechanism and without having any influence on the multinational decision-making process.
> 
> (Karakas 2006: 325)

Both the ENP and the Stabilization and Association Process with the Western Balkans rely closely on the enlargement model which the EU developed for Central and Eastern Europe. Whereas this strong path dependency can arguably be justified with reference to the 'potential candidate' status of the Western Balkans, it is more striking in the ENP context. 'EU demands for pre-accession legal and institutional alignment – however onerous, one-sided, and asymmetrical they may be – are legitimized by the prospect of full inclusion and the promise of future equality of participation' (Magen 2006: 422). This membership perspective is absent in the European Neighbourhood Policy, especially for the Southern Mediterranean partners.

The major challenges of deep integration are related to the risk of legal and political fragmentation, the homogeneity of the internal market and third countries' sovereignty concerns. The institutional features of a close affiliation with the EU must provide satisfactory solutions for a dynamic adaptation to the evolving *acquis*, the homogeneous interpretation, independent surveillance and judicial enforcement of the agreements as well as for dispute settlement. The EEA may serve as a source of inspiration, but joining or copying the EEA is in most cases unlikely to constitute a viable option.

The following conclusions can be drawn from the analysis:[5] First, many existing neighbourhood models of deep economic integration have reached their limits since they cover more and more sectors but lack efficient arrangements for ensuring the necessary market homogeneity. The Council of the European Union (2012: 5–6) underlined that any model must be guided by 'the principles of homogeneity and legal certainty' because they 'guarantee the efficiency, sustainability and ultimately the credibility of the single market'.

Second, an implicit EU strategy has been emerging as the EU increasingly attempts to ensure market homogeneity by concluding agreements with a dynamic adaptation to the *acquis*, its uniform interpretation as well as an independent surveillance and judicial enforcement.

Third, this shift towards broader, more dynamic models raises the question of the institutional pillar solution, in particular for surveillance and judicial enforcement: in principle, the main options are parallel (national or multilateral) institutions, new joint institutions with the EU or putting the relevant EU institutions in charge. The EEA negotiations had shown that real joint institutions and decision-making procedures with the EU, such as a joint EEA Court of Justice composed of EFTA and CJEU judges, are not possible (Gstöhl 1994). And in the Swiss case the EU ruled out a national pillar for surveillance and enforcement. This basically leaves the two-pillar EEA model and the 'absorption model' with a single EU pillar to choose from.

Fourth, safeguarding market homogeneity implies a measure of supranational surveillance, enforcement and dynamic adaptation to the *acquis*, which encroaches on national autonomy because of the lack of participation in the relevant EU decision-making processes. The closer a model is based on the internal market *acquis*, the less it risks creating legal and political fragmentation, yet the more likely it suffers from a participatory gap for the neighbours. This inherent dilemma tends to be bigger, the broader the scope and the higher the degree of institutionalisation. In other words, the dilemma is smaller, the fewer members and the narrower the sectoral scope of market integration, and the less dynamic and supranational the adoption and enforcement of the *acquis*. As a result, any deep economic integration with the EU's internal market needs to find an appropriate institutionalisation through which third countries adopt and apply relevant EU rules but also participate to a certain degree in the decision-making process. Even the DCFTAs provide for a limited form of 'decision-shaping' in specific areas where full internal market treatment is foreseen (Van der Loo et al. 2014: 19).

Fifth, the EEA is still referred to as the 'blueprint' model for the EU's relations with the other neighbours or as the 'second-best' model after full EU membership. On the other hand, the EEA itself suffers from growing shortcomings, as identified by the recent reviews of its performance mentioned earlier.

Sixth, as recently argued by Lavenex (2014: 898), the extension of functionalist integration to third countries in the form of sectoral, regulatory outreach constitutes a source of international influence for the EU 'that is hitherto little understood and that is only loosely coupled with the EU's evolving foreign policy actorness'. This calls for further research on the implications of the EU's neighbourhood models not only for the third countries but also for the EU itself.

Finally, for all neighbours the main alternative to deep economic integration with the internal market is, of course, full EU membership. Yet not all are equally willing or able to join the Union any time soon. The need to devise satisfactory alternatives to full membership is thus unlikely to disappear. In the end, each country has to answer for itself to what extent a democratic deficit caused by its choice of European integration poses (un)acceptable legitimacy problems.

## Notes

1 This part draws on Gstöhl (2015).
2 'New Dilemma: Serbia's EU Integrations, EU or EEA?', *Voice of Serbia*, 4 February 2013. Available at http://voiceofserbia.org/content/new-dilemma-serbia%E2%80%99s-eu-integrations-eu-or-eea, last accessed 17 December 2014.
3 'Iceland's New Coalition Government Suspends EU Accession Talks', *Financial Times*, 22 May 2013.
4 'San Marino Rejects EU Accession', *European Voice*, 24 October 2013.
5 This part draws on Gstöhl (2015).

## References

Barroso, J.M. (2012) Lettre du Président de la Commission européenne à la Présidente de la Confédération, PRES (2012) 1548156, Brussels, 21 December. Available at https://www.eda.admin.ch/content/dam/dea/de/documents/eu/Brief-BXL-CH-20121221_de.pdf, last accessed 22 December 2014.
Baudenbacher, C. (2007) 'Was ist aus dem Gutachten des EuGH 1/91 geworden?', in G. Baur (ed) *Europäer – Botschafter – Mensch: Liber Amicorum für Prinz Nikolaus von Liechtenstein*, Schaan: Liechtenstein Verlag.
Blockmans, S. and Van Vooren, B. (2012) 'Revitalizing the European "Neighbourhood Economic Community": The Case of Legally Binding Sectoral Multilateralism', *European Foreign Affairs Review*, 17(4): 577–604.
Börzel, T.A. and Risse, T. (2012) 'From Europeanisation to Diffusion: Introduction', *West European Politics*, 35(1): 1–19.
Council of the European Union (2010) 'Council Conclusions on EU Relations with EFTA Countries', 3060th General Affairs Council Meeting, Brussels, 14 December 2010.
—— (2012) 'Council Conclusions on EU Relations with EFTA Countries', 3213th Transport, Telecommunications and Energy Council Meeting, Brussels, 20 December 2012.
Cremona, M. (1994) 'The "Dynamic and Homogeneous" EEA: Byzantine Structures and Variable Geometry', *European Law Review*, 19(5): 508–526.
De Clercq, W. (1987) Speech delivered at the EC-EFTA Ministerial Meeting, Interlaken, 20 May.
Delcour, L. and Wolczuk, K. (2013) 'Eurasian Economic Integration and Implications for the EU's Policy in the Eastern Neighbourhood', in R. Dragneva and K. Wolczuk (eds) *Eurasian Economic Integration: Law, Policy, and Politics*, Cheltenham: Edward Elgar.
Delors, J. (1989) 'Statement on the Broad Lines of Commission Policy', Strasbourg, 17 January 1989, *Bulletin of the European Communities*, Supplement no. 1, 5–19.
EFTA Secretariat (2009) 'Decision Shaping in the European Economic Area', *EFTA Bulletin*, 1(June).
Eriksen, E.O. and Fossum, J.E. (eds) (2014) *Det norske paradoks: Om Norges forhold til Den europeiske union*, Oslo: Universitetsforlaget.
European Commission (2003) Communication from the Commission to the Council and the European Parliament, Wider Europe – Neighbourhood: A New Framework for Relations with Our Eastern and Southern Neighbours, COM (2003) 104 final, Brussels, 11 March.
—— (2004) Communication from the Commission, European Neighbourhood Policy: Strategy Paper, COM (2004) 373 final, Brussels, 12 May.
—— (2006) Communication from the Commission to the Council and the European Parliament on Strengthening the European Neighbourhood Policy, COM (2006) 726 final, Brussels, 4 December.

—— (2007) ENP - Thematic Dimension, Non-paper Expanding on the Proposals Contained in the Communication to the European Parliament and the Council on 'Strengthening the ENP', COM(2006) 726 final, 4 December 2006, Brussels, June.

—— (2008) Communication from the Commission to the European Parliament and the Council, Eastern Partnership, COM (2008) 823 final, Brussels, 3 December.

—— (2012a) Communication from the Commission to the European Parliament, the Council, the European Economic and Social Committee and the Committee of the Regions, EU Relations with the Principality of Andorra, the Principality of Monaco and the Republic of San Marino: Options for Closer Integration with the EU, COM (2012) 680 final, Brussels, 20 November.

—— (2012b) European Commission staff working document 'A Review of the Functioning of the European Economic Area', SWD (2012) 425 final, Brussels, 7 December.

European Commission and High Representative (2011) Joint Communication to the European Parliament, the Council, the European Economic and Social Committee and the Committee of the Regions: A New Response to the Changing Neighbourhood, COM (2011) 303 final, Brussels, 25 May.

Franck, T.M. (1988) 'Legitimacy in the International System', *American Journal of International Law*, 82(4): 705–759.

Fredriksen, H.H. (2012) 'Bridging the Widening Gap between the EU Treaties and the Agreement on the European Economic Area', *European Law Journal*, 18(6): 868–886.

Friese, K. (2011) *Die europäischen Mikrostaaten und ihre Integration in die Europäische Union: Andorra, Liechtenstein, Monaco, San Marino und Vatikanstadt auf dem Weg in die EU?*, Berlin: Duncker & Humblot.

Frommelt, C. and Gstöhl, S. (2011) 'Liechtenstein and the EEA: The Europeanization of a (Very) Small State', report to the EEA Review Committee no. 18, Oslo. Available at http://www.europautredningen.no/wp-content/uploads/2011/04/Rap18-Liechtenstein2.pdf, last accessed 17 December 2014.

Gahr Støre, J. (2011) 'Biannual address to the Storting on important EU and EEA matters', Oslo, 19 May. Available at http://www.regjeringen.no/en/dep/ud/aktuelt/taler_artikler/utenriksministeren/2011/viktige_eusaker110519.html?id=643648, last accessed 17 December 2014.

Gstöhl, S. (1994) 'EFTA and the European Economic Area or the Politics of Frustration', *Cooperation and Conflict*, 29(4): 333–366.

—— (2008) 'The Internal Market's External Dimension: Political Aspects', in J. Pelkmans, D. Hanf and M. Chang (eds) *The Internal Market in Comparative Perspective: Economic, Political and Legal Analyses*, Brussels: P.I.E. Peter Lang.

—— (2014) 'Differentiated Integration and the Prospects of a Neighbourhood Economic Community between the EU and its Eastern Partners', in P. Van Elsuwege and R. Petrov (eds) *The Application of EU Law in the Eastern Neighbourhood of the European Union: Towards a Common Regulatory Space?*, London: Routledge.

—— (2015) 'Models of External Differentiation in the EU's Neighbourhood: An Expanding Economic Community?', *Journal of European Public Policy*, 22(6): 854–870, http://dx.doi.org/10.1080/13501763.2015.1020834.

Gylfason, T. and Wijkman, P.M. (2010) 'Turkey's Road to Europe', VoxEU.org, 24 April. Available at http://www.voxeu.org/article/turkey-s-road-europe, last accessed 17 December 2014.

Karakas, C. (2006) 'Gradual Integration: An Attractive Alternative Integration Process for Turkey and the EU', *European Foreign Affairs Review*, 11(3): 311–331.

Kux, S. and Sverdrup, U. (2000) 'Fuzzy Borders and Adaptive Outsiders: Norway, Switzerland and the EU', *Journal of European Integration*, 22(3): 237–270.

Lavenex, S. (2011) 'Concentric Circles of Flexible "European" Integration: A Typology of EU External Governance Relations', *Comparative European Politics*, 9(4–5): 372–393.

―――― (2014) 'The Power of Functionalist Extension: How EU Rules Travel', *Journal of European Public Policy*, 21(6): 885–903.

Lawrence, R.Z. (1996) *Regionalism, Multilateralism, and Deeper Integration*, Washington, DC: The Brookings Institution.

Łazowski, A. (2008) 'Enhanced Multilateralism and Enhanced Bilateralism: Integration without Membership in the European Union', *Common Market Law Review*, 45(5): 1433–1458.

Magen, A. (2006) 'The Shadow of Enlargement: Can the European Neighbourhood Policy Achieve Compliance?', *Columbia Journal of European Law*, 12(2): 384–427.

―――― (2007) 'Transformative Engagement through Law: The Acquis Communautaire as an Instrument of EU External Influence', *European Journal of Law Reform*, 9(3): 383–427.

Menon, A. and Weatherill, S. (2002) 'Legitimacy, Accountability, and Delegation in the European Union', in A. Arnull and D. Wincott (eds) *Accountability and Legitimacy in the European Union*, Oxford: Oxford University Press.

Official Norwegian Report (NOU) (2012:2) 'Outside and Inside: Norway's Agreements with the European Union', delivered to the Norwegian Ministry of Foreign Affairs, 17 January.

Peers, S. (1996) 'Living in Sin: Legal Integration under the EC-Turkey Customs Union', *European Journal of International Law*, 7(3): 411–430.

Pelkmans, J. and Böhler, P. (2013) *The EEA Review and Liechtenstein's Integration Strategy*, Brussels: CEPS.

Petrov, R. (2012) 'Energy Community as a Promoter of the European Union's "Energy Acquis" to Its Neighbourhood', *Legal Issues of Economic Integration*, 39(3): 331–356.

Prodi, R. (2002) 'A Wider Europe: A Proximity Policy as the Key to Stability', Speech/02/619 delivered at Sixth ECSA-World Conference, Brussels, 5–6 December.

Scharpf, F. W. (1999) *Governing in Europe: Effective and Democratic?*, Oxford: Oxford University Press.

Schwok, R. (2009) *Switzerland–EU: An Impossible Membership?*, Brussels: P.I.E. Peter Lang.

Sverdrup, U. (2011) 'Modes of Association to the EU: The EEA as a Model?', in H. Høibraaten and J. Hille (eds) *Northern Europe and the Future of the EU [Nordeuropa und die Zukunft der EU]*, Berlin: Berliner Wissenschafts-Verlag.

Swiss Federal Council (2010) *Bericht des Bundesrates über die Evaluation der schweizerischen Europapolitik* (10.086), Bern, 17 September.

―――― (2012) 'Lettre de la Suisse à l'UE', Bern, 15 June.

Tobler, C., Hardenbol, J. and Mellár, B. (2010) 'Internal Market beyond the EU: EEA and Switzerland', Briefing Paper PE 429.993, Brussels: European Parliament.

Ülgen, S. (2012) 'Avoiding a Divorce: A Virtual EU Membership for Turkey', The Carnegie Papers, Brussels: Carnegie Europe.

Vahl, M. and Grolimund, N. (2006) *Integration without Membership: Switzerland's Bilateral Agreements with the European Union*, Brussels: Centre for European Policy Studies.

Van der Loo, G., Van Elsuwege, P. and Petrov, R. (2014) 'The EU–Ukraine Association Agreement: Assessment of an Innovative Legal Instrument', EUI Working Papers, LAW 2014/09, Florence: European University Institute.

Van Randwyck, H. (2011) *EFTA or the EU*, London: The Bruges Group.

Van Stiphout, T. (2007) 'Homogeneity vs. Decision-Making Autonomy in the EEA Agreement', *European Journal of Law Reform*, 9(3): 431–447.

# 3

# THE SWISS WAY

## The nature of Switzerland's relationship with the EU

*Sandra Lavenex and René Schwok*

Switzerland has a unique type of association with the European Union. Unlike other European Union (EU) neighbourhood policies that imply the extension of (parts of) the Union's *acquis communautaire* such as the European Economic Area (EEA) or the European Neighbourhood Policy (ENP), Swiss–EU relations are based on a set of negotiated sector-specific agreements and lack central coordinating institutions or enforcement mechanisms. At first sight, this arrangement promises a much greater degree of autonomy and self-determination towards the EU than the comprehensive and legally constraining architecture of the EEA. Indeed, official discourse in Swiss politics has tended to justify this type of association as a form of 'pragmatic bilateralism' (Steppacher 2008: 144) with Switzerland and the EU cooperating in areas of mutual interest, but in which the former basically retains its political sovereignty. This official depiction has been questioned in public and academic debates. While Eurosceptics have bemoaned Switzerland's 'creeping subjugation' to EU rule, supporters of EU accession regret that by adhering to a large part of the *acquis communautaire* yet not participating in EU decision-making institutions, Switzerland has willingly marginalised itself as a 'passive executor' of European Community (EC) law (Gabriel and Hedinger 2002: 707 [authors' translation]). Thus, there are grounds for questioning whether the difference in association makes up for a less hegemonic relationship for Switzerland than what is the case with the EEA countries.

Fifteen years after the adoption of the first round of bilateral agreements, the Swiss type of EU association is challenged from within and from without. In Switzerland, a majority of the population has voted in favour of a popular initiative which, calling for the introduction of quotas on EU immigrants, runs counter to the agreement on the free movement of persons concluded with the Union and herewith one of the basic pillars of the association. Meanwhile, in the EU, increasing dissatisfaction with the complex and particularistic Swiss solution has been voiced for nearly one decade, culminating in the determination to reform the current arrangements in the direction of an EEA-like framework agreement.

This chapter gives an overview of Swiss–EU bilateralism from its inception until today and discusses this evolution in terms of the balance among state sovereignty, integration and hegemony. Throughout this review, the argument is proposed that this balance is contingent on the tension between two partly antagonistic dynamics in Swiss–EU relations: the functionalist pressure for pragmatic, incremental and problem-oriented integration, on one hand, and the political debate on the constitutional ordering of this *de facto* membership, on the other hand. Whereas for many years, 'bottom-up' functionalism has allowed Swiss public officials to participate in the inter-administrative, transgovernmental structures underpinning European integration, thereby safeguarding the balance between subjugation and participation, with the increasing formalisation of the EU and its external relations, the boundaries between membership and non-membership have hardened, making more political solutions – and compromises – unavoidable.

## The origins of Swiss–EU bilateralism

At first glance the relations between Switzerland and the EU can be considered similar to those of the other European Free Trade Agreement (EFTA) countries. The Swiss have, however, because the outset been even more 'reluctant Europeans' than the people of Scandinavian countries have owing to their self-perception of being a *Sonderfall* or a 'special case' (Gstöhl 2002).

Traditionally a distinction has been made between functional/economic versus political integration, whereby the Swiss are strong supporters of the former but remain strongly opposed to the latter. The reluctance towards any form of political involvement with European integration already manifested itself in the negotiations between the EC and Switzerland on an associated status beginning in 1962. According to the conceptions of the EFTA states the association agreements could come to cover all the 'economic' aspects of the EC, without extending to the political elements (Zbinden 2006: 117). Neither the Swiss population nor the Swiss business association, at that time the Vorort, were in favour of such an association, and thus, the Swiss were not unhappy, when France vetoed the British entry into the Community and with it the attempt to associate the EFTA members (Zbinden 2006).

At the same time, the countries that had joined the then EC remained Switzerland's main trading partners. Apart from a number of limited agreements the first important treaty concluded to safeguard this privileged access to the EC market was the Free Trade Agreement of 1972, leading notably to the removal of customs duties and quotas on industrial products (Schwok 2010: 105–106). The free trade agreements allowed for strengthening the economic ties with the EEC without having to participate in any political activities.

At the eve of the 1986 Single European Act, that targeted the completion of the Internal Market, the EFTA countries, fearing economic marginalisation, intensified their relations with the EC. The 1984 Luxembourg Declaration on the idea of a 'European Economic Space' between the EC and EFTA was well received in Switzerland. When it became apparent that – in spite of Delors's 1989 promise of joint decision-making structures – the reinvigorated EC was not going to open up its internal decision-making processes to the non-member states in the EEA, the Swiss government became a more reluctant supporter of this association. The failure of this promise motivated the Swiss Federal Council, like the governments of most other EFTA states, to submit a formal membership application in 1991. The justification for this step was the recognition that the EEA would entail far-ranging losses of sovereignty that could only be compensated for with full membership. This realisation, however, came as a complete surprise to the Eurosceptic Swiss citizenry which, consequently, expressed its discontent with a rejection of the EEA Agreement by popular referendum on 6 December 1992.

Concerned for the future of its export-driven economy, the Swiss government embarked on the bilateral path asking the EU to open negotiations on access to the internal market. The European Commission accepted the principle of new negotiations but prevented the Swiss from taking advantage of the bilateral talks by engaging in a pick and choose tactic and controlling the negotiation agenda (Dupont and Sciarini 2007).

## The legal scope of Swiss–EU bilateralism

The legal scope of pragmatic bilateralism is limited to the issue areas in which bilateral agreements have been concluded. This stands in contrast to the 'global' nature of the EEA. In addition to the Free Trade Agreement of 1972 and more than a hundred minor ones (Vahl and Grolimund 2006: 22), a total of hitherto 16 bilateral agreements have been concluded in two rounds of negotiations. These bilateral agreements differ strongly with regard to their thematic width and hence horizontal scope; whereas some, such as the agreement on the Free Movement of Persons, cover significant sections of the EU *acquis*, others are much more specific.

### The bilateral agreements

The first bilateral agreements that were concluded in 1999 guarantee a large and unhindered access to the internal market for Switzerland and include the elimination of technical barriers to trade, the opening of public procurement markets at the municipal level, the reduction of customs duties and quotas on certain agricultural products, participation in EU research programmes, air transport; land transport and the free movement of persons (Schwok 2009: 38). The last two agreements, and in particular the one on the free movement of persons that was already controversial under the EEA negotiations, were subject to particular contention in Switzerland. Nevertheless, presenting them as a package with the other agreements facilitated their approval by 67 per cent of the Swiss voters in May 2000 in a referendum. Consequently, all these agreements entered into force at the same time in June 2002 (Schwok 2010: 38–47).

A special feature of the first round of agreements is the so-called guillotine clause stipulating that if a party terminates one agreement, the other party has the right to resign all other agreements.[1] This clause was inserted in order to avoid that Switzerland rejects the free movement of persons but benefits from the agreements in the other areas (Koch and Lavenex 2007). In addition, there is an implicit political link between the free movement of persons and Switzerland's participation in the Schengen and Dublin Agreements concluded under the second round of bilateral negotiations (see the later discussion): it is difficult to imagine that the member states would agree on the abolition of systematic controls at the Swiss–EU borders as stipulated by the Schengen provisions if Switzerland were to reject the extension of free movement to the new member states in upcoming referenda.

The market liberalisation path of the first bilateral agreements was pursued in a second round of negotiations starting in 2001 that led to the signing of a second series of bilateral agreements in October 2004. The majority of these agreements covered relatively minor issues (participation in EU education programmes and the MEDIA programme for the audiovisual industry, accession to Eurostat and the European Environmental Agency, reduced customs duties on processed agricultural products and income tax exemptions for retired EU officials living in Switzerland). The contentious negotiations concerned accession to the Schengen and Dublin Agreements, the fight against fraud and taxation of savings. Of these, the agreement on Schengen and Dublin was subject to a referendum in June 2005 but was accepted by 54.5 per cent of the Swiss electorate (Schwok 2009: 53–66). Taking into account other minor agreements, Switzerland and the EU now cooperate through a stunning number of about 120 bilateral agreements.

In view of conducting a third round of bilateral agreements the Federal Council in 2008 issued a statement declaring that Switzerland would like to cooperate on eight further issue areas with the EU (free trade in agricultural goods, cooperation in public health policy, electricity, cooperation with the European Defence Agency, participation in Galileo, participation in the EU's emission trading system and an agreement on cooperation in European Security and Defence Policy [ESDP] Missions). Despite some discussions, this eventual third round of sectoral negotiations has been stalled, mainly due to the EU's determination to reform the overarching institutional set-up of its relations with Switzerland (see the later discussion).

## *The legal nature of obligations*

The bilateral agreements between the EU and Switzerland differ from the EEA Agreement in various respects. First of all, the issue specificity of the former differs strongly from the broad scope of the latter. Bilateral agreements have only been concluded in areas in which both parties manifested an interest in furthering cooperation. What is more, the two forms of association differ with respect to their dynamism. Whereas the EEA, as an integration agreement, provides for the EEA countries' steady adaptation to the evolving EU *acquis*, the agreements concluded with Switzerland are, as a general rule, static in nature as they lay down the scope of necessary regulatory adaptation at the time of their conclusion. There are two exceptions to this general rule: the bilateral agreement on air transport and the agreement on Switzerland's association with the Schengen and Dublin agreements. Both agreements provide for dynamic alignment with future EU regulations and directives (Lazowski 2006: 168, 172) and, as such, are in stark contrast to the agreements on the taxation of savings and on fighting fraud, which are entirely 'static'.

Whereas the agreements on air transport and on Schengen and Dublin are at least partial integration agreements, most of the bilateral agreements are based on the mutual recognition of the 'equivalence of legislation'. This means that the 'equivalent' Swiss laws are explicitly listed in the annexes to the sectoral agreements. In practice, however, this requirement of 'equivalence of legislation' has led to far ranging adaptations of Swiss legislation to European standards (Honegger 2004: 43–44). The recognition of equivalence was merely a formality, provided that Switzerland has been assessing the 'euro-compatibility' of each legislative act prior to adoption since 1992; the practice of voluntary adaptation to the *acquis* (*autonomer Nachvollzug*) is one of the main sources of Europeanisation in Switzerland, also independently from the existence of the bilateral agreements (Church 2000; Jenni 2014).

The questions of how to ensure the 'equivalence of legislation' and of how to organise legislative adaptation to new developments in Community Law as propagated by the dynamic agreements were one of the key issues during the negotiations of the bilateral agreements (Lazowski 2006: 168), and it remains one of the core questions in bilateral relations to date. As in the EEA negotiations before, a balance needed to be struck between ensuring the autonomy of the parties and assuring the functioning of the agreements. From the outset it was clear that a quasi-automatic dynamic incorporation procedure as in the EEA would not be an option for Switzerland. That is why a special organisational solution was found with the key role assigned to the joint committees. The functions of the Swiss joint committees are much more limited than were those of the EEA Joint Committee, because the Swiss joint committees are only in charge of one specific sectoral agreement and not the bulk of the relations between the EU and Switzerland. Another specificity of the Swiss joint committees is that they do not all have the same competences (Honegger 2004: 85–86). The Swiss joint committees exert in part functions that come close to those of the EEA Joint Committee, for example when they make technical changes to the annexes of the bilateral agreements, that is when they incorporate new EU legislative instruments into the bilateral agreements. In some areas the joint committees have been given the competence to decide on the incorporation of new legislation into an agreement; this competence is subject to the prior consent of the Swiss Federal Council that is formally in charge of the work conducted in the committees. In other words, the joint committees do contribute to the further development of the joint '*acquis helveto-communautaire*'. Yet in contrast to the EEA case – where incorporation of new legislative acts into the EEA *acquis* constitutes the main source of adaptation to EU law – in Switzerland the decisions of the joint committees are only one source amongst others with voluntary adaptation to EU law playing a crucial role in bringing about euro-compatibility (Schweizerischer Bundesrat 2007: 5921).

Apart from new legislation, a second source of dynamism for the *acquis* is the jurisdiction of the Court of Justice of the European Union (CJEU). This is why a reference to the relevant CJEU case law was inserted into the agreement on air transport and in the agreement on the free movement of persons. The decision whether subsequent case law is to be incorporated into the *acquis* is delegated to the respective joint committees (Lazowski 2006: 168). The opinions of the Swiss courts still diverge concerning the question whether they are under an obligation to take over further developments of the EU *acquis*.

Another dimension determining the legal quality of Swiss–EU bilateralism refers to the monitoring of the implementation of the bilateral agreements. In contrast to the EEA, where a sophisticated monitoring procedure has been put in place for ensuring 'legal homogeneity', the bilateral agreements lack such formalisation. Under the bilateral agreements the contracting parties are responsible for ensuring implementation on their respective territories, with the exception of the air transport case. In essence the implementation of the bilateral agreements is based on the international law principle of 'good faith'. To ensure the good functioning of the agreements the joint committees have been endowed with the power to manage the implementation of the agreement, to exchange information on implementation and on further legislative and judicial developments in the legal order of the contracting parties and to settle disputes that may arise (Honegger 2004: 72).

At least formally, the political monitoring procedure respects Switzerland's sovereignty as it avoids subjugation under a supranational jurisdiction. The only exception to this rule is the agreement on air transport, which is a partial integration agreement. It is as noted above dynamic, because it builds on EU law and has made provisions for the dynamic incorporation of new legislative acts. The implementation of the agreement is subject to the monitoring and control functions of the supranational organs of the EU, the European Commission and the CJEU. These characteristics lead to a blurring of the distinction between EU membership and non-membership or between the EEA model and Swiss–EU bilateralism. In light of the dynamic adaptation procedure and the powers granted to the supranational institutions under the Schengen and Dublin Agreements, the latter has also been qualified as a partial integration treaty.

## The organisational scope of Swiss–EU bilateralism

The bilateral agreements with Switzerland, in contrast to the EEA, do not have a multilateral dimension. Their legal basis reflects the complexity of legal obligations and organisational forms resulting therefrom: agreements were concluded either between Switzerland and the EU (Schengen), the EC (most agreements) or the member states (free movement and fraud), individually or jointly. The contracting parties to the agreements vary in function of the internal distribution of competences between the EU/EC and the member states. This peculiar fragmentation of the bilateral agreements finds reflection in their political management on the side of the EU. In contrast to other association relations, the European External Action

Service (formerly DG Relex), which is normally responsible for managing relations with third countries, does not have the lead role in the relations with Switzerland. In practice the sectoral directorates-general (DGs) manage the everyday implementation of the bilateral agreements. These particularities are illustrations of the fact that relations between the EU and Switzerland have, at least until now, been closer to a functionalist, expert based interaction 'from below' than to classical, coordinated 'top-down' diplomacy. Another consequence of this fragmentation is a particular degree of complexity of organisational structures and a lack of political leadership which pose particular challenges to the overall strategic management of relations with Switzerland.

In the absence of a hierarchical institutional structure, the main fora to discuss regulatory approximation and eventual problems of implementation are the joint committees established under each bilateral agreement. The Swiss delegation to the joint committees consists of experts from the Swiss federal administration, a representative of the coordinating body in the Swiss administration, the integration office, a representative of the Swiss mission in Brussels and, in issues related to cantonal competence, a representative of the cantons. The EU normally sends experts from the sectoral DGs; the latter are normally accompanied by an European External Action Service (EEAS) representative in charge of the relations with Switzerland (Honegger 2004: 62–66). Below the level of the joint committees we find a number of subcommittees and expert groups that have been created to implement the agreement at the technical level. Marius Vahl and Nina Grolimund (2006) mention that ten subcommittees have been created for the implementation of the agriculture agreement alone under the bilateral agreements I. This high level of functional specialisation translates into close ties between the Swiss officials and those in charge of relations with Switzerland in the sectoral DGs. It seems as if most problems are solved in direct 'informal' contacts at administrative level, and that the meetings of the joint committees mainly 'rubber-stamp' the solutions elaborated informally. The problem-solving capacity at the expert level has also been used as an explanation why no formal dispute settlement procedures have been initiated in the various joint committees. After a first phase of implementation, however, some contention has started to arise as to how to ensure proper implementation of the *acquis* (Möckli 2008; Tobler 2008).

The bilateral agreements also foresee Switzerland's participation in the decision-shaping process. Formally the rules are similar to those established for the EEA EFTA states, but in practice opportunities for participation are more restricted. The formal rules are contained in a declaration on participation in the committees, which was annexed to the bilateral agreements. This declaration stipulates that Switzerland has the right to participate as an 'active observer' with a right to speak, but not to vote, in the areas of research, air transport, social security and the recognition of diplomas (Honegger 2004: 45; Vahl and Grolimund 2006: 47). Moreover, the Commission has to consult with Switzerland on legislative proposals that further develop the *acquis* in areas in which legislation is equivalent. Nonetheless, the possibilities to influence legislation, once it has passed the pre-pipeline stage, decrease markedly, in contrast to the arrangement found under the EEA. This holds in particular for the elaboration of the implementing legislation in the comitology committees. As under the EEA, the Commission has to consult Swiss experts when drafting legislation in the areas relevant to the bilateral agreements and it mentions the Swiss positions in the pursuant Committee discussions. However, in contrast to the EEA EFTA states the informal practice allowing EEA EFTA experts to assist comitology meetings as observers has not been extended in a general manner to Switzerland. Whereas the sectoral DGs are usually in favour of this informal practice, and have repeatedly allowed Swiss participation on an ad hoc and informal basis, the Legal Service of the Commission and DG Relex/the EEAS have been increasingly disinclined to accept these special solutions for non-members (Honegger 2004: 88).

Swiss presence in EU agencies is also significantly more limited than Norway's. Switzerland participates in the Agency for Air Transport Security and the European Environmental Agency. Association with the Schengen and Dublin agreements in Justice and Home Affairs (JHA) has also implied the conclusion of cooperation agreements with Europol, the European Police College CEPOL, the prosecution agency Eurojust and the borders agency Frontex. Although participation in agencies is still less developed than with Norway, it may be expected that more associations will be sought as the implementation of the bilateral agreements progresses and the fields of cooperation expand (Schweizerischer Eidgenossenschaft 2010). Normally the agency has the power to engage in relations with a third country and the modalities for doing so are stated in the statutes. In the case of Europol, which is merely a coordinating body, the Council of Ministers has to adopt a decision indicating the countries with which Europol can enter into negotiations. In the case of Switzerland, the Council asked Eurojust to negotiate an agreement pursuant to the conclusion of the bilateral agreements II. As in the Norwegian case, association with the Schengen and Dublin Agreements involves the most far-reaching participation rights as Swiss officials have direct access to all relevant Council working parties yet without the right to vote (Lavenex forthcoming-a; Wichmann 2009).

To sum up, the main characteristics of 'pragmatic bilateralism' between the EU and Switzerland are the fluid junctions among formal obligations, informal practices and the organisational complexity, highlighting the sectoral diversity of forms of association to EU structures. While at first sight the negotiated issue specificity of the bilateral agreements, their mainly static nature as well as the lack of supranational enforcement mechanisms promise a stronger preservation of Swiss sovereignty vis-à-vis the EU than the more comprehensive, dynamic and hierarchical EEA, in practice the scope for derogations from the dynamically evolving acquis is similarly limited, thus reducing the relevance of these formal differences.

## Political design versus bottom-up functionalism

Beyond the formal provisions of the bilateral agreements, Swiss integration into EU transgovernmental structures has traditionally occurred from the bottom up, in an informal manner, motivated by questions of interdependence and sustained by the compatibility of political-administrative structures. For instance, in the field of internal security, the Swiss Federal Department of Justice was associated to the Schengen executive committee and relevant working groups well before the formal cooperation treaty was signed (Lavenex 2006). The same is true in environmental policy, where Swiss officials from the Federal Office for the Environment have been cooperating with the European Environmental Agency from the outset, well before a formal bilateral association treaty was signed (Schweizerischer Eidgenossenschaft 2010). In the absence of an overarching hierarchical agreement such as the EEA and in the light of an evolving EU competence in many policy areas, access to relevant transgovernmental networks has become increasingly restrictive. It can be said that this level of decentred functionalist *engrenage* – or intermeshing – has entered a foreign policy logic in which the European Commission and the Council of the EU seek to control and to limit Switzerland's bottom-up integration into common regulatory structures (Lavenex forthcoming-b).

A good example for the constraining impact of evolving EU competence is the aviation sector. Here, cooperation among European states used to occur through specialised pan-European intergovernmental organisations such as the Joint Aviation Authorities or Eurocontrol. With the creation of the European Aviation Safety Agency (EASA) these organisations in which Switzerland used to be an active member have lost much of their influence. As a consequence, Switzerland has had to negotiate its accession to EASA as part of a commitment to align with the EU's evolving aviation *acquis* (Lehmkuhl and Siegrist 2009).

In other cases, Swiss access to pre-existing transgovernmental cooperation frameworks has been limited by the latter's formalisation under the auspices of the EU. In the field of health policy, the creation of an EU agency, the European Centre for Disease Prevention and Control (ECDC), has to some extent centralised the pre-existing system of transgovernmental coordination and information among European health authorities. Switzerland has traditionally played a very active role in these transgovernmental networks. With the latter's formal integration under the auspices of the ECDC, Swiss participation has increasingly been put in question and has even led to its exclusion from some of these networks, such as, for instance, the European Antimicrobial Resistance Surveillance System and the European Food- and Waterborne Diseases and Zoonoses Network (Schweizerischer Eidgenossenschaft 2010: 72). A third salient example is energy policy, where cooperation was originally based on the informal coordination of national regulators and other stakeholders in two fora, the so-called Florence Forum of regulators in the field of electricity and the Madrid Forum on gas. Besides the European Commission, national regulators, transmission system operators, member state governments, electricity traders and consumers, as well as third countries, including Switzerland participate in these fora. Over time, efficiency concerns have led to a greater formalisation of these networks in the framework of the European Regulators Group for Electricity and Gas and the Agency for the Cooperation of European Energy

Regulators. In this process, Switzerland has lost its informal access and participation has been made conditional on the conclusion of a formal bilateral agreement on energy policy. In sum, with progressive development of EU competence, '[t]he forum process has thus shifted from an informal and relatively inclusive network with very limited power to a formalised, institutionalised and more powerful, but exclusive network' (Jegen 2009: 590). In other words, the progressive institutionalisation, formalisation and supranationalisation of EU policymaking internally provides a structural limit to the flexible participation in relevant transgovernmental structures, thereby narrowing down a formerly horizontal space of coordination under more hierarchical structures.

## The end of the Swiss Sonderweg?

The EU's internal dynamics towards more formalised cooperation structures and supranational procedures, its growing assertiveness in foreign affairs, and dissatisfaction with the evolving, ever more complex and particularistic Swiss 'solution' raise – together with the contention within Switzerland – the possible limits of Bilateralism as we know it.

While Eurosceptics in Switzerland have been moaning the country's creeping membership in the EU, and only a minority of the population has maintained a wish to fully join the EU, the bilateral 'Sonderweg' has been accepted by the ruling elites as the best possible compromise between the formal retention of national sovereignty and the necessary policy integration into the common European space.

Thus, Swiss–EU bilateralism that started as a pragmatic reaction to the failure to ratify the EEA subsequently became largely accepted in Switzerland as a stable basis for its genuine path to European integration. Long ignored on the part of the Swiss decision makers, this accommodation has not been shared by their EU counterparts. Rather than accepting the pragmatic Sonderweg as a compromise, EU partners originally perceived Swiss–EU bilateralism as an interim solution to an eventual full membership or another, EEA-type framework agreement. This difference in perspectives is partly due to the fact that notwithstanding the rejection of the EEA and the conclusion of the bilateral agreements instead, the Swiss demand for EU accession, tabled in 1991, was never officially withdrawn, but merely 'frozen'. At the latest with the massive rejection of a popular initiative 'Yes to Europe' calling for EU accession in 2001 and the proliferation of bilateral negotiations, those with EU hopes for an eventual Swiss accession have been deceived. The admission of 12 new member states in 2004 and 2007 who – in contrast to Switzerland's selective approach – had had to adopt the *acquis communautaire* in full in order to qualify for membership, further diminished the scope of tolerance for this kind of particularism. The hardening of the EU's position towards Switzerland's incremental *de facto* integration, finally, is linked to the former's determination to develop a more cohesive foreign policy, including a coherent strategy of association relations with its neighbours to the east, south and west (Lavenex 2009).

## Renovation of the bilateral way: Progress and setbacks

Since the mid-2000s, the Federal Council has uttered its wish to have other agreements with the Union. This request was met with reluctance from Brussels because the EU demanded a better institutional mechanism before granting additional access to its internal market to Swiss products and services (Council of the European Union 2010, 2012). This EU reluctance came from a concern that Switzerland might take advantage of this relatively loose legal framework in order to gain a comparative advantage over other European economic competitors.[2] To put it clearly, the EU wanted to adapt the institutional mechanism with Switzerland to a new one closer to what is done at the level of EEA. The idea is to be sure that agreements between Switzerland and the EU would adapt in a quasi-automatic way to the evolution of the relevant Community acquis, as well as to ensure its homogenous legal interpretation. The EU also insisted on setting up a supranational mechanism for controlling the enforcement by Switzerland of new EU regulations on a model close to the EEA/EFTA surveillance authority. Furthermore, Brussels underlined the necessity to have a judicial mechanism rather similar to the one in Luxembourg for the EEA/EFTA states (Council of the European Union 2010, 2012). The Swiss government reacted in June 2012 by making counter-proposals (Widmer-Schlumpf 2012):

> *The issue of surveillance.* A surveillance authority shall be established to control a proper implementation of the new EU legislations with the Swiss bilateral order. This body should be independent from the Swiss bureaucracy but composed only of Swiss citizens.
> *Contractual violations.* In case of a violation of the terms of agreement, this new surveillance authority could open a court procedure. To ensure homogeneity of interpretation, the EU and Swiss highest courts would set up an 'institutionalised dialogue'.
> *Not automatic but 'dynamic' adoption of new EU rules.* The provisions of the Swiss constitution, including the possibility to organise referendums, must be ensured when adjusting to the evolution of the relevant *acquis*.
> *Participation in the phase of 'decision-shaping'.* Switzerland, like the EEA EFTA States, should be allowed to take part in the early stage of the EU decision mechanism for the body of legislation, which is relevant to Switzerland.
> *In case of persisting litigation,* the involved agreement must not become automatically terminated. Instead, there might be some rebalancing measures decided by the offended party. An arbitration court composed on parity between Swiss and EU citizens shall review the scope, duration and proportionality of those measures if asked by one of the parties.
> *The Swiss–EU Joint Committee as the only mechanism of settlement of disputes must be.* This function should not be attributed to the CJEU.

Brussels expressed disappointment with the Swiss counterproposals. An unpublished report by the European External Action Service (2012) showed even some irritation. This text of September 2012 qualified Berne's proposals as 'unbalanced' and 'not corresponding to the requirements expressed by the Council'. It rejected the Swiss' views because they did not provide uniform interpretation and application, that is sufficient elements in order to create homogeneity (European External Action Service 2012).

The report underlined that a Swiss surveillance authority, even if it is independent from the traditional Swiss bureaucracy, cannot meet the criteria of impartiality, which should be monitored by either the ESA or the EFTA Court in relation to the EEA/EFTA countries, or by the Commission and the CJEU in relation to the EU member states (European External Action Service 2012). In addition, the EU was not satisfied because Switzerland proposed an illusion of a mechanism of arbitration. The Swiss suggestion would only assess the proportionality of the countermeasures which could be adopted by the EU against Switzerland in case of non-adoption by Berne of the evolution of the EU *acquis*. But Brussels wanted of course a mechanism which applies as soon as there is a point of divergence between the EU and Switzerland. Because, otherwise its original goal to re-establish homogeneity and to avoid that the divergence in legal regimes would persist. Thus, the goal of re-establishing homogeneity would not be met, as the divergence in legal regimes would persist. For all those reasons, the European Commission officially rejected the Swiss proposals in December 2012 (Barroso 2012).

In order to get out of the deadlock, the top Swiss and EU negotiators produced in 2013 another unpublished document called the O'Sullivan/Rossier non-paper (O'Sullivan and Rossier 2013). David O'Sullivan was then the chief operating officer at EEAS, and Yves Rossier, the state secretary at Federal Department of Foreign Affairs. This is again a compromise between the positions of both camps. Thus, on the issue of the adoption of new EU legislation by Switzerland, they accepted that it should not be automatic but 'dynamic' and that it shall respect Swiss constitutional requirements, especially those related to direct democracy.

On the issue of control of the implementation of EU regulations by Switzerland, they agreed in the non-paper that it was not necessary to set up a new surveillance authority. It means that Switzerland shall therefore primarily continue to monitor the implementation of the bilateral agreements on its own territory. The European Commission is nevertheless mentioned in this context. Depending on the needs of the sectors, it could also have the possibility to conduct investigations. EU agencies and other bodies may also have a role in the implementation of the agreements. Consequently, a few voices were raised in Switzerland to express their dissatisfaction with a proposal that gives too many rights of investigation to the Commission, a body composed of foreign officials and widely considered as the epitome of a supranational bureaucracy hostile to Swiss sovereignty.

As for the settlement of disputes, the mixed committees shall remain the main bodies for solving the issues. Interestingly, the non-paper contemplated that, in case of non-agreement, either party may refer to the CJEU, which would decide the matter. Note that its judgement will be 'binding' on both parties, that is including Switzerland. This sentence has obviously generated much criticism in Switzerland, especially from the Swiss People's Party, who saw in it the triumph of foreign judges. Keep in mind that in the Swiss political mythology, 'the foreign judge' is assimilated to the enemy that William Tell had fought.

To make the whole compromise more ambiguous, the non-paper stated that, although the CJEU ruling will be binding for Switzerland, this latter country could still have the possibility not to implement the new relevant EU legislation. In this case, it is anticipated that the EU could take rebalancing measures, including the suspension or the cancellation of the agreement.

Finally, nothing was mentioned about the monitoring of the proportionality of the potential rebalancing measures (O'Sullivan and Rossier 2013). This point was left to later negotiations.

Relations between Switzerland and the European Union have become even more of a headache after the popular vote of 9 February 2014 anchoring in the Federal Constitution (Art. 121a) a limitation of immigration. The 'yes' was certainly very low, 50.3 per cent, but it was neither disputed nor relativised. This new constitutional article stipulates that the number of permits issued for the residence of foreigners in Switzerland may be limited by ceilings and quotas. These should be set according to the overall economic interests of Switzerland and in accordance with the principle of national preference.

Consequently, the EEAS considered that the implementation of quotas affecting EU immigration to Switzerland would be a violation of the bilateral agreement on free movement of persons. Formally, this would entitle the EU to activate the 'guillotine clause' according to which the unilateral denouncement of one bilateral agreement by one party permits the other party to suspend all other bilateral agreements I (see the earlier discussion). This popular initiative thus constitutes a new stumbling block in Swiss–EU relations, and the EU has made it clear that there would be no solving of the institutional dimension as long as Switzerland does not offer guarantees for securing the continuation of free movement of persons.[3]

In sum, this episode shows not only the delicate relationship of Swiss direct democracy and commitment to supranational EU law (see Blatter in Chapter 4 in this volume), it also points at the political context in which negotiations on a framework agreement unfold.

## Conclusion

From the Swiss perspective, the bilateral Sonderweg was a compromise between the functional necessity of integration and the political infeasibility of an EU accession. First, the bilateral agreements provide for a highly selective and issue-specific extension of the EU's regulatory boundary. The horizontal scope of regulatory adaptation is also circumscribed by the static nature of most bilateral agreements. Also the fact that each sectoral agreement is the outcome of a process of bilateral negotiations enhances the chances for Swiss negotiators to maximise their interests. Finally, at the organisational level, the absence of a juridical monitoring system (with the exception of the Air Transport Agreement) can be interpreted as an additional safeguard for Switzerland's sovereignty.

In practice, however, these advantages have had to be qualified and adherence to the bilateral agreements has generated obligations that are similar to those contained in the EEA EFTA agreement. Even though Swiss adaptation to EU regulations is for the most part not the result of the incorporation of EU legal acts under a bilateral agreement but of the voluntary alignment of Swiss legislation with EU standards (euro-compatibility), strong functional pressure for voluntary alignment is a structural fact. This *de facto* pressure also applies to the formally 'static' bilateral agreements and their adaption to the dynamic *acquis*. While formally more protective of Swiss de jure sovereignty, these distinctive features of the bilateral model: their negotiated, static and non-enforceable character have increasingly become artefacts in what de facto is a much more dynamic form of association.

In sum, Swiss bilateralism – while apparently more tailored – does not necessarily imply that the EU exerts less influence on Swiss policies than it does in the formally more constraining EEA. Nevertheless, it should be highlighted that much of this EU influence results from shared structural patterns of interdependence rather than from intentional attempts at domination (see also Chapter 1 in this volume). From the outset of European integration, Switzerland has followed this process from the fringes: politically as an outsider, functionally however very much at the core of cooperation endeavours, be it in trade, in transport, in environmental matters or in internal security. For many years, Swiss regulators and public officials have been able to liaise with their counterparts from the EU member states on an informal basis, joining relevant policy networks and transgovernmental bodies before negotiating the corresponding agreements. This functionalist integration from below has to a certain extent acted as a counterweight to the dominance of the *acquis communautaire* in the mutual relationship. With the increasing communitarisation of EU policymaking, and the enlarged EU's enhanced aspirations towards coherent and cohesive foreign policy relations, the scope for flexible, apparently apolitical arrangements has been reduced. With or without a continuation of the bilateral path, it seems certain that what some have seen as a 'Swiss model' is losing much of its exceptionalism. Even without the formal constraints put on state independence by the dynamic scope and enforcement mechanisms of the EEA, de facto interdependence, coupled with an increasingly supranational EU, question the very basis of the notion of Swiss sovereignty.

## Notes

1 The first round of bilateral treaties was formally concluded as an 'association agreement' based on Art. 301 and 310 of the Treaty on the European Communities.
2 Philipps, L. (2010) 'EU to Switzerland: where are we going with this relationship', *EUobserver*, 15 December 2010. Available at http://bit.ly/PzjdGB, last accessed 18 December 2014.

3 O'Sullivan, D. (2014) 'Les négotiations Suisses sont dans l'impasse', *Radio Télévision Suisse*, 29 October. Available at http://bit.ly/10NUK7I, last accessed 18 December 2014.

## References

Barroso, J.M. (2012) Lettre du Président de la Commission européenne à la Présidente de la Confédération, PRES (2012) 1548156, Brussels, 21 December. Available at https://www.eda.admin.ch/content/dam/dea/de/documents/eu/Brief-BXL-CH-20121221_de.pdf, last accessed 18 December 2014.

Church, C. (2000) 'Switzerland: an Overlooked Case of Europeanization?', Queen's Paper on Europeanization 3/2000, Belfast: Queen's University.

Council of the European Union (2010), Council Conclusions on EU Relations with EFTA Countries, 3060th General Affairs Council meeting, Brussels, 14 December.

────── (2012), Council Conclusions on EU Relations with EFTA Countries, 3213th Transport, Telecommunications and Energy Council meeting, Brussels, 20 December.

Dupont, C. and Sciarini, P. (2007) 'Back to the Future: The First Round of Bilateral Negotiations with Europe', in C. Church (ed) *Switzerland and the European Union*, London: Routledge.

European External Action Service (2012) 'Letter of the President of the Swiss Confederation of 15 June 2012; analysis of the Swiss proposals; document to the attention of Member States', confidential and unpublished, Brussels, 11 September.

Gabriel, J. and Hedinger, S. (2002) 'Außen- und Sicherheitspolitik', in U. Klöti, P. Knoepfel, H. Kriesi, W. Linder, Y. Papadopoulos and P. Sciarini (eds) *Handbuch der Schweizer Politik*, Zürich: Verlag Neue Zürcher Zeitung.

Gstöhl, S. (2002) *Reluctant Europeans: Norway, Sweden, and Switzerland in the Process of Integration*, Boulder, CO: Lynne Rienner Publishers.

Honegger, E. (2004) 'Die Gemischten Ausschüsse in den Sektoriellen Abkommen zwischen der Schweiz und der EG', IDHEAP Report 216/2004, Lausanne: IDHEAP.

Jegen, M. (2009) 'Swiss Energy Policy and the Challenge of European Governance', *Swiss Political Science Review*, 15(4): 577–602.

Jenni, S. (2014) 'Europeanization of Swiss Law-Making: Empirics and Rhetorics Are Drifting Apart', *Swiss Political Science Review*, 20(2): 208–215.

Koch, P. and Lavenex, S. (2007) 'The (Contentious) Face of Europeanization: Free Movement and Immigration', in C. Church (ed) *Switzerland and the European Union*, London: Routledge.

Lavenex, S. (2006) 'Switzerland: Between Intergovernmental Co-operation and Schengen Association', in M. Caparini and O. Marenin (eds) *Borders and Security Governance, Managing Borders in a Globalised World*, Zürich: LIT Verlag.

────── (2009) 'Switzerland's Flexible Integration in the EU: A Conceptual Framework', *Swiss Political Science Review*, 15(4): 547–476.

────── (forthcoming-a) 'The External Face of Differentiated Integration: Third Country Participation in EU Sectoral Bodies', *Journal of European Public Policy*.

────── (forthcoming-b) 'Experimentalist Governance in EU Neighbourhood Policies: Functionalist versus Political Logics', in J. Zeitlin (ed) *Extending EU Experimentalist Governance*, Oxford: Oxford University Press.

Lazowski, A. (2006) 'Switzerland', in S. Blockmans and A. Lazowski (eds) *The European Union and Its Neighbours: A Legal Appraisal of the EU's Policies of Stabilisation, Partnership and Integration*, The Hague: TMC Asser Press.

Lehmkuhl, D. and Siegrist, O. (2009) 'Conditioned Networking: Swiss–EU Relations in Transport', *Swiss Political Science Review*, 15(4): 603–627.

Möckli, D. (2008) 'Schweizer Europapolitik: Wie tragfähig ist der Bilateralismus?', CSS Analysen zur Sicherheitspolitik Nr. 37, Zurich: Centre for Security Studies.

O'Sullivan, D. and Rossier, Y. (2013) 'Eléments de discussion sur les questions institutionelles entre l'Union européenne et la Confédération helvétique', confidential and unpublished, Bern, 13 May.

Schweizerischer Bundesrat (2007) 'Bericht des Bundesrates zu den Auswirkungen verschiedener europapolitischer Instrumente auf den Föderalismus in der Schweiz', 15 June.

Schweizerischer Eidgenossenschaft (2010) Bericht des Bundesrates zum Verhältnis der Schweiz zu den europäischen Agenturen, Bern, September.

Schwok, R. (2009) *Switzerland–European Union: An Impossible Membership?*, Brussels: P.I.E. Peter Lang.

——— (2010) 'Specificities of Switzerland's Relations with EFTA', in K. Bryn and G. Einarsson (eds) *EFTA 1960–2010: Elements of 50 Years of European History*, Reykjavik: University of Iceland Press.

Steppacher, B. (2008) 'Naher fremder Nachbar Schweiz. Szenarien der Schweizpolitik der Europäischen Union', in F. Breuss, T. Cottier and P.C. Müller-Graff (eds) *Die Schweiz im europäischen Integrationsprozess*, Baden-Baden: Nomos.

Tobler, C. (2008) 'Der Acquis der rechtlichen Verbindung der Schweiz zur EG und EU: Eine unsichere Grösse?', in F. Breuss, T. Cottier and P.C. Müller-Graff (eds) *Die Schweiz im europäischen Integrationsprozess*, Baden-Baden: Nomos.

Vahl, M. and Grolimund, N. (2006) *Integration without Membership: Switzerland's Bilateral Agreements with the European Union*, Brussels: Centre for European Policy Studies.

Wichmann, N. (2009) '"More in Than Out": Switzerland's Association with Schengen/Dublin Cooperation', *Swiss Political Science Review*, 15(4): 653–682.

Widmer-Schlumpf, E. (2012) Lettre de la présidente de la Confédération au Président de la Commission européenne José Manuel Barroso, Bern, 15 June.

Zbinden, M. (2006) *Der Assoziationsversuch der Schweiz mit der EWG 1961–1963: Ein Lehrstück schweizerischer Europapolitik*, Bern: Haupt.

# 4

# SWITZERLAND

Bilateralism's polarising consequences in a very particular/ist democracy

*Joachim Blatter*

Switzerland qualifies for European Union (EU) membership but is not a member and has rejected membership in the European Economic Area (EEA). It has developed a close, albeit unique, form of association with the EU – generally referred to as sectorial bilateralism. In this chapter I focus on the democratic implications of Switzerland's bilateral relationship with the EU, with particular emphasis on autonomy and accountability. The assessment must take proper heed of the fact that Swiss democracy is strongly shaped by classical republican ideas of popular sovereignty and that liberal or constitutional understandings of democracy have not taken hold in a similar way.

In the next section I provide an overview of the Swiss model of democracy and show how this ideologically and institutionally enshrined understanding of democracy to a large extent accounts for why a majority of the Swiss people refused to exchange direct-democratic veto rights with rights to be represented in rule-shaping and -making in Brussels, because that would represent a paradigmatic shift from republicanism to liberalism.

The republican tradition can explain Swiss hesitance to establish closer political ties with the EU. Nevertheless, I believe it cannot justify Switzerland's distinct association with the EU, because it draws on a very traditional understanding of republicanism, one that is not adequate anymore for understanding political autonomy in times of massive trans-boundary flows and interdependencies. A neo-republican approach, in contrast, takes these conditions better into account, reconceptualises political autonomy and introduces non-domination as a core concept. When we apply such a neo-republican understanding of political autonomy, Switzerland's bilateralism has to be evaluated much more critically, because it combines strong resistance against interference from neighbouring states and international organisations with an extreme opportunism towards the demands of multinational corporations. Such a stance undermines the capacities of larger polities like the EU to secure political self-determination against private capital holders and multinational corporations.

In the final section, I focus on the concept of accountability and argue that in Switzerland, an 'elective' understanding of how representatives should be held accountable has never played a role of similar importance as it does in representative democracies. Instead, an 'identity' approach which implies that rulers serve as trustees, and a 'deliberative' approach emphasising the justificatory and constitutive nature of communicative processes between the rulers and all affected parties, have been characteristic features of Swiss democracy. The configuration of strong trans-boundary interdependence and bilateralism undermine those ways of holding representatives accountable: first, they contribute to the erosion of trust in the national government and thereby undermine identity-based accountability; second, in the present context, direct democracy is losing (again) its integrative and problem-solving qualities in terms of deliberative accountability.

## Swiss democracy

Switzerland's model of democracy is characterised by the fact that core features of republicanism are (still) very strong, whereas central elements of liberalism are comparatively weak. The first and most well-known republican feature of Swiss democracy is the fact that the Swiss people can decide directly on many issues on all levels of government. Switzerland is the country with the strongest institutionalisation – and the most extensive use of – direct-democratic instruments in the world (Vatter 2014: 343). The direct-democratic instrument of the popular initiative gives the people the opportunity to put an issue on the agenda, and the referendum provides them with a veto right.

The second, less well-known, but at least as important, classical republican feature is that Switzerland holds dear the principle of identity not only among the members of the political community but also between the rulers and the ruled. The first, communitarian, aspect of the principle of identity explains the fact that Switzerland remains the most decentralised and federalised country in Europe so that the cantons, which have their distinct cultures, still have many competences and capacities (see the following discussion). The second, more clearly republican, aspect is embodied in the so-called *Milizsystem*. It expresses the idea that the citizens themselves and not any agents or representatives defend and rule themselves. Its strong ideological anchorage prevented the strong professionalisation of the military and of the political elite, as well as the functional specialisation of the bureaucracy. Normatively, it is not even acceptable for the members of the national parliament to perform their position as a full-time job (although *de facto* it is often the case; see Z'graggen 2009).

The Swiss political system, as noted, is the most decentralised and federalised one in Europe (Vatter 2014: 343, 427, 465). In contrast to other federations, where the federal structure has been established in order to contribute to the liberal ideas of institutional checks and balances, Swiss federalism is much more the result of communitarian and republican thinking. The cantons, where cultural homogeneity is much more prevalent than on the national level, are the basic building blocks of the political system, and the federal government was only reluctantly established in order to secure political autonomy from the European neighbours. The prevalence of these ideas shows up in the following structural features of Swiss federalism (Vatter 2014: 427–438):

- Multiplicity: the small country with a population of about 8 million people is divided up in 26 cantons and about 2,500 municipalities;
- Diversity in size: the largest canton (ZH) has 1,425,538 inhabitants and the smallest 15,778 (AI);
- Diversity in function: similar to the US, in Switzerland, municipalities as general purpose and territorially defined jurisdictions are accompanied by many policy-specific forms of governance like school districts and parentage-based *Bürgergemeinden*, as well as
- Smallness: the majority of cantons have less than 270,000 inhabitants, and the majority of municipalities have less than 1,300 inhabitants.

Despite their small size and great diversity, Swiss municipalities and cantons have been able to keep more competences and resources on the subnational level than in any other federal state (with the exception of Canada). The horizontal relationship among the entities of the Swiss nation-state is primarily determined by an ideology that values economic and fiscal competition. Competitive federalism is accompanied by limited forms of functional cooperation. The cantons have used formal forms of inter-cantonal cooperation much less than other federations; functionalist bi- and multilateral cooperation clearly trumps nationwide horizontal coordination; the latter is only accepted if it can be sold as an attempt to avoid regulation at the federal level (Parker forthcoming). The picture is different, though, when we look at informal and technocratic forms of cooperation and coordination – more than 500 bodies exist, staffed with cantonal members of government and bureaucrats (Iff et al. 2010). The vertical relationship among the entities of the Swiss state is also characterised by unusually successful attempts at preserving competences on a lower level of government and keeping the competences of the different layers of government separate. All attempts at changing the fundamental structure of the Swiss confederation by arguing that the socio-economic interdependencies among the particular municipalities and cantons are very strong, have never found much resonance, neither among the elites nor among the people. For example, a recent attempt to reunite the two half-cantons of Basel-Stadt and Basel-Land has been stopped by a referendum before detailed negotiations could even start.

Whereas republican (and communitarian) features of democracy are strongly institutionalised in the Swiss political system this is not the case with liberal principles. First, the direct-democratic instruments and the important role of the cantons in the Swiss federation have had a strong influence on the functioning of representative democracy. The availability of direct democratic instruments has reduced the importance of general elections, so that Switzerland has a very low turnout rate in parliamentary elections. It stimulated the formation of the well-known consociational form of democracy in which all major parties are included in the federal government and parliamentary elections usually do not lead to any changes in government. Furthermore, competitive federalism entails that political cleavages and competition are strongly defined along territorial lines and comparatively less so in terms of interest groups, ideology or party politics. In addition, the foundational role of the cantons is reflected in the fact that the second chamber of the national parliament (Ständerat), which represents the cantons, has competences and powers equivalent to the first chamber of parliament which represents the Swiss people. Each canton is equally represented in the Ständerat (by two directly elected representatives) despite tremendous differences in size. In consequence, the equality between the two principals of the Swiss *Eidgenossenschaft* (the cantons and the people) entails that the liberal principle of formal equality of all individual persons is severely compromised. Equal opportunity in the political process is also compromised by the fact that the hegemonic conservatives and liberals have blocked all attempts to provide public money for political parties. Even more, they turn a deaf ear to demands from internal and external critics (the Group of States against Corruption has launched numerous criticisms) that Switzerland should provide some transparency when it comes to the financing of campaigns for general elections and popular votes.[1] The Swiss model of democracy has flaws not only in terms of formal equality and transparency but also with regard to inclusion. Not by accident, it was the last Western democracy to give women the right to vote; restrictive naturalisation regulations led to the fact that currently almost 25 per cent of the adult population are foreigners and therefore are excluded from voting on the national level. Further, it is important to realise that Switzerland has neither a strong constitution – the constitution is getting modified with every successful popular initiative – nor a constitutional court. Neither popular votes nor federal legislation is subject to legal scrutiny (Blatter 2015; Linder 2012). Finally, it is important to underline that whereas political liberalism plays a minor role, the same cannot be said of economic liberalism, which plays a central role, as will be seen in the next section.

## Switzerland's form of European Integration

The principles and institutions of Swiss democracy shape the normative-cognitive framework by which the Swiss – at least in their majority – look at the external world, and it influences their preferences in respect to how Switzerland should relate to the external world (especially to the EU). In the following, I want to show why the Swiss bilateral relationship to the EU can be explained by the prevalence of political republicanism and economic liberalism.

In economic terms, Switzerland is one of the most integrated countries in Europe.[2] Nevertheless, a majority of the Swiss apply their internal experience to deal with socio-economic integration and political (inter-)dependence also to their external relations: They defend the neo-liberal principle that national autonomy, competition and (mutual) adjustment is the best way to deal with socio-economic (inter)dependence.[3] In consequence, in Europe they prefer 'negative integration' (deregulation and free trade) and oppose 'positive integration' (reregulation and harmonisation).

The entire foreign policy has been dominated by the twofold goal not to get excluded from the European market and not to get included in any larger political community. In consequence, Switzerland joined the European Free Trade Association (EFTA) in 1960 as a reaction to the Treaty of Rome and signed a free trade agreement with the European Community in 1973 after Great Britain joined the EC. After a narrow majority of the people but a clear majority of the cantons rejected Swiss membership in the multilateral EEA in 1992, the Swiss government negotiated bilateral, primarily market opening, treaties with the EU until the beginning of the twenty-first century (Freiburghaus 2009). In 2001, the Swiss people clearly rejected a popular initiative that demanded a start of negotiations with the EU to become a fully fledged member (Schwok 2009: 88–89). Based on the bilateral treaties and despite the clear anti-EU stance of the population, the Swiss government has tried to get included (in most cases successfully) in the intergovernmental networks and agencies of the EU that are set up to smoothen the socio-economic and political interactions (Lavenex 2009, forthcoming).

This strategy has proven to be very successful in economic terms, because Switzerland has profited from the integration in the European common market without being obliged to contribute much when it comes to financing cohesion measures[4] or to stimulate growth through public spending programmes. Furthermore, the Swiss government has used the negotiations for the bilateral treaties with the EU in order to overcome resistance of entrenched domestic interests and to modernise regulations in many policy fields, which have contributed to its economic success since the turn of the millennium. Switzerland could smoothen the internal adjustment process by getting many substantial (e.g. in the field of agriculture) and temporal concessions (especially in respect to free movement of people) from the EU, and it is very plausible that the threat of a potential referendum made the Swiss bargaining position stronger (Freiburghaus 2009).

Sectorial bilateralism has until now not only proved to be economically profitable but also to safeguard the traditional republican forms of political participation. The fact that Swiss diplomats and bureaucrats are taking part in many intergovernmental networks/agencies – although often without a formal voting right (Lavenex 2009, forthcoming) – and that the Swiss government has introduced a 'euro-compatibility' examination in the lawmaking process, should not be interpreted as a case of Swiss obedience to the EU. It is primarily an extension of established forms of governance in the decentralised and competitive Swiss federation: for the Swiss cantons (especially the smaller ones) observing the policies and regulations of others and adjusting to them is nothing unusual and not seen as a loss of autonomy as long as they can secure autonomy in core areas (e.g. taxation), and as long as they keep some leeway in how exactly they adjust to external rules and regulations. The same is true for functionalist collaboration and rule transformation through intergovernmental networks and institutions, which are established in the Swiss federation in a similarly extensive way as in the multilevel system of the EU.

There are two preconditions that make these modes of governance legitimate from a classical republican point of view:

First, in order to secure the 'identity' of the rulers and the ruled, bureaucrats and politicians must not be decoupled from the people. Their closeness and similarity to 'normal' people is what makes them seen as legitimate trustees.

Second, the people have the right to intervene through popular initiatives and referenda. In Switzerland, the internationalisation of the lawmaking process has been accompanied by an expansion of popular and cantonal rights in external affairs (the cantonal rights had been dominant until the confederation turned into a federation in 1848). At the beginning of the twentieth century, foreign policy was the competence of the federal executives, but only briefly, because in a first step the role of the parliament has been strengthened in three constitutional revisions (1921, 1977, 2003) and, in a second step, the rights of the people have been expanded, as well. Today, the constitution grants direct participation of the people in international affairs similarly to domestic laws: the most important treaties are subject to the obligatory referendum, and the optional referendum was extended to all treaties containing important legal norms or demanding federal legislation for implementation (Linder 2014: 229).[5]

The adjustments of the political rights of the people in the field of foreign affairs to the ones they have in domestic politics entail that 'there have been more popular votes on European integration in Switzerland than in any EU member state' (Gava et al. 2014: 197). This is true even if we count only those popular votes which can be described as explicit integration decisions (as will be made clear in later sections, there are many more popular votes which target or affect the Swiss relations to the external world).

In 1992, the Swiss people rejected membership in the EEA, but in 2000 they accepted the first bilateral treaties with the EU as a package. The seven treaties facilitated the integration of Switzerland in the common market, and the most important one brought the freedom for EU citizens to settle in Switzerland. In 2005, they voted on one of the nine treaties of the second round of bilateral treaties, the so-called Schengen/Dublin Agreements, which brought the elimination of border controls for individuals within the Schengen Area.

At the beginning of the 1990s, the Swiss government saw the EEA only as a first step for fully fledged membership in the EU. A few weeks before the people decided on the EEA in 1992, the government sent an official application letter to Brussels. This letter probably contributed to the peoples' rejection of the EEA, and the government has not come back to it, but officially the application is still pending. In 1997, a popular initiative demanded that the Federal Council would withdraw its application for membership. The people dismissed it with a clear majority, but in 2001, they rejected with a similar strong majority an initiative that asked the government to reopen membership negotiations with the EU. In 2005 and 2009, the Swiss people accepted the extension of the bilateral treaties to eight Central and Eastern European Countries and then to Bulgaria and Romania (Schwok 2009).

During the first decade of the twenty-first century, it looked as if sectorial bilateralism would be a stable pathway for a relationship with the EU that safeguards economic liberalism and political republicanism in times of intensified socio-economic exchanges and interdependencies, but as is shown in the last section, this turns out to be an illusion.

Before ending this section I address the argument that membership in the EU would be a gain in respect to securing autonomy through participation. This is so, the argument goes, because membership would make it possible for the Swiss to vote for the European Parliament and for Swiss representatives to have a say (actually, a vote) in all EU institutions and the ability to influence the policymaking process in Brussels (e.g. Kellenberger 2014). First, from a classical republican view, indirect participation through representatives in distant, large and heterogeneous decision-making bodies is seen as clearly inferior in comparison to direct participation in closer, smaller and more homogeneous arenas. Second, for a country that has secured a profitable niche in a globalised world economy it is clear that having a little bit of influence in respect to all policy fields is an unsatisfactory substitute for having a lot of influence in just a few, but very important, ones. Third, because of the fact that since 1848 political republicanism has been moulded together with economic liberalism, the fact that bilateralism restricts the participation of Swiss politicians (and bureaucrats/diplomats) in agenda setting, decision shaping and decision-making on the European level is a price that many are more than willing to pay, and it is not seen as an important loss of autonomy. Much more valued is that bilateralism allows the Swiss more leeway in the later stages of the policy process (deciding which policies and how to implement them without judicial oversight) and that they can fend off those policies that would restrict their economic freedom. After all, the Swiss brand of republicanism values the autonomy of particularistic political communities, but not the autonomy of politics. This is a very particular and rather conservative understanding of republican democracy, which does not represent the current state of the art in republican theories of democracy, as is shown in the next section.

## Swiss sovereignty and the selective stance against domination

In recent years, we have witnessed the rise of a neo-republican theory of democracy. In contrast to what can be called 'developmental' or 'communitarian' republicanism[6] that draws on the Greek tradition and on continental European thinkers like Rousseau, emphasising identification and participation, the 'protective' or 'liberal' strand of republicanism refers to the Roman tradition, makes reminiscence not only to Italian thinkers such as Machiavelli but also to 'Atlantic' ones such as the writers of the Federalist Papers, and focuses on the concept of non-domination (Pettit 2012: 5–8, 16).[7] Republican autonomy demands in this view that individuals (and states on an international level) are embedded in a social structure and are provided with a legal status that shields them from arbitrary interference by others (from alien control in the case of nation states). In contrast to liberal or libertarian views of autonomy, interference or control as such is not seen as problematic per se, but only if it is 'arbitrary' or 'alien' (Pettit 2012: 56–59). Protective republicans are 'less sceptical of the possibility of state intervention, and they will be more radical in their view of the social ills that the state ought to rectify', because 'they do not view state action, provided that it is properly constrained, as an inherent affront to liberty' (Pettit 1997: 148, 276). For Philip Pettit, there are two options to make interference non-arbitrary and control non-alien: first, if interference is justified, control takes place in a non-coercive deliberative form and second, if interference can be resisted, control can be checked by the controlled so that it ultimately relies on consent (Pettit 2010: 73–75). Other neo-republicans emphasise the malevolent effects of private *dominium* even more in comparison to the danger of public *imperium*. In consequence, they advocate a strong majoritarian government based on competitive elections instead of consensus and checks-and-balances for mitigating domination (Shapiro 2012: 329, 335).

In the article 'A Republican Law of Peoples' Pettit spells out three potential sources of domination that nation states face within the international system (Pettit 2010: 77–79):

a. Powerful states, which use military threats or interventions and economic or diplomatic pressure to exercise direct or indirect control of other states;
b. Resourceful private bodies like multinational corporations and rich individuals which use their resources directly for having an undue influence in public policy-making by financing and lobbying or using their property rights for wielding influence on national policies by threatening to move offshore.
c. International public bodies, which are set up by states but have escaped their control and reduce the states' autonomy directly or indirectly in an arbitrary manner.[8]

In the following, I want to show that Switzerland takes a highly selective stance in respect to these sources of domination and is only selectively successful in shielding itself from alien control. On one hand, Switzerland rejects in principle and resists in practise alien control from neighbouring European states and the EU. On the other, it accepts in principle the control of powerful private actors and is not able anymore to resist in practise the interference of those states that wield hegemonic market power (the US – and increasingly China). What makes things worse from a neo-republican democratic point of view is that Switzerland undermines the capacities of its European neighbouring states and the EU to protect themselves from domination by resourceful private individuals/corporations and hegemonic states.

In the following section I substantiate these claims by first pointing to a general Swiss reluctance to sign up to binding international collaboration and thereafter go through the important example of Switzerland's banking secrecy and the important role Switzerland has played for many years – thanks to its non-member status – in helping to block all attempts within the EU to reach coordinated measures in the field of taxation of private savings.

## Switzerland's selective stance towards external sources of domination

Switzerland's reluctance to join international political organisations is not limited to the EU. Although Switzerland had been hosting many institutions of the United Nations in Geneva for a long time, it joined the United Nations only recently. As late as 1986 three-quarters of the Swiss voters decided not to join the United Nations, and only in 2002 a majority of the Swiss could be won over. Whereas the reluctance to join politically oriented international organisations is justified with the notion of 'neutrality', another trope makes it difficult to accept any judicialisation of its external relations: traditional narratives not to accept any 'foreign judges' have popped up already during the campaigns against the membership in the EEA. In recent years it has been a major hindrance in the negotiations with the EU, because the EU makes its willingness to sign further bilateral treaties conditional upon Swiss willingness to accept judicial oversight over the implementation of the bilateral treaties. Furthermore, resistance is mounting against the rulings of the European Court of Human Rights. Critics argue that Switzerland has signed and ratified the European Convention on Human Rights without the consent of the people. As I discuss in the last section in more detail, not only international organisations but also international law are framed more and more as antagonistic to popular sovereignty.

In sharp contrast to the traditional and in recent years once again growing aversion against international political organisation and international courts, Switzerland has joined many technically or economically oriented international organisations. For example, in 1948 it was a founding member of the Organisation for Economic Co-operation and Development (OECD). But even more important in our context is the fact that Switzerland has a long tradition of being very accommodating towards private holders of financial capital and multinational corporations.

Mobile private capital and international corporations (at least their headquarters) are attracted by a combination of political stability/conservatism, low taxation, liberal or non-existing regulation, and the Swiss reluctance to cooperate and share information with other states (famously symbolised in Swiss banking secrecy). These ingredients made it possible for Switzerland to become the largest offshore financial centre in the world. Swiss banks manage about one-fourth of the global offshore wealth, about twice as much as the second-largest place, Singapore (Boston Consulting Group 2013: 12). But it is not only in the financial sector that Switzerland plays a key role in the globalised economy. The same is true for other economic sectors that are strongly globalised; for example, commodity trading and the marketing of sports and arts.

Swiss non-membership in the EU made it possible to pursue a tax and regulatory policy that undermines the capacity of other states to tax and regulate private and corporate actors. With reference to its sovereignty, for half a century Switzerland was able to resist all external attempts to force it to give up its most harmful practices (Freiburghaus 2009: 316–323; Steinlin and Trampusch 2012). What is more, its non-membership provided it with a status that gave it 'alien control' over the EU. This became most obvious when the EU undertook another attempt to fight tax evasion by private capital holders at the end of the 1990s (the first attempts date back to the 1960s). The large member states (which suffer most from tax evasion) and the European Commission pushed for the introduction of a system of autonomous information exchange. Smaller member states such as Luxembourg, Belgium and Austria – which had followed Switzerland's lead by introducing bank secrecy laws and which profited from the existing system – could no longer resist the pressure of the other member states after Great Britain joined the coalition in favour of the information exchange. They accepted the automatic reporting system in principle but would only implement it after Switzerland (and other tax havens) would give up banking secrecy, as well. Switzerland refused, which allowed these countries to uphold their banking secrecy for many further years, which in turn lessened the capabilities of the EU states to reduce tax evasion (Holzinger 2005). In other words, Swiss banking secrecy not only undermined the taxing capabilities of other countries indirectly by serving as a tax haven, but also directly by providing the excuse for those that had an interest in escaping the common norm.

Both forms of interference have to be judged as unjustified because they violate the transparency and cooperation norms that have taken hold not only within the EU but on a global level in the last 20 years also. Because it had become clear that the interdependency of tax regimes generates external effects that undermine the de facto sovereignty of states and that tax competition exacerbates inequalities of income and wealth both within countries and across borders (Dietsch and Rixen 2014), the OECD, backed later on by the G20, started to develop an initiative against harmful tax competition (Sharman 2008). Also here, 'Switzerland ultimately contributed to the initiative's (partial) failure' (Emmenegger 2014: 8). Ironically, this time because Switzerland is a member of the OECD, and the OECD in its first attempt to fight tax havens targeted only non-member states. This allowed the attacked tax havens to accuse the OECD of hypocrisy as long as it left countries like Switzerland off the list of tax havens (Sharman 2006).

Despite many attempts, neither the EU nor any of its member states (nor the OECD) was able to curb Switzerland's unjustified interference in their policy-making in the field of taxation. Only later, when the US used its legal and market power to threaten to deny them access to the US market, in effect threatening the existence of the Swiss banks, did Switzerland give up its uncooperative policy and some core elements of banking secrecy (Emmenegger 2014).

The taxation of private capital income is one important field of international tax policy; the even more important one is the taxation of international corporations. Also, here Switzerland plays an important role as a country that offers not only low tax rates, but a regulatory context that makes it very attractive for multinational corporations which aim to reduce their tax loads. Once again, Switzerland's non-membership status (and its extremely federalised structure) made it possible for a long time to resist the pressure of the EU to eliminate taxation rules on the cantonal level which contain massive discounts for foreign multinationals. Nevertheless, it seems that Switzerland cannot uphold this resistance anymore. The federal government promised to erase those rules that the EU judged to be unfair. But the way the government proposed to make the adjustment to EU demands is very telling: The first and most important proposed measure is to import those taxation rules (such as 'patent boxes') that EU member states use in order to reduce the tax loads of multinationals. The second important measure is to lower the taxes for all corporations close to the level that until now only the multinationals enjoy.[9] For the minister of finance it is clear: Switzerland will use the necessary adjustment as an opportunity to strengthen its international competitiveness.[10] This, of course, will lead to massive gaps in the tax revenue of the Swiss cantons. The federal government has promised to partly compensate the cantons for their losses, but it is highly likely that the cantons will be forced to introduce further cost-cutting measures (most cantons had to cut services and costs already in the last few years, since a fierce round of inter-cantonal tax competition forced them to lower taxation for corporations and individuals during the last 10 years). In other words, when Switzerland is no longer able to fend off the demands from the EU to reduce its harmful tax regimes, the way it adjusts to this demand fuels massively the 'race to the bottom' in respect to corporate taxation.

In the context of our analysis of republican autonomy as non-domination, we can interpret this as follows: when threatened by the EU and by private corporations and capital holders at the same time, its embedding in the global socio-economic structure and its status as a non-member contribute to the result that Switzerland obeys much more to the demands of the latter than to the demands of the former. More precisely, Switzerland adjusts its adaptation to EU demands in such a way that the control of political communities over private corporations is not strengthened. It seems that this model might have come to an end since subservience to the demands of private corporations/capital seems not to pay off anymore for the Swiss population. *De facto*, the autonomy of the Swiss population is limited to choose between either higher taxes for individuals/consumers or lower public services in order to make up for the reduced financial contributions of corporations. Nevertheless, it might well be that – like in 1814 and 1848 – tectonic shifts in the wider international environment make it possible for Switzerland to uphold its very selective stance against domination. The private capital-/corporation-friendly way to adjust to EU pressure makes Switzerland even more competitive in the globalised economy. Furthermore, the combination of having access to the common European market coupled with full formal autonomy to forge international trade agreements with emerging markets, might make it once again possible that obeying to the wishes of an external power might be perceived not as 'alien control' but as profitable for both and therefore based on consent. Switzerland's foreign economic policy has already turned very much towards China with the explicit goal of reducing its economic dependence on Europe. Switzerland's embassy in Peking has been staffed up so much that it is now the largest embassy that Switzerland maintains in the world, and Switzerland is very proud of being the first European country with whom China has signed a free trade agreement. Not much attention was paid to the fact that China wants to use Switzerland as a side-entry into the European market.[11] So, once again the Swiss selective stance towards external domination might indeed shield it from being dominated by the Europeans and obedience towards other external powers is turned into a profitable and therefore acceptable relationship for the Swiss. As has been the case in earlier times,[12] the price for the autonomy of a particular and small polity is the weakening of the self-determining capacity of other and more encompassing polities like the EU.

## The Swiss form of political accountability between republicanism and regional integration

In the introductory chapter of this volume accountability is defined as a 'justificatory process that rests on a reason-giving practice, where the decision-makers can be held responsible to the citizenry, and where, in the last resort, it is possible, to dismiss incompetent rulers' (Eriksen and Fossum 2012: 20). This definition combines two understandings of how representatives should be held accountable that we find in the literature on representation:[13] First, an 'electoral' approach focussing on the formal authorisation of representatives by the represented and on the opportunities to sanction them through regular elections (e.g. Ferejohn 1999), and second, a 'discursive' or 'deliberative' approach which does not only demand that representatives have to justify their decisions to all affected parties (and not just to their electorate) but which also highlights the constitutive dimension of the communicative acts that are taking place in the process of representation (e.g. Dryzek and Niemeyer 2008; Saward 2006). Nevertheless, it misses a third understanding of accountability, which has traditionally played a major role in Swiss democracy: an 'identical/identificatory' approach which implies that representatives share descriptive traits with the represented; a common social background and shared experiences lead to confidence that a representative that resembles the represented functions as their authentic voice (Mansbridge 1999; Philipps 1995).

As noted above, in Switzerland's consociational democracy electoral accountability does not play as important a role as it does in majoritarian forms of parliamentary democracy. Parliamentary elections do not lead to a change in government, and the prime means of controlling rulers is not to dismiss them but to challenge their decisions in a referendum. Accountability has been secured by selecting 'identical' rulers and by an inclusive and consensus-oriented public discourse. In the following section, I show how bilateralism as an institutional form to deal with strong trans-boundary interdependencies is undermining and transforming those traditional republican means of holding representatives accountable: first, it contributes to the erosion of trust in government and thereby undermines identity-based accountability; second, direct democracy is losing its integrative and pragmatic qualities for deliberative accountability.

## Holding Swiss rulers accountable: From trustees to traitors?

Over time, there has been a slow but clear change in the logic of political representation in Switzerland. In the beginning, politicians on the national level primarily represented the interests/values of their cantons. Later on the ideology of political parties became the main point of reference, and Switzerland developed one of the most polarised party systems in Europe (Vatter 2014: 95–158). Nevertheless, when it comes to executives, the role model for political rulers has always been the 'trustee' and not the 'delegate'.[14] Institutionally, this shows up most strongly in the rule that the members of the Swiss national government (Bundesrat) cannot be dismissed by the parliament after they have been elected by the two chambers of parliament at the beginning of a legislative period. This makes the executive much less dependent on and responsive to the parliament than is the case in parliamentary systems. Beyond formal institutional rules, there are further features which indicate the prevalence of the trustee concept (the selection model) over the delegate concept (the sanctioning model) of representation: in the second half of the twentieth century there has been a fixed formula for the composition of the Bundesrat based on two consociational dimensions: all major parties and all major cultural/linguistic parts of the country had to be represented. But the parties were not free to decide autonomously who should be their representative in the executive branch; especially in the case of the Social Democrats, the majority of the parliament dismissed profiled party candidates and selected more mainstream candidates instead. Furthermore, until recently it was very uncommon that incumbent members of parliament or members of the executive were not re-elected. In other words, whereas there is a sophisticated set of criteria and a comprehensive process to select the adequate people to govern Switzerland in an inclusive and consensual way, after being elected those rulers usually do not have to fear any sanctions. The parliament has no right to dismiss them and during the twentieth century never refused to re-elect those that wanted to serve another term (Vatter 2014: 222). The people cannot dismiss the government either, and nobody expects a resignation if the people do not follow the government in a referendum or initiative.

Nevertheless, the trustee model has become destabilised during the last 20 years. After Christoph Blocher made it possible with strong anti-EU and anti-immigrant campaigns to elevate the Swiss Peoples' Party (Schweizer Volkspartei [SVP]) to the rank of the largest party in parliament, he not only challenged the traditional 'magic formula' for the Bundesrat by demanding a further seat for the SVP. In 2003, he managed to be elected as one of the seven members of the Bundesrat himself. The inclusion of such a polarising figure in the federal executive produced stark tension within an institution that has been designed for being populated by consensus-oriented trustees. After one unruly legislature, the federal parliament did not re-elect Blocher but preferred a more moderate SVP candidate. The SVP did not accept this verdict of the parliament and expelled the two elected SVP magistrates from their party. This resulted in the SVP not being included in the Bundesrat at all for one year. Afterwards, the parliament accepted the former party president,

Ulrich Maurer, as a member of the Bundesrat, but the SVP remains underrepresented in the federal executive (Vatter 2014: 207–208, 225).

Against this background, the federal government has been under attack in recent years. The SVP put an initiative on the agenda demanding the direct election of the members of the Bundesrat by the Swiss people. They launched this initiative despite the fact that experience from the direct election of executives on the cantonal level has proved that SVP candidates do not profit from this election modus because they are usually too radical for getting a majority of votes. Nevertheless and although they could not win over a majority at the ballot box, with this initiative the populist party could bring to the fore that the members of the Bundesrat are the only rulers in the Swiss political system who are not directly elected. They are elected by the two chambers of the national parliament. Within the traditional republican understanding of democracy that dominates in Switzerland, such an election does not produce as much democratic legitimacy as a direct election by the people.

Whereas the most direct attack on the institutional setup of the Bundesrat could be repelled, the national government is nevertheless on the defensive. Longstanding plans to reform the 165-year-old organisational structure of the government with the goal to strengthen the leadership capacity of the national executive were defeated in parliament (Vatter 2014: 249). Furthermore, not only is its agenda-setting role in the legislative process eroding (Vatter 2014: 235); in parliament governmental proposals are getting rejected much more often than in the last century. Finally, the government is not able anymore to counter popular initiatives with arguments or with alternative proposals as had been the case during the time when the 'magic formula' was intact. We should remember that between the Second World War and the end of the 1970s, not a single popular initiative was successful. From the 1980s until 2003 the success rate rose to about 6 per cent, whereby it is striking that only one specific kind of initiative was successful: initiatives which demanded a stronger protection of the natural environment. With the breakdown of the traditional 'magic formula', this changed dramatically. From 2003 onwards, about every fourth popular initiative succeeded against the will of the Bundesrat, and all successful initiatives have a nationalist/conservative leaning (Linder et al. 2010; Vatter 2014: 351, 352).[15]

These developments indicate that the Swiss government is no longer accepted as the trustee it had been earlier on. And there are signs that this traditional form of accountability will be shattered even more in the upcoming years. For the 2015 parliamentary election campaign, Christoph Blocher and the SVP have developed a strategy that puts the Bundesrat and its role in the Swiss relationship with the EU in the spotlight. Blocher has started a similar tour through Switzerland as he did in 1992 when he played a major role in defeating the EEA treaty. The main message is that the current members of the Bundesrat are 'traitors' who try to lead Switzerland through the backdoor into the EU. He asks the people to use the next parliamentary elections to stop such a betrayal.[16] This discursive focus on the national executive is accompanied by launching popular initiatives that put the Swiss relationship with the external world at centre stage in the election year (more details are provided in the next section). This means that the established Swiss system of accountability is put on its head: popular initiatives are instrumentalised as campaign tools by the strongest party in order to gain more seats in parliament, and the latter, in turn, is primarily framed as a necessary condition for changing the composition of the executive. In other words, issue-specific direct democratic decision-making is not decoupled anymore from the questions of political power and party politics. As in parliamentary systems, elections are seen primarily through the prism of gaining power in government. The relationship with the EU (and the external world in general) plays an important role in making this radical makeover of the Swiss political system possible. In the next section, I want to show that this is also true the other way around: the internal changes in the Swiss political system have potentially massive implications for the Swiss form of political integration in Europe and beyond.

To sum up this section, in contrast to what has been diagnosed for Norway (and for EU member countries), for Switzerland the main finding is that the bilateral form of European political integration has not led to a strengthening of the national executives. There were some tendencies in this direction during the negotiations of the bilateral treaties at the turn of the century, but soon a strong counter-current set in to avoid that the national executives could use their gatekeeper position between domestic and international politics for expanding their leeway and power. Bilateralism puts the national executives in a precarious position, since they represent the points of contact with an external other in a constellation that is framed and perceived not only as bipolar (Switzerland against the EU) but as strongly asymmetric and endangering (a large EU threatens a small Switzerland). The institutional design makes the Bundesrat predestined for fulfilling a mediating role – but only for mediating among the divergent groups within Switzerland. When the challenge changes towards mediating between internal and external demands, the organisational weakness of the Bundesrat does not allow a leadership role similar to that of national executives in many EU member countries.

This suggests that the bilateral form of European affiliation does not lead to similar changes in respect to political accountability as in other European states, but it does not leave intact those forms of political accountability that dominated in the second half of the twentieth century in Switzerland either. The traditional form of accountability, which had been based on an imagined identity between rulers and the ruled, is under attack. Furthermore, the combination of bilateralism and increasing importance of popular democracy in foreign affairs not only contributes to the demise of 'identical' accountability; it also reduces the productivity of direct-democratic instruments for 'deliberative' accountability.

## Deliberative accountability within a popular democracy: From inclusiveness and pragmatism back to exclusiveness and populism?

In order to interpret the current developments it is revealing to look back into history. The introduction of direct-democratic instruments during the nineteenth century first on the cantonal and soon after on the federal level was the result of the mobilisation of rural-conservative and later on urban-social democratic masses against the ruling liberal elites. Those liberal elites did not only promote economic openness but tried also to preserve representative forms of government as well. Whereas the Conservatives used forms of popular democracy to exclude migrants and religious minorities, the Social Democrats tried to use them in order to gain social rights and benefits for the growing but still excluded working class. The Conservatives were not only much more successful at the ballot box; they were also included in the federal government much earlier.

Only after the Second World War, the famous consociational form of democracy (*Konkordanzdemokratie*) emerged, characterised primarily by the inclusion of all major parties in government according to the 'magic formula' and by the proportional representation of political parties and cultural segments of the country in all public institutions. This structural element was complemented by a very cooperative culture among the political elites, characterised by extensive formal and informal consultation and the maxim of 'amicable agreement', so that Switzerland came to be seen as a showcase for what has been called 'consensus democracy' (Lehmbruch 1975; Lijphart 1984; Linder 2012). Within this structural and cultural embedding, direct democratic instruments have unfolded their potential most productively: the decoupling of specific policy decisions from questions of who holds power positions makes it possible for the public discourse to be very problem-centred and usually the solutions represent pragmatic compromises (Blatter 2015). Given this configuration of structural and cultural features, it comes as no surprise that empirical studies found that the deliberative quality of public campaigns and the quality of parliamentarian debates are high in Switzerland compared to other democracies (Hänggli and Kriesi 2012: 275; Steiner et al. 2004: 111–119).

Currently, it seems that popular democracy is losing it productive features for deliberative accountability and shows once again its conservative, exclusive and polarising face. We can discover many similarities between developments in the second half of the nineteenth century/at the beginning of the twentieth century and those in more recent times. Since the 1980s/1990s, liberals have tried once again to stimulate and facilitate stronger socio-economic exchanges by introducing exchange-facilitating regulations on a higher level of government (earlier on from the cantonal to the federal level, now from the national to the European level). Nationalists as the current day conservatives use direct democratic instruments to block the centralisation of rule making and to send strong exclusionary signals. And once again they are very successful: the rejection of Switzerland's membership in the EEA and the clear dismissal of the initiative that demanded to start membership negotiations with the EU exemplify the resistance against any attempts to transfer political decision-making power to higher levels. And there are similar exclusionary decisions which resemble those in the second half of the nineteenth century: In 2004, a majority of the Swiss voters rejected a federal law aimed at facilitating naturalisation for third-generation immigrants; and in 2009, they approved an initiative to ban the building of new minarets. The fact that only four minarets exist in Switzerland and that none is used to lead the prayers, indicate the primarily symbolic feature of this vote. The Muslims have taken over from the Jews the role of the cultural/religious 'other'.[17]

The current day equivalents to the working-class interests of the late nineteenth and early twentieth centuries are the interests of the immigrants, but even more so the interests of the affected others beyond the boundaries of the nation state. The tendency of popular democracy to be exclusive towards non-established groups and external interests has not only shown up in the nineteenth century but also in the twentieth century. The most prominent example for the former is its role in making Switzerland the last country in Europe to establish suffrage for women. Attempts to reduce the political exclusion of immigrants by liberalising the very restrictive naturalisation regulations or through the introduction of alien voting rights on a local or cantonal level have not fared better at the ballot box so that Switzerland ends up at the lower end when the political inclusion of immigrants is compared across European democracies (Blatter et al. 2014).

If we interpret the EU as the most important attempt to take the external effects of national policymaking systematically into account, and to complement deregulation on the national level with democratically legitimised reregulation on a continental level, Switzerland's unwillingness to join and strengthen the EU is the first and most important indicator for its neglect of the interests of the externally affected. The exclusivity of popular democracy in respect to external interest has shown up not only in these polity decisions but also when it comes to specific policy decisions. For example, when the Social Democrats tried to abolish Swiss banking secrecy in 1984 by referring to its massive negative effects for neighbouring and developing countries, they suffered a crushing defeat at the ballot box (Blatter 2015).

The latest development has been that popular initiatives are instrumentalised by resourceful national interest groups and the SVP to deliberatively target the legal foundations which embed Swiss popular democracy in an international contractual and constitutional environment. In 2012, an initiative was put on the ballot box which would have made the referendum not just facultative but obligatory for most international treaties; it would also have made international treaty making for the Swiss government cumbersome, time-consuming and risky. This initiative was rejected, but in February 2014, a narrow majority of the voters accepted the anti-mass-immigration initiative, which demands that the national government has to reduce the inflow of people through the establishment of quotas for immigrants. This initiative was drafted very skilfully: explicitly, it addresses only a specific issue which has been salient for many Swiss given the high numbers of people who have moved to Switzerland during the last 10 years. But implicitly, the target has been the bilateral relationship with the EU in total, since immigration quotas violate the right of EU citizens to settle in Switzerland. This fundamental right had been established in the first package of bilateral treaties which contains the so-called guillotine clause to ensure they are put into effect together. If one of the agreements is not extended or is cancelled, either party has the right to terminate the others. Given the fact that the freedom of movement (or more correctly the freedom of settlement) had been the major price that Switzerland had to pay for the gains it received by the other treaties (access to the European market), the accepted initiative represents a fundamental challenge to the package deal that the bilateral treaties resemble. This reinforces Switzerland's reputation as a 'cherry picker'. But even more, there is a danger that the Swiss government is losing its standing as a reliable contractual partner in international relations.

The next attack on Switzerland's legal embedding in an international environment is already in the making. The SVP is currently launching an initiative that demands an explicit clarification of the relationship between the Swiss constitution and international law. The party proposes to anchor explicitly in the Swiss constitution that the Swiss constitution is the highest legal norm in Switzerland and that it supersedes international law and international accords. Because the Swiss constitution is changed by every successful popular initiative, such a clarification would have much more potential consequences in comparison to other countries with similar clauses. If the majority of the citizens vote for an initiative that stands in opposition to an international treaty, the clarification would mean that the government has to terminate the treaty. The aim of the initiative is to reduce the leeway of the national government. Currently, the government tries to deal with such a situation (produced by the anti-mass-immigration initiative) by searching for innovative solutions that are compatible both with the verdict of the people, on one hand, and with the obligations that result from the international accords, on the other.

But the initiative is not only aiming at limiting the mediating role of the federal government, it also targets the transmitter role of the federal court. According to its main drafter, an SVP politician who is professor of private and economic law, the initiative was stimulated when a chamber of the federal court declared the European Convention of Human Rights as binding for its decisions and superior to the Swiss constitution.[18] After the SVP has launched the initiative, constitutional lawyers laid out the complex and differentiated interplay between international law and national law as it is currently practiced by Swiss courts,[19] but for Christoph Blocher it has to be clarified 'to whom the federal court is primarily accountable – to the parliament and the people or to the European Court of Human Rights (ECHR)?'[20] Observers warn that the initiative is flawed because it would press a differentiated and balanced relationship into a simple hierarchy. But it is not only the content but also the instrument which has problematic consequences. The popular initiative leads to a public debate that is characterised by simplification and polarisation.[21]

In sum, the recent popular initiatives launched by the nationalist Swiss Peoples Party display the dangers of popular democracy for the quality of deliberative accountability in Switzerland: They try to (re)install the verdicts of the Swiss people as the only points of reference to which governments and judges have to justify their decisions. This is supposed to take place at the expense of human rights which are embodied in international conventions/courts and at the expense of external interests which are taken into account in international treaties/organisations.

## Conclusion

Switzerland's form of democracy and its corresponding bilateral relationship with the European Union are so distinct as to render them very difficult to imitate from a practical perspective. With its strong republican form of democracy it shows that liberal-constitutionalism is not the only way how democratic self-determination can be understood and institutionalised in the twenty-first century. Furthermore, Swiss bilateralism has made it possible for the Swiss to reap the economic profits from a common European market without having to give up its specific form of democracy.

Nevertheless, when we do not ignore the interdependencies among different models of democracy and different models of European integration, the judgement is not as positive anymore. Thus, there are also normative reasons to caution against imitating the Swiss model. The Swiss traditional and particularistic understanding of republican self-determination leads to a very selective stance against external domination. Strong resistance against any interference of neighbouring states and international organisations is combined with an extreme opportunism towards the demands of multinational corporations. From the perspective of cosmopolitan republicanism, the price for the autonomy of a particular and small polity is the weakening of the self-determining capacity of other and more encompassing polities like the EU.

Bilateralism has made it possible to conserve the traditional form of popular democracy. Nevertheless, that does not mean that strong transnational interdependencies and the bilateral treaties with the EU have not had any impact on the quality of the Swiss democracy. The *problematique* is very different from most other countries within and outside the EU. In Switzerland, we do not observe the strengthening of the executive and the judiciary. On the contrary, the Bundesrat has lost its traditional grip on the political process and is less able to function successfully as a mediator. One of the main reasons is that the federal executives (and the judiciary) are the only points of contact to external interests and universal norms. Within the national domain, they (are portrayed to) represent the external interests, but they do not have a corresponding constituency in the direct-democratic decision-making process, where only Swiss nationals have a vote. In the 1990s, the instruments of popular democracy have allowed a charismatic leader who embodies the combination of political conservatism and economic liberalism to block any form of political integration beyond bilateralism. Bilateralism as an institutional form of dealing with the external world strengthens dichotomous frames (Switzerland against the EU, the people against the elites) in the public discourse. This, in turn, makes the relationship between Switzerland and the EU (external polities in general) a perfect issue for popular campaigns. Overall, we can conclude that the Swiss form of popular democracy leads to a dichotomous and polarised relationship with the external world and this in turn feeds into the trend towards a more extreme and fundamentalist practice of popular democracy.

## Notes

1 'Kein Gesetz zur Finanzierung der Parteien', *Neue Zürcher Zeitung*, 13 November 2014.
2 König, J. and Ohr, R., 'Schweiz ist stärker EU-integriert als viele Mitgliedsländer. Der Integrations-Index zeigt Stärke und Verletzlichkeit der Schweizer Wirtschaft im EU-Raum', *Neue Zürcher Zeitung*, 12 August 2014.
3 As an ideal-typical mode of interaction, adjustments are mutual (Lindblom 1965). This symmetric concept is based on the assumption that both sides depend on the other side – in other words, that they are really *inter*dependent. By putting both terms – *inter* and *mutual* – in brackets, I would like to signal that this assumption might not hold.
4 In 2006, 53.4 per cent of the Swiss voters accepted to contribute 'voluntarily' to a cohesion fund for the Central and Eastern European Countries, but Switzerland insisted on implementing their contribution bilaterally (Schwok 2009).
5 Whereas the growing involvement of the people follows the established lines of the Swiss political system, the demand of the cantons to be more strongly involved in foreign affairs has led to a structural change – the governments of the cantons have created a joint representation in Bern for this purpose and challenge the second chamber of parliament in representing subnational interests – thereby bringing the Swiss multilevel system closer to the ones that we see in Germany and in the EU (Blatter 2002).
6 David Held (2006) introduced the terms *protective* and *developmental* in his description of republicanism as well as liberalism.
7 Major contributions are Bohman (2007), Pettit (1997, 2012) and Shapiro (2012).
8 For Philip Pettit (2010: 85–86) it is clear that '[i]nternational agencies do not represent a threat on a par with the dangers from other states and from private bodies like corporations, despite the outcries about the democratic deficit that those agencies display [...] There may still be dangers of domination associated with international agencies, of course, but only a perverted sense of priority would suggest that they are the principal problems in the area'.
9 Daepp, M. (2014) 'Die steuerlichen Massnahmen der Unternehmenssteuerreform III erhöhen Rechtssicherheit und Standortattraktivität', *Die Volkswirtschaft. Das Magazin für Wirtschaftspolitik*, Eidgenössisches Departement für Wirtschaft, Bildung und Forschung (WBF), Staatssekretariat für Wirtschaft (SECO) 11.
10 Widmer-Schlumpf, E. (2014) 'Editorial: Die Unternehmenssteuerreform III – für einen attraktiven Wirtschaftsstandort Schweiz', *Die Volkswirtschaft. Das Magazin für Wirtschaftspolitik*, Eidgenössisches Departement für Wirtschaft, Bildung und Forschung (WBF), Staatssekretariat für Wirtschaft (SECO) 11.
11 Zhang, J., 'Die Schweiz als zweites Hongkong', *Neue Zürcher Zeitung*, 19 July 2013.
12 Viktor Parma and Werner Vontobel (2009: 28–47) describe in detail how Swiss bankers have used Swiss sovereignty and secrecy already at the beginning of the twentieth century to help capital holders from neighbouring countries to escape higher taxation that new democratic governments introduced at home. They argue that this contributed massively to destabilising the Weimar Republic in Germany and the Third Republic in France.
13 For an overview on the concept of representation in contemporary democratic theory see Urbinati and Warren (2008) and Shapiro et al. (2009).
14 Andrew Rehfeld (2009: 215) provides the following criteria for this distinction: (a) whether the representative aims at the good of all or the good of a part (particularly district or party), (b) whether he or she relies on his or her own judgement or on the judgement of a third party and (c) whether he or she is responsive to sanctions or not. I deliberately stick to the traditional term *trustee* and do not exchange it with the newer concept of a

'selection model' exactly because this term implies elitism and not egalitarianism in the relationship between representative and represented (Mansbridge 2011: 621–624). Traditionally, economic elites have dominated all political institutions, and even today, the socio-structural incongruence between population and parliamentarians is very strong: in the two chambers of parliament less than 20 per cent are female, almost nobody is younger than 40 years and the lower professions are minimally represented: 8 per cent in the first chamber, 2 per cent in the second chamber, 50 per cent in the population (Vatter 2014: 324–325).

15 Hermann, M., 'Die Zauberformel', *Neue Zürcher Zeitung*, 16 November 2014.
16 For example 'Schlacht um Europa: Wie 1992 tourt Blocher durchs Land. Er ist bereit, die bilateralen Verträge mit der EU aufzugeben. Unter seinen Gegnern fehlt eine starke Figur. Und es herrscht Streit', *Neue Zürcher Zeitung*, 18 October 2014.
17 See Vatter (2011) and Vatter and Danaci (2010) for more detailed analyses of the relationship between direct democracy and religious minorities in Switzerland.
18 'Ich glaube an die Weisheit des Volkes', *Neue Zürcher Zeitung*, 27 November 2014.
19 For example Nay, G., 'Rechte der Bürger schützen', *Neue Zürcher Zeitung*, 10 July 2014; and Thürer, D., 'Kein undifferenzierter Vorrang', *Neue Zürcher Zeitung*, 29 September 2014.
20 Blocher, C., 'Politische Klärung tut not', *Neue Zürcher Zeitung*, 29 September 2014 (author's translation).
21 Vischer, B., 'Tückischer Traum von der wohlgeordneten Welt', *Neue Zürcher Zeitung*, 28 November 2014.

## References

Blatter, J. (2002) 'Zurück ins Mittelalter? Westfälische Souveränität als nationalstaatliche Monopolisierung der Außenpolitik. Historische Entwicklung und Unterschiede in den Bundesstaaten Deutschland, Österreich und der Schweiz', *Österreichische Zeitschrift für Politikwissenschaft*, 31(3): 337–361.

Blatter, J. (2015) 'Kritik der Schweizer Demokratie', Working Paper Series 'Glocal Governance and Democracy' 09, Luzern: University of Luzern. Available at: https://www.unilu.ch/fileadmin/fakultaeten/ksf/institute/polsem/Dok/WP9_Kritik-der-Schweizer-Demokratie.pdf

Blatter, J., Schmid, S.D. and Blättler, A. (2014) 'The Immigrant Inclusion Index (IMIX): A Tool for Assessing the Electoral Inclusiveness of Democracies with Respect to Immigrants', Working Paper Series 'Glocal Governance and Democracy' 08, Luzern: University of Luzern. Available at: https://www.unilu.ch/fileadmin/fakultaeten/ksf/institute/polsem/WP8_The_Immigrant_Inclusion_Index.pdf

Bohman, J. (2007) *Democracy across Borders: From Dêmos to Dêmoi*, Cambridge, MA: MIT Press.

Boston Consulting Group (2013) 'Global Wealth 2013: Maintaining Momentum in a Complex World', Boston, MA, May.

Dietsch, P. and Rixen, T. (2014) 'Tax Competition and Global Background Justice', *Journal of Political Philosophy*, 22(2):150–177.

Dryzek, J. and Niemeyer, S. (2008) 'Discursive Representation', *American Political Science Review*, 102(4): 481–493.

Emmenegger, P. (2014) '"A Nut Too Hard to Crack": Swiss Banking Secrecy and Automatic Exchange of Information in Tax Matters', paper presented at the SVPW Jahreskongress, Bern, 30 January.

Eriksen, E.O. and Fossum, J.E. (2012) *Rethinking Democracy and the European Union*, London: Routledge.

Ferejohn, J. (1999) 'Accountability and Authority: Toward a Political Theory of Electoral Accountability', in A. Przeworski, S.C. Stokes and B. Manin (eds) *Democracy, Accountability, and Representation*, Volume 2, New York: Cambridge University Press.

Freiburghaus, D. (2009) *Königsweg oder Sackgasse? Sechzig Jahre schweizerische Europapolitik*, Zürich: Verlag Neue Zürcher Zeitung.

Gava, R., Sciarini, P. and Varone, F. (2014) 'Twenty Years after the EEA Vote: The Europeanization of Swiss Policy-Making', *Swiss Political Science Review*, 20(2): 197–207.

Hänggli, R. and Kriesi, H. (2012) 'Frame Construction and Frame Promotion (Strategic Framing Choices)', *American Behavioral Scientist*, 56(3): 260–278.

Held, D. (2006) *Models of Democracy*, 3rd Edition, Stanford, CA: Stanford University Press.

Holzinger, K. (2005) 'Tax Competition and Tax Co-Operation in the EU: The Case of Savings Taxation', *Rationality and Society*, 17(4): 475–510.

Iff, A., Sager, F., Hermann, E. and Wirz, R. (2010) *Interkantonale und interkommunale Zusammenarbeit: Defizite bezüglich parlamentarischer und direktdemokratischer Mitwirkung (unter besonderer Berücksichtigung des Kantons Bern)*, Bern: KPM Verlag.

Kellenberger, J. (2014) *Wo liegt die Schweiz? Gedanken zum Verhältnis CH – EU*, Zürich: Verlag Neue Zürcher Zeitung.

Lavenex, S. (2009) 'Switzerland's Flexibel Interation in the EU: A Conceptual Framework', *Swiss Political Science Review*, 15(4): 547–575.

Lavenex, S. (forthcoming) 'The External Face of Differentiated Integration: Third Country Participation in EU Sectoral Bodies', *Journal of European Public Policy*.

Lehmbruch, G. (1975) 'Consociational Democracy in the International System', *European Journal of Political Research*, 3(4): 377–391.

Lijphart, A. (1984) *Democracies: Patterns of Majoritarian and Consensus Government in Twenty-One Countries*, New Haven, CT: Yale University Press.

Lindblom, C. (1965) *The Intelligence of Democracy: Decision Making through Mutual Adjustment*, New York: Free Press.

Linder, W. (2012) *Schweizerische Demokratie: Institutionen, Prozesse, Perspektiven*, Bern: Haupt.

Linder, W. (2014) 'Swiss Legislation in the Era of Globalisation: A Quantitative Assessment of Federal Legislation (1983–2007)', *Swiss Political Science Review*, 20(2): 223–231.

Linder, W., Bolliger, C. and Rielle, Y. (2010) *Handbuch der eidgenössischen Volksabstimmungen 1848 bis 2007*, Bern: Haupt.

Mansbridge, J. (1999) 'Should Blacks Represent Blacks and Women Represent Women? A Contingent Yes', *Journal of Politics*, 61(3): 628–657.

Mansbridge, J. (2011) 'Clarifying the Concept of Representation', *American Political Science Review*, 105(3): 621–630.

Parker, J. (forthcoming) 'Switzerland', in J. Parker (ed) *Comparative Federalism and Intergovernmental Agreements: Analyzing Australia, Canada, Germany, South Africa, Switzerland and the United States*, London: Routledge.

Parma, V. and Vontobel, W. (2009) *Schurkenstaat Schweiz? Steuerflucht: wie sich der grösste Bankenstaat der Welt korrumpiert und andere Länder destabilisiert*, München: Bertelsmann.

Pettit, P. (1997) *Republicanism: A Theory of Freedom and Government*, Oxford: Oxford University Press.

Pettit, P. (2010) 'A Republican Law of Peoples', *European Journal of Political Theory*, 9(1): 70–94.

Pettit, P. (2012) *On the People's Terms: A Republican Theory and Model of Democracy*, Cambridge: Cambridge University Press.

Phillips, A. (1995) *The Politics of Presence*, Oxford: Oxford University Press.

Rehfeld, A. (2009) 'Representation Rethought: On Trustees, Delegates, and Gyroscopes in the Study of Political Representation and Democracy', *American Political Science Review*, 103(2): 214–230.

Saward, M. (2006) 'The Representative Claim', *Contemporary Political Theory*, 5(3): 297–318.

Schwok, R. (2009) *Switzerland–European Union: An Impossible Membership?*, Brussels: P.I.E. Peter Lang.

Shapiro, I. (2012) 'On Non-domination', *University of Toronto Law Journal*, 62(3): 293–335.

Shapiro, I., Stokes, S.C., Wood, E.J. and Kirshner, A.S. (2009) *Political Representation*, Cambridge: Cambridge University Press.

Sharman, J.C. (2006) *Havens in a Storm: The Struggle for Global Tax Regulation*, Ithaca, NY: Cornell University Press.

Sharman, J.C. (2008) 'Regional Deals and the Global Imperative: The External Dimension of the European Union Savings Tax Directive', *Journal of Common Market Studies*, 46(5): 1049–1069.

Steiner, J., Bächtiger, A., Spörndli, M. and Steenbergen, M.R. (eds) (2004) *Deliberative Politics in Action: Analyzing Parliamentary Discourse*, Cambridge: Cambridge University Press.

Steinlin, S. and Trampusch, C. (2012) 'Institutional Shrinkage: The Deviant Case of Swiss Banking Secrecy', *Regulation & Governance*, 6(2): 242–259.

Urbinati, N. and Warren, M.E. (2008) 'The Concept of Representation in Contemporary Democratic Theory', *Annual Review of Political Science*, 11: 387–412.

Vatter, A. (2011) *Vom Schächt- zum Minarettverbot. Religiöse Minderheiten in der direkten Demokratie*, Zürich: Verlag Neue Zürcher Zeitung.

Vatter, A. (2014) *Das politische System der Schweiz*, Baden-Baden: Nomos.

Vatter, A. and Danaci, D. (2010) 'Mehrheitstyrannei durch Volksentscheide? Zum Spannungsverhältnis zwischen direkter Demokratie und Minderheitenschutz', *Politische Vierteljahresschrift*, 51(2): 205–222.

Z'graggen, H. (2009) *Die Professionalisierung von Parlamenten im historischen und internationalen Vergleich*, Bern: Haupt.

# PART II
# Welcomed, inside, but still unwilling
## TWO EEA COUNTRIES ASSESSED

# 5

# DESPOILING NORWEGIAN DEMOCRACY[1]

*Erik O. Eriksen*

> The Kingdom of Norway is free, independent, indivisible, and inalienable.[2]

In 1994, the most important argument against European Union (EU) membership for Norway concerned the right to self-determination, popular rule and democracy.[3] Basically, it was felt that Norwegians should have to follow laws or regulations enacted by themselves and only themselves.[4] With the negative referendum result that year, the already ratified temporary agreement, the European Economic Area (EEA) Agreement, became Norway's permanent formal affiliation to the EU. The agreement had entered into force less than a year before the referendum. Many of those who were sceptical to full membership perceived the EEA Agreement as the lesser evil – a deal which would secure Norwegian access to the EU's internal market, while at the same time minimising the loss of sovereignty. The EEA Agreement is a general framework agreement, its main body containing 129 articles, with protocols, attachments and declarations, as well as more than 9,000 legal documents. Its dynamic development ensures that the set of rules and regulations are uniformly applied across the EU and EEA.

Some claim that the Norwegian 'No' campaigners won in 1994 but have lost a little every day since then. Norway today is a member not only of an increasingly comprehensive internal market but also of the Schengen Agreement on border controls, as well as taking part in the defence cooperation of the EU, with Norwegian troops at the disposal of EU-led battle groups. The treaty register of the Norwegian Ministry of Foreign Affairs currently includes some 130 agreements with the EU. The idea that Norway must have a close and well-functioning association with the EU has become an established truism of all governments, regardless of how many anti-EU membership parties have featured in governing coalitions. As a rule, also anti-accession parties have voted in favour of further extending the agreements with the EU. How can this be, when a majority of the Norwegian population voted *against* EU membership in the 1994 referendum? What right do the Norwegian authorities have to operate in this fashion?

In this chapter I investigate the implications of Norway's EU affiliation, the EEA Agreement in particular, with regard to the constitutional right of self-determination. What are the effects for the democratic chain of rule? Through this chain the citizens authorise political power through public debate and elections and may hold the decision makers to account. Intrinsic to this chain is the separation of powers – between the legislative, judicial and executive branches. It may seem curious that a sovereign state should make itself subject to an organisation of which it is not a member, committing itself to incorporate most of that organisation's rules and regulations with no time limit. Is this a case of relinquishment of sovereignty on a grand scale and dominance as a consequence? That would be so if Norwegian citizens are not able to co-determine the conditions to which they are subjected.

In this chapter I analyse Norway's peculiar EU affiliation, emphasising the effects on the democratic chain of rule. Much of the debate on supranationalism relates to how we should understand democracy and how the ideals of representative government can be realised under conditions of complex interdependence and juridification beyond the nation state. Furthermore, I analyse Norway's relationship with the EU, focusing on the type of *contract* on which the EEA Agreement can be said to rest. Norway's relations with the EU are characterised by dependence and a broken democratic procedure. Relinquishing sovereignty can be necessary to solve problems and realise collective goals – to increase system effectiveness – but is loss of democratic legitimacy unavoidable? I therefore finally examine Norway–EU relations in light of the process of *cosmopolitanisation of nation states*, where principles of human rights and other stipulations of supranational rights stipulations are incorporated into national legislation. Sovereignty has become a question of complying with international standards of democracy and human rights. But first, the concept of democracy must be properly defined.

## Democracy and congruence

Democracy implies a specific kind of relationship between those who make decisions, and those who are affected. But does it mean that those who authorise the execution of power – the political community – must necessarily constitute a territorially based people?

### Citizens' self-rule

The international order, as we have come to know it since the Peace of Westphalia in 1648, is based on the territorial sovereignty of states and their unchecked authority in internal affairs. In the classical doctrine, sovereignty is understood as actors' exclusive control over themselves and their conditions for action. Sovereignty depicts the legal capacity to act independently on common action norms and 'the right to issue orders backed by threats which are generally obeyed' (Hart 1997: 25). It indicates the state's primary legal and judicial authority to maintain law and order within a given territory, and to be independent of external authorities (Morgenthau 1993: 321). A sovereign group controls its own agenda.[5]

This classic understanding has been heavily criticised for being merely nominal, as well as undergoing change.[6] Robert Jackson (1990) claims that states are only rarely truly sovereign, because great amounts of power (and resources) are necessary to realise real 'positive freedom'. States can have negative, *de jure* freedom, but only to a limited degree *real sovereignty*. For example, Norway emerges as not very sovereign when compared to the US. In this sense, modern states are mostly 'quasi-states'. Second, whilst the *de jure* sovereignty of nation states is rooted in the United Nations (UN) Charter, their *de facto* sovereignty is today under external pressure. As the world economy is opened up, gradually becoming more integrated, the number of transnational transactions increases; the flow of capital is globalised; transport and communication channels multiply. The ability to maintain national control over the economy is increasingly limited, at the same time as the world is facing new challenges – challenges extremely difficult to handle within the borders of a nation state. Even the mightiest state cannot control the world's financial markets. The international situation is characterised by *intense mutual dependence* between states, and many problems and challenges require coordinated efforts across borders. Among the examples are instable financial markets, tax evaders, ecological crisis, unregulated migration, refugee issues, terrorism and human rights violations. This has led to the establishment of many international conventions, institutions and transnational networks. Denationalisation[7] and transnational forms of government entail that no national communities are fully sovereign in terms of deciding their own action norms and that no state has the exclusive right to define which rules should apply to its citizens.

Denationalisation also undermines the two symmetries that are necessary for effective participation: the correspondence between the citizens and the decision makers (*input congruence*) and between the decisions and the territory within which they apply (*output congruence*). Without people's participation in the decisions that affect them, there is no real self-determination, and without correspondence between the political system and the territory that is under control, there is no effective participation. We are dealing with *dominance* when there is a lack of input congruence: when the people are subject to arbitrary power and when they are unable to influence the decisions by which they are affected or to which they are subjected.

Under conditions of complex interdependence – in a denationalised and globalised world – nation states cannot realise citizens' freedom and welfare alone, with their own resources. Therefore, dominance is a necessary consequence of globalisation. Even if the internal market of the EU contributes to economic globalisation, the EU also represents an effort towards mitigating this. It represents a contribution to *global governance* through the establishment of supranational governing structures.

Such structures increase output congruence and may as such have democratic merit. But according to which conception of democracy?

## Law and democracy

Democracy understood as a sovereign people's right of self-determination – as it is expressed in a communitarian reading of republicanism – is fundamentally problematic (Habermas 1996: 279ff.). Basically, it understands politics as a form of deliberation which takes place within groups that are already socially and culturally integrated. In this perspective, *democratic legitimacy* springs from the free will of the people. The popular will comes into existence when citizens gather and are allowed to deliberate freely, and when they obey only the laws passed by themselves. In the communitarian-republican tradition, only *the citizens of political communities* have rights, not *human beings* in general. Hence, the problem of republicanism is how to ensure an inalienable status for human rights.

In this model of democracy, individual freedom entails nothing more than the right to participate in processes of collective self-determination, with the implication that the principles of popular and of nation state sovereignty are conflated. When the nation-state is seen to ensure constitutional rule, which in turn renders possible and legitimises democracy, and hence the protection of citizens' rights and interests, there is no independent basis for securing individual rights. They become the subject of collective will formation. In this reading, *post-national democracy* becomes impossible. However, this perspective is not only difficult to maintain under conditions of interdependence and international institution building, it is also problematic in principle.

The conflation of the principles of nation-state and popular sovereignty is because of a special historical construction. It was the formation of nation states that led to the myth of citizens as macro-subject – as *one people* – that could govern themselves by controlling the state apparatuses. Herein prevails the image of *one people* based on national belonging or ethnic homogeneity, a *Volksgemeinschaft* that can be expressed and realised. The people come about as an agent with a will and mode of action of its own.

However, 'the people' does not constitute a specific entity capable of action.[8] It appears only in the plural: 'the People' consists of many peoples. It is made up of several groups, each with its own collective consciousness.[9] Most states are *multicultural* and every nationality is territorially dispersed. Rather than as a collective subject, a people should be understood as an association of individuals who share identifications but who are also granted the right to disagree by the liberal state.

Democracy must thus be viewed as a question of citizens' self-legislation, as seen in the civic republicanism of Kant. Here we have to do with an intersubjective interpretation of the principle of popular sovereignty where the will of the people is not conceived of as a collective subject, as 'the people', but as a procedural principle (Maus 1994). According to the Kantian interpretation of the principle of popular sovereignty, it can only be understood as anonymous and subjectless – as an expression of citizens' right to collective self-determination. The principle of popular sovereignty refers to the autonomy citizens require in order to form independent opinions and take part in political deliberations about what ought or ought not to be done. It stems from the procedures and institutions that provide the conditions for legitimate opinion and will formation (see Eriksen and Weigård 2003: 197; Habermas 1996: 474). The principle of popular sovereignty is linked to respect for individual freedom – subjective rights – and to the procedures for participation, deliberation and free will formation, rather than to a specific community's collective values or its capacity for action. 'The people' is a 'bodiless category', to quote Claude LeFort (1988). Therefore, modern democracies are constitutional; they are governed through constitutions that guarantee equal individual freedom and that divide the branches of government into separate powers.[10] Today rights upheld by judicial review comprise the prime component of constitutionalism.

By *constitution* is meant, higher law that regulates the establishment and execution of political power and that is devised through political decision. This understanding of constitution is of later origin – it arose through the American and French revolutions. Earlier constitutions existed as a description of countries' specific conventions, as they were shaped by territory, historical development and prevailing power relations. The premodern constitution described the existing legal basis and the operation of political institutions. It was understood as an empirical fact and custom. With the aforementioned revolutions, constitutions became normative and were linked to the rights of the individual. The constitution is now seen as constituting a horizontal association of free and equal citizens. All are equal before the law!

This new interpretation of the term *constitution* originates from efforts to limit power and bind it to the freedom of citizens, as well as to the democratic idea that all power stems from the citizens. Political legitimation was released from tradition and religion, and the protection of the individual, its dignity, freedom and well-being, became the modern principle of justification. A constitution was no longer viewed simply as a set of norms but, rather, as the conditions under which they were made. National constitutions were thus linked to democracy, and the conditions for legitimately made law. Here we see the internal link between law and politics. It is the legislative process that furnishes the judicial system with its normative premises, whereas political decision-making is governed by the law. It must follow the procedures and laws that the courts enforce. No law without politics; no policy without law. Law is the lingua franca of democracy, and democracy is increasingly viewed as the only form of government that justifies the use of political power (Lipset 1960; Sen 2012). According to this, no law is justifiable unless it also takes into account the minority and the rights of individuals, and protects the opposition so that it can work to become 'the position'. The power of the majority is subject to judicial review and thus limited, and the law is bound by principles of freedom, human dignity, tolerance, the rule of law and so on. Constitutions are expected to deal with three rather conflicting considerations:

- To define the political unit
- To balance the fear of 'the tyranny of the majority' against the fear of oligarchy
- To decide who should decide

Given this understanding of constitutional self-government, it is important to distinguish between the sovereignty of the state and that of its citizens. There is a great difference between the conditions for ensuring the capacity to act efficiently, and those for ensuring autonomous opinion-formation. In such a perspective, then, post-national democracy is not impossible. However, there is also a connection between the two forms of sovereignty.

## State or popular sovereignty?

*State sovereignty* and *popular sovereignty* are conceptually different terms. They refer to different units – to different tasks and obligations. State sovereignty refers to the interests and willpower – to *Willkür* and *Staatsraison* – and refers to the status that states are granted under classic international law. It reflects the unitary concept of sovereignty, of external sovereignty, which has an explicit anti-democratic source. Jean Bodin (1577) stated, 'We see the principal point of sovereign majesty and absolute power to consist in giving laws to subjects in general, *without their consent*' (cited in Keohane 2002: 747 [italics in the original]). Today the unitary concept of sovereignty reflects the constellation of constraints and opportunities of interdependent states, viz., the largely *self-help international system* and its tit-for-tat logic of reciprocity and countermeasures. It is the right that states have in relation to other states, concerning their control of territory and inhabitants, which includes the right to issue orders backed by threats.

State sovereignty is therefore clearly different from the rights that citizens have as free and equal members of the legislative body. Citizens are assigned the right to participate in the joint exercise of self-government. They have the rights to govern themselves cooperatively. Popular sovereignty revolves on the freedoms and possibilities required for citizens' autonomous opinion and will formation, which make it possible for them to be the authors of the laws they are do abide by. It is only when relieved from force and the power constellations of decision-making that the people can autonomously discuss and form an opinion of what ought to be done.

However, there is an empirical link between the two types of sovereignty. State sovereignty entails capacity – the resources and means needed to protect citizens' freedoms and the ability to achieve collective goals. In order to protect the citizenry – its freedom and integrity – a state with capabilities is needed. It must control its task environment in order to be able to protect the rights of its citizens. Formal, negative freedom is not worth much without clout, the organised capacity to act. This means that limitations in state sovereignty need not necessarily infringe on popular rule. It might be the other way around: renouncing state sovereignty – pooling sovereignty – might be necessary in order to achieve international cooperation and problem-solving, to increase capacity for action and, hence the ability to protect the citizenry. In Europe states have accepted restrictions on their sovereignty not only for the sake of cooperation with other states but also for the establishment of a 'legal system of peace and justice between nations' as it is stated in the Italian constitution, Art. 11. Other European states' constitutions contain similar articles. Such ceding of sovereignty may contribute to the lowering of barriers to national goal achievement and increase system effectiveness. It may also increase citizens' ability to maintain control of their own agenda (Dahl 1994; Dahl and Tufte 1973). Such cession of state sovereignty, or such pooling thereof, does not constitute cession of the people's sovereignty, as long as the democratic procedures remain intact. The establishment of supranational political orders does not constitute a loss of democratic legitimacy as long as the state continues to function as the constitutional guardian of rights and freedom (Habermas 2012: 14ff.; Linklater 1998).

Normatively speaking, democracy also requires that citizens can file complaints to superior bodies when their rights are violated. Any political community may make mistakes and may be in need of correctives. Majority decisions may violate individual or minority rights and interests, and national courts – the Supreme Court – may not always constitute a safeguard against the tyranny of the majority or against popular opinion running rampant. Supranational organs may be needed in order to prevent nation states from violating citizens' rights, to prevent one state from infringing on another or so that the policy of one nation state does not produce externalities that others end up paying for. Even democratic states sometimes operate as freeloaders, and inflict costs on others without compensation.

Thus, the normative meaning of democracy does not stop at national borders. In any instance where the political community is affected by decisions it is not in control over, demands for political representation and influence of the affected parties will arise. Democracy requires that the political community be enlarged to take into consideration the interests of all those affected. In order to prevent *dominance* and to keep decision makers accountable, citizens need to be granted opportunities to influence relevant decision-making bodies on relevant levels. Dominance is rule without justification. It is to be subject to arbitrary power or alien control. The right not to be dominated is a fundamental one, hence dominance is illicit (Forst 2011; Pettit 1999, 2010; Richardson 2002; Shapiro 2012). The right not to be dominated stems from the claim that actors and institutions are responsible for the inflicted harms of their wilful actions. Injustice, inequality and humiliation are all symptoms of dominance. The right not to be dominated is a right to have ones autonomy protected.

Autonomy is the basis for dignity and is, according to Kant, located in the lawmaking procedure. The law must be self-given, and this is the core of dignity: to obey only those laws one has been involved in making – as set out in Kant's *Groundwork of the Metaphysics of Reason* (1785/1996). Autonomy refers to the basic democratic principle that those subjected to laws should also be authorised to make them. This is the basic democratic criterion and means that the citizen *is* the legislator – either in person or through representation. *Democratic autonomy* refers not only to the conditions for free and equal opportunities to participate but also to authoritative institutions that can make binding decisions and allocate resources. This last part relates to the capacity for political action – to exercise social control and rational calculation. Capability – in the form of power, resources and competence – is necessary to protect the freedom and integrity of the political community. Intrinsic to this criterion is the capability of the authorised decision-making bodies to react adequately to public support, to determine the development of the political community in such a way that the citizens can be seen to act upon themselves.

Accountability is a secondary democratic principle. It designates a relationship in which the decision makers can be held responsible to the citizenry, and, in the last resort, it is possible to dismiss incompetent rulers. Accountability rests on the foundation of the right of the public to get proper justifications for the actions of officials and professionals as officials. It requires transparency and openness as well as activity on the part of those in authority, and misconduct is met with reactions. It refers to a relationship that is multilateral rather than unilateral, dialogical rather than monological. Accountability is deliberative, involving two-way communication between the representative and the represented, with both sides asking questions and giving answers. The core of accountability is justification, and the core of justification is good arguments. Its bottom line is the *obligation to provide good arguments for one's judgements*, decisions and actions to the public (Grimen et al. 2012).

In order to meet the requirements of autonomy and accountability – to ensure that citizens are allowed to govern themselves through law and political institutions – *congruence* is needed between *de jure* areas of competence and the actual reach of political institutions. To be in control of one's own agenda, to possess the political capacity to solve problems and realise collective goals, there must be output congruence, viz., correspondence between the decisions and the territory within which they apply and between political and social space.

## Self-inflicted harm to democratic procedure

Exactly what is it with Norway's EU affiliation that creates problems for the democratic procedure?

### Greater system effectiveness

Norwegian–EU relations are regulated through the EEA Agreement. Negotiations with the European Free Trade Association (EFTA) started already in 1989, and the EEA Agreement was implemented almost one year before the 1994 referendum. This agreement was originally intended as a temporary arrangement, but it has remained Norway's link to the internal market. While EFTA negotiations were underway, the world was changing. The Soviet Union and the Iron Curtain fell. Nation-states that had not been able to apply for EU membership now started accession negotiations. Finland and Austria joined in 1994, as did Sweden.

When Norwegians voted 'No' in the 1994 referendum, the EEA Agreement was already in force. Thanks to the large number of countries involved in the initial negotiations, the agreement is considered to be better than it would have been, should the negotiations have taken place between the EU and the remaining EFTA countries. Of these, Switzerland rejected the EEA Agreement, so the agreement is applicable only to Norway, Iceland and Liechtenstein. It is the most comprehensive agreement Norway has ever signed: it has its own court and its own surveillance body ESA (the European Surveillance Authority). Within the EU, the EEA Agreement is increasingly viewed as an annoying hindrance to effective implementation of directives and regulations (European Commission 2012).

The EEA Agreement regulates access to the internal market for all goods, capital, services and people, although Norwegian fisheries and agriculture are exempted here. The core of the agreement lies in the four freedoms of EU law and regulation of competition, public procurement and government subsidies. In addition come certain fields that do not specifically relate to the four freedoms but are seen needed to enhance their effectiveness, as well as a few adjoining areas. However, Norway's affiliation does not begin and end with the EEA and the internal market. Art. 1 of the Agreement states that its objectives include 'closer cooperation in other fields, such as research and development, environment, education and social policy'.[11] The body of rules and regulations continues to change and develop, and new areas are steadily being incorporated. The agreement now also includes areas such as gender equality, consumer protection, working environment, tourism and contingency planning. The EEA Agreement gives Norwegians citizens as well as Norwegian businesses the same rights and duties as those of citizens of EU member states when it comes to trade, investment, banking and insurance, services and to live, work and study in other countries. Norwegians are accounted 'members' of the EU as employers and employees, as customers, clients and users of services. Nearly all groups are included, except fishers, farmers and politicians.

When it was approved by the Storting (the Norwegian parliament) in 1992, the EEA Agreement contained 1875 legal provisions (directives, regulations, decisions and recommendations). A further 530 came in 1994. Since then, between 200 and 400 legal provisions have been included each year: some 10,000 in total. Between 70 and 80 per cent of these are additional explanatory rules in connection with earlier provisions. It has been estimated that Norway has adopted three-fourths of the EU's systems of regulations and laws and that 73 per cent of the motions passed in local governmental bodies in Norway stems from the EEA.[12]

Strictly speaking, it is correct to say that the EEA is an agreement that respects the sovereignty of the participating parties. The EFTA countries have not delegated decision-making authority to international bodies. The Norwegian parliament, the Storting, has entered into the agreement voluntarily and is free to leave it as well. On the other hand, the EFTA surveillance body, the ESA, does have direct authority in matter concerning competition, public procurement and agricultural subsidies and, from 2012, in the enforcement of EC regulations on aviation safety.[13] The ESA passes resolutions with direct effect for Norwegian businesses and can punish violations of rules or resolutions which are tried and confirmed by the EFTA Court. In these areas, the ESA has authority similar to that of the European Commission. Thereby Norway can be said to have ceded sovereignty.

From a constitutional perspective, decisions to cede sovereignty are of utmost importance, since they affect the status and legal standing of the constitution. There are three different legal procedures specified in the Norwegian constitution for the transfer of competence:

- Consent of the Storting by simple majority, Art. 26, second paragraph
- Approval by the Storting with a three-fourths majority, Art. 115 (previously Art. 93)
- Amendments to the Constitution by a two-thirds majority, to be dealt with by two consecutive parliaments, Art. 121 (previously Art. 112)

The EEA Agreement was approved by a three-fourths majority in the Storting in 1992, under Art. 115 of the Constitution. This article was adopted in 1962, as part of the process of Norway's first application to join the European Economic Community, now part of the European Union. It states that the Storting may transfer power to 'an international organisation to which Norway belongs or will belong [...] within specified fields'.[14] The problem is that Norway is not a member of this association – the EU – and this article cannot be seen to allow for transference of competence to pure EU bodies. Art. 115 therefore could not, and was not, used in order to adopt the agreement on border controls and police cooperation under the Schengen Agreement. The choice of procedure was in this case justified by stating that it was 'not too inventionary' and that it 'did not transfer legislative power in a constitutional sense'. The Schengen Agreement was adopted under Art. 26, by 85 to 19 votes. Here, both the controversial and very open and discretionary thesis of 'limited transfer of competence' as well as Norway's right to veto were used as arguments for this not being an unconstitutional transfer of power (Official Norwegian Report [NOU] 2012:2: 235f., 239). The basis for making this argument was very thin, however – a point to which I will return.

Every Norwegian government since 1994 has brought the country closer and closer to the EU, and more parallel agreements outside the EEA have been made (Schengen, Dublin I and II, Interreg and Europol). What was at the time viewed as a minor transfer of sovereignty has now grown out of proportion. The Schengen Agreement, which applies to border control, visas, police cooperation, return of migrants and personal privacy, binds Norway to EU policies in the field of justice and home affairs. Another matter is that in an increasingly extensive, complex and interdependent judicial Europe, *de jure* sovereignty is not worth so very much. National impotence and incapacity are the features of the day. It has become blatantly clear that the formal right to veto holds little value. The Schengen Agreement would cease to exist as soon as Norway refused to implement a directive. Because of this threat, Norway *de facto* becomes a member of the Schengen Agreement in the same respects as any full EU member.[15]

In summation, all these agreements lead to Norway being heavily involved in the day-to-day business of the EU, and especially as regards economic, administrative and judicial maters. The cumulative effect is massive, and difficult to grasp. New agreements come into being, and those already in place are further developed and expanded.

## Homogeneity and dynamics

Iceland, Liechtenstein and Norway, which now make up the EEA Group, have chosen to stand outside of the EU while benefitting from the internal market through the EEA Agreement. The intention is to achieve two goals: system effectiveness is to be ensured through access to the market, while at the same time only limited sovereignty is ceded by not having formal EU membership. Norway retains the status of a sovereign state that is free to pursue its own foreign policy; it is seen as able to protect its own vital interests, as fisheries and agriculture have been excluded from the cooperative agreement.

The EEA Agreement is a dynamic framework agreement that does not need to be renegotiated whenever the EU adopts a new regulation. The agreement is continually updated so that the laws and regulations remain consistent throughout the EEA. This dynamic aspect of the agreement is important for realisation of the basic intention: the maintenance of a homogeneous market throughout the whole area. A principle of homogeneity applies. As is also pointed to in Chapter 2 by Gstöhl and Chapter 6 by Haukeland Fredriksen in this volume, *homogeneity trumps sovereignty* as it excludes the legal norms of the EEA countries as a legal basis for the interpretation of EU market rules. Regulations and directives are to be uniform and to have the same effect for all EU member states as well as the EEA countries. The homogeneity requirement can be found in the preamble of the EEA Agreement but is also an 'unwritten rule' governing the Schengen and other agreements. This means that Norway is obliged not only to adopt EU regulations but also to interpret, uphold and live by them, in the same way as EU member states.

EU law has 'direct effect' on its member states: it does not need to be passed or voted on by the member states themselves. In contrast, under the EEA Agreement all laws and regulations must be adopted by national legislators, although it is their right and duty to interpret national law so as to avoid conflict. Therefore, there is no practical difference between how regulations are practised in Norway and in EU member states – implementation is to be 'loyal' and 'correct'. The judicial reality is in all practical aspects identical for Norway/the EEA countries and the EU member states. EEA law may, as we shall see to, claim to be the primary source of law for Norwegian courts.

The better portion of new EU law is included in the EEA Agreement each year. This agreement is the most extensive arrangement Norway has ever signed, and it is a special agreement. It is exceptional, not only because it involves very different parties – three small EFTA countries with a total population of approximately 5.5 million, on one side, and 28 EU member states with a total population of 500 million, on the other – but also because its purpose is to incorporate EFTA countries automatically into the EU's internal market – indefinitely. To this end, Norway is not only expected to incorporate current EU law into national legislation – but also to incorporate *any future law*. It is an expansive agreement, and makes the EEA signatories subject to an organisation they have no influence over – an organisation that has developed into quasi-federation with state-like features.

The EEA Agreement and other framework agreements are exceptional also because the EU itself is exceptional. It is not an ordinary international organisation, but a supranational unit with its own criteria for legitimacy. The EU is based on a special type of contract, which spills over to the EEA Agreement.

## An indigent contract

In stark opposition to the case with an ordinary international contract, where presumably equal parties enter into, terminate or renegotiate an agreement, the EU is based on a *status contract*, where the goal is to change the status of one of the parties. Such a contract has the intent to change the state's status from *nation states* to *member states*. A distinctive feature of certain institutions (such as the state or the family) is that one is part of these not as an independent individual but as a *member*. Status contracts involve a legal change in civil status. Membership gives rise to new identities and conceptions of self – conceptions about how one views and evaluates oneself. Evaluation standards, status and identity all change (Hegel 1921/2006: par. 75).

By contrast, in a normal contractual relationship, the parties freely enter into a legally binding agreement that can be terminated or amended by parties, with veto right. Nothing changes unless all those specified in the contract agree. An agreement under international law is a *gentleman's agreement*, which respects the formal rights to freedom of contract. It presupposes equality and independence, and does not touch upon sovereignty or identity issues. The parties remain the same after the contract enters into effect. Accordingly, an international organisation based on an international contract – on international law – does not invoke its own standards and criteria for legitimacy. Its legitimacy stems from the agreement of its members.

That the EU is more than an international organisation controlled by its members helps to shed light on the dynamics of the European integration process – which is the process of changing the states' legal status and domesticating international relations. The EU, with its supranational structures, is perhaps best characterised as a Bund – more than an international organisation or confederation, yet less than a federation. The member states have a strong position within a quasi-federal structure that positions EU law over national law. The European integration process has been developed and ensured through the Court of Justice of the European Union (CJEU) and its rulings. To an increasing degree the court may claim that compliance with EU law is a prerequisite for equal treatment of citizens. Here we have to do with *functional supremacy* and not supremacy of validity: it is not settled who has the final word in European arbitration but, in order for citizens to be treated equally, EU law must rank higher (on this see Bogdandy [2006] and Franzius [2010]).

But there is more. In critical court rulings during the 1960s it was affirmed that Community law takes precedence over national law, and is to be granted immediate effect in member states. In *Costa v ENEL*, the CJEU ruled that, in establishing a union, states restrict their own sovereign rights and create an order of indefinite duration.[16] The doctrine of direct effect grants EU law status equal to that of domestic, national law. The doctrine of EU law supremacy over national law ensures that in case of conflict between national and EU law, EU law wins out. Furthermore, in contrast to international organisations, the EU has its own source of legitimacy through representative bodies that make decisions by qualified majority and through the CJEU having monopoly on the interpretation of treaties. The EU makes law that most Europeans are bound by through institutions committed to the Union itself. Unlike international organisations, the EU has a constitutional identity and a legal personality.

However, the EU lacks the instruments of power. Member states have retained a 'monopoly on violence and taxes', and the EU lacks *Kompetenz-Kompetenz*: the competence to increase its competence. Still, over the past 20 years, the structure of decision-making has become increasingly supranational, in line with the increased scale of the cooperation. Through the co-decision procedure the elected officials of the European Parliament have gained more power. This could balance the Council and to a greater extent keep the Commission accountable. The EU then has its own legal basis, supranational institutions and direct links to citizens, based on the expansive status contract that alters the states' legal identity and self-perception.

The EEA Agreement, which integrates Iceland, Norway and Liechtenstein into the internal market, is marked by this construction. For these countries to be able to act on equal terms with the EU member states, most of the common legal framework known as the EU *acquis communitaire*[17] was incorporated into the respective national legal systems. But, since neither the governments nor the citizens of the EEA countries are represented in EU decision-making processes, the contract more closely resembles an *indigent contract*: an asymmetric contract which privileges the one part – the EU. It subjects EEA countries and their citizens to an authority over which they hold no sway. The EEA countries are left in a take-it-or-leave-it position, EU law in effect ranks higher and the EU stands as a hegemon vis-à-vis the EEA countries.

## *Hegemony by default*

The superiority of the EU is established in the EEA Act of 1992, which specifies how the EEA Agreement is to be implemented in Norwegian law.[18] Art. 2 reads

> Legal provisions that serve to fulfil Norway's commitments according to the Agreement, shall in the case of conflict take precedence over other provisions regulating the same matter. The same goes for cases in which a regulation that serves to fulfil Norway's according to the Agreement, conflicts with another regulation or runs into conflict with a later law.

Legally speaking, this article grants no precedence to EEA regulations in relation to other laws. The Storting may at any time legislate against EU/EEA regulations, and this would be binding on Norwegian courts even though it would also imply being in breach of the Agreement (Arnesen 2004: 245). The Storting's legislative power is, in contrast to the earlier-cited EEA article, guaranteed by the Norwegian Constitution. Therefore, Art. 2 of the EEA Agreement must be viewed as an interpretation principle. Whether national or EU sources of law rank higher is a question of judgement, of weighing the pros and cons. But as a general rule, in case of conflict, EU law has precedence – in those areas that fall under its jurisdiction. EU supremacy is a collision norm. The EFTA Court has previously determined that the EEA Agreement does not lay down the same principles of direct effect and supremacy as EU law does in the member states. However, in a 1998 decision the court characterised the EEA Agreement as a treaty *sui generis* – in a class of its own – with its own legal order. The EEA Agreement is unusual, and more than just an international agreement – in terms of intent and reach (see B.EFTA Court 2000). Furthermore, the 1998 decision underlines the importance of homogeny between law in the EEA and in the EU. Therefore, Norway could be sued for treaty breach – but in any case, it will be difficult for the Storting to enact laws that go against the EEA.[19] For most practical purposes EEA law, as implemented in Norwegian law, enjoys supremacy over other Norwegian legislation. Freedom and autonomy are more formal than real,[20] and the EU comes across as a hegemon towards the EEA countries. The citizens of EEA countries are, to a considerable degree, subjected to the decisions of the EU. Being dependent on the goodwill of other is not freedom (Pettit 1999).

The EU has the real power to interpret what falls under the EEA Agreement. Furthermore, competency to interpret whether a Norwegian law breaches EEA rules rests with the EFTA Court, not with the Storting or Norwegian courts.[21] According to Art. 31 of the EEA Agreement, a state can be brought before the EFTA Court on allegations of treaty breach. Formally, Norway has the opportunity to influence or resist the EU's decisions. New EU rules do not automatically become part of the EEA Agreement but must be adopted in the EEA Committee, where the EEA countries and the EU are represented. However, that Committee enjoys very little leverage regarding the content of the legislation. Negotiations in the EEA Committee, in which the legal act is formally adopted, provide an opportunity to arrive at interim and accommodative arrangements – but not changes in or additions to the substantial content of the EU legal act in question.

When it comes to preventing new EU rules from being incorporated into the EEA Agreement, the possibilities for influence are greater. Decisions in the Committee are made unanimously, and if agreement is not reached with regard to the implementation of a legal act, the EEA countries can reserve themselves collectively (but not individually) against the inclusion of the act in the agreement. This means that Norway can prevent legislation from being incorporated into the EEA Agreement but has no means of stopping the EU from adopting its own legislation. Therefore, the EEA countries do not have a veto right, but rather, as mentioned, a reservation right. However, this right is very difficult to apply in practice. If it were to be used, the entire EEA arrangement, and thus the interests of Iceland and Liechtenstein, would come under threat. Reservations would create imbalance in the internal market, which could again lead to counter-reactions from the EU in the form of protective measures, that is measures to handle the practical problems that would ensue from such an imbalance. The reservation right has therefore remained latent in the 20 years that the EEA Agreement has been in force, and it is doubtful whether any government would be willing to risk the uncertain consequences of using it.[22] In reality, therefore, EU dominates EEA countries, not by intention but by *default*. Because they have rejected membership in the EU, but seek access to the internal market, the EEA members become subjected to the EU. It is so to say a default strategy on part of the EU which undermines national self-determination. EU law must apply and take precedence in order to safeguard the integrity of the internal market and the equal treatment of actors.

## *Rule without justification*

Technically, Norway is free to withdraw from the EEA Agreement. However, the negative implications for the country's trade and industry, and for the people's welfare and safety, has by those in government been viewed as too great and too severe to consider. Nor is it tempting for Norway to go solo (Sjursen 2008). There is a need to be recognised as a partner and Norwegian governments would like to be considered part of the European family. Norway subscribes to the same values and, one may add, that it may be risky to only rely on North Atlantic Treaty Organization when it comes to security issues.

Norway's affiliation with the EU entails the establishment of political power relations that conflict with the principle of sovereignty laid out the Constitution. Norway has voluntarily, though parliamentary decisions, subjected itself to a hegemon. Norway is dominated by the EU because it prioritises access to the European common goods within a framework of international law. It is an asymmetric power relationship in breach with the idea of a fair bargaining process. A majority of Norwegians have rejected membership but cannot back their claims by credible threats while the EU one-sidedly can destroy the whole arrangement without perceptible costs. Dominance occurs because neither is there parity of power to render the use of threats or countermeasures credible under international law, nor possibilities for participation in co-decision-making to wield influence or demand justifications under EU law.

Once we realise the nature of the EU, it becomes clear that adopting EU regulations through Art. 26 of the Norwegian Constitution is problematic. Competency that according to the Constitution is awarded a Norwegian state body is transferred to an international organ though simple majority vote. This is a relinquishment of sovereignty of constitutional character – yet Art. 121, which is required for constitutional change, has not been applied. Art. 26 does not authorise ceding sovereignty to EU bodies. Also, Art. 115 has been deemed inappropriate. The latter is a 'haste article' actually restricted to accession to an association that Norway is or intends to become a member of. We must ask, should Art. 115 have been used in 1992 to adopt the EEA Agreement? Moreover, is it constitutionally justifiable to adopt an increasingly stronger link to the EU, the internal market and its flanking areas, through Art. 26 and simple majority?

The effects of EU legal acts are extensive, but principled reflections have been lacking:

> In the [Norwegian] Government's view, balanced and well-functioning cooperation requires a pragmatic approach from all parties to the agreement. Practical solutions should be sought that will in the best possible way take account of the institutional structure of the EEA Agreement, the desire for legislative homogeneity and national interests.
>
> (Parliament White Paper no. 5 2012–2013: 19 [author's translation])

In the handling of Norway's EU affiliation, quasi-legal theory and Staatsraison – reason of state, power holders' considerations of what serves the nation best – rather than constitutional principles have prevailed. What is the legal status and legal standing of the principle of 'limited transfer of competence'? The legal basis for these decisions is thin indeed, as noted by Holmøyvik in Chapter 8 of this volume. They are in breach with the legal system of the Norwegian constitution and its prioritisation of popular sovereignty. The consequence is that the status of the Norwegian Constitution as the 'most important law of the land' is undermined. The system in place is hard to justify on constitutional grounds, and it is even harder to find a principled argument for it.

What we are witnessing is not only the 'the impotence of popular rule' due to general globalisation and Europeanisation, but also *democratic harm to self*, all the while Norwegians means of association remains based on choices that could have been different. The damages to the democratic chain of rule could have been reduced by organising the relationship in other ways than through the EEA Agreement. The present legal relationships with the EU is clearly in tension with the idea of Norway as a sovereign and independent state, in which the important cases are decided by the executive, the cabinet (Art. 3); the people exercise lawmaking power through the Storting, the Storting that gives the laws (Art. 49, 75), and the supreme court of Norway is the final arbitrator of the law (Art. 8) (Eriksen 2013: 379). In reality the legislative power of the Storting is weakened because it does not control EEA lawmaking. Thereby, the citizens' ability to govern themselves through control of its own institutions is reduced.[23] What is urgently needed is a new *constitutional debate* regarding whether Norway's EU affiliation requires changes to the country's constitution, as is the case for EU member states. When transfer of competence or ceding sovereignty is outside of what the constitution allows for, there is a need for changing it on the basis of Art. 121. This is needed in order to establish a secure basis for other bodies than those of the Norwegian state to make decisions that affect the interest and preferences of Norwegian citizens. There is no political freedom outside the association that makes the binding rules.

## Cosmopolitanisation of nation states

The term *globalisation* has connotations of liberalisation, deregulation and free movement of capital: economic globalisation. In fact, however, modernity itself is inherently globalising and manifests itself in international human rights movements and supranational rulemaking: in political globalisation.

### Juridical supranationalism

Today most legal areas are affected by internationalisation. There are no lawless areas left, as all human beings have been assigned rights. New decision-making bodies and courts have been established, constraining the power of states and bonding the relationship between them. A formidable build-up of international law has taken place in the wake of the establishment of the UN – especially with the Universal Declaration of Human Rights, the European Convention on Human Rights (ECHR) and the International Criminal Court (ICC) – which in reality has curbed the sovereignty of nation states. The European Court of Human Rights in Strasbourg protects the rights of European citizens – now they can sue their own state. The ICC sets limits to governments' room for manoeuvre. Moreover, war criminals risk being taken to The Hague for trial. National interests are from time to time overruled. The World Trade Organization, through its dispute settlement body, can make decisions that are binding on all its member states, even those that may not agree to the particular decision. The tradition of quoting international legal sources in national court rulings allows norms that have not been explicitly accepted by the citizens of a state to become part of *de lege lata*. Furthermore, the EU's regulatory policies regarding working standards, environmental standards and human rights standards, go beyond national legislative processes, hence protect the rights and status of the individual. Generally speaking, private autonomy – citizens' freedom and opportunity to seek realisation of their wants and beliefs – increases, whilst their public, political autonomy as participants in popular rule, decreases.

On the face of it, the EEA, Schengen, Dublin and other agreements are international agreements that bind only the contracting parties, viz., the states. What is special about these agreements is that they contain a set of rules that assign Norwegian legal subjects – individuals and companies – rights and duties that are enforced by Norwegian courts. Increasingly EU/EEA regulations serve as the basis for Norwegian court rulings. EEA law, as mentioned, takes the upper hand, and the EU grants citizens' rights, which implies duties for the Norwegian state. Claimants can use EU law against the Norwegian administration.[24] The agreements strengthen the protection of individual rights and bind Norway to the European legal system. EU law works together with other European lawmakers, first and foremost the ECHR – which is increasingly recognised by Norwegian citizens. Already in 1960 human rights were cited in cases brought before the Norwegian supreme court (Høyesterett). In 1990 the European Court of Human Rights decided on one case where Norway was the defendant, but it was not until 1999 that the central conventions – in particular the ECHR – were incorporated into Norwegian law.

Just as the main principle of the EEA Agreement is that a legal rule that does not implement an EU legal act is to be set aside in case of conflict, so there is a rule of supremacy in human rights law, according to which human rights are to have precedence in case of conflict with other rules and regulations. The incorporation of a complex set of international human right obligations supplements the Norwegian constitutional regulations in this field and may at times overrule them.

To establish the range of government duties, as well as the limits of state action, is today not a national constitutional question but, rather, is a question of the interpretation of international conventions. Moreover, the situation is one where human rights clauses are being developed when constitutions are revised – also the minor Norwegian revision in 2014. Revisions echo cosmopolitanism, in that the decisive units of concern are *persons* – not groups, nations or states. 'Man is the measure of all things' (Protagoras) and persons are ultimate units of concern for *everyone*. The status of ultimate unit of concern attaches to *every* living human being *equal* status, and this special status has global force (Pogge 1994: 89). Every human being has equal worth and deserves impartial consideration of his or hers claims upon us.

What we are witnessing is a *cosmopolitanisation of nation states*, of their constitutions, and an alteration of sovereignty (Niesen 2012). Increased legal protection, better protection of individual rights and the incorporation of human rights into the national constitution limits the state's sovereign use of force in internal affairs. Legal developments and institution building since the Second World War have contributed to systematic change, in that states are deemed sovereign only if they uphold and enforce democratic principles and human rights. No longer is state sovereignty to exist at the expense of the rights and freedoms of the individual. However, the consequence is juridification.

## *The right to co-determination*

Juridification beyond the nation-state has many advantages, as law is what ultimately prevents *bellum omnium contra omnes*. It also increases citizens' legal protection. But it is not the mandate of lawyers to make the laws. Saddling individuals with a load of rights may be an expression of benign paternalism and compassion, but it does not serve to respect the individual right to self-determination. It amounts to dominance because individuals are subject to the discretion of others. Merely assigning rights to people does not turn them into self-determining, self-governing, enlightened citizens capable of taking part in the political process.[25] All have rights – children and slaves have rights, as do people living under dictatorships. Granting individuals civil and economic rights without due process amounts to dominance – of being subject to arbitrary rule. One is not free if one is dependent on the will, even the goodwill, of others. Juridification is in breach with the idea of a self-governed society where legislative power lies with the citizens. Citizens' dignity is respected only when they are included as equal members of a self-governing association (Kant 1785/1996).

The relationship between democracy and fundamental rights is indeed complicated but is most often understood as one of interdependence. No rights, no democracy – no democracy, no rights. What is exceptional about modern states – states that have experienced the democratic revolution – is that their citizens have been granted the *right of rights*: the right to co-grant themselves rights. That is why legislation without participation is inherently problematic. Liberalisation from heteronomy – from arbitrary power, from suppression and paternalism – are the mantras of the democratic movement. Under conditions of legal dominance and decisional exclusion these are again brought to the table.

In a democratic *Rechtsstaat*, the right to participate in public debate and in elections to representative institutions exists in order to ensure that the democratic principles of *autonomy* and *accountability* are upheld. Decision makers authorised through election can be held accountable, and be removed from office at the next election. In Europe, many citizens are no longer simply members of nation states but also members of the EU and an international legal framework. Equal compliance with EU law has become a precondition for equal rights, equal citizenship. Here we are talking of a *shared sovereignty*, as citizens are members of two units at the same time – of a member state and of the EU – where there is no talk of superiorities/subordinates (Bogdandy 2006; Franzius 2010; Habermas 2012).[26] All EU member states have an equal place at the table in the Council, and their citizens are represented in the European Parliament (EP). We are talking of pooling and sharing of sovereignty: of co-determination and multilevel governance. From a situation with dwindling influence, and only nominal right to participate in decision-making processes, European citizens have through the integration process been empowered, in particular by the rising clout of the EP. That is not the case for the signatories to the EEA Agreement and their citizens.

Today's EU is more than an international organisation, and this makes the status of EEA members particularly problematic. The EU is not based on the delegation of power that can be controlled and called back by the contracting parties. In particular, the elected EP, the Commission, the CJEU and the co-decision procedure do not sit well with the delegation model for democratic control. Also the Council is developing into a more supranational creature (Curtin 2009). These institutions do not fit with the view of the EU as something controlled by the signatories to its treaties. The EU has a direct link to the citizens of its member states. Even though the requirements of autonomy and accountability are not met (Lord 2013; Stie 2013). In addition to the difficulty of holding the supranational institutions accountable there is a further challenge: the EU's intergovernmental bodies, which should be controlled by the member states, have *decisional autonomy*. Within these bodies there is an opinion- and will-formation process of a certain magnitude. They enjoy discretionary powers and take a stand on political controversies. *Agency or preference drift* is well known from the literature. Decision makers – in the Council, in committees, in expert groups and interest groups represented under the Commission – find that they must 'drift away' from legislators' intent in order to find agreement on solutions.

Norwegian citizens are not represented in the bodies that pass EU legislation: the EP and the Council. Norway's sole way of influencing decisions is through diplomacy and lobbying. It is true that Norwegian experts participate in many of the Commission's expert groups that prepare and develop proposals for regulations – but such experts do not represent the Norwegian people but their epistemic community. Bureaucrats and experts also take part in more than 200 committees in the EU system, but they do not have access to all committees, and certainly not all the important ones under the Council. The general way to wield influence is through lobbying. Obviously, such 'participation' cannot compensate for the lack of formal access to decision-making processes in the EP or in the Council. Norway's link to the EU makes Norwegian citizens *receivers* of policy, rather than its creators.

Even if the people's right to self-government clearly suffers under Norway's current relationship of dependency to the EU, it is not so that other countries' autonomy is unaffected. Some form of external dominance is always to be expected: it is a necessary consequence of denationalisation; of increased interdependence, international juridification and institution building. Ceding state sovereignty in order to increase system effectiveness also has democratic value, as democracy has not only the deontological requirement to ensure political equality: it also has an epistemological requirement. Simply put, it is there in order to make rational decisions. Without good results, no legitimacy. No effective democracy without congruence between social and political space. Democracy implies that political capacity is extended beyond national borders when necessary in order to control the political agenda. Democratic legitimacy depends not only on meeting the autonomy requirement, but also on being in control of the conditions for action – including the possibility to influence external environments that are vital for achieving important goals.

It is in this light that we must view the active efforts of Norwegian governments to link the country more and more tightly with the EU. Nationally bound democracy is not worth much if it does not also have the capacity to act and 'get things done'. Small nation states today have scant capacity to influence the conditions for action on their own, making their sovereignty and autonomy often merely nominal and symbolical. Under conditions of globalisation and intense, complex dependence, one could therefore argue that large units are more democratic than small ones are. Larger units, larger states, can provide citizens with better chances of cooperatively handling challenges and solving problems.

## Conclusion

In relations between states it is so, as Thucydides wrote, that 'while the strong do what they can, the weak endure what they must'. The European integration process was intended to change this by domesticating international relations. For Norway, however, it would seem that Thucydides's words still ring true. The special thing about Norway's situation is its EU affiliation, where the state has entered into a set of agreements that regulate border controls and access to the EU internal market thoroughly. Norwegian legislation today originates in the EU, and Norway is entwined in a fine-mesh net of regulations, rights and duties over which its own citizens have no direct control. Here we are dealing with a classic case of dominance and a despoiled democratic procedure. The democratic chain of government – where, through elections and public debate, the citizens authorise political power, which they in turn can punish or reward through new elections – has been broken.

This is a paradox, because in two consultative referendums a majority of Norwegian voters came out rejecting joining the EU and being part of its formal decision-making channels and processes. On the 'no' side, the arguments for democratic self-rule were strong. Yet successive Norwegian governments, with broad parliamentary support, have chosen to incorporate the EU's directives and decrees into national law in order to get access to the internal market and other European public goods.

With what right and with a basis in what law has this come to pass? The results of the referendums were acknowledged in that Norway did not formally join the EU – but its comprehensive adaptation to and involvement in the EU has never been constitutionally clarified.

The Norwegian EU affiliation is an extreme example of increased system effectiveness at the expense of popular participation. In complex, modern societies there will always be dilemmas and considerations linked to the balance between effectiveness and popular participation – but there must also be a limit: *No participation, no democracy!*

## Notes

1 I am grateful to Eirik Holmøyvik for comments on an earlier version of this chapter.
2 The Norwegian Constitution Art. 1 (author's translation).
3 Norway has applied for membership three times, first in 1962 when France said no, then in 1972 and 1994 a majority of Norwegian citizens voted no in referenda.
4 See Ringdal (1995: 51) and Esborg (2008: 189ff.).
5 The classical doctrine states that 'first, no one can be the subject of more than one sovereign, second, only one sovereign power can prevail within a territory, third, all citizens possess the same status and rights, and fourth, the bond between citizen and sovereign excludes the alien' (Linklater 1996: 95).
6 Sovereignty is today perceived as multidimensional and at times irrelevant (Koskenniemi 1989/2005; Ruggie 1993; Slaughter 2004: 190). However, the classic doctrine of sovereignty as control over one's self and one's conditions for action has never been absolute: no state exists in isolation, and the Westphalian order rests on intersubjective norms and mutual recognition, which Hegel (1921/2006) realised and Carl Schmidt (2003: 167) attests to. Even in their most Hobbesian moments, states must follow procedures of crisis management.
7 Denationalisation indicates a weakening of the relationship between territorial states and their corresponding national societies – a somewhat less dramatic description of the disintegration of national borders and increased commodity trade and communication (Zürn 2000: 187).
8 'The word "people" is ambiguous, because it can refer to the people considered as a collective body, or to people considered in their several or plural identities. Even in talk of "we, the people", it is not clear whether the reference is to "we, the single American people", or "we, the people of America". E pluribus unum, the motto goes. But which are the people? The plures or the unum, the plurality or the singular, the many or the one?' (Pettit 2006: 301).

9   Likewise, 'supra-individual entities, such as a people, a majority or a state, are not self-authenticating sources of valid claims' (Michelman 1997: 152).
10  In Norway, legislative authority is exercised by the Storting through Art. 49 and 75 of the Constitution. According to Art. 3, the government (meeting with the monarch) has executive power, whereas Art. 88 and 90 grant judicial power to the courts, with the Supreme Court as the highest authority.
11  Art. 1.2, law no. 109 of 27 November 1992, EEA Agreement.
12  About 75 per cent of the laws and regulations of the EU apply to Norway as well (Official Norwegian Report [NOU 2012:2]).
13  Prior to the incorporation of EC Regulation No 216/2008 on common rules in the field of civil aviation and establishing a European Aviation Safety Agency (EASA), the implications for the Constitution were considered. The regulation authorises EASA to request the Commission to impose fines on national companies for breaches of the provisions of EASA rules. On 18 January 2010, the Legislation Department of the Norwegian Ministry of Justice concluded that '[i]n principle, transferring the power to impose sanctions directly on Norwegian undertakings [to a body outside Norway] must be regarded as a considerable encroachment on Norway's administrative authority. On the other hand, the transfer of powers in this case has limited substantive scope, in that it will only have an impact on undertakings that already have or later obtain certificates issued by the European Aviation Safety Agency. Currently, this only affects four Norwegian undertakings. Furthermore, it does not appear to be politically controversial to put further sanctions at the disposal of the European Aviation Safety Agency in addition to its already existing power to withdraw certificates. This would make it possible to respond in a more balanced and proportionate way to breaches of the rules, and would be beneficial for the Agency's work on aviation safety. On this basis, we are inclined to conclude that, all in all, the transfer of powers set out in Art. 25 of Regulation (EC) No 216/2008 is not too much of an encroachment on constitutional powers, so that the Regulation can be incorporated into the EEA Agreement, provided that the Storting gives its consent in accordance with Art. 26 (second paragraph), of the Constitution. As mentioned initially, however, the Storting's views on the constitutional assessment will be of importance in cases of doubt' (Parliament White Paper no. 5 2012–2013: 18).
14  Art. 115 of the Constitution reads, 'In order to safeguard international peace and security or to promote the international rule of law and cooperation, the Storting may, by a three-fourths majority, consent that an international organisation to which Norway belongs or will belong shall have the right, within specified fields, to exercise powers which in accordance with this Constitution are normally vested in the authorities of the state, although not the power to alter this Constitution. For the Storting to grant such consent, at least two-thirds of its Members shall be present, as required for proceedings for amending the Constitution. The provisions of this Article do not apply in cases of membership in an international organisation whose decisions only have application for Norway exclusively under international law.' See the English translation of the Norwegian Constitution, including the latest changes as of May 2014, available at https://www.stortinget.no/Global/pdf/Constitutionenglish.pdf?epslanguage=no, last accessed 17 December 2014.
15  In the Schengen Area, there is no reservation/veto right. The Schengen Agreement simply ceases to exist for countries that do not incorporate it into national legislation. Here, however, Norway has been accorded observer status with a right to speak.
16  Case 6/64 *Flaminio Costa v ENEL* [1964] ECR 585.
17  This is a French expression, roughly translatable as 'the EU as it is', that is the rights and duties the EU member states share. This includes all EU laws and treaties, declarations

and resolutions and decisions made by the CJEU. For a state to be accepted as an EU member, it must fulfil the *acquis* requirements.
18  See also Stavang (2002: 118ff.).
19  The Norwegian Supreme Court has postponed one case, awaiting decision in the CJEU.
20  See Arnesen (2004: 245). Henrik Bull refers to a long list of sources that claim the EEA Agreement involves the same principles of precedence and direct effect as EU law, but the EFTA Court has not been willing to accept this (Bull 2011: 260).
21  As the two-pillar system is in place, the rulings of the EFTA Court do not have direct effect on Norwegian law. They must be adopted by the Storting as well, as mentioned earlier.
22  Moreover, the EEA Agreement is increasingly perceived as a burden where the EU does not get enough in return. Within the EU, there is waning interest in maintaining it (European Commission 2012).
23  The constitutional lawyer Eivind Smith characterised the EEA Agreement as a constitutional catastrophe (Parliament Recommendation no. 229 1996–1997: 37).
24  '[W]hen international law is used as the primary legal foundation, this means that the courts view international law as directed towards courts as well, and not solely to the state as legislator, and that rights for the individual can be granted without any decision in Norwegian law (Arnesen and Stenvik 2009: 51 [author's translation]).
25  '[Y]ou could create rights and afford judicial remedies to slaves. The ability to go to court to enjoy a right bestowed on you by the pleasure of the other does not emancipate you, does not make you a citizen. Long before women and Jews were made citizens they enjoyed direct effect' (Weiler 1997: 503).
26  For a critique see E.O. Eriksen (2014: 91ff.).

## References

Arnesen, F. (2004) 'EØS-reglenes betydning i norsk rett', in F. Arnesen, S. Foyn, O. Kolstad, O.-A. Rognstad and F. Sejersted, *EØS-law*, 2nd Edition, Oslo: Universitetsforlaget.

Arnesen, F. and Stenvik, A. (2009) *Internasjonalisering og juridiske metode. Særlig om EØS-rettens betydning i norsk rett*, Oslo: Universitetsforlaget.

B.EFTA Court (2000) 'Case E-9/97 – Erla Maria Sveinbjörnsdóttir v the Government of Iceland. Advisory Opinion of the EFTA Court of 10 December 1998, Report of the EFTA Court, 97', *Common Market Law Review*, 37(1): 187–207.

Bodin, J. (1577) *Les six livres de la Republique*, Paris.

Bogdandy, A. von (2006) 'Constitutional Principles', in A. von Bogdandy and J. Bast (eds) *Principles of European Constitutional Law*, Oxford: Hart Publishing.

Bull, H. (2011) 'One Market, Two Courts: The Case Law of the EFTA Court', in F. Carbonell, A.J. Menédez and J.E. Fossum (eds) *Hope, Reluctance or Fear? The Democratic Consequences of Case Law of the European Court of Justice*, ARENA Report 5/11, Oslo: ARENA.

Curtin, D. (2009) *Executive Power of the European Union: Law, Practices and the Living Constitution*, Oxford: Oxford University Press.

Dahl, R.A. (1994) 'A Democratic Dilemma: System Effectiveness versus Citizen Participation', *Political Science Quarterly*, 109(1): 23–34.

Dahl, R.A. and Tufte, E.R. (1973) *Size and Democracy*, Stanford, CA: Stanford University Press.

Eriksen, C.C. (2013) 'Den norske forfatningen og forholdet utenfor Norges grenser: Unntakstilstandens eksterne dimensjoner', in D. Mikalsen (ed) *Unntakstilstand og forfatning: Brudd og kontinuitet i konstitusjonell rett*, Olso: Pax.

Eriksen, E.O. (2014) *The Normativity of the European Union*, Houndsmills: Palgrave Macmillan.

Eriksen, E.O. and Weigård, J. (2003) *Understanding Habermas: Communicative Action and Deliberative Democracy*, London: Continuum Press.

Esborg, L. (2008) *Det norske nei til EU: En studie av motstand som kulturell praksis*, Ph.D. thesis, Department for Culture Studies and Oriental Languages, University of Oslo.

European Commission (2012) Commission Staff Working Document: A Review of the Functioning of the European Economic Area, SWD (2012) 425 final, Brussels, 7 December.

Forst, R. (2011) *The Right to Justification: Elements of Constructivist Theory of Justice*, New York: Columbia University Press.

Franzius, C. (2010) *Europäisches Verfassungsrechtsdenken*, Tübingen: Mohr Siebeck.

Grimen, H., Molander, A. and Eriksen, E.O. (2012) 'Professional Discretion and Accountability in the Welfare State', *Journal of Applied Philosophy*, 29(3): 214–230.

Habermas, J. (1996) *Between Facts and Norms: Contributions to a Discourse Theory of Law*, Cambridge, MA: MIT Press.

—— (2012) *The Crisis of the European Union: A Response*, Cambridge: Polity Press.

Hart, H.L.A. (1997) *The Concept of Law*, Oxford: Oxford University Press.

Hegel, G.W.F. (1921/2006) *Rettsfilosofien*, Oslo: Vidarforlaget.

Jackson, R.H. (1990) *Quasi-States: Sovereignty, International Relations and the Third World*, Cambridge: Cambridge University Press.

Kant, I. (1785/1996) 'Groundwork of the Metaphysics of Morals', in M. Gregor (ed) *Practical Philosophy*, Cambridge: Cambridge University Press.

Keohane, R.O. (2002) 'Ironies of Sovereignty: The European Union and the United States', *Journal of Common Market Studies*, 40(4): 743–765.

Koskenniemi, M. (1989/2005) *From Apology to Utopia: The Structure of International Legal Argument*, Cambridge: Cambridge University Press.

LeFort, C. (1988) *Democracy and Political Theory*, Cambridge: Polity Press.

Linklater, A. (1996) 'Citizenship and Sovereignty in the Post-Westphalian State', *European Journal of International Relations*, 2(1): 77–103.

—— (1998) *The Transformation of Political Community*, Cambridge: Polity Press.

Lipset, S.M. (1960) *Political Man: The Social Basis for Modern Politics*, New York: Doubleday.

Lord, C. (2013) 'The Democratic Legitimacy of Co-Decision', *Journal of European Public Policy*, 20(7): 1056–1073.

Maus, I. (1994) *Zur Aufklärung der Demokratietheorie*, Frankfurt: Suhrkamp.

Michelman, F.I. (1997) 'How Can the People Ever Make the Laws? A Critique of Deliberative Democracy', in J. Boham and W. Regh (eds) *Deliberative Democracy: Essays on Reason and Politics*, Cambridge, MA: MIT Press.

Morgenthau, H.J. (1993) *Politics among Nations: The Struggle for Power and Peace*, New York: McGraw-Hill.

Niesen, P. (2012) 'Kosmopolitismus in einem Land', in P. Niesen (ed) *Transnationale Gerechtigkeit und Demokratie*, Frankfurt: Campus.

Official Norwegian Report (NOU) (2012:2) 'Outside and Inside: Norway's Agreements with the European Union', delivered to the Norwegian Ministry of Foreign Affairs, 17 January.

Parliament Recommendation no. 229 (1996–1997) Recommendation from the Parliament Foreign Committee [Innst. S. nr. 229 (1996–1997) Innstilling fra utenrikskomiteen om samtykke til ratifikasjon av samarbeidsavtale av 19. desember 1996 mellom partene i Schengen-avtalen og Schengen-konvensjonen, og Island og Norge om avskaffelse av personkontroll på de felles grenser], Oslo: Stortinget.

Parliament White Paper no. 5 (2012–2013) The EEA Agreement and Norway's Other Agreements with the EU [Meld. St. 5 (2012–2013) EØS-avtalen og Norges øvrige avtaler med EU], Oslo: Ministry of Foreign Affairs.

Pettit, P. (1999) *Republicanism: Theory of Freedom and Government*, Oxford: Oxford University Press.

────── (2006) 'Democracy, National and International', *The Monist*, 89(2): 301–324.

────── (2010) 'A Republican Law of Peoples', *European Journal of Political Theory*, 9(1): 70–94.

Pogge, T.W. (1994) 'An Egalitarian Law of Peoples', *Philosophy and Public Affairs*, 23(3): 195–224.

Richardson, H.S. (2002) *Democratic Autonomy: Public Reasoning about the End of Policy*, Oxford: Oxford University Press.

Ringdal, K. (1995) 'Velgernes argumenter', in A.T. Jenssen and H. Valen (eds) *Brussel midt imot*, Oslo: Ad Notam Gyldendal.

Ruggie, J.G. (1993) 'Territoriality and Beyond: Problematizing Modernity in International Relations', *International Organization*, 47(1): 139–174.

Schmidt, C. (2003) *The Nomos of the Earth in the International Law of the Jus Publicum Europaeum*, New York: Telos Press.

Sen, A. (2012) *The Idea of Justice*, Cambridge, MA: Harvard University Press.

Shapiro, I. (2012) 'On Non-Domination', *University of Toronto Law Journal*, 62(3): 293–335.

Sjursen, H. (2008) 'Fra bremsekloss til medløper: Norge i EUs utenriks- og sikkerhetspolitikk', *Nytt Norsk Tidsskrift*, 25(4): 323–335.

Slaughter, A.-M. (2004) *A New World Order*, Princeton, NJ: Princeton University Press.

Stavang, P. (2002) *Parlamentarisme og folkestyre. Utvalde statsrettslege emne*, 4th Edition, Bergen: Fagbokforlaget.

Stie, A.E. (2013) *Democratic Decision-Making in the EU: Technocracy in Disguise?*, London: Routledge.

Weiler, J.H.H. (1997) 'To Be a European Citizen: Eros and Civilisation?', *Journal of European Public Policy*, 4(4): 495–519.

Zürn, M. (2000) 'Democratic Governance beyond the Nation-State: The EU and Other International Institutions', *European Journal of International Relations*, 6(2): 183–221.

# 6

# THE EEA AND THE CASE LAW OF THE CJEU

## Incorporation without participation?

*Halvard Haukeland Fredriksen*

The authority of the Court of Justice of the European Union (CJEU) over the interpretation of the Agreement on the European Economic Area (EEA) is a politically sensitive as well as a legally difficult matter. In this chapter, an attempt is made not only to present the origins and the inherent tensions of the complex judicial architecture of the EEA but also to reveal how it works in practice. As the analysis will show that the authority on the interpretation of the substantive rules of the European Economic Area *de facto* rests firmly with the CJEU, it is further discussed to what extent the participating member states of the European Free Trade Association (EFTA) may influence the CJEU's development of the law. Towards the end follow some brief thoughts on how the judicial architecture of the EEA Agreement would cope with a scenario where either Switzerland or the UK (or both) were to join in on the EFTA side of the EEA.

### The origins of the complex judicial architecture of the EEA

During the EEA negotiations, both the European Union (EU) and the EFTA states were well aware that to achieve the objective of full integration of the latter into the EU internal market, it was not enough to make sure that the wording of the EEA Agreement and the relevant provisions of EU law were identical: a homogeneous EEA with equal conditions of competition (Art. 1 EEA Agreement) could only be achieved if the relevant provisions of EU and EEA law were also interpreted and applied in a uniform manner.

Originally, the contracting parties agreed that a common EEA Court of Justice should be established. Among other things, this court was to have jurisdiction to settle disputes between the contracting parties. This would have guaranteed that the EEA rules *as such* were interpreted and applied in a uniform manner in the EU and in the participating EFTA states. Still, the existence of a common EEA court could not in itself guarantee homogeneity between its interpretation of EEA law and the CJEU's authoritative interpretation of the corresponding provisions of EU law. Acknowledging this, the contracting parties agreed that provisions of the EEA Agreement which were taken over from EU law were to be interpreted 'in conformity with the relevant rulings of the Court of Justice of the European Communities given prior to the date of signature of this Agreement' (Art. 6 EEA Agreement). For reasons of sovereignty, however, it was impossible for the EFTA states to accept an extension of this obligation to encompass future CJEU case law. Instead, a provision of the draft agreement obliged the EEA Court and the CJEU (as well as the highest courts of the EFTA states) to pay 'due account' to each other's decisions. However, the centrepiece in the attempt to secure homogeneity lay at the institutional level: the contracting parties agreed that the EEA Court should be integrated into the CJEU. It was to be composed of eight judges, of which only three were to come from the EFTA states and a majority of five from the CJEU. Furthermore, the draft agreement introduced a possibility for the national courts of the EFTA states to ask the CJEU 'to express itself' on the interpretation of a provision of the EEA Agreement. The EFTA states originally argued for this competence to be assigned to the EEA Court, but this was rejected by the EU side.

To the surprise of the Contracting Parties, the CJEU was not satisfied by the compromises found. In its (in)famous Opinion 1/91, the CJEU declared the whole system of judicial supervision in the draft agreement incompatible with the (then) European Economic Community (EEC) Treaty.[1] The CJEU stressed that it, as an institution of one of the contracting parties, would be bound by the EEA Court's interpretation of EEA law and that this – via the objective of homogeneity – would determine the interpretation of the corresponding provisions of EU law. The obligation on the EEA Court to follow the CJEU's case law did not alter this as it was limited to rulings given prior to the date of signature of the agreement. According to the CJEU, an agreement which in this way would condition the future interpretation of the EU rules on free movement and competition conflicted with 'the very foundations of the Community'. The fact that the majority of the members of the EEA Court were to come from the CJEU did not remedy this. Rather to the contrary, the CJEU was of the opinion that these 'organic links' made things even worse as it would 'be very difficult, if not impossible, for those judges, when sitting in the CJEU, to tackle questions with completely open minds where they have taken part in determining those questions as members of the EEA Court'. Furthermore, the CJEU held it to be 'unacceptable' that answers given to questions on the interpretation of the EEA Agreement from the national courts of the EFTA states were to be advisory only. According to the CJEU, this would change the nature of its function as it was conceived by the (then) EEC Treaty, namely that of a court whose judgements were binding.

As noted at the time by leading commentators, the essence of the CJEU's objections to the draft EEA Agreement was that it saw the common EEA Court as a threat to its own position as the supreme authority on EU law (Hartley 1992: 847).

Acknowledging this, the contracting parties returned to the negotiating table and came up with a solution which left the position of the CJEU untouched. Instead of a common EEA Court, an EFTA Court without any functional or personal connections to the CJEU was set up by the Agreement between the EFTA States on the establishment of a Surveillance Authority and a Court of Justice.[2] The EFTA Court's competences extend to the EFTA States alone – it has no jurisdiction over the EU or the EU member states.

Furthermore, the obligation on the CJEU to pay due account to the rulings of the courts on the EFTA side of the EEA was removed and it was agreed that the CJEU's answers to any questions put by the national courts of the EFTA States would be binding.

Without a common EEA Court, the contracting parties acknowledged that any disputes between one or more of the EFTA states on the one side and the EU and the EU member states on the other would have to be settled by diplomatic means in the EEA Joint Committee (Art. 111 EEA Agreement). However, the EFTA states accepted that in cases concerning the interpretation of EEA provisions taken over from EU law, the contracting parties to the dispute can agree to refer the matter to the CJEU. In addition, disputes concerning the scope or duration of safeguard measures or the proportionality of any rebalancing measures taken can be referred to arbitration, but not questions of interpretation of EEA provisions taken over from EU law, may be dealt with in such procedures.

The contracting parties were, of course, fully aware of the risk that a system with two courts at the international level, the CJEU and the EFTA Court, interpreting the same rules, poses to the objective of homogeneity. In order to reach 'the most uniform interpretation possible' of the provisions of the agreement and of the corresponding provisions of EU law, the Joint Committee was therefore vested with competence to keep the development of the case-law of the CJEU and of the EFTA Court under constant review (Art. 105 EEA Agreement). The Joint Committee is to act to preserve the homogeneous interpretation of the agreement. However, the EFTA states had to accept that in no case may decisions taken by the Joint Committee affect rulings of the CJEU.[3]

In its Opinion 1/92, the CJEU approved the renegotiated agreement, stressing that the EFTA Court would exercise its jurisdiction only within EFTA and highlighting the abovementioned limitation on the competences of the EEA Joint Committee as 'an essential safeguard which is indispensable for the autonomy of the Community legal order'.[4]

## The core of the problem: Independence vs homogeneity

The CJEU's insistence on the autonomy of the EU legal order and its own untouchable position as the supreme authority on not only the EU rules as such, but also on the corresponding EEA rules as they are to be applied within the EU, left the EFTA States with only bad alternatives. As candidly stated by the Commission, the best solution from the perspective of homogeneity would have been for the EFTA states simply to accept future rulings of the CJEU.[5] However, reasons of sovereignty left this alternative untenable for the EFTA States. On the other hand, if the EFTA states reacted by stressing the complete independence of 'their' courts (the EFTA Court as well as their own national courts) from the future developments of CJEU case law, the result could only be the gradual undermining of the objective to create a homogeneous EEA with equal conditions of competition. Thus, as noted by one commentator at the time, the EFTA states acknowledged the need to accord a *de facto* pre-eminence in the judicial structure to the CJEU *without making this explicit* (Cremona 1994: 517 [author's emphasis]).

An important element in this attempt to 'square the circle' is Art. 3(2) of the Agreement between the EFTA States on the establishment of a Surveillance Authority and a Court of Justice. This provision, which was introduced unilaterally by the EFTA states, obliges the EFTA Court (and the EFTA Surveillance Authority) to pay 'due account' to the principles laid down by the 'relevant rulings' of the CJEU given *after* the date of signature of the EEA. Importantly, this obligation encompasses not only the CJEU's interpretation of EU rules, which are copied into the EEA Agreement, but also the CJEU's interpretation of EEA law as such.

Equally important is the earlier-mentioned role of the EEA Joint Committee under Art. 105 EEA. The agreement that no decision of the Joint Committee may affect the case law of the CJEU (Protocol 48) essentially means that in the case of diverging case law from the CJEU and the EFTA Court, the Joint Committee can only preserve homogeneity by letting the view of the CJEU prevail. The Joint Committee, then, ostensibly given the task of reconciling differences between the two judicial organs, is in fact, in the words of one commentator, 'intended to preserve the case-law of the Court [the CJEU], and not to substitute its own political decision' (Cremona 1994: 517). As candidly admitted by the Commission, Art. 105 EEA 'provides for the "reception" of new rulings of the Court of Justice by means of measures taken by the Joint Committee'.[6]

Of course, from a legal point of view, Art. 105 and Protocol 48 EEA may not be interpreted as to impose the case law of the CJEU on the EFTA states. If a case of diverging case law of the EFTA Court and the CJEU is to be raised by the EU in the EEA Joint Committee, the EFTA states remain free under Art. 105 to refuse to adopt the interpretation maintained by the CJEU. Similarly, the EFTA States may block any attempt by the EU to refer the disputed question to the CJEU in accordance with Art. 111 EEA. Still, refusal to accept the CJEU's view will open up for safeguard measures from the EU or the suspension of the affected part of the agreement. Thus, as noted by one commentator, the EFTA states cannot enforce opposition to CJEU case law except at the risk of pulling down part of the EEA structure (Cremona 1994: 524).

Perhaps the most important practical effect of Art. 105 and Protocol 48 is the message this arrangement sends to the EFTA Court: a case of judicial conflict between it and the CJEU is one which the EFTA Court cannot win. According to the president of the EFTA Court, this is a threat of which the EFTA Court has always been aware (Baudenbacher 2010: 5).

## The EFTA Court's approach

More than 20 years after the entry into force of the EEA Agreement, the track record of the EFTA Court reveals that it has consistently let the objective of a homogeneous EEA prevail over any temptation it may have had to pursue an independent interpretation of the EEA Agreement within the EFTA pillar of the EEA. In its very first case, the *Restamark* case from 1994 concerning the Finnish import monopoly for alcoholic beverages, the EFTA Court adopted the CJEU's method of interpretation and essentially decided that the objective of homogeneity had to prevail over any expectations the (Nordic) EFTA states might have had as to the possibility to keep their strict policy on the import of alcohol.[7] Since *Restamark*, the EFTA Court has continued to disprove the widespread fear that differences in context and purpose would inevitably undermine the objective of an interpretation of EEA rules in conformity with corresponding rules of EU law (Fredriksen 2010b: 740). In *Restamark*, the CJEU case law relied on by the EFTA Court predated the signing of the EEA Agreement, but subsequent cases soon revealed that the temporal limitation of Art. 6 EEA had no impact on the EFTA Court's adherence to CJEU case law. As the EFTA Court itself noted in the *L'Oréal* case from 2008, it has 'consistently taken into account the relevant rulings of the CJEU given after the said date'.[8] In essence, as noted with satisfaction by the president of the CJEU on the occasion of the EFTA Court's twentieth anniversary, 'it does not appear that the EFTA Court has treated the CJEU case-law differently depending on when the pertinent judgments were rendered' (Skouris 2014: 35).

A prominent example illustrating this is the so-called *Reversion* case, concerning the legality of the almost century-old Norwegian regime for acquisition of hydropower resources under which private undertakings have to surrender all installations to the Norwegian state without compensation at the expiry of the concession period.[9] The EFTA Surveillance Authority argued that the regime violated both Art. 31 EEA Agreement on the freedom of establishment and Art. 40 on the free movement of capital because undertakings in which Norwegian public entities owned at least two-thirds of the shares were exempted from the system of reversion. In its defence, the Norwegian government argued, *inter alia*, that the rules at issue were a part of the basic ownership structure in the hydropower sector, and as such fell under Art. 125 EEA Agreement. According to Art. 125, the EEA Agreement 'shall in no way prejudice the rules of the Contracting Parties governing the system of property ownership'. The provision is copied verbatim from what is now Art. 345 TFEU. At the date of the signing of the EEA Agreement, the CJEU had not clarified the reach of this exemption. Subsequent case law, however, revealed that the CJEU was of the view that Art. 345 TFEU does not exempt the member states' systems of property ownership from the fundamental rules of the EU Treaties.[10] Supported by Iceland, and highlighting their common understanding of Art. 125 EEA Agreement at the time of the EEA negotiations, the Norwegian government argued that Art. 125 should not be interpreted in conformity with the CJEU's interpretation of Art. 345 TFEU. The

EFTA Court was not persuaded, however, holding that there were no 'specific circumstances' in the case which would warrant such a break with the homogeneity objective. In particular, the EFTA Court stressed that '[u]nilateral expressions of understanding of the kind claimed to have been made by Norway and Iceland cannot constitute such circumstances'.[11] Closely following CJEU case law, the EFTA Court thereafter found the system of reversion to be incompatible with the EEA Agreement.[12]

Of course, a policy of adherence to CJEU case law is only helpful in cases where guidance may be found in existing rulings from the CJEU. In cases where the EFTA Court has to tackle questions of internal market law not yet decided by the CJEU (so-called *going first* cases), the EFTA Court's judges are in reality asked to second-guess the CJEU: by applying the CJEU's method of interpretation, the EFTA Court will – to the best of its ability – try do identify how the CJEU would have decided the case at hand.

Experience after twenty years of the EEA reveals that the EFTA Court has won subsequent approbation of the CJEU in several of the cases where it had to go first (Fredriksen 2010b: 747–749). This is a considerable achievement for which the EFTA Court deserves praise. However, it is inevitable that the EFTA Court (like everyone else) sometimes fail to second-guess the CJEU.

The question of how to proceed in such situations was raised before the EFTA Court in in the *L'Oréal* case from 2008. In a remarkable open and straightforward manner, the EFTA Court conceded that the consequences for the internal market within the EEA 'call for an interpretation of EEA law in line with new case-law of the CJEU regardless of whether the EFTA Court has previously ruled on the question'.[13] Acknowledging that the CJEU's interpretation of the Trademark Directive (89/104/EEC) in the cases *Silhouette* and *Sebago* was based on arguments which were equally valid in an EEA law context and an EU law context, the EFTA Court simply abandoned the interpretation of the Trade Mark Directive which it had previously favoured in the *Maglite* case.[14] Of particular interest is the fact that the EFTA Court at no point admitted that the interpretation preferred by the CJEU was any better, or the reasoning more convincing, than the one originally favoured by the EFTA Court. On the contrary, the EFTA Court expressly stated that both alternatives were supported by 'weighty arguments' and that the EFTA Court and the CJEU simply had 'opted' for different solutions.[15] Thus, it was merely the authority of the CJEU's case law which caused the EFTA Court to overrule *Maglite*. As a result, as noted by one commentator, the *L'Oréal* case suggests that the EFTA Court is of the opinion that its own decisions only have 'provisional authority pending a decision of the CJEU'(Van Stiphout 2009: 15).

In the wake of its U-turn in *L'Oréal*, the EFTA Court has been charged with having relegated itself to 'junior partner' in the EEA judicial system, a subordination which was 'neither the intention of the Contracting Parties in general nor that of the EFTA States in particular' (Van Stiphout 2009). There is some merit to this criticism from an institutional perspective, but from the perspective of homogeneity the EFTA Court's open deference to the CJEU may only be applauded

(Fredriksen 2010a: 496). As has been shown, the EFTA Court may only exercise its institutional equality with the CJEU at the expense of the overall goal of uniform interpretation and application of the common EEA rules in all of the EEA States. In short, *L'Oréal* confirms and strengthens the impression left by the case law of the EFTA Court ever since its establishment that the objective of a homogeneous EEA prevails over any pluralistic suggestions left by the judicial structure of the EEA. Even though not invoked as justification by the EFTA Court, the previously mentioned acceptance from the EFTA States of the untouchable position of the CJEU (as most clearly evidenced in Protocol 48) suggests that the decision in *L'Oréal* only made explicit an inconvenient truth which was deliberately hidden by the contracting parties in the complex judicial architecture of the EEA.

Unfortunately for the EFTA Court, the loyal deference to the CJEU has diminished the demand for its services considerably. The number of preliminary references to the Court from the national courts of the EFTA States is very low, with an annual average of only a little more than four cases altogether from Icelandic, Liechtenstein and Norwegian courts.[16] Most strikingly, it is now more than 12(!) years since the last occasion on which the Supreme Court of Norway bothered to ask the EFTA Court for guidance on the proper interpretation of EEA law.[17] Even though there may be several different factors contributing to this result, the EFTA Court's deference to the CJEU certainly has to be recognised as one of them (Fredriksen 2012: 203–206). Once it is acknowledged that the authority on the interpretation of the substantive rules of the internal market essentially rests with the CJEU, the national judges may perhaps be excused if they ask themselves how much there really is to gain from a preliminary reference to the EFTA Court and if the advantages outweigh the delay, work and cost entailed. The acknowledgement of the authority of the CJEU may also explain why the parties appearing before Norwegian courts are not very keen on a reference to be made to the EFTA Court. Even though there are several cases in which a party has pleaded for a reference to be made, it is striking that this seems not to be the case in the majority of the EEA-related cases (Fredriksen 2012: 205). It is tempting to speculate that parties with an interest in general clarification of the substantive rules of the internal market (such as consumer organisations, labour unions, business federations, public agencies etc.) would be keener on such references to be made if the recipient was the CJEU rather than the EFTA Court.

Furthermore, in situations where similar questions of EEA law arise at the same time in the EFTA pillar and in the EU (which they often do), there seem to be a quiet understanding between the EFTA states and the EFTA Surveillance Authority to let the matter be decided by the CJEU (Baudenbacher 2010: 14). Rather than parallel proceedings before the EFTA Court, both the EFTA Surveillance Authority and the EFTA states concerned make use of their right to take part in EEA-related proceedings before the CJEU. As long as the EFTA states loyally adhere to the subsequent ruling of the CJEU, there is hardly any reason for the EU to object to this indirect seizure of the CJEU as a forum to decide such disputes. But there is no denial that the practice demonstrates that the EFTA Surveillance

Authority and the EFTA states acknowledges that the authority on the interpretation of the common EU/EEA rules rests with the CJEU.

In an interesting attempt to increase the demand for its services, the EFTA Court has in the last couple of years highlighted the 'EEA specific' character of certain matters of EEA law – parts of EEA law where the agreement is not merely a copy of EU law and where the quest for equal conditions for competition throughout the EEA allows for more creativity from the EFTA Court. This is particularly true for the thorny issue of the effect of EEA law in the legal orders of the EFTA states, where the EFTA Court recently warned that the principle of state liability for breaches of EEA law differs from the development, in the case law of the CJEU, of the principle of state liability under EU law and that the application of the principles therefore 'may not necessarily be coextensive in all respects'.[18]

However, as far as the substantive rules of the internal market are concerned, the approach revealed in *L'Oréal* still prevails (even though the EFTA Court's reluctance to quote the decision in subsequent cases perhaps suggests that it regrets how explicit it was in its deference to the CJEU). Thus, based on 20 years of experience, the EFTA Court's approach to CJEU case law may be summarized in the following statement by the president of the CJEU on the occasion of the EFTA Court's twentieth anniversary: There is general agreement that the EFTA Court 'strictly respects the obligations imposed upon it by the [EEA] Agreement and respects the precedence of the CJEU' (Skouris 2014: 36). As a telling result, twenty years on there are still no examples of the EU calling on the EEA Joint Committee to deal with a case of diverging case law from the EFTA Court and the CJEU.

## The approach of the national courts of the EFTA states

As noted in the introduction, it was a *sine qua non* for the EFTA states during the EEA negotiations that they would not have to relinquish judicial sovereignty to the 'foreign judges' of the CJEU. From this background, one would perhaps expect a somewhat reluctant reception of CJEU case law in the EFTA states, perhaps with the national courts sticking to 'their' EFTA Court or even pursuing a more independent interpretation of EEA law on their own. However, this is not how things have turned out. Rather on the contrary, CJEU precedents are cited and followed by Icelandic, Norwegian and Liechtenstein courts, including the supreme courts, in much the same manner as in the EU member states (Batliner 2004; Fredriksen 2012; Hannesson 2012).[19]

In Norway, the Supreme Court played down the significance of the temporal limit of Art. 6 EEA at the first opportunity. In two important cases from 1997, *Eidesund* and *Løten*, concerning the interpretation of Directive 77/187/EEC on employees' rights in the event of transfers of undertakings, the Supreme Court held that CJEU judgements rendered after the date of signature of the agreement still would have 'direct consequences' for the interpretation of the Norwegian legislation implementing the directive[20] and that the temporal limit in Art. 6 EEA was 'of little interest'.[21] A later statement to the same effect is found in the 2002 judgement in the *Jo-Bolaget* case, where the Supreme Court referred to *Eidesund* as authority for the opinion that it was clear that more recent case law of the CJEU had to be taken into account.[22] After this, the Supreme Court simply stopped referring to Art. 6 EEA, clearly indicating that the temporal limit of that provision is without any practical significance (Graver 2005: 91).

Furthermore, the jurisprudence of the Supreme Court shows that CJEU case-law is not only taken into account when interpreting EEA law – it is *de facto* followed as binding authority. Evidence suggests that the Supreme Court will disregard even clear assumptions in the *travaux préparatoires* and overrule both its own and the EFTA Court's precedents if deemed necessary in order to comply with CJEU case-law.

Thus, in the *Norsk Dental Depot* case from 2004 the Supreme Court simply referred to CJEU's interpretation of the Product Liability Directive (85/374/EEC) in *Sánchez*[23] to the effect that established Norwegian jurisprudence on strict liability for dangerous products could no longer be relied on in addition to the liability regime established by Art. 6 of the said directive.[24] The fact that the Norwegian legislator in the *travaux préparatoires* to the act implementing the Directive into the 1988 Act on Product Liability clearly assumed that there would still be room for the established Norwegian regime of strict liability was simply disregarded.

Similarly, in the *Vesta Forsikring* case from 2006, concerning bad faith of the applicant as a condition for refusal to register a trademark, the Supreme Court openly overruled an earlier decision on the interpretation of Art. 4(4) of the Trademark Directive (89/104/EEC).[25] Nothing in the judgement indicates that the Supreme Court accorded its own previous judgement any authority in this respect – the court simply stated that subsequent clarification through decisions of the EU's Office of Harmonization for the Internal Market called for an interpretation deviating from the one previously held.

Further, both the *Finanger (No 1)* case from 2000 and the *Edquist* case from 2010 clearly suggested that the Supreme Court would be prepared to deviate from the case law of the EFTA Court if it deemed this to be necessary in order to follow the CJEU's lead.[26] The Supreme Court confirmed this in its controversial judgement in the *STX* case from 2013.[27] In this judgement, the Supreme Court made it painfully clear that it disagreed with the EFTA Court's interpretation of the Posted Workers Directive (96/71/EC).[28] In a way, the judgement may rightly be portrayed as the Norwegian Supreme Court demonstrating its sovereignty from the EFTA Court. However, it is important to add that the judgement is dotted with references to CJEU case law and clearly based on the assumption that the directive in question is to be interpreted and applied in Norway in accordance with the (presumed) view of the CJEU. Thus, the Supreme Court only exercised its independence vis-à-vis the EFTA Court in order to adhere to what it believed to be 'the ECJ version of EEA law'.

The loyal reception of CJEU case law is equally striking in cases where no clear precedent may be found. Avoiding any temptation it may have had to pursue its own interpretation of EEA law, the Supreme Court's approach in such cases is to analyse existing CJEU case law to try to deduce whatever guidelines it can from the reasoning of the CJEU in cases involving more or less similar questions. In the two fairly recent judgements *Nye Kystlink* and *Bottolvs* concerning alleged age discrimination, the Supreme Court stated that Norwegian courts should interpret the ban against age discrimination in Directive 2000/78/EC as would the CJEU if the case had been referred to it.[29] As Directive 2000/78/EC is not part of the EEA Agreement, a reference to the EFTA Court was no alternative. Even though the court was careful to tie its adherence to CJEU case law to the presumed intentions of the legislator when voluntarily implementing the directive into Norwegian law, both judgements show that the reception of CJEU case law is extended even beyond the scope of EEA law.

Striking is certainly too the decision to stay the proceedings before the Supreme Court in the age discrimination case *CHC Norway* in order to await the preliminary judgement of the CJEU in *Prigge*.[30] A better illustration of the Supreme Court's adherence to the 'foreign judges' of the CJEU than staying a pending case for more than a full year and against the will of one of the parties to the case, in order to make sure that Norwegian law is interpreted and applied in conformity with CJEU case law, is hard to imagine.[31]

Of course, general acceptance of the authority of the CJEU does not guarantee that the national courts of the EFTA states always get it right in their interpretation of EEA law in concrete cases. Unsurprisingly, it is not difficult after twenty years of the EEA to find examples from Iceland, Liechtenstein and Norway where it may well be questioned whether the national judges succeeded in their attempts to follow CJEU case law (Batliner 2004; Fredriksen 2012; Hannesson 2012). A recent and much debated example is the Norwegian supreme court's reliance on CJEU case law in the earlier mentioned *STX* case from 2013. Subsequent developments suggest that the supreme court overestimated the reach of the CJEU case law it relied on in order to justify several deviations from the EFTA Court's opinion.[32] This is, of course, unfortunate, not only to the parties to the case but also with a view to the damage mistakes like this can do to the credibility of the judicial mechanism in the EFTA pillar of the EEA. Still, a single judgement is hardly enough to charge the Supreme Court with a strategy to establish a distinct (state-friendly) 'Norwegian version of EEA law'.[33] As mentioned previously, the judgement is dotted with references to CJEU case law and clearly based on the view that the Posted Worker Directive was to be interpreted and applied in Norway in accordance with what the Supreme Court sincerely believed to be the view of the CJEU. Furthermore, the Supreme Court was careful to claim support from the observations which the Commission and the EFTA Surveillance Authority submitted to the EFTA Court as the case was pending before it.

Furthermore, if subsequent rulings from the CJEU indeed should reveal that the Norwegian Supreme Court got it wrong in the *STX* case, Norwegian authorities will have no choice but to adjust their policies against social dumping accordingly. Failure to do so will certainly prompt the EFTA Surveillance Authority to take action, if need be by bringing an infringement action against Norway before the

EFTA Court. This will give the EFTA Court the possibility to have the final say on the matter in the form of a binding judgement. And as demonstrated above, the ruling of the EFTA Court may safely be expected to follow the CJEU's lead. Thus, in one way or the other, the view of the CJEU will prevail in the end.

## Influencing the CJEU's development of the common rules for the internal market?

Even though the authority of the interpretation of the common rules for the EEA internal market rests with the CJEU, if not *de jure* then certainly *de facto*, the judicial architecture of the EEA still leaves the EFTA side with some opportunities to influence the judicial development in the CJEU.

First, the EEA Agreement provides the EFTA states (and the EFTA Surveillance Authority) with the right to appear before the CJEU in cases of relevance to the EEA.[34] This is an opportunity which the Norwegian government has highlighted as an important way to 'influence' the development of EEA law and of which it makes use on a fairly regular basis (Parliament White Paper no. 5 [2012–2013]: 22–24). Submissions made by the EFTA states are considered by the CJEU on an equal footing with submissions made by EU member states – it is the quality of the submission and the strength of the arguments that determine whether the views put forward gain acceptance. As admitted by the Norwegian government, it is difficult to gauge the extent to which a submission has influenced the CJEU in its final decision, but there are several examples in which it is apparent that the CJEU has based its decision directly on arguments put forward by Norway, including in cases where Norway's views have differed from those of other actors (Parliament White Paper no. 5 ([2012–2013]). Still, the right to appear before the CJEU hardly compares to the existence of a common EEA Court which would have included members representing the legal traditions of the EFTA States. And furthermore, in 2010 the president of the CJEU changed his practice concerning the EFTA states' right to intervene in EEA-related cases between EU member states and EU institutions (e.g. infringement proceedings initiated by the Commission against an EU member state).[35] The EFTA states have reportedly raised the issue with the EU, both in the EEA Joint Committee and in the EEA Council, and the Norwegian government has vowed to 'continue to work actively to gain acceptance for its view on this matter' (Parliament White Paper no. 5 [2012–2013]: 22–24), but essentially all they can do is to hope for the president of the CJEU to change his mind.[36] For the time being, the EFTA states' right to appear before the CJEU is thus limited to other categories of cases (of which preliminary references are by far the most important).

Second, and perhaps somewhat unexpectedly, the EFTA Court has managed to establish itself as a fairly regular dialogue partner of the CJEU. Over the past twenty years, the CJEU and its advocate generals have referred to decisions from the EFTA Court in more than 200 cases.[37] This is a remarkable achievement for a small court from the equally small EFTA pillar of the EEA, not least in view of the importance the CJEU attached to its position as the supreme authority on the rules of the internal market in its previously mentioned opinions on the EEA

Agreement. Indeed, together with the powerful European Court of Human Rights in Strasbourg, the EFTA Court is the only court with which the CJEU engages in such a dialogue on a regular basis.[38]

Still, the extent to which decisions from the EFTA Court have influenced the CJEU is hard to gauge. While some commentators take the view that the CJEU only cite decisions from the EFTA Court as a source of inspiration, others believe the EFTA Court's influence to be substantial.[39] Interestingly, members of the CJEU tend to fall in the latter category when they – in an extra-judicial capacity – on various occasions over the last twenty years have paid salute to the EFTA Court. On the occasion of the EFTA Court's tenth anniversary in 2004, the president of the CJEU described the dialogue between the CJEU and the EFTA Court as 'a paradigm for international cooperation between judicial institutions' and stated that 'ignoring EFTA Court precedents would simply be incompatible with the overriding objective of the EEA Agreement which is homogeneity' (Skouris 2005: 123–129). Ten years later, he repeated the same words and even took the view that the CJEU in some cases had referred to decisions of the EFTA Court as 'leading authority' (Skouris 2014: 28). Still, cases in which the CJEU departs from the case law of the EFTA Court without even mentioning the latter's decisions certainly confirm that the CJEU may well allow itself to be inspired or even influenced by the case law of the EFTA Court but that it decides by itself if, when and to what extent this will be the case. Indeed, that the dialogue is not one between equals has explicitly been acknowledged by the president of the EFTA Court: The CJEU is 'in the driver's seat' (Baudenbacher 2012: 12).

Even if the EFTA Court may be able to influence the CJEU, it is questionable how interested the EFTA states are in such a 'judicial dialogue'. Experience reveals that is almost only in cases where the EFTA Court has taken the lead in the development towards further realisation of the fundamental freedoms of the internal market that the CJEU sees fit to quote its decisions (Fredriksen 2010b: 757). Arguably, this might be part of the reason why the EFTA states, Norway, in particular, seem rather reluctant to take steps in order to increase the number of cases which reach the EFTA Court. Both the tendency to suggest that the EFTA Surveillance Authority ought to await the CJEU's decision in a similar case or the mostly firm opposition to suggestions that national courts ought to refer a case to the EFTA Court may be seen as part of a strategy to prevent the EFTA Court from taking the lead in the judicial evolution of EU/EEA law. In Norway, the government's lawyers seem to fear that the EFTA Court will seize any such opportunity to make an impression on the CJEU and that it will do so through dynamic interpretation of EEA law against the interest of the state. The chilling response to the EFTA Court's recent call for two additional judges and an advocate general in order to reinforce its standing and credibility hints in the same direction.[40] The same applies to the governments' disinterest in proposals for the jurisdiction of the EFTA Court to be broadened to encompass other agreements between the EU and the EFTA states.

Part of the problem for the EFTA states is that the homogeneity objective leaves no room for the legal traditions of the EFTA states as a relevant consideration in the interpretation of the substantive rules of the internal market. Seen from the

CJEU's perspective, it is plain that a distinction has to be drawn between the legal traditions of the member states and those of third countries such as the EFTA states: the former are recognized as relevant sources of EU law; the latter are not. It follows that the use of legal traditions characteristic to the EFTA states as sources of EEA law would, in any situation where they differ from the traditions of the EU member states, *per se* conflict with the agreement's overarching goal of homogeneity between EEA and EU law. Thus, it is hardly surprising that there are no cases where the EFTA Court has advocated the legal traditions of the EFTA states as a relevant source for the judicial development of EEA law: the only way the EFTA Court can gain and keep the position of a dialogue partner of the CJEU is by adopting the CJEU's method of interpretation and its selection of relevant sources. Thus, the judicial dialogue between the EFTA Court and the CJEU hardly compares to the existence of a common EEA Court in which judges from the EFTA states would have been participating on equal footing with colleagues from the CJEU.

## What if Switzerland and the UK were to join to the EFTA pillar of the EEA?

Given the current debate in both Switzerland and the UK, it is tempting to end by contemplating how the judicial architecture of the EEA Agreement would cope with a scenario where one or both of these countries were to join in on the EFTA side of the EEA. The immediate result would obviously be a strengthening of the EFTA Court with two new members and, presumably, a welcome increase in its caseload. This again could possibly reinforce the EFTA Court's standing and credibility, leading to more cases being referred to it both from the national courts of the existing members of the EFTA pillar and from the EFTA Surveillance Authority. Further, it may lead to an intensified and perhaps even more equal dialogue with the CJEU. Still, Swiss and/or UK accession to the EFTA side of the EEA may also reignite the inherent tensions in the judicial architecture of the EEA. It is hardly given that neither the courts nor the governments of Switzerland and the UK will adhere to the decisions of the 'foreign judges' of the CJEU as readily as have the much smaller EFTA states of Iceland, Liechtenstein and Norway. Should the EFTA States, be it their governments or courts, become more self-assertive and demand a greater say in the judicial development of the common rules of the internal market, then the maintenance of equal conditions for competition throughout the EEA would depend on the EU being willing to accept this. Opinion 1/91 and 1/92 suggest that any such expectations from the EFTA side, even in the rather unlikely scenario that it was to be enforced by Switzerland or the UK (or both), will be frustrated by the CJEU.

## Conclusion

Despite the gradual development of a judicial dialogue between the CJEU and the EFTA Court, the reality of the EEA is that the EFTA states have to play by the rules of the internal market as they are interpreted by the 'foreign judges' of the CJEU.

The fact that the EEA Agreement for more than 20 years now has defied the discouraging predictions made by leading commentators at the time of its birth[41] is more than anything due to the fact that the remaining EFTA states have accepted the hegemony of the EU and its Court of Justice. From a political perspective, this may perhaps be explained by the increasingly unequal strength between the diminished EFTA pillar and the ever-growing EU pillar of the EEA; the perceived importance of the EEA Agreement to the economy of the remaining EFTA States and their lack of viable alternatives to the current association to the EU. Thus, the survival of the EEA Agreement is hardly due to its judicial architecture being so much better than perceived by those predicting its demise more than twenty years ago but, rather, to the fact that the remaining EFTA states have proved to be far more pragmatic than any commentator back in the early 1990s could have expected them to be. In a way, the EFTA states have grown accustomed to life under the hegemony of the CJEU, a fact which is now demonstrated by their adherence to CJEU case law even outside the reach of the EEA Agreement.

## Notes

1 Opinion 1/91 *EEA I*, ECLI:EU:C:1991:490.
2 OJ [1994] L 344, 3.
3 Originally, this followed from an agreed minute by the contracting parties, but its binding effect was later strengthened by moving it to a protocol (Protocol 48).
4 Opinion 1/92, *EEA II*, ECLI:EU:C:1992:189.
5 See the submission of the Commission before the CJEU in Opinion 1/92, above n. 4 at p. 2833.
6 The submissions of the Commission in Opinion 1/92, above n. 5, at p. 2833.
7 Case E-1/94 *Restamark* [1994–1995] EFTA Court Report 15. See the telling question posed by Kronenberger: 'Does the EFTA Court interpret the EEA Agreement as if it were the EC Treaty?' (Kronenberger 1996).
8 Joined cases E-9/07 and E-10/07 *L'Oréal* [2008] EFTA Court Report 258, para. 28.
9 Case E-2/06 *EFTA Surveillance Authority v Norway* [2007] EFTA Court Report 167.
10 See, for example, Case C-302/97 *Klaus Konle v Australian Republic* [1999] ECLI:EU:C:1999: 271, par. 38.
11 Ibid., para. 59.
12 For the sake of completeness, it ought to be added that the Norwegian government reacted by eliminating completely the possibility for undertakings in which Norwegian public entities do not own at least two-thirds of the shares to obtain concessions for acquisition of hydropower resources.
13 Joined cases E-9/07 and E-10/07 *L'Oréal* [2008] EFTA Court Report 258, para. 29.
14 In Case E-2/97 *Maglite* [1997] EFTA Court Report 129, the EFTA Court opted for an interpretation of Art. 7(1) of the Trademark Directive which allowed for so-called international exhaustion of trademarks. Shortly thereafter, however, the CJEU opted for mandatory EEA-wide exhaustion in Case C-355/96 *Silhouette*, ECLI:EU:C:1998:374 and then upheld that interpretation in Case C-173/98 *Sebago*, ECLI:EU:C:1999:347 (which concerned goods originating from outside the EEA).
15 *L'Oréal*, para. 24–25. Whereas the EFTA Court attached particular importance to considerations relating to free trade and competition in the interest of consumers, the CJEU

emphasised the overall objective of facilitating the free movement of goods and services and in that regard the directive's objective of ensuring the same protection for registered trademarks within the whole of the internal market.
16 See the EFTA Court's annual report for 2013, p. 1035ff. The report is available at www.eftacourt.int, last accessed 18 December 2014.
17 Case E-3/02 *Paranova* [2003] EFTA Court Report 101.
18 Case E-2/12, *HOB-vín* [2012] EFTA Court Report 1092, par. 120 and Case E-7/12 *DB Schenker v EFTA Surveillance Authority* [2013] EFTA Court Report 356, par. 120.
19 For Icelandic courts see Hannesson (2012), for Norwegian courts see Fredriksen (2012) and for Liechtenstein courts see Batliner (2004).
20 Rt. 1997 p. 1954 *Eidesund*, at 1960.
21 Rt. 1997 p. 1965 *Løten*, at 1970.
22 Rt. 2002 p. 391 *Jo-Bolaget* (often referred to in Norway as the *God Morgon* case), at 395–396.
23 Case C-183/00 *Sánchez*, ECLI:EU:C:2002:255.
24 Rt. 2004 p. 122, para. 31.
25 Rt. 2006 p. 1473 *Vesta Forsikring* (often referred to in Norway as the *Lifebuoy* case), overruling Rt. 1998 p. 1809 *BUD*. It the earlier decision, the Supreme Court had held that mere knowledge of existing use of a similar mark by another meant that the trademark could not be registered, whereas the court in the 2006 case clarified that registration may only be refused if the applicant was acting in bad faith at the date of the application.
26 Rt. 2000 p. 1811 *Finanger (No 1)*, at p. 1825 and Rt. 2010 p. 1500 *Edquist*, para. 113.
27 Rt. 2013 p. 258 *STX*. For a recent comment in the English language, see Barnard (2014).
28 Case E- 2/11, *STX Norway Offshore* [2012] EFTA Court Report 4.
29 Rt. 2010 p. 202, para. 56, and Rt. 2011 p. 609, para. 72.
30 Rt. 2010 p. 944, staying the proceedings in order to await the outcome of Case C-447/09 *Prigge*, ECLI:EU:C:2011:573.
31 In its final judgement (Rt. 2012 p. 291), the Supreme Court closely followed the CJEU's findings in *Prigge*.
32 See the opinion of Advocate General Wahl in the pending Case C-396/13 *Sähköalojen ammattiliitto*, ECLI:EU:C:2014:2236.
33 As the EFTA Court's president did in a remarkable onslaught in the wake of the Supreme Court's judgement in the *STX* case, see Baudenbacher (2013).
34 See the Statute of the CJEU Art. 23 (3) (observations in preliminary reference cases) and Art. 40 (3) (right to intervene in certain other types of cases).
35 See the orders of the CJEU's president in Case C-542/09 *Commission v Netherlands* and in Case C-493/09 *Commission v Portugal*.
36 Of course, the EU Council can force a reversal of this practice on the CJEU through an amendment of the CJEU's statute, but it is to be doubted if the EU member states will take such action just for the benefit of the three small EFTA states (in particular because the decision of the CJEU president is to be seen as part of the court's efforts to handle its ever increasing workload).
37 Source: The CJEU's InfoCuria database (http://curia.europa.eu/juris/).
38 It is thus hardly surprising that the 'judicial dialogue' with the CJEU (and its Advocate Generals) is a favourite topic for the EFTA Court's president, see Baudenbacher (2008).
39 Compare Bekkedal (2008) with Baudenbacher (2008).
40 See Press Release 11/11 of 8 December 2011 *An Extended EFTA Court? The EFTA Court proposes amendments to the Surveillance and Court Agreement*. For unknown reasons, the proposal is no longer available at the EFTA Court's homepage, but if may be obtained from the court upon request to the registrar. The response from the Norwegian government

came in Parliament White Paper no. 5 (2012–2013: 22–24): 'Thus far, the Government has not seen a need to make amendments to the institutional setup of the EFTA Court'.
41 See Cremona 1994:524: 'the compromises reached are unlikely to prove satisfactory'.

## References

Barnard, C. (2014) 'Reciprocity, Homogeneity and Loyal Cooperation: Dealing with Recalcitrant National Courts?', in EFTA Court (ed), *The EEA and the EFTA Court: Decentred Integration*, Oxford: Hart Publishing.

Batliner, A. (2004) 'Die Anwendung des EWR-Rechts durch liechtensteinische Gerichte – Erfahrungen eines Richters', *Liechtensteinische Juristen-Zeitung*, 25: 139–141.

Baudenbacher, C. (2008) 'The EFTA Court, the ECJ, and the Latter's Advocates General – a Tale of Judicial Dialogue', in A. Arnull, P. Eeckhout and T. Tridimas (eds), *Continuity and Change in EU Law: Essays in Honour of Sir Francis Jacobs*, Oxford: Oxford University Press.

—— (2010) *The EFTA Court in Action*, Stuttgart: German Law Publishers.

—— (2012) 'Some Thoughts on the EFTA Court's Phases of Life', in EFTA Court (ed) *Judicial Protection in the European Economic Area*, Stuttgart: German Law Publishers.

—— (2013) 'EFTA-domstolen og dens samhandling med de norske domstolene', *Lov og Rett*, 52(8): 515–534.

Bekkedal, T. (2008) *Frihet, likhet og fellesskap*, Bergen: Fagbokforlaget.

Cremona, M. (1994) 'The "Dynamic and Homogeneous" EEA: Byzantine Structures and Various Geometry', *European Law Review*, 19: 508–526.

Fredriksen, H.H. (2010a) 'One Market, Two Courts – Legal Pluralism vs. Homogeneity in the European Economic Area', *Nordic Journal of International Law*, 79(4): 481–499.

—— (2010b) 'The EFTA Court 15 Years On', *International and Comparative Law Quarterly*, 59(3): 731–760.

—— (2012) 'The Two EEA Courts – A Norwegian Perspective', in EFTA Court (ed) *Judicial Protection in the European Economic Area*, Stuttgart: German Law Publishers.

Graver, H.P. (2005) 'The Effects of EFTA Court Jurisprudence on the Legal Orders of the EFTA States', in C. Baudenbacher, P. Tresselt and T. Orlygsson (eds) *The EFTA Court Ten Years On*, Oxford: Hart Publishing.

Hannesson, O.I. (2012) *Giving Effect to EEA Law – Examining and Rethinking the Role and Relationship between the EFTA Court and the Icelandic National Courts in the EEA Legal Order*, Florence: European University Institute.

Hartley, T. (1992) 'The European Court and the EEA', *International and Comparative Law Quarterly*, 41(4): 841–848.

Kronenberger, V. (1996) 'Does the EFTA Court Interpret the EEA Agreement as if it Were the EC Treaty?', *International and Comparative Law Quarterly*, 45(1): 198–212.

Parliament White Paper no. 5 (2012–2013) 'The EEA Agreement and Norway's Other Agreements with the EU' [Meld. St. 5 (2012–2013) EØS-avtalen og Norges øvrige avtaler med EU], Oslo: Ministry of Foreign Affairs.

Skouris, V. (2005) 'The ECJ and the EFTA Court under the EEA Agreement: A Paradigm for International Cooperation between Judicial Institutions', in C. Baudenbacher, P. Tresselt and T. Orlygsson (eds) *The EFTA Court Ten Years On*, Oxford: Hart Publishing.

—— (2014) 'The Role of the Court of Justice of the European Union in the Development of the EEA Single Market', in EFTA Court (ed) *The EEA and the EFTA Court – Decentred Integration*, Oxford: Hart Publishing.

Van Stiphout, T. (2009) 'The L'Oréal Cases – Some Thoughts on the Role of the EFTA Court in the EEA Legal Framework: Because it Is Worth It!', *Jus & News*, 1: 7–18.

# 7

# ICELAND

## A reluctant European

*Baldur Thorhallsson*

The main aim of this book is to address the question of whether the people in closely associated non-member states are able to govern themselves through law and politics or whether they are subject to alien rule. Are the effects different from those of European Union (EU) members? Do they through their distinct form of EU association, in effect, experience some form of *submission*, whose effects could resemble living under hegemony?

In this chapter, I examine this question by first considering the key features of Iceland's relationship with the EU, with focus on the EEA Agreement and the Schengen Agreement. The assessment shows that the structure of the relationship is very similar to that of Norway, but there are also broader effects that set Iceland apart from Norway. I discuss three such effects. One pertains to *size*: Does Iceland's considerably smaller size than Norway's matter? Another is the structure of the Icelandic economy and its greater reliance on primary sectors. The third is Iceland's traditionally close relationship with – and dependence on – the US.

In the first section, I provide an overview of Iceland's relationship to the EU and an assessment of the constitutional democratic effects. The next section discusses the question of size, including the role of the public administration; I discuss Iceland's relationship with the US in the subsequent sections.

### Background

Icelandic politicians have been reluctant to participate in European integration but have nevertheless taken decisive steps to ensure involvement when Icelandic interests have been at stake.[1] This was the case with European Free Trade Association (EFTA) membership in 1970. It paved the way for a free trade agreement with the European Economic Community (EEC) two years later, the EEA Agreement twenty years later, and the Schengen Agreement in 1999 (Iceland's privileges under the Nordic Passport Union were here at risk). Accordingly, Iceland has been swept by Europeanisation despite the fact that it is not a member of the EU. Iceland's and Norway's association with the EU is basically the same.

Memberships of EFTA and the EEA were very controversial amongst both the political elite and the public in Iceland. The small Social Democratic Party was the only political party that fully supported membership of the EEA – all other parties had considerable reservations about the four freedoms and transfer of sovereignty to the EEA decision-making bodies. Opponents of EEA membership frequently argued that Iceland would sacrifice its freedom and independence by joining the EEA and that the Icelandic constitution did not allow transfer of sovereignty to supranational institutions (Thorhallsson 2004). The EEA Agreement was narrowly approved in the Icelandic national parliament – the Althingi. The president of Iceland considered to use her *veto power* for the first time and initiate a referendum on the EEA Agreement. However, she came to the conclusion that the tradition of parliamentary governance should prevail and claimed that the agreement would give Icelandic students access to university education within the EEA, move Iceland closer to Europe and limit American influence (Thorhallsson 2008). Iceland's largest political party, the centre-right Independence Party, came out in support of EFTA and the EEA membership when the private sector was largely united in taking part in these aspects of the European project – Iceland's economic interests were at stake. Supporters of membership denied that any transfer of power was taking place and claimed that the Althingi still had the final say on whether EEA rules would be implemented in the country. Until recently, it has been near taboo for Icelandic politicians to acknowledge and speak for transfer of power from Reykjavik to regional and international organisations.

In the summer of 2009, Iceland applied for membership of the EU just nine months after its economic collapse. The membership application has now been put on hold after the Independence Party and the centrist agrarian party, the Progressive Party, came back to power in the general election in 2013. Their firm opposition to EU membership is based on objections of *transfer of sovereignty* to supranational institutions and the economic damage membership would mean for the fisheries and agrarian sectors (Thorhallsson 2008). Furthermore, Icelandic politicians, except for the Social Democrats, have never accepted that the country's defence would be bolstered by taking part in the EU's Common Foreign and Security Policy and the development of the European Security and Defence Policy. This is contrary to the case in Norway, where governments have been attracted to the EU for security reasons (Archer and Sogner 1998; see also Sjursen in Chapter 11). The centre-right in Iceland still looks to the US for defence – though European countries increasingly patrol Iceland's airspace.

## Constitutional implications

Iceland's constitutional democracy is greatly affected by its current affiliation with the European project. Given that both Iceland and Norway are part of the EEA and Schengen Agreements, the implications for Iceland and Norway seem to be similar in terms of autonomy and accountability. There are also differences: Iceland's smallness, special domestic features and unique relationship to the US have had special consequences in Iceland. The case of Iceland further strengthens the claim of Egeberg and Trondal in Chapter 10 that the EU's administrative system challenges administrative sovereignty at the national level in the EFTA/EEA states. Lawmaking without Icelandic representation within the EEA and Schengen Agreements is a norm which Iceland would be unlikely to experience under full membership. Icelandic politicians lack access to proper procedures within these settings to influence decision-making, and there is no explicit authority under which they can be held to account.

Constitutional challenges associated with membership of the EEA are still a hot topic in Icelandic politics, as discussed in the case of Norway in Chapters 6 and 8. The 2008 economic crash highlighted these and other democratic challenges. This is the case despite the fact that Icelandic governments have largely followed international democratic developments, and the country fully satisfies the political criteria for membership of the EU. The opinion and the first progress report of the European Commission on Iceland's application for membership of the EU state that Iceland has 'deeply rooted traditions of representative democracy. Its institutions are effective and respect the limits of their competences. Iceland's constitutional and legal order is stable. The rule of law and respect for human rights are guaranteed' (European Commission 2010a). The progress report only identified a handful of shortcomings regarding the county's governance (e.g. as regards judicial appointments, conflict of interest, the independence of the data protection authorities from interference by the government and EU's citizens' rights to vote and stand in local elections; Thorhallsson and Thorarensen 2014).

The report, however, fails to take into account the democratic deficit associated with membership of the EEA and Schengen Agreements and many other democratic challenges facing Icelanders at present. The democratic challenges are given added impetus through the political uproar and lack of trust in governmental institutions in the aftermath of the crash (Capacent 2009; Hardarson and Onnudottir 2009). In the wake of the crisis, many Icelanders started to question the morality and work practices of the national administration and political sector (Althingi n.d.). Furthermore, the Commission fails to address the smallness and weakness of the public administration and political patronage, as it states that 'Iceland's public administration remains, in general, efficient and free of political interference' (European Commission 2010b).

## *Side-lining the parliament*

In order to shed further light on these concerns, it is interesting to examine the Althingi's attempts to have a say on EEA rules. On one hand, according to a new working procedure it has a chance of stating its opinion on upcoming EEA rules, that is before they are approved in the EEA Joint Committee (Althingi 2008, 2010a,

2011). On the other hand, when EU legislation reaches the Joint Committee it has already been approved by all relevant bodies on the EU side. To complicate matters, the EFTA/EEA states (Iceland, Norway and Liechtenstein) have to speak with one voice within the Joint Committee. This has largely undermined the Icelandic standpoint, because Norway is normally eager to incorporate EU law in line with the EU treaties signed after the completion of the EEA Agreement, whereas Iceland has been reluctant in this respect.

Membership of the EEA and Schengen led to fundamental changes in lawmaking in Iceland. The handling of EEA and Schengen legislation is more in the hands of decision makers in the institutions of the European Union and Icelandic civil servants than of elected representatives in Iceland (Lægreid et al. 2004). Iceland, just like the other EFTA/EEA states, does not have access to the Council of the European Union and the European Parliament, that is the legislative bodies of the EU. Moreover, the EEA decision-making framework does not include Icelandic ministers and parliamentarians in its day-to-day processes. The structure of the EEA Agreement makes it very difficult for Iceland to influence EU/EEA decision-making. Icelandic civil servants only have access to the European Commission, which is supposed to take their views into account, and the EEA Joint Committee, where decisions are taken, by consensus, to incorporate EU legislation into the EEA Agreement.

Icelandic ministers have not been able to utilize the EEA Council, which is officially composed of the foreign ministers of the EEA/EFTA countries and the EU countries (in the 'troika' format of the EU Council presidency), and is supposed to provide political impetus for the development of the agreement and solve disputes within the Joint Committee, because its scope has turned out to be very limited. This is because of a lack of interest in its work on the EU side. Also, the EEA Joint Parliamentary Committee, which is composed of members of parliament (MPs) from both sides, is only a talking club and has no powers. Moreover, these EEA bodies are largely unknown to anyone in Iceland, except for a few public officials who work with them, and politicians who show an interest in their operations.

The Althingi has been absent from the decision-making process and has simply *rubber-stamped* the Joint Committee's incorporation of EU legislation. The normal working procedure is that ministries implement the European legislation without any decisive involvement of ministers and parliamentarians. This may be according to 'best practice' in terms of the agreement and may even limit the traditional *political favouritism* in Iceland (Lægreid et al. 2004). Nevertheless, this decision-making procedure sidelines democratically elected officials. It has created a much larger democratic deficit in Iceland than that which has been identified by many academics within member states of the European Union (e.g. see Follesdal and Hix 2006). In the case of Iceland, membership of the EEA has increased bureaucratic control since the executive and the national parliament are largely absent from the decision-making process; Iceland's electorate does not have the right to vote in the European Parliamentary elections, nor does it choose other EU decision makers; EU decision-making is even more distant from Icelandic voters than it is from the

European electorates, and, finally, membership of the EEA is even more likely than membership of the EU to lead to the adoption of policies that are not Icelanders' ideal policy preferences.

The Althingi's new working procedure is unlikely to have much of a democratically certificatory effect, because the Althingi can only raise its concerns at the final stage of the EU/EEA decision-making process. However, it may be able to have a say on declarations from the EEA Joint Committee concerning exemptions from strict implementation of some EEA rules in Iceland.

## Passive integration

Iceland is better placed within the Schengen scheme, because its minister of the interior can attend Council meetings composed of ministers from all the member states. Also, Icelandic officials have a voice in the Council, but the minister is not allowed to vote on EU legislation even though it is applicable to Iceland. Formally speaking, the non-EU members of the Schengen scheme (also including Norway, Switzerland and Liechtenstein) take a separate decision in a 'Mixed Committee', composed of representatives from all the Schengen members) to incorporate Schengen legislation and decisions. Icelandic ministers of the interior have not sought active participation within Schengen despite the fact they can voice their opinion in the Council and some of them are even known to have been ignorant of this entitlement. Furthermore, the public at large and, for instance, the media are more or less unaware of this possibility of participation in decision shaping in Schengen. Occasionally, some politicians and active social media bloggers may criticise Iceland's membership of Schengen and claim that it opens up the country to foreigners and criminal activity, but in this they are unaware of the fact that free movement of people is part of the EEA Agreement, not of the Schengen scheme. Discussions on whether Iceland could have a say on the running of Schengen never take place.

Nevertheless, the Althingi can reject Schengen and EEA legislation. However, the Althingi (like the Storting in Norway and the Landtag of Lichtenstein), the Joint Committee and the Mixed Committee have very limited room for manoeuvre due to Iceland's clear obligations, under the agreements, to ensure the harmonious development of its legislation in line with that of the EU. Also, EEA legislation is rarely a matter of public debate. The national electorates and parliamentarians are hardly ever aware of upcoming legislation, and they first encounter it after it has been approved within the EU decision-making bodies.

Occasional debates take place about implementation, and demands are raised concerning exemptions from strict application. In the first years of EEA membership, members of local councils were sometimes critical of the costs involved in the implementation of EEA rules. Their common claim was that the smallness of Icelandic municipalities made EEA rules very costly to handle, and thus, they should be exempted from strict application. Also, the business community at large has been critical of many of the EEA rules, which it feels restrict its scope of action, while the main labour unions, which were highly critical of EEA membership in the beginning, changed course, welcome most new EEA rules, and regard them as beneficial for workers.

Furthermore, many of those who oppose Iceland's membership of the EU have always been critical of EEA rules and stepped up their opposition to their implementation in the wake of the EU accession process between 2009 and 2013. Critical assessments of new rules in parliamentary committees and the reluctance of some ministers to enforce implementation partly explain Iceland's implementation deficit at the end of this period. Interestingly, pro-Europeans are also among the critical voices, but their criticism has largely been focused on Iceland's lack of influence within the EEA. Their arguments have not gained ground in the debate on membership of the EU.

That said, the EFTA Surveillance Authority (with the informal approval of the EU) has allowed Iceland to keep its strict capital controls in force – introduced at the eve of the economic crash – despite the fact that they curb one of the four freedoms of the EU/EEA. This indicates a greater flexibility in the EEA Agreement than many anticipated, through the possibility of an exception from one of its core elements, at least temporarily. It is, however, hard to foresee that Iceland will be able to lift its capital restrictions in the foreseeable future without a fall of the króna.

Formally speaking, EU law is not directly applicable in the EEA/EFTA states. Under the EEA Agreement, the EFTA Court only provides national courts with an advisory opinion, though, in practice, they have followed its guidance. That said, politicians and others who oppose Iceland's engagement with European integration commonly claim that Icelandic courts should not follow rulings by the EFTA Court. Furthermore, the Court of Justice of the European Union (CJEU) has taken an active part in establishing the primacy of EU law over national law. In practice, as is also underlined in Chapters 5 and 6, the EEA/EFTA states in effect follow the EU's direction by ensuring harmonisation within the EEA.

To summarise, Iceland has outsourced a large part of its lawmaking, with negative constitutional implications. Formally speaking, as stated before, Iceland can refuse to adopt EU laws that are applicable to the EEA and Schengen Areas. But there is a consensus amongst political parties in Iceland that a refusal would directly challenge the country's membership of these agreements. Hence, Iceland is in practice obliged to implement the EU's decisions. There seem to be two ways for Iceland to regain its sovereignty and independence in policy sectors that fall within the EEA and Schengen. First, it could withdraw from these arrangements with the EU – but the economic cost might be high in terms of a loss of near-tariff-free access to the internal market. The second option would be to join the EU. Membership of the European Union would at least give Iceland a seat at the negotiating table and a chance to influence the EU legislation which ultimately takes effect in the country. However, this would be at the expense of full domestic control over policy sectors of huge economic and political importance; for example, those of fisheries and agriculture. These sectors are sceptical of any changes that might alter their close working relationship with the government, which has often been characterised as *sectoral corporatism*, and has largely allowed them to regulate themselves – as are discussed later (Thorhallsson 2010). That said, these sectors have to apply many items of EEA legislation; for example, in the fields of environmental, health and labour market rules, without the democratic ability to have a say on them. This leads us to Iceland's position, as a small entity dominated by larger entities on either side of the Atlantic, and the implications for its policy choices.

## Does size matter?

Iceland is a small state according to all traditional variables used to define the size of states. It is the second smallest of all the 31 EEA states. This gives a distinctive shape to Iceland's relationship with the EU. Norway and Iceland are both small states but smallness is likely to matter more in the case of Iceland, because it is so much smaller than Norway. Iceland's smallness and its location on the geographical map – one could also say the geopolitical map – has had a profound influence on its domestic and foreign affairs. It is closely associated with European integration and was under American hegemony in the North Atlantic throughout the cold war – as is discussed in the last section.

Small states have to adapt to *realpolitik*, and make special domestic and external arrangements in order to prosper, according to the small-states literature. It argues that small states are vulnerable due to the smallness of their domestic market, limited military capability and small diplomatic corps. Small states need to realise their weaknesses in order to compensate for them. Accordingly, they have to acknowledge their limited capabilities compared with their larger neighbours in terms of their populations and the size of their gross domestic product (GDP), territory, military and public administration (including their foreign service). We may not need 'a final definition' of what constitutes a small state, because a state's 'size' may vary in importance according to which states they are compared with, for example, whether we are comparing Norway with Sweden or with Germany.

Among the three EFTA/EEA countries, Iceland is considerably 'smaller' than Norway, having only 321,000 inhabitants (in contrast to Norway's of 5,089,000), a territory of 103,000 square kilometres, GSP of USD 13.1 billion in 2013, per capita GDP of USD 40,300,[2] 134 people working in the foreign service in October 2014 (excluding locally hired personnel abroad and people working in the Translation Centre of the Ministry for Foreign Affairs; there is usually a correlation between states' populations and the size of their foreign services in Europe; Thorhallsson 2004) and without a military. That said, Liechtenstein (the third EFTA/EEA country) has a considerably smaller capacity than Iceland according to these indicators, except for GDP per capita. In fact, all the Nordic states are most often defined as small states in Europe, and in the international system in general. In practice, however, the small size of the Icelandic Foreign Service and the public administration, in general, restricts its scope of action within the EEA and Schengen. It has a much smaller presence within their decision-making frameworks compared with that of Norway, and it relies on the EFTA Secretariat for information gathering and participation within the EEA/EU institutions.

Katzenstein (1984, 1985) argues that small states need to make special domestic arrangements in order to compensate for their small domestic markets and greater economic fluctuations compared to larger markets. Hence, several small European states (Norway, Sweden, Denmark, the Netherlands, Belgium, Switzerland and Austria) adopted what Katzenstein has termed *democratic corporatism* as a domestic buffer against the vagaries of the international economy. This emphasises consensual decision-making between all key actors in the society. Labour market organisations and the government come to joint decisions regarding economic policy and finances. They have succeeded and created a stable political system and a relatively stable economy. Recent findings indicate that Katzenstein's seven corporatist states were not as badly hit as four non-corporatist or sectoral corporatist states (Iceland, Estonia, Latvia and Lithuania), and adjusted much better to the latest international economic crisis than the latter group (Thorhallsson and Kattel 2013). Iceland's small domestic market has had a profound influence on its operation within the EEA, due to severe challenges posed by the free flow of capital. Iceland's participation in the internal market without any concerns given to its small domestic market and the government's ability to defend it from external market pressure contributed to the scale of the latest economic crisis (Thorhallsson and Kirby 2012).

Democratic corporatism or other forms of domestic arrangements may not be sufficient for small states to deal with the challenges associated with the liberal international economy of today, which is characterised by the free flow of capital. Generally, small-state studies claim that small states need a protector. Historically, small entities/states have always sought protection by their larger neighbouring states (Alesina and Spolaore 2005). Nowadays, small states are more inclined to seek political, economic and societal security within regional and international organisations than to rely on a single protecting power. The forms and rules of these bodies in the international system, according to the literature, provide protection from aggressive neighbours (Bailes and Thorhallsson 2013). In autumn 2008, Iceland found itself without an ally when the financial crash hit the country with full force. No one was willing to come to its rescue and, in Brussels, Iceland was told that it was not part of the club. This was the situation when it sought assistance in the period leading up to the economic crash, during the crash (when nearly the entire financial sector collapsed) and in trying to secure rescue packages in cleaning up after the event.

No one any longer contests small states' ability to govern themselves, that is to run the necessary domestic apparatus and a basic foreign service. However, small states have to be aware of their more limited administrative capacity and adopt particular administrative working practices in terms of prioritisation, informality, flexibility and the autonomy of their officials in order to cope with the workload involved in membership of regional and international organisations, such as the EU and the United Nations. Many small states have demonstrated that they can form a coherent domestic policy stand, take full part in decision-making, defend their interests in organisations such as the EU and implement their rules without greater difficulties than larger states (Panke 2010; Thorhallsson 2000).

Small states primarily seek political and economic shelter through their membership of regional and international organisations such as the North American Treaty Organization (NATO), the EFTA, the EU, the International Monetary Fund (IMF), and the World Bank (Thorhallsson 2011). Membership grants them access to benefits, such as larger markets, economic assistance in times of need, and hard and soft security. However, these organisations often provide shelter at the cost of domestic autonomy. Most recently, for example, the EU has offered some of its member states economic aid and important political shelter in terms of diplomatic backing for receiving IMF assistance but at the cost of strict austerity measures (Bailes et al. 2013). For instance, David Vital (1967: 5) claims that when a small state joins an alliance with other states 'a price must normally be paid in terms of sacrifice of autonomy in the control of national resources and loss of freedom or political maneuver and choice'. This is the case of small states seeking to join the EU (Bailes and Thorhallsson 2013), and to a lesser extent – though in very different ways – for members of NATO and the Nordic Council. The EFTA/EEA states' engagements with European integration are largely an unexplored territory in this respect.

Katzenstein (1997: 259–271) argues that the EU, and Germany, as a key European player, provides a *soft institutional environment* for small states with considerable leeway for distinct national choices. However, small European states experience German and EU effects different – depending on the depth of their involvement in the European project. Small states that are deeply involved in the EU, such as the Benelux states, experience theses influences as soft constraints. Their domestic policies have basically become more or less similar to Germany's, and they have an easier time adjusting to the EU's and Germany's economic policies and political manoeuvres than small states that diverge or take less part in the European project. These experience German and EU influences as harder constrains. For instance, the Scandinavian states, Denmark, Sweden and Norway, have hesitated taking full part in the EU because of various reasons related to its economic and political features. They experience these influences as firmer European and German constraints because their domestic policymaking and policies differ more than do the Benelux countries from the EU's and Germany's policymaking procedures and policies. This is also the case of Iceland. Icelandic policymakers have had to response to the ongoing European integration process and reluctantly take part in it, by joining EFTA, the EEA and Schengen, in order to secure their interests. They have gained access to the internal market at the cost of constitutional implications and limited influence on its rules. On the other hand, Iceland has managed to preserve its control over the economically important fishing sector and the politically important agrarian sector.

Finally, Iceland's small size in terms of its population, its GDP and the size of its public administration (foreign service) affects its position within the EEA and Schengen. Iceland lacks the expertise, and an adequate bureaucracy and a foreign service, to take an active part in decision shaping within the EEA and Schengen. However, it is remarkable how smoothly Iceland has been able to implement the EEA rules despite its small administrative capacity (see next section). Iceland's small domestic market has also had a profound influence on its functioning within the EEA due to severe challenges posed by the requirement regarding the free flow of capital – as is briefly discussed later.

The implicit implication of these discussions is that there is a 'critical mass' required for effective function stateness, and the question is whether the small Iceland really possesses that. This is the topic of the next section.

## Administrative capacity: Opportunities and challenges

The lack of expertise and limited human resources in Iceland's central bureaucracy have hindered it from engaging in long-term policymaking concerning European and security affairs, and foreign policy in general. The central bureaucracy cannot be blamed, however, and it is remarkable how much the Icelandic Foreign Service has achieved despite its smallness; for example, in the EFTA negotiations in the 1960s and the negotiations leading to the EEA Agreement (only 85 people worked in the Foreign Service in 1985). However, its limitations become nowhere more obvious than in the Icesave negotiations with Britain and the Netherlands; that is it did not have the expertise needed to engage in such detailed negotiations and had to hire foreign experts. In 2010, 160 people were employed in the Icelandic Foreign Service, and Iceland had 21 embassies and missions abroad. The numbers had dropped somewhat after the financial crisis, due to drastic cuts in the budget.

Ministers and governments have obviously not given priority to developing a reliable or comprehensive knowledge of European and security affairs within the bureaucracy. The foreign service has barely had sufficient resources to concentrate on Iceland's core interests, as defined by the government, such as the extension of the fisheries zone, and finding a suitable solution for Icelandic marine exports to the EU. Moreover, the limited focus on long-term policymaking in the central bureaucracy has made ministries highly dependent on interest groups and other external assistance (Kristinsson et al. 1992). For this reason, the powerful fisheries and agricultural lobbies have enjoyed a privileged position in Iceland's international negotiations, when these touched upon their interests, as they perceived them. For instance, the foreign service and other governmental departments relied on these and other powerful interest groups in formulating Iceland's negotiating objectives during the EU membership talks. This is due to the traditional official and unofficial outsourcing of policymaking of the administration to the primary sectors. Moreover, Iceland would have difficulty in covering meetings and taking an active part in the EU's activities. This is the case with small states in the EU (Thorhallsson 2000). Hence, Iceland would have to prioritise its most important economic sectors.

The administration has already shown that it is capable of implementing the EEA and Schengen rules. However, these rules are most often implemented without any consideration being given to Iceland's unique features, such as its smallness (Althingi n.d.). On the other hand, Iceland has had considerable difficulties in meeting the 1 per cent interim target but in 2011 reached the target for the first time since 2003 (EFTA Surveillance Authority 2011). In the last few years, Iceland's implementation deficit has risen because of the increased workload on the administration in connection with the EU negotiations and greater opposition to the implementation process in the Althingi. In July 2014, Iceland had the highest implementation deficit of all the 31 EEA states. Its deficit stood at 3.1 per cent, a similar level as in the last scoreboard. It corresponds to 34 directives not being fully transposed into national law within the foreseen deadlines. Norway's deficit was 1.9 per cent, the second-highest deficit in the whole EEA, and corresponds to 21 overdue directives. The countries had their worst scores since the introduction of the Scoreboard in 1997. The EFTA Surveillance Authority 'finds the current trend of Iceland and Norway alarming and strongly urges them to do their utmost to reverse it' (EFTA Surveillance Authority 2014: 2).

The government and the public administration have encountered immense criticism since the 2008 economic crash. This touches on all aspects of society, some of them fundamental to democratic decision-making. According to several experts' reports, the national administration lacks capacity and credibility (Althingi 2010b; Prime Minister's Office 2010). Its smallness and lack of expertise made it unable to supervise the financial sector properly. The government not only allowed the banks to grow beyond governmental control; it also permitted 'the bankers largely to regulate themselves' (Althingi 2010b). For instance, the Working Group on Ethics, which was part of the Special Investigation Commission appointed to investigate and analyse the processes leading to the collapse of the financial sector, concludes that

> although several individuals, in the financial, administrative, political and the public sphere, showed negligence and sometimes reprehensible action, the most important lessons to draw from these events are about weak social structures, political culture, and public institutions. It is the common responsibility of the Icelandic nation to work towards strengthening them and constructing a well functioning democratic society.
>
> (Althingi n.d.)

Membership of the European Union would be unlikely to alter most of the topics under criticism but could have profound consequences for the small bureaucracy and lead to closer engagement with European continental culture and the European democratic way of life. For instance, Europeanisation of the public administration, related to membership of EEA and Schengen, has led to more professionalism when it comes to employing officials. Ministries and their agencies have felt pressure to hire staff with expertise in the field of European affairs instead of political favourites. This pressure will inevitably become stronger within the EU. This may help address the most fundamental criticism of an independent expert committee appointed by the prime minister to address the conclusions of the Special Investigation Commission. This identified a lack of professional competence due to political interference, small staff sizes, reliance on personal connections and a limited emphasis on 'best practice'. The committee criticised the government's working methods, which have created a decision-making framework characterised by a lack of united leadership and an *absence of accountability* on the part of senior executives. At the same time, ministers are not effectively restrained by the public administration and other domestic actors such as the Althingi, the media and educational and research institutes (Prime Minister's Office 2010). The committee made several recommendations on how to improve the public administration, and these are in the process of being implemented by the government. In addition, the Special Investigation Commission pointed out the need for a preceding evaluation of lawmaking with regard to existing laws, the constitution, international human rights treaties/conventions and EU law. In other words, there has been a lack of a comprehensive policymaking process to ensure respect for the rule of law (Prime Minister's Office 2010).

Interestingly, the Commission's opinion and first progress report fail to address these concerns, and comes to the conclusion that the public administration is 'free of political interference' (European Commission 2010a). The failure of the Commission's reports to demand changes in the structure and working methods of the public administration casts doubt on the likelihood that membership of the EU would result in the appropriate changes. One could argue that EU member states are left to dictate their own policymaking, as long as they respect the broad Copenhagen criteria. Hence, domestic governmental policymaking, which is increasingly being questioned in the political aftermath of the economic crash, would be unlikely to be improved by EU membership.

It may be the case that supranational institutions are needed to guarantee that states will respect citizens' rights and ensure that they will run an accountable bureaucracy. However, Icelanders are divided on whether this is the case. The vast majority of politicians consider that the state should be the guarantor of the core principles of democratic constitutionalism. Those that think otherwise still have to convince voters that the EU can uphold and embed these principles and is capable of ensuring the citizens' freedom and equality. Having said that, membership of the EEA and Schengen have led to better bureaucratic practices in Iceland, even though citizens are subject to rules that they have not participated in making.

This leads to the next section which will, among other things, deal with how the primary sectors have avoided being accountable in terms of professional bureaucratic practices by declining to participate fully in the EU.

## Challenging political patronage

Traditionally, Icelandic politicians have interfered greatly in the day-to-day work of the public administration, and it has not possessed the strength to prevent patronage (Kristinsson 1996; Kristinsson et al. 1992). The Europeanisation of the decision-making process has made it more difficult for politicians to maintain the political patronage system. This is mainly due to the absence of politicians from the EEA's decision-making. Ministers interfere to a very limited degree in the administration's work concerning EEA affairs. The handling of European affairs is more in the hands of civil servants in the EEA states than is the case in the EU states. Also, Icelandic civil servants have more influence, compared to politicians, in EEA cases than in other cases (Lægreid et al. 2004). Accordingly, membership of the EEA and Schengen has led to greater *professionalism* within the national administration. One could say that the policy areas that fall within the agreements are subject to a greater degree of good governance than prior to their existence.

Three policy sectors have largely escaped this Europeanisation process due to their not being included in the EEA framework, that is fisheries, agriculture and rural development. Strong political patronage has existed in these areas, and it is often difficult to determine where the role of interest groups ends and the work of the bureaucracy begins (Kristinsson et al. 1992). Political favouritism still prevails in these three areas (Ríkisendurskodun 2011a). The primary sectors have largely created their own legislative framework and are partly responsible for implementing it (Ríkisenduskodun 2011b; Thorhallsson 2010). The continuation of political patronage is due to the strong position of politicians from the rural regions, which are greatly over-represented in the Althingi, and a lack of expertise and capacity in the public administration. For instance, the Commission's 2010 progress report on agriculture stated that '[t]he limited administrative capacity has not been addressed' (European Commission 2010b). The firm opposition of the primary sectors to membership of the EU is partly based on the uncertainty that membership would involve regarding their influence within a new decision-making framework within the Union. These sectors oppose any changes to their privilege relationship with the government often characterised as sectoral corporatism (Thorhallsson 2010). The primary sectors have largely regulated themselves and managed to avoid Europeanisation within their own fields and the domestic decision-making process. Membership of the EU would be bound to continue the Europeanisation, particularly in the fields of fisheries, agriculture and rural development, and the traditional political patronage system would face challenges and be unlikely to continue to the same extent as before.

That said, a considerable number of members of council municipalities have been sympathetic to the question of EU membership, and consider that the country's potential membership of the Regional Policy would grant them greater access to decision-making in the field of rural development within the framework of its Structural Fund than the current centralized decision-making system in Reykjavik. Two-thirds of the population live in the Greater Reykjavik area – Reykjavik itself being by far the largest local authority. In the last twenty years, the central government has transferred considerable powers to the local authorities, many of which have been too small to meet the responsibilities involved. The many local authorities in the sparsely populated regions are further weakened by the lack of regional authorities. The most powerful lobby in the field of rural development, the agrarian lobby, opposes moves towards broadening the rural development policy that would be bound to take place with EU membership.

The EEA Agreement has led to closer cooperation and consultation between labour market organisations, on one hand, and the government on the other. This is because the agreement requires the state to involve the organisations of labour and the employers in the implementation process. The agreement has also widened the scope of cooperation to include social and welfare measures (Gudmundsdottir 2002).[3] These changes have been welcomed by labour unions, while the employers' associations have been somewhat sceptical about this new process of decision-making regarding implementation of rules affecting the labour market. Hence, the EEA framework has given the unions a new platform to have a say on labour market laws and associated social and welfare measures.

To summarise, membership of the EEA challenged political favouritism in the economic sectors that were part of the agreement but not in the sectors that were not included in the agreements. Based on these observations it is likely that citizens might be better able to hold decision makers in the primary sectors accountable within the EU framework. The next section deals with the legacy of another dominant actor, the US, in Iceland and its implications for the country's engagement with the European project.

## The legacy of the US hegemony

US hegemony in the North Atlantic has had a profound influence on Iceland's domestic affairs and external relations. In 1941, Iceland made an extensive defence, economic and trade agreement with the US. The emerging superpower promised to support the creation of a Republic in 1944. Iceland had become a sovereign state in 1918, although it still received considerable economic and diplomatic backing within the Danish kingdom until the states' relations were severed by the German occupation of Denmark in spring 1940. Britain occupied Iceland soon thereafter, and American forces took over the country's defence a year later.

Importantly, Iceland was part of the US defence territory and remained so up until 2002. The special relationship included provisions on trade and other commercial benefits, which laid the foundation for *economic assistance* – the highest, per capita, that the US provided in Europe – and flourishing trade relations between the two countries. The superpower provided Iceland with direct economic assistance until the late 1960s and continued to pay for the running of its international airport at Keflavik, the expensive radar surveillance system around the island, and its defences until 2006. US economic assistance kept up living standards on the island and governments did not have to take part in trade liberalisation in Europe. Governments could postpone participation in the European project and difficult decisions concerning economic modernisation until the 1960s (Thorhallsson and Vignisson 2004).

Icelandic governments have never spent a penny on military defence and relied totally on US forces and NATO membership. Moreover, Iceland's defence policy has relied entirely on policymaking within the US administration and NATO.

Limited knowledge in the field of defence among Icelandic politicians and civil servants prevented Iceland from developing a comprehensive defence policy. For instance, one person in the Ministry for Foreign Affairs handled all relations with NATO in 1989, and the Icelandic delegation to NATO consisted of three officials and two staff secretaries. The Norwegian and Danish delegations were much larger at this time, composed of 30 and 40 officials, respectively (Thorhallsson and Vignisson 2004).

In the designing of defence and economic arrangements between the two countries in the 1940s, some Icelandic politicians found it appealing that Iceland was no longer in the British sphere of influence in the North Atlantic. This later became evident in the Cod Wars with Britain in the decades following the Second World War. However, after the end of the cold war, the weakness of Iceland's bilateral arrangement with the US was exposed, as the changed geopolitical landscape reduced Iceland's significance and eventually led to the withdrawal of US forces in 2006. Icelandic governments – with two exceptions – fought hard against any reduction in the US military presence in the country until the closure of the military base.

Since the closure of the US military base, Iceland has made civil security arrangements (mainly concerning its waters) with Britain, Denmark, Norway and Canada and, concerning airspace surveillance, with various NATO member states such as France, Germany and Britain and, more radically, the non-NATO Nordic states Sweden and Finland, allowing the temporary presence of their jet fighters in the country. Icelanders saw the US decision to close its base and two years later, not to help Iceland out in the 2008 credit crunch, as a clear sign of a lack of willingness to provide the country with political, defence and economic *shelter* (Thorhallsson 2011). This is a sharp break with the past, when the US not only provided the country with a military presence to defend it but also always came to its economic rescue up until the late 1960s. Iceland was suddenly on its own in the middle of the North Atlantic.

Icelandic–US relations are not likely to return to what they were prior to the closure of the base – despite the existence of the defence treaty between the two states. Icelandic governments have already started to look to the east, to their European neighbours, for security and defence cooperation. Interestingly, this was not a deliberate choice. They were forced to turn to Europe after the US abandoned the country. These shifts have been welcomed by the Social Democratic Party but the coalition government, consisting of the Independence Party and the Progressive Party, has made it clear that it would like to restore the good working relationship with the US.

Iceland benefitted, politically and economically, from its subjection to US hegemony in the North Atlantic. Icelandic governments were more or less satisfied with their reliance on US defence and economic assistance and fought hard to maintain it. Iceland's loss of independence under US hegemony and dominance did not worry most politicians as long as Icelanders benefitted from the arrangements. The government was able to delay modernisation in the politically important agrarian sector, secure market access for its fishing industry with US assistance, and distribute American 'goods' to favourites. One could say that the EEA and Schengen arrangements include similar elements. Iceland receives access for its fisheries exports (by far its most important industry) on the European markets (which account for more than 80 per cent of Iceland's export of goods) and is able to maintain autonomy in the agrarian sector and rural development. Moreover, Icelandic fisheries moguls operate within the internal market and buy up companies and associated fisheries quotas while Europeans and others are more or less denied access to the fishing industry on the island. Furthermore, Icelandic politicians continue to benefit from *favouritism* in these sectors, which do not have to submit to the supranational scrutiny of the EEA/EU. The primary sectors are not accountable in terms of the same democratic practices and good governance as other sectors. Iceland's loss of independence within the EEA and Schengen is simply regarded as the cost that is necessary to pay for keeping the status quo in the primary sectors. Politicians can live with the EEA/Schengen hegemony as long as they see Iceland benefit economically from the deal and they are not forced to alter their practices in these political important sectors.

## Conclusion

Most Icelandic politicians consider that full membership of the European Union would impose hard constraints on Iceland. This is because Icelandic domestic policymaking and policies in the fields outside the EEA and Schengen Agreements differ strongly from EU policymaking and polices. Icelandic politicians can accept a loss of independence and sovereignty as long as it does not touch upon the policy sectors that they regard as most important. The cost of full access to the internal market has created a structure of *inbuilt democratic deficit* within the EEA and Schengen. Furthermore, the dynamic character of the EEA Agreement means in practice that Iceland becomes drawn ever deeper into this decision-making structure characterised by the transfer of sovereignty from the EFTA/EEA states to the European Union. Hence, the closer Iceland's affiliation with the EU – within the EEA and Schengen Agreements – the more vulnerable to hegemony the relationship will be. Public debates in Iceland (or one could say, debates within its political public sphere) have no influence at all on decision makers within the EU.

Iceland's current engagement with the European project has strengthened the public administration (e.g. improved its competence), limited political patronage in many sectors and led to somewhat closer cooperation between the government and the labour market organisations. However, it has not challenged the traditional political culture, which has been heavily criticised since the economic collapse of 2008. The opinion and the first progress report of the European Commission on Iceland's application for membership of the EU failed to grasp crucial aspects of Iceland's democratic dilemma. They neglected a number of shortcomings such as those regarding political patronage, the political culture, the weak national administration and the democratic deficit.

Iceland's sovereignty and conditions for democratic governance are greatly affected by its current affiliation with the EU. The case of Iceland indicates that the EU's administrative system challenges administrative sovereignty at the national level in the EFTA/EEA states. Iceland is also similar to Norway in that there is lawmaking without Icelandic representation within the EEA and Schengen Agreements. That is a situation that Iceland would be unlikely to experience under full membership. Icelandic politicians lack access to proper procedures within these settings to influence decision-making, and there is no explicit authority under which they can be held to account. Hence, Iceland experiences constitutional and democratic effects from its current affiliations with the EU. It has only been able to sustain its independence within the few areas that are outside the scope of the agreements. However, these sectors are not accountable in terms of normal European democratic practices, and citizens may be in a better position to call them to account in terms of good governance norms if Iceland were to gain full EU membership.

The question that requires further attention is whether the post-crisis EU can provide a legal rights–based infrastructure to ensure that decision-making processes will be protected from undue incursions by powerful groups and actors.

## Notes

1 The first two sections are partly based on the author's detailed study on how membership of the EU might affect Iceland's democracy, published in the book *European Institutions, Democratization, and Human Rights Protection in the European Periphery* (Carey 2014).
2 "Iceland," *CIA World Factbook*. Available at https://www.cia.gov/library/publications/the-world-factbook/geos/ic.html, last accessed 22 December 2014.
3 Interview with a Labour leader in Iceland, 24 March 2011.

## References

Alesina, A. and Spolaore, E. (2005) *The Size of Nations*, Cambridge, MA: The MIT Press.
Althingi (2008) *Skýrsla utanríkismálanefndar um fyrirkomulag á þinglegri meðferð EES-mála*. Unpublished report by the Standing Committee on Foreign Affairs, 8 October.
——— (2010a) 'Reglur um þinglega meðferð EES-mála'. Available at http://www.althingi.is/vefur/EESmal_reglur, last accessed 22 December 2014.
——— (2010b) Report of the Special Investiation Commission – Chapter 2: Summary of the Report's Main Conclusions. Available at http://sic.althingi.is/pdf/RNAvefKafli2Enska.pdf, last accessed 22 December 2014.
——— (2011) 'Verklagsreglur skrifstofu Alþingis um framkvæmd reglna um þinglega meðferð EES-mála (EES-reglur)'. Available at http://www.althingi.is/vefur/EESmal_verklagsreglur, last accessed 22 December 2014.
——— (n.d.) The Main Conclusion of the Working group on Ethics. Available at http://sic.althingi.is/pdf/WorkingGroupOnEthics_Summary.pdf, last accessed 22 December 2014.
Archer, C. and Sogner, I. (1998) *Norway, European Integration and Atlantic Security*, London: Sage Publications.
Bailes, A.J.K. and Thorhallsson, B. (2013) 'Instrumentalizing the European Union in Small State Strategy', *Journal of European Integration*, 35(2): 99–115.

Bailes, A.J.K., Thorhallsson, B. and Johnstone, R.L. (2013) 'Scotland as an Independent Small State: Where Would it Seek Shelter?', *Icelandic Review of Politics and Administration*, 9(1): 1–20.

Capacent (2009) *Þjóðarpúlsinn: Traust til stofnana og embætta minnkar verulega*. Available at http://www.capacent.is/frettir/nr/587, last accessed 29 December 2014.

Carey, H.F. (ed) (2014) *European Institutions, Democratization, and Human Rights Protection in the European Periphery*, London: Lexington Books.

EFTA Surveillance Authority (2011) Internal Market Scoreboard No. 37: EEA EFTA States of the European Economic Area. Available at http://www.eftasurv.int/media/scoreboard/Scoreboard-No.-27--March-2011.pdf, last accessed 22 December 2014.

——— (2014) Internal Market Scoreboard No. 34: EEA EFTA States of the European Economic Area. Available at http://www.eftasurv.int/media/scoreboard/Internal_Market_Scoreboard_No_34.pdf, last accessed 22 December 2014.

European Commission (2010a) Communication from the Commission to the European Parliament and the Council: Commission Opinion on Iceland's Application for Membership of the European Union Opinion, COM (2010) 62, Brussels, 24 February.

——— (2010b) Commission Staff Working Document: Iceland 2010 Progress Report Accompanying the Communication from the Commission to the European Parliament and the Council: Enlargement Strategy and Main Challenges 2010–2011, SEC (2010) 1328, Brussels, 9 November.

Follesdal, A. and Hix, S. (2006) 'Why There Is a Democratic Deficit in the EU: A Response to Majone and Moravcsik', *Journal of Common Market Studies*, 44(3): 533–562.

Gudmundsdottir, A.E. (2002) *Íslenskur vinnumarkaður á umbrotatímum: Sveigjanleiki fyrirtækja, stjórnun og samskipti aðila vinnumarkaðarins*, Reykjavik: Reykjavik University.

Hardarson, O.Th. and Onnudottir, E.H. (2009). 'Óánægðir lýðræðissinnar: Afstaða Íslendinga til lýðræðis', in H.S. Gudmundsson and S.B. Omarsdottir (eds) *Rannsóknir í félagsvísindum X – Félagsráðgjafardeild og stjórnmálafræðideild* [Electronic version], Reykjavik: The Social Science Research Institute.

Katzenstein, P. (1984) *Corporatism and Change: Austria, Switzerland and the Politics of Industry*, Ithaca, NY: Cornell University Press.

——— (1985) *Small States in World Markets: Industrial Policy in Europe*, Ithaca, NY: Cornell University Press.

——— (1997) 'The Smaller European States, Germany and Europe', in P. Katzenstein (ed.) *Tamed Power: Germany in Europe*. London: Cornell University Press.

Kristinsson, G.H. (1996) 'Parties, States and Patronage', *West European Politics*, 19(3): 433–457.

Kristinsson, G.H., Jonsson, H. and Sveinsdottir, H. Th. (1992) *Atvinnustefna á Íslandi 1959–1991*, Reykjavik: Institute of Social Sciences – University of Iceland.

Lægreid, P., Steinthorsson, R.S. and Thorhallsson, B. (2004) 'Europeanization of Central Government Administration in the Nordic States', *Journal of Common Market Studies*, 42(2): 347–369.

Panke, D. (2010) *Small States in the European Union: Coping with Structural Disadvantages*, London: Ashgate.

Prime Minister's Office (2010) Viðbrögð stjórnsýslunnar við skýrslu rannsóknarnefndar Alþingis: Skýrsla starfshóps forsætisráðuneytisins. Available at http://www.forsaetisraduneyti.is/media/Skyrslur/Skyrsla-starfshops-6-mai2010.pdf, last accessed 22 December 2014.

Rikisenduskodun (2011a) *Skýrsla um eftirfylgni: Stjórnarráðið mars 2011*. (Skýrsla til Alþingis). Reykjavik: Rikisenduskodun. Available at http://www.rikisendurskodun.is/fileadmin/media/skyrslur/Stjornarradid_eftirfylgni_22.03.pdf, last accessed 29 December 2014.

—— (2011b) Skýrsla til Alþingis: Útvistun opinberra verkefna til Bændasamtaka Íslands, Reykjavik: Rikisendurskodun Available at http://www.rikisendurskodun.is/fileadmin/media/skyrslur/baendasamtokin.pdf, last accessed 22 December 2014.

Thorhallsson, B. (2000) *Small States in the European Union*, London: Ashgate.

—— (2004) 'Shackled by Smallness: A Weak Administration as a Determinant of Policy Choice', in B. Thorhallsson (ed) *Iceland and European Integration: On the Edge*. London: Routledge.

—— (2008) 'Evrópustefna íslenskra stjórnvalda: Stefnumótun, átök og afleiðingar', in V. Ingimundason (ed) *Uppbrot hugmyndakerfis: Endurmótun íslenskrar utanríkisstefnu 1991–2007*, Reykjavík: Hið íslenska bókmenntafélag.

—— (2010) 'The Corporatist Model and its Value in Understanding Small European States in the Neo-Liberal World of the Twenty-First Century: The Case of Iceland', *European Political Science*, 3(9): 375–386.

—— (2011) 'Domestic Buffer versus External Shelter: Viability of Small States in the New Globalized Economy', *European Political Science*, 10(3): 324–336.

Thorhallsson, B. and Kattel, R. (2013) 'Neo-Liberal Small States and Economic Crisis: Lessons for Democratic Corporatism', *Journal of Baltic Studies*, 44(1): 83–103.

Thorhallsson, B. and Kirby, P. (2012) 'Financial Crisis in Iceland and Ireland: Does EU and Euro Membership Matter?', *Journal of Common Market Studies*, 50(5): 801–818.

Thorhallsson, B. and Thorarensen, B. (2014) 'Iceland's Democratic Challenges and Human Rights Implications', in H.F. Carey (ed) *European Institutions, Democratization, and Human Rights Protection in the European Periphery*, London: Lexington Books.

Thorhallsson, B. and Vignisson, H.Th. (2004) 'The Special Relationship between Iceland and the United States of America', in B. Thorhallsson (ed) *Iceland and European Integration: On the Edge*, London: Routledge.

Vital, D. (1967) *The Inequality of States: A Study of the Small Power in International Relations*, Oxford: Clarendon Press.

# 8

# NORWAY'S CONSTITUTIONAL ACROBATICS UNDER THE EEA AGREEMENT

*Eirik Holmøyvik*

### The EEA Agreement's promise of sovereignty

That Norway is not a member of the European Union (EU) can be interpreted to mean that Norwegians are more concerned about national sovereignty than the rest of Europe. In contrast to the EU, which is supranational in the sense that EU bodies can made decisions with direct effect in member states, the European Economic Area (EEA) is predominantly an instrument of international law. The purpose of the 1992 EEA Agreement, in place of EU membership, was for Norway and other EFTA states to participate in the EU's internal market without having to give up sovereignty. In spite of this starting point, Norwegian sovereignty is not unaffected by the EU. The ever-closer European integration increasingly requires Norway to transfer sovereignty – formal and substantive – to both EU and EEA bodies. This gives Norway's affiliation with the EU a constitutional dimension. A key question is this: What requirements and limits does the Norwegian constitution impose on transfers of sovereignty?

As Norway's affiliation with the EU through the EEA Agreement is built on a premise of Norwegian sovereignty, it is especially important that transfers of sovereignty are made in compliance with the requirements laid down in the Norwegian constitution. For transfers of sovereignty the constitution provides a specific decision-making procedure in Art. 115, which, inter alia, requires a three-quarter majority in the Norwegian parliament, the Storting.[1] The problem is that Art. 115 and its requirements are disregarded in practice. In the past 20 years, consecutive parliaments and governments have consistently interpreted the constitution such that the special decision-making procedure for transfers of sovereignty in Art. 115 is not required for transfers of sovereignty. Instead, the Storting has made decisions about transfers of sovereignty in accordance with the general treaty-making rules in the second paragraph of Art. 26 which only requires a simple majority.

The striking difference between the constitution's text and the Storting's practice is the topic of this chapter. I argue that the Storting's interpretation of the constitution is far from judicially sound. Rather, it is a pragmatic interpretation due to Norway's troubled view on the EU as well as an increasing political pressure on the non-member Norway to keep up with the institutional development in the EU. The Norwegian practice on transfers of sovereignty thus illustrates the increasing constitutional difficulties of integrating Norway into the EU under the EEA Agreement's premise of national sovereignty.

## Law in books: What does the constitution say?
### Formal and substantive transfers of sovereignty

The constitutional starting point for Norwegian participation in international cooperation is the distinction between international agreements about formal transfers of sovereignty and agreements that merely impose obligations on Norway under international law. By formal transfers of sovereignty, I mean that an international organisation is granted authority to make decisions with direct effect in Norway. If such authority is not transferred, and it rarely is, decisions by international organisations are only binding on Norway under international law. Such agreements can only take effect in Norway through decisions made by Norwegian state bodies. These agreements may nevertheless place such extensive international law obligations on Norway that the formal constitutional powers of Norwegian state bodies takes on a *pro forma* character.[2]

The difference between having an effect in domestic or international law is a crucial constitutional criterion for deciding which decision-making procedure the Storting must use to enter an international agreement. According to the Constitution Art. 115, second paragraph, the stricter decision-making procedure therein does not apply 'in cases of membership in an international organisation whose decisions only have application for Norway exclusively under international law'. In such cases, the government is free to enter agreements even without the consent of the Storting. Pursuant to Art. 26, second paragraph, it is only when the agreement is of 'special importance' or requires a new statute or decisions by the Storting, that the consent of the Storting is required.

In the grand scheme of things, however, it is often less important whether or not the decisions of an international organisation have direct effect in Norway. The purpose of the EEA Agreement is precisely to give Norway access to the EU's internal market while simultaneously limiting the formal transfer of sovereignty to the EU to a minimum. Formally, the EEA Agreement provides that EU legal acts and decisions are only given effect in Norway through decisions made by competent Norwegian state bodies in accordance with the procedures laid down in the constitution. In other words, under the EEA Agreement the Norwegian Storting, government and courts of law retain their constitutional powers formally unabridged.

Yet, the EEA Agreement and Norway's other agreements with the EU have constitutional consequences, in the sense that they have had profound implications on the actual exercise of legislative, executive and judicial power in Norway. In practice, the EEA Agreement's requirement for homogeneity between EU law and EEA law means that the Storting must exercise its legislative power so that Norwegian legislation conforms to EU legislation.[3] Of about 6000 EU legal acts incorporated into Norwegian law through the EEA Agreement between 1992 and 2011, Norway has only been given 55 material exemptions. About one-third of all Norwegian statutes now contain elements of EU law. Moreover, Norway has yet to make reservations against EU legal acts pursuant to Art. 102 of the EEA Agreement. Clearly, the EEA Agreement has had a significant impact on Norway's substantive sovereignty.[4]

Yet none of this raises formal constitutional issues in Norway due to the strict division in Art. 115, second paragraph, between decisions from international bodies with direct effect in Norway and decisions that are only binding for Norway under international law. Even agreements with wide-ranging implications for Norway's substantive sovereignty can be and indeed are approved by the Storting using the general treaty-making procedure in Art. 26. An example is the important 1998 Schengen Agreement, in which Norway became a member of the borderless Schengen Area. As with the EEA Agreement, Norway is not formally required to accept the EU's later amendments to the Schengen Agreement. Nevertheless, a clause in Norway's particular affiliation agreement effectively prevents Norway from refusing any future amendments since that would instantly terminate Norway's entire membership to the Schengen Area.[5]

The constitutional issues discussed in this chapter, however, only concern the agreements with the EU that allows for EU or EEA bodies to make decisions with direct effect in Norway and thus require the use of the special procedure in Art. 115. Such agreements have been steadily growing in numbers and importance in the recent years and are likely to continue to do so in the coming years.

## *The necessity of a specific procedure for formal transfers of sovereignty*

Like other constitutions, the Norwegian constitution presupposes that state power shall be exercised by the bodies stipulated therein and in the manner stipulated therein. This premise follows not only from Art. 1 saying that Norway is a 'free, independent [. . .] realm', but also directly from the various competency provisions in the constitution. According to Art. 49 and Art. 75(a) of the constitution, legislative power rests with the Storting; according to Art. 3 and other provisions, the executive power rests with the king and the government; and according to Art. 88, judicial power rests with the courts with the supreme court at the apex. This distribution of power in the constitution is the starting point when discussing transfers of sovereignty to international organisations. When the constitution allocates authority to Norwegian state bodies, it simultaneously prohibits international bodies from exercising the same authority in Norway.

Thus, a transfer of sovereignty is effectively a material exception from the constitution, even though it leaves no trace in the constitution's text (Smith 2012: 151–152). This means that unless the Storting amends the constitution using the special amendment procedure in Art. 121, transfers of sovereignty require a special constitutional authority. Such authority is provided in Art. 115.[6]

Pursuant to Art. 115, the Storting can, by a three-fourths majority, decide that an international organisation shall have the right 'to exercise powers which in accordance with this Constitution are normally vested in the authorities of the state'. This provision also sets some material limitations on the transfer of sovereignty that Art. 121 does not. The transfer of sovereignty must fulfil specific goals, must relate to 'specified fields', cannot include the power to amend the constitution, and Norway must be a member of or be about to become a member of the organisation in question. The latter requirement is particularly important as it means that Art. 115 cannot be used to transfer sovereignty to the EU because Norway is not currently a member.

So far, so good. The problem is, however, as mentioned in the introduction, that the Storting has only used the decision-making procedure in Art. 115 once since its adoption in 1962. This was when Norway adopted the EEA Agreement in 1992. Because the enforcement system for the competition rules in the EEA Agreement required a formal transfer of sovereignty to EFTA's Surveillance Authority (ESA) and the EFTA Court, the Storting applied Art. 115 and decided with a three-quarters majority. In the enforcement of the competition rules, the ESA can order enterprises in Norway to supply information, inspect enterprises in Norway, make individual exemptions from the general prohibitory provisions in Art. 53 of the EEA Agreement and impose penalties in the form of fines.[7] Appeals to the ESA's decisions are decided by the EFTA Court.

That was in 1992. Since then, and particularly during the last 10 years, the Storting has on several occasions formally transferred decision-making powers not only to EEA bodies and to other international organisations of which Norway is a member but also to the EU, of which Norway is not a member. None of these agreements has been adopted by the Storting using the special procedure in Art. 115. Rather, the Storting as well as the government argues that the general treaty-making procedure in Art. 26, second paragraph, allows for the transfer of sovereignty as long as it has only a 'minimal impact' on the exercise of legislative, executive and judicial power according to the constitution.

## Law in action: Current Norwegian practice for transfers of sovereignty

Since the EEA Agreement in 1992, Norway has entered into eight agreements, which in one way or another allows an international organisation to make decisions with direct effect in Norway. All of these agreements have been approved by the Storting pursuant to the general treaty-making provision in Art. 26, second paragraph, as if they did not entail a transfer of sovereignty.[8]

The Storting's 2012 decision related to an EU regulation about common rules for civilian aviation is especially illustrative of the constitutional development since 1992.[9] In this decision, the Storting transferred to the ESA the authority to impose fines on aviation enterprises in Norway for violations of individual licences or provisions in the said EU regulation. At the same time, the EFTA Court was granted judicial authority over these cases. Given that it is precisely this type of transfer of sovereignty that was determinative for the use of Art. 115 for the EEA Agreement in 1992, it is surprising that the identical 2012 case did not fall under Art. 115. In the constitutional assessment, the government nevertheless concluded that the transfer of sovereignty had 'minimal impact' on the constitutional powers of Norwegian state bodies.[10] Therefore, the Storting considered a decision pursuant to Art. 115 unnecessary. The reasons given for this were that the EU regulation in question was not politically controversial and that this particular transfer of decision-making powers to the ESA had a more limited scope of applicability than the EEA Agreement.[11] The latter is not actually correct, as the ESA has only fined Norwegian companies for violations of the competition rules in the EEA Agreement twice in 20 years. Nevertheless, the Storting unanimously and with no debate decided that this time, the ESA could have such competency transferred based on Art. 26, second paragraph.[12]

I should add that the same kind of transfer to the ESA of the authority to impose fines using the second paragraph of Art. 26 has been accepted in two other cases by the Department of the Ministry of Justice and Public Security. It is the Legislation Department which in these cases provide constitutional assessments for the government. In one case from 2004, the Norwegian government eventually reached an agreement with the EU to avoid a formal transfer of sovereignty.[13] A 2012 case has not yet been heard by the government and Storting but will most likely be decided pursuant to Art. 26, second paragraph.[14] In a 2014 case, however, the Legislation Department concluded that the specific authority for the ESA to impose fines on enterprises in Norway was so far-reaching that it could not be considered to have 'minimal impact'.[15] This last case must then be decided using Art. 115. This last case shows that Norwegian constitutional law concerning the transfer of sovereignty has become quite uncertain.

In all events, the cases since 1992 demonstrate how the government and the Storting interprets the constitution differently today than in 1992. Today, unlike in 1992, the use of Art. 115 is not necessarily required when transferring to international bodies the authority to impose fines on enterprises in Norway.

To complicate things even more, a number of recent cases relate to the transfer of sovereignty to an EU body. This is due to the institutional development in the EU often called 'agencification'.[16] To an increasing extent EU law is being enforced at the supranational level by independent administrative agencies and supervisory bodies (Craig and De Búrca 2011: 69–70).[17] In some cases, these EU agencies can make decisions that are directly binding on enterprises in the member states.

Consecutive Norwegian governments have indicated that it is important for the non-member Norway to be a part of the EU agency system. As a result of this policy, Norway is currently affiliated with 26 of 43 EU agencies. The same policy has, however, created constitutional challenges for Norway in line with the growing importance of these agencies and supervisory bodies in the EU. The reason is that Art. 115 in the constitution requires Norwegian membership, which means that it cannot be used for transfers of sovereignty to EU bodies.[18] In some cases the government has attempted to evade the constitutional requirements in Art. 115 by allowing Norwegian state bodies to make *pro forma* decisions based on EU decisions, but such clever legal tricks are not always possible.[19] The only practical constitutional alternative for Norwegian participation in EU agencies and supervisory bodies is thus to transfer decision-making powers directly to these EU institutions. Since such a transfer is barred in Art. 115, the only viable way is by the ordinary treaty-making procedure in Art. 26, second paragraph, interpreted to allow for so-called minimal impact transfers of sovereignty.

In the recent years there have been three cases of the Storting transferring sovereignty to EU bodies pursuant to the second paragraph of Art. 26. In 2005 the Storting granted the European Aviation Safety Agency (EASA) the competency to make decisions with direct effect for Norwegian air carriers.[20] These decisions concerns granting licences on type certification for new aircraft and imposing requirements regarding repairs or controls of aircraft prior to their use. At the same time, the Court of Justice of the European Union (CJEU) was granted judicial authority over disputes arising from EASA's decisions.

In 2007, the European Chemicals Agency was granted the authority to make a variety of decisions related to the registration of chemicals in the EEA area.[21] Decisions on terms, rejections, information requirements and so on apply directly for enterprises in Norway.

Also, in 2012 the Storting transferred to the European Commission the authority to make decisions on applications from Norwegian enterprises for the use and production of recycled plastic as food contact materials.[22]

Finally, it must be mentioned that the 1992 transfer of sovereignty to the ESA and EFTA Court for the enforcement of the competition rules in the EEA Agreement also extended to the European Commission and CJEU in all cases affecting trade between an EU state and an EFTA state.[23] In practice, it is the Commission rather than the ESA that processes most of these cases (Sejersted et al. 2011: 154). Despite the Storting having consented to the transfer of sovereignty to the ESA and the EFTA Court pursuant to Art. 115, the government considered the equivalent transfer of sovereignty to the Commission and the CJEU to have sufficiently 'minimal impact' as to allow the decision to be made pursuant to the second paragraph of Art. 26.[24] This mind-bogglingly paradoxical conclusion was justified by Norway having made reservations in the EEA Agreement against the enforcement of EU decisions on fines. This meant that the transfer of decision-making powers to the EU was practically though not constitutionally limited to decisions for orders regarding information and inspections and regarding exemptions from the prohibitory provisions of the EEA Agreement. In turn, the remaining decision-making powers were considered to be of 'minimal impact' on the constitutional powers.

Politically, it was of course exceedingly convenient for the government that the legal distinction between transfers of sovereignty with 'minimal impact' and those requiring the use of Art. 115 just happened to be drawn precisely here. Indeed, the government made it clear that if the Storting could not transfer sovereignty to the EU pursuant to Art. 26, second paragraph, then 'this would in reality mean that Norway could not sign the EEA Agreement'.[25]

Here we have reached the core of Norway's constitutional difficulties in its affiliation with the EU through the EEA Treaty: the ever-closer institutional integration in the EU increasingly requires Norway to transfer formal sovereignty directly to EU bodies. The growth of special EU administrative bodies and agencies are examples of this. In turn, this puts significant political pressure on the constitution and on the interpretation of Art. 26, second paragraph, because Art. 115 cannot authorise transfers of sovereignty to EU bodies.

Moreover, at the time of writing several similar agreements are in the pipeline. The anticipated Norwegian participation in the EU Body of European Regulators for Electronic Communications and the EU Agency for the Cooperation of Energy Regulators is expected to require formal transfers of sovereignty, either directly to these EU bodies or to the ESA.[26] Furthermore, the anticipated incorporation into the EEA Agreement of several EU regulations will extend the ESA's power to fine enterprises in Norway to new areas.[27] It thus appears that the rise in recent years of cases requiring Norway to transfer decision-making powers to EEA or EU bodies will only continue in the years to come.

## Legal basis for the current practice

Having demonstrated how the Storting consistently avoids using Art. 115 in the constitution when transferring sovereignty to EEA and EU bodies, what then is the legal argument supporting this practice?

The constitution does not make any reference to 'minimal impact' transfers of sovereignty in Art. 26, second paragraph. If we look at the second paragraph of Art. 26, this provision simply states that international treaties on matters 'of special importance' and treaties that require a statute or a decision by the Storting require the Storting's consent before being binding in Norway. The text does not address whether the Storting can or cannot consent to treaties that transfer formal sovereignty. Yet the second paragraph of Art. 26 must be read in light of the constitution's clear presumption that formal transfers of sovereignty require a special legal basis, which we find in Art. 115.

Indeed, the government and the Storting has recognised the fact that Art. 26, second paragraph, was never intended to authorise agreements on the transfer of sovereignty. Instead, their legal argument rests on different legal sources than the constitution itself.

First of all, what we can call the Norwegian doctrine on 'minimal impact' transfers of sovereignty was established by law professor Carl August Fleischer in an academic article published in 1963, the year after Art. 115 was adopted.[28] In this article Fleischer argued that despite the clear wording in Art. 115, it would simply be too severe to impose a three-quarter majority requirement on limited transfers of formal sovereignty. Instead, he suggested that the Storting could consent to such 'minimal impact' transfers of formal sovereignty pursuant to the ordinary treaty-making procedure in Art. 26, second paragraph. Fleischer's interpretation clearly ran contrary to the Storting's intentions when it adopted Art. 115 in 1962, as it considered Art. 115 to be the sole authority for transfers of sovereignty. Nevertheless, Fleischer's minimal impact doctrine proved politically convenient and was later adopted by the Storting, the government and the Legislation Department. Subsequent legal theory has also uncritically and without further discussion conveyed Fleischer's minimal impact doctrine.[29]

Second, and most important, the government and the Storting justify their use of Art. 26, second paragraph, by their own long-standing non-use of Art. 115. As the Storting has consistently built on the doctrine of minimal impact transfers of sovereignty in all cases following the EEA Agreement in 1992, this practice has itself become an argument for an expansive reading of the second paragraph of Art. 26 in the constitution. Though such a conspicuous departure from the constitution's text may seem alien to foreign lawyers, and admittedly I find it peculiar myself, when interpreting the constitution Norwegian lawyers often tend to emphasise the Storting's own practice and understanding of the constitution more than the text.[30]

It is on this basis that the government, in a 2012 White Paper to the Storting, *The EEA Agreement and Norway's Other Agreements with the EU*, stated that the legal basis for transfer of sovereignty pursuant to Art. 26, second paragraph is a 'firm constitutional practice'.[31] The Legislative Department repeatedly says the same in the constitutional assessments that form the basis for the Storting's decisions on transfers of sovereignty.[32]

## Problems with the current practice

Despite the government's claim that the current practice of transferring sovereignty pursuant to the constitution, Art. 26, second paragraph, rests on a 'firm constitutional practice', this constitutional interpretation is riddled with problems.

First of all, the current practice runs counter to the clear and univocal wording of the constitution. Neither the special procedure in Art. 115 nor the general treaty-making procedure in the second paragraph of Art. 26 makes any reference whatsoever to minimal impact transfers of sovereignty. Clearly, no such exception from Art. 115 was intended when this special procedure for transfers of sovereignty was adopted in 1962. In fact, Art. 115 was introduced in order to remedy doubts in previous cases on whether the constitution at all permitted transfers of sovereignty.[33] At the time of the adoption of Art. 115, the Standing Committee on Foreign Affairs stated that there was 'an obvious need for clearer guidelines in this area and that the proposal for a new Art. 115 must be seen in light of this consideration'.[34] In other words, Art. 115 was to clear the way of the constitutional doubts that transfers of sovereignty had previously caused, and that were anticipated in connection with a possible Norwegian membership in the then EEC, now the EU. Although the committee did not explicitly state that Art. 115 barred future transfers of sovereignty pursuant to Art. 26, second paragraph, it left no doubt that Art. 115 was meant to be the general provision for transfers of sovereignty.

Second, whatever the legal basis for the minimal impact doctrine, it is evident that the view on what constitutes a 'minimal impact' on the constitutional powers has changed. Today, the use of Art. 26 second paragraph for transfers of sovereignty extends far beyond what even Fleischer envisioned when he formulated the 'minimal impact' doctrine in 1963. For example, Fleischer believed that granting an international organisation the power to issue licences to operate in a specific industry would normally require a decision pursuant to Art. 115 (Fleischer 1963: 92). Precisely this competency was transferred to EASA in 2005 without applying Art. 115. When the government and the Storting now accepts that the power to fine enterprises in Norway is transferred to ESA, this not only goes further than Fleischer envisioned but also further than the Storting was willing to go in 1992 in relation to the EEA Agreement. For this agreement it was precisely the transfer to the ESA of the competency to impose fines that necessitated the use of Art. 115. We see, then, that the interpretation of what constitutes a minimal impact on the constitutional powers is being expanded concurrently with the political demands due to Norway's desire to keep up with the institutional developments in the EU.

Another and more practical problem is that the limit to transfers of sovereignty pursuant to Art. 26(2) is notoriously unclear: what constitutes a minimal impact on the constitutional powers? The text of the constitution obviously does not provide any hints, because the evaluation criteria are entirely based on legal theory and state practice. Today, the evaluation is made based on a number of elements that the Legislative Department has outlined, and leaving a wide room for discretion. The prime example is the previously mentioned shifting views on the transfer to ESA of the competency to impose fines.

Moreover, in the few cases where the Legislation Department has concluded that a transfer of sovereignty is not of minimal impact and thus must be decided pursuant to Art. 115, the deciding factor seems to have been whether the transfer of decision-making powers concerns areas of significant social and political interest. Such cases involve the transfer of decision-making powers concerning the use of foodstuff based on genetically modified organisms, hazardous chemicals and, last, Norwegian participation in the EU system of financial supervision (European Banking Authority [EBA], European Insurance and Occupational Pensions Authority [EIOPA] and European Securities and Markets Authority [ESMA]).[35] What this means is that in practice, the applicability of Art. 115, and thus the necessity of passing transfers of sovereignty by a three-quarter majority in the Storting, rests on a bureaucratic consideration beforehand whether the case is politically and socially controversial. This does not make much sense constitutionally as the entire purpose of supermajority requirements such as the one in Art. 115 is precisely to democratically settle politically controversial issues.

The result of the minimal impact doctrine and the corresponding use of the second paragraph of Art. 26 for transfers of sovereignty is that it effectively renders Art. 115 ineffective. What we see are multiple incremental transfers of sovereignty from case to case, that are individually considered to be of minimal impact, but combined they constitute or will eventually constitute a significant impact on the constitutional powers. For example, the Norwegian adoption of an EU regulation about common rules for civilian aviation[36] has on two occasions led to transfers of sovereignty: first in 2005 to the EASA and then in 2012 to the ESA. In both cases, the transfer of sovereignty was considered individually to be of minimal impact. But what about the overall transfer of sovereignty as a result of the EU regulation about common rules for civilian aviation? According to the minimal impact doctrine, however, there are no limits as to how much sovereignty the Storting can transfer without using Art. 115 as long as each case considered individually has only a minimal impact on the constitutional powers. The result is that the Storting by simple majority can set aside a decision-making procedure in the constitution that requires a three-quarter majority.

The last, but perhaps gravest problem with the 'minimal transfer' doctrine and the current state practice is that it allows for the transfer of sovereignty to EU bodies. Since 1992, there have been four cases of Norway transferring decision-making powers to EU bodies. As we recall, Art. 115 expressly requires Norwegian membership in the organisation receiving decision-making powers in Norway. Thus, the Storting's decisions in these cases violate a clear and univocal prohibition in the constitution. Even if we accept the minimal impact doctrine and the use of Art. 26, second paragraph, in cases where Norway is a member of the organisation receiving decision-making powers in Norway, one simply cannot extend the minimal impact doctrine to cases where such a transfer is expressly forbidden in Art. 115. That would be to defy basic juridical logic. How can the Storting by simple majority according to an unwritten doctrine and a 'firm constitutional practice' do something that is expressly forbidden even with a three-quarter majority according to the *lex specialis* Art. 115? Such an interpretation of the Norwegian constitution simply does not make sense, yet this interpretation has consistently been applied by both the Storting and the government since the adoption of the EEA Agreement.

## Why all the constitutional acrobatics under the EEA Agreement?

Given the numerous legal objections to be made against the Norwegian minimal impact doctrine, one may ask why the Storting consistently resort to Art. 26, second paragraph, and not Art. 115 when transferring sovereignty to international organisations.

On one hand, it is clear that the Storting's embrace of the 'minimal impact' doctrine is a pragmatic solution to a specific constitutional problem. The problem is the institutional development in the EU of autonomous administrative agencies and supervisory bodies with decision-making powers in the member states. This development puts Norway in a squeeze, because the EEA Agreement is an instrument of international law that presumes that authority will be exercised through national institutions or at least through EEA institutions such as the ESA. Because Art. 115 does not allow transfers of sovereignty to EU bodies, the pressure on the constitution is particularly strong in cases where Norway fails to reach an agreement with the EU that allows for an EEA body such as the ESA to exercise the decision-making powers of EU bodies in Norway. Here we find an absolute constitutional barrier for Norwegian integration in the EU as a non-member: The Storting cannot allow EU bodies to make decisions with direct effect in Norway. Yet this barrier has been breached several times and increasingly in recent years as Norwegian participation in the EU agencies and supervisory bodies is a policy with widespread support in the Storting.

Nevertheless, it is noteworthy that the Storting consistently and expressly opts for the decision-making procedure in Art. 26, second paragraph, and the minimal impact doctrine even in cases where the requirements in Art. 115 are met. In fact, in most if not all of these cases, the Storting has voted unanimously for the transfer of decision-making powers to the ESA or non-EEA bodies such as the European Organisation for the Safety of Air Navigation and the European Patent Office.[37] Thus, the supermajority requirement in Art. 115 would not have prevented any of these decisions. This fact suggests that the reasons for sidelining Art. 115 are more fundamental than merely context-specific political pragmatism to overcome constitutional barriers.

The non-use of Art. 115 even in cases where its requirements are met is evidence of a high political–psychological threshold for its use.[38] It may well be that by using the general treaty-making provision in Art. 26, second paragraph, rather than the special provision for transfers of sovereignty in Art. 115, the Storting hope to avoid admitting to the public that transfers of sovereignty takes place under the EEA Agreement and its premise of unabridged Norwegian sovereignty. This is of course a self-deception, but it is a self-deception for which there appears to be political agreement over several decades. This self-deception seems to be inseparably linked to the EU being a highly sensitive issue in Norwegian politics, as evidenced by referendums in 1972 and 1994 rejecting Norwegian membership in the EU.

Whatever the reason, the Norwegian self-deception is about to come to an end. In 2014, following years of delay due to constitutional and institutional difficulties, the Norwegian Government and the other EEA EFTA states Iceland and Lichtenstein reached an agreement with the EU on participation in the EU system of financial supervision and its three regulatory bodies EBA, EIOPA and ESMA.[39] According to the agreement, all legally binding decisions for banks and financial services in Norway are to be made by the ESA on behalf of the EU bodies. Already in 2010 the Legislation Department concluded that the powers granted to these bodies were so extensive that an equivalent transfer of decision-making powers to the ESA could not be considered to have only minimal impact on the constitutional powers in Norway.[40] Thus, it appears likely that the Storting, for the first time since the EEA Agreement in 1992, will transfer decision-making powers to the ESA with a three-quarter majority pursuant to Art. 115.

It remains to be seen whether or not the Storting's use of Art. 115 for Norway's accession to the EU system of financial supervision is a one-off or if it will embolden the Storting to apply Art. 115 in future cases. Most likely the Storting will continue to apply Art. 26 second paragraph if needed. That is when the political majority's desire for Norway to keep up with European integration dictates a transfer of decision-making powers to EU bodies. Despite the EEA Agreement's premise of unabridged Norwegian sovereignty, the institutional development in the EU will require the Storting to deal with many more cases of transfer of sovereignty in the years to come. Thus, the Norwegian constitutional acrobatics discussed in this chapter also seem likely to continue in the years to come.

## Notes

1 In this chapter I refer to the Norwegian constitution as amended by the Storting in May 2014. An English translation is available at https://www.stortinget.no/Global/pdf/Constitutionenglish.pdf?epslanguage=no, last accessed 29 December 2014.
2 One example of *pro forma* Norwegian decision-making powers is the 2005 agreement that regulates Norwegian participation in the EU Battlegroups; see Holmøyvik (2012: 209–214) and Sjursen (2008: 323–332).
3 The homogeneity objective follows from the EEA Agreement's preamble as well as Art. 1(1).
4 The Official Norwegian Report (NOU) (2012:2) concludes that the Storting's last word on legislation under the EEA Agreement, the 1998 Schengen Agreement and Norway's other agreement with the EU has been little more than a formality. The report further concludes that this effective transfer of legislative power to the EU without corresponding Norwegian representation in the EU legislative process is a fundamental democratic problem for Norway; see Official Norwegian Report (NOU) (2012:2: 829–831).
5 For a legal analysis of the Schengen Agreement in relation to the Norwegian constitution, see Boe (1999) and Sejersted (1999).
6 On the background and context of Art. 115, see Opsahl (1969: 490–510) and Holmøyvik (2011: 451–453).
7 See Parliamentary Proposition no. 100 (1991–1992: 335–336, 344). Pursuant to Art. 110 of the EEA Agreement, decisions from ESA and the EFTA Court, as well as decisions by the Commission and the CJEU, that impose fines on Norwegian companies are in and of themselves grounds for enforcement. In Norwegian law, the same follows from Art. 4–1(2)(h) of the Act of 26 June 1992 no. 86 (Enforcement Act). The ESA's and the EFTA Court's authority to make decisions with direct effect in Norwegian law follows from the Act of 3 May 2004 no. 11 (Act on the implementation and enforcement of the EEA Agreement's competition rules). See further Fredriksen and Mathisen (2012: 152–157).
8 For further discussions of this practice, see Holmøyvik (2011: 458–467) and Lilleby (2010).
9 Regulation (EC) no. 216/2008.
10 See Ministry of Justice and Public Security Legislation Department 2010.
11 See Parliament Proposition no. 27 (2012–2013) Proposition to the Storting.
12 See Parliament Recommendation no. 146 S (2012–2013) Recommendation to the Storting.

13 This case concerned the introduction of regulation (EC) 1228/2003/EC into the EEA Agreement, see Ministry of Justice and Public Security, Legislation Department (2004).
14 This case concerned the introduction of the introduction of regulation (EC) no. 1901/2006 into the EEA Agreement, see Ministry of Justice and Public Security, Legislation Department (2012a).
15 See the Legislation Department's legal memorandum on the amendment of regulation (EC) 659/1999 (Ministry of Justice and Public Security, Legislation Department 2014).
16 There is a growing body of work on the agencification of the EU, see, inter alia, Busuioc (2013: 13–23).
17 This development and its consequences for Norway have been thoroughly described in the Official Norwegian Report (NOU) (2012:2: 240–242).
18 A different and controversial question is whether EU bodies can functionally be considered EEA bodies if Norway is represented in these bodies without formally being a member; see Bull (2013), section 4 note 7. In connection with the EEA Agreement in 1992, the Government presumed that Art. 115 in the constitution entailed membership; see Parliamentary Proposition. no. 100 (1991–1992: 344–345). However, a possible exception from the membership requirement in Art. 115 may where Norway is not formally a member but is represented and participates in the EU body on equal footing with the members.
19 One way the government has avoided a formal transfer of sovereignty is by instructing Norwegian state bodies to replicate decisions from EU bodies within 30 days. The decision by the EU body is then formally binding on Norway under international law only, but in reality the decision by the EU body determines the subsequent decision of the Norwegian state body. Examples of such arrangements can be found in the EEA Committee's adaptations to Regulation (EC) no. 726/2004 about medicinal products for human and veterinary uses and Regulation (EC) no. 1907/2006 about chemicals (the REACH regulations; see Parliamentary Proposition no. 115 (2008–2009) appendix 1 and Parliamentary Proposition no. 49 (2007–2008: 4).
20 Regulation (EC) 1228/2003, see Parliamentary Proposition no. 44 (2004–2005) and Parliamentary Recommendation no. 164 (2004–2005).
21 Regulation (EC) 1907/2006.
22 Regulation (EC) no. 282/2008. See Parliamentary Proposition no. 133 S (2011–2012: 2–3) and Parliamentary Recommendation no. 86 S (2012–2013).
23 Art. 53 of the EEA Agreement.
24 See Parliamentary Proposition no. 100 (1991–1992: 342–347).
25 See Parliamentary Proposition no. 100 (1991–1992: 346).
26 A 'road map' for future Norwegian participation in EU agencies was outlined by Minister of EEA and EU Affair Vidar Helgesen in his address to the Storting on important EU and EEA matters on 20. November 2014, see Helgesen (2014).
27 See Ministry of Justice and Public Security, Legislation Department 2012a (concerning the incorporation of regulation (EC) 1901/2006 on medicinal products for paediatric use). See also Ministry of Justice and Public Security, Legislation Department 2014 (concerning the incorporation of regulation (EU) 734/2013 amending Regulation (EC) No 659/1999).
28 See Fleischer (1963). For the background to and content of the doctrine, see Holmøyvik (2011: 453) et seq.
29 For a recent and reasoned defence for the minimal impact doctrine, see Sejersted (2013).
30 For an example of this particular view on constitutional interpretation in Norway, see Fleischer (1969: 433–452). Generally on Norwegian constitutional interpretation, see

Holmøyvik (2013c: 11–26). For a critical (and English-language) perspective on customary constitutional law in Norway, see Smith (2008: 493–506).
31 Parliament White Paper no. 5 (2012–2013).
32 Inter alia, the legal memorandum on a possible introduction to the EEA Agreement of the EU timber regulation (regulation (EU) 995/2010), see Ministry of Justice and Public Safety Legislative Department (2012b).
33 For a discussion on cases before the adoption of Art. 115, see Holmøyvik (2013a: 51–52).
34 Parliamentary Recommendation no. 100 (1961–1962: 138).
35 For an overview and discussion, see Holmøyvik (2011: 461–463).
36 Regulation (EC) no. 216/2008.
37 On Norwegian transfers of sovereignty to non-EEA and EU institutions, see Holmøyvik (2013b: 55–58).
38 See also Holmøyvik (2011: 470) and the Official Norwegian Report (NOU) (2012: 2: 267).
39 See the press release at http://www.efta.int/about-efta/news/eea-efta-and-eu-ministers-reach-agreement-european-supervisory-authorities-3211, last accessed 29 December 2014.
40 See Ministry of Foreign Affairs Legislation Department (2010).

## References

Boe, E. (1999) 'Norges Schengenavtale fra 1998 og Grunnloven', in E. Boe and F. Sejersted (eds) *Schengen og Grunnloven*, Oslo: Universitetsforlaget.
Bull, H. (2013) *Norsk lovkommentar: EØS-loven (inkludert EØS-avtalen og ODA)*, 14 March. Accessed 27 March 2013 on http://www.rettsdata.no.
Busuioc, E.M. (2013) *European Agencies: Law and Practices of Accountability*, Oxford: Oxford University Press.
Craig, P.P. and De Búrca, G. (2011) *EU Law: Text, Cases and Materials*, 5th Edition, Oxford: Oxford University Press.
Fleischer, C.A. (1963) 'Grunnloven § 93', *Jussens Venner*, series Y (4): 74–110.
―――― (1969) 'Prinsipper for grunnlovsfortolkning', *Lov og Rett*, 8: 433–452.
Fredriksen, H.H. and Mathiesen, G. (2012) *EØS-rett*, Bergen: Fagbokforlaget.
Helgesen, V. (2014) 'Address to the Storting on Important EU and EEA Matters', speech at the Storting on 20 November.
Holmøyvik, E. (2011) 'Grunnlova § 115 og læra om "lite inngripende" myndigheitsoverføring i lys av nyare konstitusjonell praksis', *Lov og Rett*, 50(8): 447–471.
―――― (2012) 'Bruk av norske styrkar utanfor Noreg – statsrettslege utfordringar i fortid og notid', *Jussens venner*, 47(3): 184–215.
―――― (2013a) '"Sikker konstitusjonell praksis"? Grunnlova og Noregs avtaler om suverenitetsoverføring', *Nytt Norsk Tidsskrift*, 30(2): 117–125.
―――― (2013b) 'Grunnlova og avtalene med EU: Pragmatismens siger, det konstitusjonelle demokratiets tap', in E.O. Eriksen and J.E. Fossum (eds) *Det norske paradoks: Om Norges forhold til Den europeiske union*, Oslo: Universitetsforlaget.
―――― (2013c) 'Tolkingar av Grunnlova', in E. Holmøyvik (ed) *Tolkingar av Grunnlova: Om forfatningsutviklinga i Noreg 1814–2014*, Oslo: Pax Forlag.
Lilleby, F.L. (2010) 'Grunnloven § 115 og unntaket for "lite inngripende" myndighetsoverføring', *Perspektiv*, 3, Oslo: Stortinget.
Ministry of Justice and Public Security, Legislation Department (2004) Legal Memorandum dated 08/12/2004, *Grunnloven § 93 mv*, Case number 2004/05639.

—— (2010) Legal Memorandum dated 18/01/2010, *Konstitusjonelle spørsmål ved en eventuell innlemmelse i EØS-avtalen av forordninger om ny europeisk tilsynsstruktur på finansmarkedsområdet*, Case number 2010/10039.

—— (2012a) Legal Memorandum dated 06/06/2012, *Konstitusjonelle spørsmål ved eventuell innlemmelse i EØS-avtalen av forordning (EF) nr. 1901/2006 om legemidler til pediatrisk bruk*, Case number 2012/001153.

—— (2012b) Legal Memorandum dated 05/06/2012, *Konstitusjonelle sider ved eventuell innlemmelse av EUs tømmerforordning i EØS-avtalen*, Case number 2011/06651.

—— (2014) Legal Memorandum dated 23/01/2014, *Nye prosedyreregler for offentlig støtte – forholdet til Grunnloven §§ 26 og 93*, Case number 13/6526.

Official Norwegian Report (NOU) (2012:2) 'Outside and Inside: Norway's Agreements with the European Union', delivered to the Norwegian Ministry of Foreign Affairs, 17 January.

Opsahl, T. (1969) 'Selvstendighet og kongedømme: Den norske grunnlovs faneparagraf og dogmatikken 1814–2014', *Tidsskrift for Rettsvitenskap*, 82: 490–510.

Parliament Proposition no. 100 (1991–1992) 'Consenting the Ratification of the EEA Agreement' [St. prp. nr. 100 (1991–1992) Om samtykke til ratifikasjon av Avtale om Det europeiske økonomiske samarbeidsområde (EØS)], Oslo: Ministry of Foreign Affairs.

Parliament Proposition no. 44 (2004–2005) Consenting the approval Approval of the EEA Committee Decision' [St. prp. nr. 44 (2004–2005) Om samtykke til godkjenning av EØS-komiteens beslutning nr. 179/2004 av 9. desember 2004 om innlemmelse i EØS-avtalen av europaparlaments- og rådsforordning (EF) nr. 1592/2002 om felles regler for sivil luftfart og om opprettelse av et europeisk byrå for flysikkerhet (EASA)], Oslo: Ministry of Foreign Affairs.

Parliament Proposition no. 49 (2007–2008) 'Consenting the Approval of the EEA Committee Decision' [St. prp. nr. 49 (2007–2008) Om samtykke til godkjennelse av EØS-komiteens beslutning nr. 25/2008 av 14. mars 2008 om innlemmelse i EØS-avtalen av forordning (EF) nr. 1907/2006 om registrering, vurdering, godkjenning og restriksjoner av kjemikalier (REACH) og etablering], Oslo: Ministry of Foreign Affairs.

Parliament Proposition no. 115 (2008–2009) 'Consenting the Approval of the EEA Committee decision' [St. prp. nr. 115 (2008–2009) Om samtykke til godkjennelse av EØS-komiteens beslutning nr. 61/2009 av 29. mai 2009 om innlemmelse i EØS-avtalen av direktiv 2004/24/EF, direktiv 2004/27/EF, direktiv 2004/28/EF og forordning (EF) nr. 726/2004, om legemidler til mennesker og dyr (legemiddelpakken), samt tilhørende rettsakter], Oslo: Ministry of Foreign Affairs.

Parliament Proposition no. 133 S (2011–2012) 'Consenting the Approval of the EEA Committee Decision' [St. prp. nr. 133 S (2011–2012) Samtykke til godkjenning av avgjerd i EØS-komiteen nr. 9/2012 av 10. februar 2012 om innlemming i EØS-avtala av forordning (EF) nr. 282/2008 om materiale og gjenstandar av resirkulert plast som er meinte for å kome i kontakt med næringsmiddel], Oslo: Ministry of Foreign Affairs.

Parliament Proposition no. 27 (2012–2013) 'Consenting the approval Approval of the EEA Committee Decision' [St. prp. nr. 27 (2012–2013) Samtykke til godkjenning av EØS-komiteens beslutning 163/2011 av 19. desember 2011 om innlemmelse i EØS-avtalen av forordning (EF) nr. 216/2008 om felles regler for sivil luftfart og om opprettelse av et europeisk byrå for flysikkerhet (EASA)], Oslo: Ministry of Foreign Affairs.

Parliament Recommendation no. 100 (1961–1962) 'Recommendation from the Foreign Affairs and Constitutional Committee' [Innst. S. nr. 100 (1961–1962) Innstilling fra utenriks- og konstitusjonskomitéen om forslag til ny § 115 i Grunnloven], Oslo: Stortinget.

Parliament Recommendation no. 164 (2004–2005) 'Recommendation from the Standing Committee on Transport and Communications' [Innst. S nr. 164 (2004–2005) Innstilling fra samferdselskomiteen om samtykke til godkjenning av EØS-komiteens beslutning nr. 179/2004 av 9. desember 2004 om innlemmelse i EØS-avtalen av europaparlaments- og rådsforordning (EF) nr. 1592/2002 om felles regler for sivil luftfart og om opprettelse av et europeisk byrå for flysikkerhet (EASA)] Oslo: Stortinget.

Parliament Recommendation no. 86 S (2012–2013) 'Recommendation from the Business and Industry Committee' [Innst. S. nr. 86 S (2012–2013) Innstilling frå næringskomiteen om samtykke til godkjenning av avgjerd i EØS-komiteen nr. 9/2012 av 10. februar 2012 om innlemming i EØS-avtala av forordning (EF) nr. 282/2008 om materiale og gjenstandar av resirkulert plast som er meinte for å kome i kontakt med næringsmiddel], Oslo: Stortinget.

Parliament Recommendation no. 146 S (2012–2013) 'Recommendation from the Business and Industry Committee' [Innstilling fra transport- og kommunikasjonskomiteen om samtykke til godkjenning av EØS-komiteens beslutning nr. 163/2011 av 19. desember 2011 om innlemmelse i EØS-avtalen av forordning (EF) nr. 216/2008 om felles regler for sivil luftfart og om opprettelse av et europeisk byrå for flysikkerhet (EASA)], Oslo: Norwegian Parliament.

Parliament White Paper no. 5 (2012–2013) 'The EEA-agreement and Norway Other Agreements with the EU' [Meld. St. 5 (2012–2013) EØS-avtalen og Norges øvrige avtaler med EU. Sentrale prioriteringer og virkemidler i norsk europapolitikk], Oslo: Ministry of Foreign Affairs.

Sejersted, F. (1999) 'Schengen og Grunnloven', in E. Boe and F. Sejersted (eds) *Schengen og Grunnloven*, Oslo: Universitetsforlaget.

——— (2013) 'Læren om 'lite inngripende' myndighetsoverføring – statsrettslig selvbedrag eller fornuftig grunnlovstolkning?', *Nytt Norsk Tidsskrift*, 30(4): 416–421.

Sejersted, F., Arnesen, F., Rognstad, O.-A. and Kolstad, O. (2011) *EØS-rett*, 3rd Edition, Oslo: Universitetsforlaget.

Sjursen, H. (2008) 'Fra bremsekloss til medløper: Norge i EUs utenriks- og sikkerhetspolitikk', *Nytt Norsk Tidsskrift*, 25(4): 323–335.

Smith, E. (2008) 'A Lawyer's Disease? Customary Change of Constitutions', in S. Heckscher and A. Eka (eds) *Festskrift till Johan Hirschfeldt*, Uppsala: Iustus förlag.

——— (2012) *Konstitusjonelt demokrati*, 2nd Edition, Bergen: Fagbokforlaget.

# 9

# REPRESENTATION UNDER HEGEMONY?

## On Norway's relationship to the EU

*John Erik Fossum*

The purpose of this book is to discern the democratic constitutional effects of EU integration on states that are closely affiliated with the European Union (EU) but are not EU members. Are they able to retain their sovereignty? Or do they experience negative effects from these forms of affiliation on their systems of constitutional democracy?

In this chapter, I focus on Norway. The chapter seeks to shed light on the broader question of constitutional democratic implications through paying special attention to political representation. The focus is on (a) how Norway is represented in the EU and (b) how the EU affects domestic Norwegian representative-democratic arrangements and practice. With regard to how Norway is represented in the EU it is important to understand what type of representation this is and whether there are specific democratic constitutional implications from the relationship. That, of course, means establishing what the lack of political representation signifies, not the least because it brings up questions of hegemony and domination. Placing the onus on what this signifies implies that the effort to establish more precisely what form or label of representation we see is part of a broader examination of whether the main problem is lack of political representation or whether there are deeper constitutional implications that can be traced back not only to the nature of Norway's relationship but to more fundamental aspects of the EU itself.

With regard to Norway's relationship to the EU it is imbued with hegemonic traits that, in turn, will rub off on the domestic workings of Norwegian representative democracy. Precisely how is important to establish.

In order to address these two aspects of political representation, as cast in a broader operational constitutional framework, in the next section, I start the chapter by providing a brief overview of the nature of Norway's relationship to the EU, with particular emphasis on how Norway is represented there. In the subsequent section I establish what this situation means for sovereignty. It is difficult to understand the nature of Norway's relationship with the EU and the implications for autonomy and accountability unless we take into account how the EU alters or reconfigures state sovereignty, more broadly speaking. In the subsequent section I query the democratic implications, with particular focus on the will-formation and opinion-formation processes within Norway. These elements are intrinsically linked to the criteria of autonomy and accountability that this book uses to evaluate the constitutional-democratic effects of the EU on closely affiliated non-member states. In the final section I present my conclusion.

## Norway's representation and presence in the EU

Norwegian citizens are subject to EU legislation within the bounds of the EEA Agreement, the Schengen Agreement and the other agreements that regulate this very close relationship. Norwegian citizens are bearers of EU rights, especially economic mobility-related ones, and could even be said to be *de facto* transnational EU market citizens (Olsen 2014). Norway has obligations towards the EU, not the least, of course, to those EU citizens that are residing in Norway.

Nevertheless, formally speaking, with regard to Norway the EU's legislation – in contrast to the situation in the member states – is not formally anchored in the legal precepts of supremacy and direct effect. But as the contributions to this book show, reality is not as different as the formal structure would suggest.[1] In the member states, EU law trumps national law in those issue areas where the EU has been conferred competence. That includes member states' constitutional law. In Norway the EFTA Surveillance Authority (ESA[2]) will ensure that legal incorporation is in accordance with EU law, and the European Free Trade Association (EFTA) Court will in practice ensure the incorporation of EU law. This relationship is clearly one-way; Norwegian citizens are pure recipients of decisions made outside of Norway. There is no form of reciprocity or 'export' of Norwegian decisions to the EU. The Norwegian process of incorporating legislation starts *after* a decision has been reached in the EU. Through Norway's dense relationship with the EU, Norway is not only subject to far more legislation from the EU than from any other international organisation; it is a recipient of legal norms from a system with obvious constitutional features—however that system is defined. As it is pointed out by many analysts, Norwegian popularly elected representatives and the Norwegian government have lost the right of initiative that Art. 76 of the Norwegian Constitution confers on them (Stavang 2002: 135).[3]

With regard to the constitutional effects on Norway, it is important to try to get a sense of the cumulative effects of the process of EU adaptation because we are not talking about a number of isolated instances but a constant flow. The process is in effect one in which Norway ties itself to an external constitutional order, an order that increasingly shapes Norway's relations to the world and that also increasingly programmes what takes place within Norway. As part of that we see that an increasing number of the legal rules in operation in Norway have their origins beyond Norway's borders.

Norway is being represented, even if the Norwegian representatives are not politically elected by Norwegian citizens. To illustrate, within the framework of the EEA Agreement Norway has a number of experts in EU bodies and committees, especially under the Commission (Official Norwegian Report [NOU] 2012:2: 824, 829–830). In issues regulated by the Schengen Agreement, Norway has the right to participate in meetings (without voting rights) in the Council, and has representatives in the committees under the Council. The issue of access and participation is raised with every new arrangement that Norway signs with the EU. The new EU crisis combatting measures in the areas of financial services and banking regulations are a case in point. As the Norwegian government notes,

> [i]n order to ensure uniform surveillance and application of the legislation in the financial services field, representatives of the EFTA Surveillance Authority and of the national competent authorities in the three EEA-EFTA States shall participate to the fullest extent possible, without voting rights, in the Boards of Supervisors of the EU ESAs and their preparatory bodies. The EU ESAs shall also participate to the fullest extent possible, without voting rights, in the work of the EFTA Surveillance Authority and its preparatory bodies in so far it is related to their activities.[4]

The Norwegian parliament has six representatives in the EEA Parliamentary Committee, gets access (through invitation) to the EU's system of interparliamentary coordination (COSAC) and has the right to participate in the interparliamentary committee on foreign and security policy.

There are also explicit measures taken by Norway to get better access to the EU system. For instance, the Norwegian parliament has recently established an office in Brussels that is located in the EU Parliament. The Norwegian EU delegation in Brussels understands itself as a spokesperson for Norwegian interests, and Norwegian regions and local government bodies also have representatives present in Brussels. The same applies to various business and trade union interests.

This system of representation and the various forms of presence are important for Norwegian authorities who are naturally anxious to know and understand what is going on in the EU. It is also the case that Norwegian experts furnish the EU with important sources of knowledge and expertise of relevance to the EU's decision-making processes. But given that we are talking about Norway being subject to an ever-increasing body of European law, these venues into the EU are qualitatively different from the systems of political representation that tie the EU's member states and citizens to the institutions at the EU level.

Norwegian decision makers and expert assessments (Official Norwegian Report [NOU] 2012: 2) generally conclude that the EEA Agreement and Norway's other arrangements with the EU have served Norway well. As a recent evaluation produced by the Norwegian Ministry of Foreign Affairs stated, 'Generally speaking, Norway benefits from the development of common rules and standards for the European market'. This is hardly surprising given that '[t]here are close links between

Norway and the EU countries due to historical and cultural ties, geographical proximity, common values and a shared commitment to the rule of law and human rights. Norway has therefore also chosen to develop its cooperation and agreements with the EU in areas outside the framework of the EEA Agreement' (Parliament White Paper no. 5 2012–2013: 55). In a similar vein the government-appointed EEA Review Committee that evaluated Norway's relationship to the EU and produced the comprehensive report *Outside and Inside: Norway's Agreements with the European Union* noted that 'the agreements [that Norway has entered into] with the EU have to a large extent ensured basic Norwegian values and material interests' (Official Norwegian Report [NOU] 2012:2: 817). The report underlines that this is a mutually held view in Norway and in the EU. That is also reflected in the fact that Norway has obtained a 'privileged partnership' with the EU (Official Norwegian Report [NOU] 2012:2: 845–846).

## Virtual representation

How then can we describe Norway's relationship with the EU from the perspective of *political* representation? The previous statements which refer to a commonality of interests, feelings and desires suggest that Norway's affiliation with the EU is marked by what Edmund Burke has termed *virtual representation*. He defined it in the following manner:

> Virtual representation is that in which there is a communion of interests and sympathy in feelings and desires between those who act in the name of any description of people and the people in whose name they act, though the trustees are not actually chosen by them. This is virtual representation.
> 
> (Burke 1792: 23)

An important point that Burke underlined is that the representatives function as *trustees*, with considerable freedom or leverage to define what they consider the interests of those they represent, and how those interests are to be promoted. Such freedom is important for the process of deliberation which representatives undertake in order to reach agreement on what is in the best interest of all (in the nation's best interest):

> Since the purpose of representation is to obtain representatives capable of pursuing the public interest better than the people themselves, election is not an essential criterion of representation. Indeed, as long as there is a mutuality of interests between the representative and all his constituents, a select group of voters may actually choose a better representative of the people's true interests than the people themselves.
> 
> (Yarbrough 1979: 80)

Burke discussed virtual representation in relation to the role of Catholics in the UK and in relation to the American colonists in the latter part of the 1700s.

Both were groups/collectives that were subject to British legislation without having politically elected representatives in the UK Parliament. Burke queried if they could nevertheless consider their basic interests to be adequately represented in the UK Parliament. His concern was whether their basic interests were taken care of in a spirit of sympathy in feelings and desires, and the benchmark was whether there were serious substantive grievances (Pitkin 1967: 178). He notes that '[t]he people may err in its choice; but common interest and common sentiment are rarely mistaken' (Burke 1792). In both these two cases the basic interests had not been well taken care of. For instance, with regard to the American colonists the relations were not based on any 'communion of interests and sympathy in feelings and desires' (Yarbrough 1979: 80).

These examples show that if virtual representation is to work, there must be well-established forms of contact, commonly shared interests, and some form of affinity. Such factors are necessary to establish the requisite trust. It should also be noted that all democracies, even modern ones, contain groups or sections of the population that do not have the right to vote. In modern democracies, children below a fixed voting age do not have voting rights; the assumption is that they are virtually represented.

To what extent, then, is Norway's relationship to the EU to be understood as a case of virtual representation? Norway is, as noted, subject to EU legislation, and the EU affects in fundamental ways Norwegian citizens' abilities to realise their interests at the same time that they are not politically represented in the EU. Thus, the basic structure of the relationship is akin to what we should expect from virtual representation, not the least because Norwegian authorities underline commonality in interests and values, and because a clear majority of the Norwegian population supports Norway's present affiliation with the EU.

The main problem with Burke's notion applied to Norway's present situation is not the structure of the relationship which is clearly in line with what Burke was referring to but, rather, Burke's notion of interest, which he understands as something quite permanent and easily identifiable. In a democracy, who defines what constitutes key interests is a core democratic issue and must be subject to and determined by the democratic procedure. The democratic procedure must also leave space for a continuous assessment of what a given community's core interests are.[5] None of these considerations is adequately dealt with in circumstances of virtual representation and is not present in Norway's relations to the EU.

## *Surrogate representation*

The Norwegian government is, of course, aware of this and has then taken more active measures to promote Norwegian interests and concerns. One such pertains to the government's active efforts at benefitting from surrogate representation. Surrogate representation is defined as 'representation by a representative with whom one has no electoral relationship – that is, a representative in another district [. . .]. In surrogate representation, legislators represent constituencies that did not elect them. They cannot therefore be accountable in traditional ways' (Mansbridge 2003: 522, 524).

Applied to Norway this suggests that there are elected representatives in the EU (MEPs in the EP or members of the Council structures) that consider themselves as spokespersons for Norwegian interests or that speak on behalf of Norway. Consider the following statement by Swedish MEP Christofer Fjellner:

> I think a lot of how various EU decisions affect Norway and have previously supported Norway in a number of cases. For instance in the case of the EU's anti-dumping measures against Norwegian salmon I spoke out against them because I thought the measures were unfair.[6]

The Norwegian newspaper that quoted Fjellner characteristically labelled him 'a friend of Norway in the EU'. The concrete occasion that prompted this statement was that he was enraged by the Norwegian introduction of high protective tariffs on cheese and beef.

Norwegian authorities are known to have actively searched for such surrogate representatives, especially in the Nordic countries. In the concrete case, Ine Marie Eriksen Søreide (then Chair of the Standing Committee on Foreign Affairs and Defence) commented that

> [w]hat Norway now did – correctly or not – entails that it will be more difficult for him to propound Norway's concerns in a new case. We have several issues under discussion with the EU where we depend on support from parliamentarians [MEPs]. They may be from different countries and with different partisan affiliations but we depend on them. We are also encouraged – in Parliament – to contact our MEPs in order to encourage them to promote Norway's case, even if we are not EU members. What strategy is there to ensure that the contact is sustained with those MEPs that feel that Norway's decision in the tariffs issue does not correspond well with the work they have done to support Norway in other circumstances?[7]

The Norwegian situation clearly exhibits features of surrogate representation (Fossum 2014). At the same time, there are also some differences from how Mansbridge depicts this notion. In her depiction of surrogate representation, Mansbridge places the emphasis on the representatives: it is they who single out persons or issues outside their constituency that they want to support. In Norway's case, Norwegian authorities take an active role in *seeking out* surrogate representation behaviour. The question is what that does to the representative relationship: Does it induce representatives to support Norway, or does it make for a less reliable form of representation?

Obviously every form of surrogate representation is structurally speaking a very weak form of representation and ultimately depends on the representative's inclinations. But representatives often do speak on behalf of those that are not directly represented and often come up with excellent justifications for doing that. In the Norwegian case, the close affinity between the Nordic states is a case in point. Just after the EEA Agreement was signed in 1994, Norwegian authorities then also pinned great hopes on support from the other Nordic countries that were directly represented in the EU (Olsen and Sverdrup 1998). The record since then has shown that this was overly optimistic.

We see from this that both virtual representation and surrogate representation share commonalities; they are both about representing the views and interests of persons and communities that do not have voting rights and who therefore cannot hold the representatives accountable. There are, nevertheless, also important differences between the two forms: virtual representation is based on the notion of the representative as a trustee, whereas surrogate representation is based on a closer association, where the surrogate understands him- or herself to be acting on behalf of those singled out. But the link to Norwegian citizens is indirect, at best, because the latter cannot instruct foreign representatives what to do or in any way hold them accountable. In Norway's case it is reasonable to assert that the nature of Norway's relationship to the EU renders surrogate representation *more* unpredictable and unreliable, because the representatives in question will be well cognisant of the fact that Norwegian citizens have voluntarily chosen this form of representation. Simply put, Norway has voluntarily chosen a form of affiliation that makes it dependent on others, but because Norway qualifies for EU membership and can at any time alter its formal membership status, these others do not have any strong compunctions to fill the void and propound Norway's case.

The analysis thus far shows that the nature of Norway's relationship with the EU is highly asymmetrical. It is also readily apparent that the dynamic process of Norwegian adaptation to the EU has cumulative effects that will, over time, exacerbate the problems. How and in what sense that will occur requires attention to the EU as a political system because the EU is not configured as a hierarchical state-type structure. What might the cumulative effects of that be? In order to address that we need to look at how the EU reconfigures sovereignty.

## Contending conceptions of sovereignty and constitutional implications

To what extent would Norway's form of EU representation be problematic from a constitutional democratic perspective? Is it mainly a matter of lack of political access and presence, or are there additional elements of more direct relevance for Norwegian constitutional democracy? In order to assess that, we need to look more closely at the question of sovereignty, in terms of it serving as a vital precondition for democratic self-governing.

We have long been accustomed to thinking of state sovereignty as synonymous with a territorially based system of self-governing. That entails 'internal supremacy over all other authorities within a given territory and external independence of outside authorities' (Keohane 2002: 746). The EU alters this notion in that it places far more weight on forging joint decisions in common EU-level institutions (where states and citizens are directly represented).

In order to get a grip on how EU integration reconfigures sovereignty in Europe, with democratic implications, it is important to recall that the European integration process takes place in a setting of already existing states, and EU democratisation unfolds within this system of states. The EU supranational system is solidly anchored in the member states. These states do not agree on what form of system the EU should become, not the least because many member states prefer a weak EU that harmonises interstate interaction and cooperation rather than supranational integration. The strong member-state presence in the institutions at the EU level also structures the integration process: it is a matter of fusing levels (EU and member state) and sharing competencies rather than singling out a distinct European level of government with exclusive competencies (Wessels 1997). States cede sovereignty *not* to a distant entity but to a common unit in which they all directly participate. In EU parlance this is generally referred to as *pooling of sovereignty*. This process of pooling has profound implications for the ensuing notion of sovereignty:

> States that are members of the European Union have broken sharply with the classical tradition of state sovereignty. Sovereignty is pooled, in the sense that, in many areas, states' legal authority over internal and external affairs is transferred to the Community as a whole, authorising action through procedures not involving state vetoes [. . .]. Under conditions of extensive and intensive interdependence, formal sovereignty becomes less a territorially defined barrier than a bargaining resource.
>
> (Keohane 2002: 748)

Pooling and sharing of sovereignty condition the structure of political representation that has emerged at the EU level, a structure that has taken on a distinctive shape. It is commonplace to think of two broad institutional patterns in multilevel systems, but in the EU they take on a highly distinct shape, precisely because they reflect this pooling of sovereignty. One channel connects the EU directly to the citizens through the EP, and is a vertical process of EP parliamentarisation.[8] This process is far from complete, and has its own distinctive features. It should also be noted that it has been weakened and set back by the Eurozone crisis.[9]

The other channel connects citizens to the EU through *two* sets of collectives. The main one goes through the many Council formations. But there is also a further, more informal and less tightly structured link that goes through direct national parliamentary involvement in the institutions at the EU level (notably through the Early Warning Mechanism [EWM]) coupled with a broad web of interparliamentary interaction (across the EU and member-state levels).[10]

This complex and composite representative structure testifies to the strong onus that is placed on incorporating member states' institutions in the decision-making processes at the EU level. That includes, as noted, both politically elected government representatives and national parliaments. This representative structure mirrors the broader EU systemic trait of institutional fusion or interweaving of levels.[11]

The EU is the most advanced instance of transforming the substantive contents of state sovereignty in a *relational* direction. The onus is placed on participation in common institutions rather than on self-governing, the hallmark of the classical notion of state sovereignty. The turn to participation is clearly a part of a global development towards heightened interdependence, which implies that '[t]he only way most states can realise and express their sovereignty is through participation in the various regimes that regulate and order the international system' (Chayes and Chayes 1995: 27).

Within the EU context, the more the member states' concerns are made subject to joint decisions the more important it is to be present and to participate in making these decisions. The European Council is a case in point. The European Council (when operating as the core body of an Intergovernmental Conference (IGC)) is in charge of treaty making/change and has taken on a more prominent role in the EU's crisis handling.

In this EU structure that weaves actors from different levels together (and where an activist Court of Justice of the European Union [CJEU] gives added integrationist impetus to the process), the forums and procedures that determine joint decisions increasingly also shape the nature and scope of each state's self-governing. Or, to put it differently, the reneging of external sovereign control transforms the state's ability to exercise internal sovereignty. The state is no longer capable of distinguishing between domestic and international affairs, as both sets of issues are increasingly determined (jointly) in common intergovernmental and supranational bodies.

That turns the classical approach to state sovereignty as a case of self-governing on its head. If it is necessary to participate in common institutions in order to wield influence in those decisions that actors have agreed to undertake in common *and*, notably, if such participation in common institutions is needed for the state to influence the scope and conditions of its self-governing, then a qualitative change is taking place. The EU appears to be moving towards a system where institutions of joint decision-making increasingly shape and set the terms of domestic sovereign rule. Such a system is based in an altered conception of sovereignty which seeks to balance shared rule with self-rule in a distinct formation of strong fusion of levels of governing.

For Norway, such a structure is doubly ominous. It is problematic because Norway is incorporated in this structure without real co-decision power. Norway is locked out from the forums where joint decisions are made. That is well known and widely recognised. But the constitutional implications – understood in terms of the functioning, not the formality, of Norwegian constitutional democracy – have not been equally well recognised. Two such implications are highlighted here. The first is that because Norway does not participate in common EU institutions also means that it lacks access to the sites that increasingly determine the terms and scope of Norwegian self-governing.[12] In such a context Norway will increasingly experience the EU as a hegemonic power because the EU sets the terms of Norway's collaboration with other states *as well as* increasingly shapes those issues that Norway has deliberatively sought to withhold from external influence, and the terms under which both sets of issues are to be handled.[13] It is the latter point of the terms under which these issues are handled that is the key constitutional dimension.

The second aspect with constitutional democratic implications and which is further developed later is that EU integration affects the state's ability to define what issues are domestic and what issues are international. Domestic democratic arrangements are hard-wired to deal with certain issue constellations; if these patterns are sufficiently upset domestic systems of authorisation and accountability are thrown off kilter. Here the lack of EU-level political representation becomes a problem because EU-level representative arrangements are an important means for member states to steer or to make up for these transformations.

The upshot of the analysis thus far is as follows: Norway in its relations with the EU has opted to stay out of the EU because Norway has sought to preserve the traditional conception of state sovereignty as autonomy. That decision has not served as an effective defence of autonomy. The nature of Norway's relationship to the EU – its privileged partnership – effectively deprives Norway of joint decision power and challenges Norway's ability to set the terms of self-rule. The more that the EU integration process proceeds, and with it Norway's further incorporation in the EU, the more acute this problem becomes. The effect is voluntary submission under a system of arbitrary domination because Norwegian citizens lack access to those institutions that *de facto* set the terms of their constitutional sovereignty. But arbitrariness not only stems from a lack of access; it also stems from uncertainties and discrepancies in how the relationship is structured and operates. The Schengen Agreement is a case in point. For the EU the general trend has been that much of the substance of the initially intergovernmental Schengen Agreement has been incorporated in the EU treaties, whereas Norway's agreement with the EU is delimited to the range of issues that were in the initial agreement. That leads to uncertainty for Norway with regard to which issues are included and which are not; with regard to the issues that are not included, Norway is in a very weak bargaining position (Bøckman-Finstad 2014). To reduce uncertainty Norway then simply shadows EU regulations. In this situation *both* being included in agreements *and* not being included engenders domination.

In the next and final section, I look more closely at what this entails for processes internally in Norway, with a focus on will-formation and opinion-formation.

## Internal workings of Norwegian representative democracy

Thus far, I have looked at Norway's external access and representation in EU-level institutions; in this section, I look more closely at the *internal* workings of Norwegian representative democracy, with emphasis on effects on domestic democratic will-formation and opinion-formation processes.

In order to understand what is meant by will formation and opinion formation in a representative democracy,[14] it is useful to draw on Nadia Urbinati who underlines that

> [r]epresentative democracy is a *diarchic system* in which 'will' (by which I mean the right to vote and the procedures and institutions that regulate the making of authoritative decisions) and 'opinion' (by which I mean the extra-institutional domain of political opinions) influence each other and cooperate without merging.
>
> (Urbinati 2014: 2)

Both democratic will formation and opinion formation are required to ensure citizens' autonomy and citizens' ability to hold the leaders to account.

The key argument I present here is that Norway's arrangement with the EU distorts Norwegian democracy's diarchy (of will and opinion) along both dimensions of the diarchy. The focus here is on those political bodies that are directly involved in the representative system of will-formation through elections; they operate as key receivers of opinion formation in society and funnel it into the political system.[15] Parliaments are quintessential strong publics, that is bodies that combine deliberation (as part of opinion and will formation) with decision-making (Fraser 1992). A similar argument applies to political parties, which programme the entire chain of representation from citizens in civil society to the exercise of executive power in government. A lack of space prevents paying attention to the general opinion formation processes in the public sphere, even if democracy is crucially dependent on them.

In order to understand the manner in which Norway's relationship to the EU affects the internal workings of Norwegian constitutional democracy, it is useful to go back to the manner in which the EU transforms state sovereignty because that has direct bearings on domestic patterns of democratic governing, and not only the state's access to external – EU-level – institutions. We should expect those effects to be different from what would have been the case if Norway's relationship to the EU had been programmed according to the standard conception of sovereignty (which incidentally is normally the manner in which the issue is discussed in Norway). In that case, the question would be one of magnitude of transfer of real sovereignty and autonomy from Norway to the EU level. But EU integration, as shown earlier, is not about the formation of a distinct – separate – level of governing; member-state representatives are much more directly included in the workings of the EU-level institutions; this difference has implications for domestic governing arrangements, including those in Norway.

## Executive dominance

The first point to note is that domestic processes of will formation and opinion formation are affected by the manner in which the EU process of pooling of sovereignty reconfigures internal executive-legislative relations in all member and affiliated states. In effect, the EU system of pooling of sovereignty is a process that privileges executives and experts, hence the frequently referred-to problems of executive dominance and technocracy.[16] In the member states, popularly elected bodies such as the EP as well as the member states' national parliaments have consistently sought to catch up with and subject this executive-expert-driven integration process to democratic norms and principles. We should therefore expect this pattern of executive dominance also to be affecting domestic governing arrangements in Norway. If anything, Norway's lack of democratic representation at the EU level suggests that executive dominance will be *more pronounced* in Norway than what is the case in the member states where provisions are in place for democratically elected bodies at the domestic *and* at the EU level to rein in executives.

The structure of Norway's relationship to the EU naturally locates the Norwegian government in a prominent position, because the structure of the relationship situates the government in a position of privileged access and information. This does not necessarily mean that the government is so very proactive; the Norwegian government has been frequently criticised for dragging its feet on EU issues. There is therefore the onus on the government to be more proactive. Consider the following quote from the Foreign Ministry's white paper on Norway's relationship to the EU:

> Within the framework of Norway's agreements with the EU, Norway has greatest opportunity to participate in the development of EU policy and legislation at an early stage of the legislative process, i.e. during the preparation of Commission proposals and during preliminary discussions in the Council of the EU (the Council) and the European Parliament [. . .] It is important to ensure early involvement in legislative processes so that we can carry out a preliminary assessment of EEA relevance when the EU is preparing new legislation. Moreover, by being actively involved at an early stage we can develop insight that will help us to clarify and make use of the options that are available as we implement and apply the legislation in Norway.
>
> (Parliament White Paper no. 5 [2012–13]: 9)

The irony is that a more pro-active government role will further exacerbate not ameliorate executive dominance. The structure of the relationship is such that when Norway seeks early involvement in EU-level processes the participants will typically be executives and experts. In such circumstances it is difficult to ensure an open public-opinion formation process because the onus is on the government to come up with a clear position as early as possible in the process. The government's position can be subsequently tested in parliament but that can only take place ex post facto. How effective that is requires attention to the role of parliament and political parties.

## *Inadequate parliamentary oversight and control*

The previous paragraph showed that the structure of Norway's EU relationship greatly favours the government in relation to Parliament. This point is further underlined when we consider the structure and conduct of parliamentary oversight and control.

Again, we need to start by looking at how the EU reconfigures domestic politics. An important trait of the EU (which has made Joseph Weiler [2001] label it an upside-down type of federation) is the fact that many of the issues that are typically handled by the EU are issues that have traditionally been understood as domestic issues and regulated by domestic political processes. EU integration entails that member states open their domestic societies to each other and regulate a broad range of issues in common, at the EU level. In this sense, we could say that the EU externalises many of the member (and affiliated) states' internal affairs. How these issues are handled matters to democratic governing. In contrast to what is the case in Sweden, Denmark and Finland whose systems of parliamentary oversight and scrutiny increasingly deal with EU issues in the same manner as they deal with domestic issues, the Norwegian parliament deals with these issues in a manner much more similar to how it deals with foreign policy issues, which naturally locates the government in a central position (Claes 2003: 289; Hegeland 2011). Norway lacks EU-level political representation, the Norwegian parliament enters the decision-making process far later than do EU member states' parliaments and the Norwegian parliament has no recourse to the EWM that gives member states' parliaments early access to (aspects of) EU-level decision-making processes. Thus, the democratic problem is far more pronounced for Norway than for the member states.[17]

A general effect of Norway's EU arrangement is to depoliticise Norway's handling of EU issues within the Norwegian political system. This is readily apparent when we consider how the Storting's European Consultative Committee relates to EU issues. This body is mandated to conduct consultations with the government on EEA and related matters (Parliament 2012). An analysis of the committee's written transcripts revealed that a distinctive feature was that there were very few debates; the general picture is one in which the executives briefed the legislators on what was taking place (Fossum and Holst 2014). The committee's work and deliberations are marked by a clear 'system-enforced consensus' and absence of debate on principled and constitutional issues that must be traced back to the nature of Norway's relationship with the EU.

The analysis thus far has shown that the domestic processes of will and opinion formation – that are of vital importance to autonomy and accountability – are affected when a state is tied up to a supranational system, even if that state is not a member of the system. The problem of executive dominance is typically reinforced, through the executive being centrally located in the process and through the parliament exercising weak scrutiny. Are there also discernible effects on Norwegian political parties and elections?

## Stymied elections and 'gagged' parties?

A key component of democratic sovereignty is that citizens must be free to choose among alternative visions of society's future development. That presupposes that politicians in formulating their future visions and partisan programmes can confidently assert a measure of control of the conditions for realising those programmes. Norway's relationship to the EU, however, distorts that because it greatly narrows the range of issues that politicians can credibly compete over during election campaigns.

One important implication is that the more closely affiliated Norway is with the EU, the greater the share of issues that get decided outside Norway's bounds, with Norway simply implementing them, and the more elections lose their role as critical moments of will formation. This is a structural issue pertaining to the range of options that politicians can credibly pursue when in office. Another similar structural effect is that the lack of upstream Norwegian influence on EU legislative processes makes the Norwegian political system stacked towards output legitimation due to the many constraints on the input side. But even output is highly influenced by external conditions; output legitimation is also vulnerable to international processes. Norway is a clear case where 'external political constraints can get in the way of representative politics by prohibiting certain forms of agency or by "forcing agents into behaviour that neither they nor their [own domestic] principals would have freely chosen"' (Mair 2009: 14, drawing on Strøm 2003).

Such constraints also shape the role and conduct of political parties. Even if Norway is not a member of the EU it is incorporated in the multilevel structure that makes up the EU. That fact conditions all political institutions, not the least political parties. The following statement by the late Peter Mair is telling: 'The same organisation that governed the citizenry also gave that citizenry voice, and the same organisation that channelled representation also managed the institutions of the polity' (Mair 2009: 5).

In Norway's case the political parties can no longer play this integrative role because the governing role is locked in by Norway's international agreements and commitments. That has implications for how the parties balance responsiveness and responsibility and how they manage conflicts and politically divisive issues notably the question of Norwegian EU membership.

An important aspect of partisan responsibility is 'to act prudently and consistently and to follow accepted procedural norms and practices [. . .] responsibility involves an acceptance that, in certain areas and in certain procedures, the leaders' hands will be tied' (Mair 2009: 12). At the same time, in the act of voting citizens express their will; they also express their segmental loyalties to particular cleavages, world views and programmes of action. In that sense for political parties, especially in multiparty systems, responsiveness has a strong expressive element built into it. The voters must understand the parties to be genuine expressions of their views and values. Parties used to combine the two roles; recent developments have driven a wedge between them; in the case of Norway, its affiliation with the EU has expanded this wedge even farther. Thus, Norway's EU affiliation exacerbates a gap in political representation between partisan responsiveness and responsibility.

Norwegian leaders must behave responsibly in terms of honouring the EEA Agreement and Norway's many other arrangements with the EU. In that sense the Norwegian government as the agent finds itself compelled to serve a set of principals outside Norway's boundaries. The rub is that the parties' greater focus on responsibility runs up against their role in ensuring responsiveness, especially in consensually based multiparty systems such as Norway's, where parties must also be understood as credible expressions of voters' values and world views. All political parties face this tension; those close to governing will tone down the expressive function, those distanced from governing will play it up. Furthermore, as Jo Saglie (2002) underlines, parties that are internally united can much more easily deal with this tension. In Norway it was really only the small Centre Party that was able to muster a coherent anti-EU policy stance.[18]

The problem in a situation of strong, pronounced, external constraints is that the scope for balancing responsibility and responsiveness is further hemmed in. In Norway's case this very trade-off is, as noted earlier, rendered democratically ominous because Norwegian citizens lack influence over the sources of the norms and the rules that the politicians must abide by in order to behave responsibly. That engenders a particular set of distortions in will formation in the realm of political elections, or more specifically, in the realm of electoral choice.

The upshot of these agreements (EEA, Schengen, etc.) is that issues become bundled together and are converted into matters of all or nothing: either you accept the current arrangement or you must advocate leaving it. It makes little sense for politicians to launch costly partisan contests over issues that they know (are being or) will be determined by Brussels. The problem of issue bundling becomes more acute with time because the affiliation arrangements are dynamic and have cumulative effects: an ever-greater number of issues become bundled together under these arrangements. Under these circumstances elections lose much of their role as moments of expression of popular will. Political contestation becomes pseudo-contestation in which real contestation – over issues that they can readily influence – covers an ever-narrower band of issues. Or rather, peripheral issues get blown up to major proportions as symbolic manifestations over disagreement.

The other point is that the parties that emphasise responsibility reap few rewards because they cannot point to successes at the EU level. Instead, they must contend with the uncertainty that stems from the fact that Norway's affiliation with the EU is based on a patchwork of agreements, and there is, as was pointed out earlier, considerable uncertainty as to precisely how far these extend and what they cover. That puts an added premium on the need to 'act responsibly' and predictably in relation to the external world and locks in the governing parties even further.[19]

Structurally speaking, Norway's EU affiliation thus makes the Norwegian political system highly vulnerable to expressive politics or responsiveness. In that sense the system is stacked in favour of populism or populist protests who not only underline the elite – mass divide – but also posit themselves as authentic expressions of 'the people'. Furthermore, as is developed further in the following, most Norwegian parties have a strong incentive to depoliticise the contentious EU membership issue. This, as I will show, actually helps to keep the dynamic EU adaptation process going.

The way in which Norwegian parties have sought to work out the relationship between responsibility and responsiveness in the complex EU affiliation issue is closely associated with the parties' role in conflict handling or better conflict dampening. The issue of Norwegian EU membership has long been deeply divisive. It splits the population but does not correspond easily with ideological lines or divisions, or even with established partisan cleavages. Most political parties are deeply divided internally on this issue and have a strong incentive to keep the issue off the political agenda.

Furthermore, the Norwegian party constellations are such that the membership issue will split most possible governing coalitions. In turn, over the last two decades governing coalitions have formulated a range of provisions for keeping the EU membership issue off the political agenda: so-called suicide clauses (if a party in a coalition government launches a campaign for EU membership or for leaving the EEA, the coalition unravels). This is based on a bipartisan agreement to base Norway's relation to the EU on the EEA Agreement. Other provisions are high thresholds for instituting a process of applying for EU membership (Fossum 2010).

Many of these measures can be characterised as 'gag rules' which refer to a particular type of issue avoidance, how actors seek to remove debate on a controversial issue that does not go away (Holmes 1995). In the Norwegian case, these provisions help to delink debate on the constitutional implications of Norway's close affiliation with the EU from the issue of ongoing EU adaptation. They permit issue-focused debate and contestation without this degenerating into political stalemate. But precisely because of this delinking the citizenry is not kept informed of the constitutional-democratic implications of what is going on. At the same time, precisely because issues are depoliticised, is it possible to conduct an ongoing policy of rapid and dynamic EU adaptation. In that sense the gag rules serve two functions: they help to keep a lid on the debate on EU membership, and at the same time they help the political system to keep alive an active process of Norwegian adaptation to the EU.

Norwegian parties' onus on conflict handling serves as a vital spur to delinking the issue of EU membership from the ongoing adaptation to and incorporation in the EU. The effect is to stymie debate on the constitutional implications of Norway's rapid and deep incorporation in the EU. The lack of debate serves to depoliticise the process which helps to foster rapid EU incorporation. Low constitutional incorporation thresholds are an intrinsic part of this picture and are a functional necessity to keep the dynamic process of adaptation going.

## Conclusion

In this chapter I focused on the effects of Norway's affiliation with the EU on Norwegian constitutional democracy. The emphasis was placed not on formal constitutional provisions but on democratic arrangements and practice. It was pointed out that we need to understand the nature of Norway's representation in the EU system and what Norway's affiliation with the EU does to the domestic system of democratic governing in Norway.

It was shown that Norway in its relations with the EU has opted to stay out of the EU because it has sought to preserve the traditional conception of state sovereignty as autonomy. It is readily apparent that that decision has not served as an effective defence of autonomy. The nature of Norway's relationship to the EU – its privileged partnership – effectively deprives Norway of joint decision power and challenges Norway's ability to set the terms of self-rule. The more that the EU integration process proceeds, and with it Norway's further incorporation in the EU, the more acute this problem becomes. The effect is voluntary submission under a system of arbitrary domination because Norwegian citizens have no access to a set of institutions that provide them with assurance of constitutional sovereignty.

Furthermore, in terms of the implications of this form of affiliation on Norway's internal workings it was shown that the affiliation exacerbates a common EU problem of executive dominance (and technocracy), amplified by a particularly weak system of parliamentary scrutiny and control. The political system is structurally speaking stacked in favour of output legitimation and leaves political parties in a difficult situation of balancing responsibility and responsiveness in a context of strong international constraints, which leaves great scope for populist politics.

The curious paradox is that little of this has really rubbed off on citizens' trust in domestic institutions. How to account for this and how impervious to change it is requires further attention. We might be in for some rude awakenings.

## Notes

1 EEA expert Hans Petter Graver noted in a parliamentary hearing on the EEA Agreement in 2002 that '[n]ow it appears that the EFTA Court has introduced some kind of quasi-direct effect of the agreement' (author's translation), hearing in the Committee on Foreign Affairs, Stortinget, 14 October 2002, available at http://www.stortinget.no/no/Saker-og-publikasjoner/Publikasjoner/Referater/Horinger/2002–2003/021014/sak/, last accessed 16 December 2014.
2 EFTA, 'About the Authority', available at http://www.eftasurv.int/about-the-authority/the-authority-at-a-glance-/, last accessed 28 November 2014.
3 Trond Nordby and Frode Veggeland (1999) have, for instance, described the EEA Agreement as the suspension of legislative authority. The EEA Review Committee underlines the lack of Norwegian representation and co-decision in EU decision-making processes (Official Norwegian Report [NOU 2012:2]: 828), and Erik O. Eriksen talks of a 'self-harmed' democratic procedure in Chapter 5 in this volume.
4 See Joint Conclusion at http://www.efta.int/sites/default/files/documents/eea/eea-news/2010–10–14-EEA-EFTA-ECOFIN-joint-conclusions.pdf, last accessed 28 November 2014.
5 The EEA Review Committee defines national interests as 'those interests that the incumbent Storting majority consider important to Norway and those that the incumbent government seeks to ensure' (Official Norwegian Report NOU [2012:2]: 808 [author's translation]). This definition is prone to ideological and partisan bias. But it does

show some of the problems in Burke's view: if the same dynamic conception is applied to the complex and multifaceted EU, the difficulty in assessing interest congruence between the EU and Norway becomes readily apparent.

6 'Norgesvenn i EU opprørt over ostetoll' [A friend of Norway in the EU enraged over cheese tariffs], *Aftenposten.no*, 29 November 2012.

7 Ine Marie Eriksen Søreide, meeting in the European Consultative Committee, Stortinget, 7 March 2013 (author's translation).

8 For a comprehensive account of the development of the EP, see Rittberger (2005). See also Hix et al. (2007) and Smith (1999).

9 The structure in place at the EU level falls well short of parliamentarianism, in the sense that the European Parliament election procedure offers no clear safeguard for European citizens' voting preferences through parliamentary elections to carry direct implications for the composition of European government and the Commission as a non-elected body is endowed with a formal monopoly of proposing legislative acts.

10 For an overview of this structure see the various contributions in Crum and Fossum (2013).

11 In the constitutional realm this has – at least up to the crisis – manifested itself in a process of *constitutional synthesis* (see Fossum and Menéndez 2011).

12 This is probably best understood as an incremental process where EU legal provisions and institutional arrangements increasingly shape Norwegian governing arrangements, and where the substantive reach of EU policies shape those issue areas that have been explicitly removed from the agreements. On the latter, agriculture is a case in point (see Official Norwegian Report [NOU 2012:2]: 645ff.). On the former, agencification is a case in point. A similar point applies to EU programming of the Norwegian public administration (see Egeberg and Trondal, Chapter 10 in this volume). The dynamism built into the agreements coupled with the steadily increased scope of arrangements contribute to drive these processes.

13 In this context, it might sound surprising, as Holmøyvik underlines in Chapter 8 in this volume, that the Norwegian parliament has systematically favoured constitutional change procedures that *reduce* the threshold for acceptance. Such low thresholds devalue the currency of the Norwegian constitution, by subjecting key constitutional concerns to ordinary legislative procedures. At the same time, I show in the next section that such low thresholds is hardly very surprising given the dilemmas that Norwegian politicians face when dealing with the difficult EU question.

14 Popular referenda are more direct expressions of popular will than elections. In Norway, popular referenda are, formally speaking, consultative only.

15 Such bodies are typically 'strong publics' that is, bodies that combine an element of deliberation (as part of opinion formation) with decision-making (Fraser 1992).

16 This is related to Robert Putnam's (1988) argument to the effect that the two-level games associated with interstate diplomacy favour executives over parliaments, because the main EU bodies in question, the European Council and the Council, have their roots in international diplomacy.

17 When EU issues are handled through the member states' foreign policy apparatuses, a double mismatch arises: on one hand, the executive dominance traditionally associated with foreign policymaking marks the handling of these issues. On the other hand, the foreign policy apparatus is left to handle a host of issues that it lacks expertise in handling, and a great internal coordination problem arises.

18 Probably the main reasons why in Norway the main right-wing populist party, the Progress Party, has not capitalised on the EU membership issue is because the party has been divided on this issue and because several of the established parties were against EU

membership, faced weak or no internal opposition and could front this issue together with a strong 'No to EU' civil society movement.
19 Art. 102 of the EEA Agreement opens the scope for suspension of new provisions. See http://www.efta.int/media/documents/legal-texts/eea/the-eea-agreement/Main%20 Text%20of%20the%20Agreement/EEAagreement.pdf, last accessed 16 December 2014. The EEA Review Committee found that of all the issues dealt with by the Storting's European Consultative Committee in the period from 1994 to 2011, there were only 17 instances where the issue was raised (Official Norwegian Report [NOU 2012:2]: 830). This provision has still not been used.

## References

Bøckman-Finstad, F. (2014) 'Norges tilknytning til EUs justis- og innenrikspolitikk', in E.O. Eriksen and J.E. Fossum (eds) *Det norske paradoks – Om Norges forhold til Den europeiske union*, Oslo: Universitetsforlaget.
Burke, E. (1792) 'On the Subject of Roman Catholics of Ireland, and the Propriety of Admitting Them to the Elective Franchise, Consistently with the Principles of the Constitution as Established at the Revolution', A Letter from the Right Hon. Edmund Burke, M.P. in the Kingdom of Great Britain, to Sir Hercules Langrishe, Bart. M.P. Available at http://www.econlib.org/library/LFBooks/Burke/brkSWv4c6.html, last accessed 21 October 2014.
Chayes, A. and Chayes, A.H. (1995) *The New Sovereignty: Compliance with International Regulatory Agreements*, Cambridge, MA: Harvard University Press.
Claes, D.H. (2003) 'EØS-avtalen – mellom diplomati og demokrati', *Internasjonal Politikk*, 61(3): 275–302.
Crum, B. and Fossum, J.E. (eds) (2013) *Practices of Inter-Parliamentary Coordination in International Politics – The European Union and Beyond*, Essex: ECPR Press.
Fossum, J.E. (2010) 'Norway's European "Gag Rules"', *European Review*, 18(1): 73–92.
—— (2014) '"Surrogatrepresentasjon?, in Eriksen, E.O. and J.E. Fossum (eds) *Det norske paradoks – Om Norges forhold til Den europeiske union*, Oslo: Universitetsforlaget.
Fossum, J.E. and Holst, C. (2014) 'Norsk konstitusjonell debatt og europeisk integrasjon', in E.O. Eriksen and J.E. Fossum (eds) *Det norske paradoks – Om Norges forhold til Den europeiske union*, Oslo: Universitetsforlaget.
Fossum, J.E. and A.J. Menéndez (2011): *The Constitution's Gift: A Constitutional Theory for a Democratic European Union*. Boulder, CO: Rowman and Littlefield.
Fraser, N. (1992) 'Rethinking the Public Sphere: A Contribution to the Critique of Actually Existing Democracy', in C. Calhoun (ed) *Habermas and the Public Sphere*, Cambridge, MA: MIT Press.
Hegeland, H. (2011) 'The European Union as Foreign Policy or Domestic Policy? EU Affairs in the Swedish Riksdag', in T. Persson and M. Wiberg (eds) *Parliamentary Government in the Nordic Countries at a Crossroads*, Stockholm: Santérus Academic Press.
Hix, S., Noury, A.G. and Roland, G. (2007) *Democratic Politics in the European Parliament*, Cambridge: Cambridge University Press.
Holmes, S. (1995) *Passions and Constraint*, Chicago: Chicago University Press.
Keohane, R.O. (2002) 'Ironies of Sovereignty: The European Union and the United States', *Journal of Common Market Studies*, 40(4): 743–765.
Mair, P. (2009) 'Representative versus Responsible Government', MPIfG Working Paper 09/8, Cologne: Max Planck Institute for the Study of Societies.

Mansbridge, J. (2003) 'Rethinking Representation', *American Political Science Review*, 97(4): 515–528.
Nordby, T. and Veggeland, F. (1999) 'Lovgivningsmyndighetens suspensjon – Stortingets rolle under EØS-avtalen', *Tidsskrift for Samfunnsforskning*, 40(1): 87–108.
Official Norwegian Report (NOU) (2012:2) 'Outside and Inside: Norway's Agreements with the European Union', delivered to the Norwegian Ministry of Foreign Affairs, 17 January.
Olsen, E.D.H. (2014) '"Utenforskapets" paradoks: mot et depolitisert statsborgerskap?', in E.O. Eriksen and J.E. Fossum (eds) *Det norske paradoks – Om Norges forhold til Den europeiske union*, Oslo: Universitetsforlaget.
Olsen, J.P. and Sverdrup, B.O. (1998) *Europa i Norden – europeisering av nordisk samarbeid*, Oslo: Tano Aschehoug.
Parliament (2012) 'Parliament's Order of Business', enacted 7 June, no. 518.
Parliament White Paper no. 5 (2012–2013) The EEA Agreement and Norway's Other Agreements with the EU [Meld. St. 5 (2012–2013) EØS-avtalen og Norges øvrige avtaler med EU], Oslo: Ministry of Foreign Affairs.
Pitkin, H. (1967) *The Concept of Representation*, Berkeley: University of California Press.
Putnam, R.D. (1988) 'Diplomacy and Domestic Politics: The Logic of Two-Level Games', *International Organization*, 42(3): 427–460.
Rittberger, B. (2005) *Building Europe's Parliament*, Oxford: Oxford University Press.
Saglie, J. (2002) *Standpunkter og strategi – EU-saken i norsk partipolitikk 1989–1994*, Oslo: Pax.
Smith, J. (1999) *Europe's Elected Parliament*, Sheffield: Sheffield Academic Press.
Stavang, P. (2002) *Parlamentarisme og folkestyre*, 4th Edition, Bergen: Fagbokforlaget.
Strøm, K. (2003) 'Parliamentary Democracy and Delegation', in K. Strøm, W.C. Müller and T. Bergmann (eds) *Delegation and Accountability in Parliamentary Democracies*, Oxford: Oxford University Press.
Urbinati, N. (2014) *Democracy Disfigured: Opinion, Truth and the People*, Harvard, MA: Harvard University Press.
Weiler, J.H.H. (2001) 'Federalism without Constitutionalism: Europe's Sonderweg', in K. Nikolaïdis and R. Howse (eds) *The Federal Vision*, Oxford: Oxford University Press.
Wessels, W. (1997) 'An Ever Closer Fusion? A Dynamic Macropolitical View on Integration Processes', *Journal of Common Market Studies*, 35(2): 267–299.
Yarbrough, J. (1979) 'Representation and Republicanism: Two Views', *Publius*, 9(2): 77–98.

# 10
# NATIONAL ADMINISTRATIVE SOVEREIGNTY

## Under pressure

*Morten Egeberg and Jarle Trondal*

The Norwegian constitution states that Norway shall be an independent state. How this should be interpreted in practice in a world characterised by mutual dependence among states in a number of policy areas is less clear. Based on formal considerations, the assessment is somewhat easier; 'independent' can then mean the absence of formal supranationality in important policy areas. Through the European Economic Area (EEA) Agreement, Norway, in contrast to the member states of the European Union (EU), has steered away from formal supranationality. Despite the EU's supranational nature in most policy areas, it is still generally accepted that member states should enjoy a form of administrative sovereignty. This means that even though EU policies (e.g. in the form of laws) are created in a supranational way, it has still been mainly up to the national authorities to administer the required implementation. Given that EU's laws have been mainly supplied in the form of directives, this may have given national authorities ample room for adaptation in the implementation phase. There are many indications, however, that this administrative sovereignty is also under pressure, and this is expressed in at least three ways. First, we see a tendency for the European Commission, often supported by a rapidly growing number of EU agencies, to get directly involved in the ways in which EU legislation is to be applied by cooperating closely with national agencies (directorates and supervisory authorities), usually without incorporating national ministries to an equivalent extent. The EU's executive branch of government does not have its own agencies at the national level but seem instead to have strong ties to already relatively independent national agencies, which thereby adopt a 'two-hatted' role relative to their own ministry, on one hand, and to the European Commission and the EU agencies on the other. Thus, in a certain sense national agencies become part of two administrations: both a national and a general EU administration. This challenges the parliamentary chain of command, parliament–government–ministry–agency (see Olsen 1978). Second, there are signs that EU legislation in the form of regulations is applied more often, and this also results in less room of manoeuvre for national authorities in the implementation phase (Brandsma 2013: 11; Official Norwegian Report [NOU] 2012:2: 110). Third, the European Commission and certain EU agencies have the right to make binding decisions in certain individual cases (see Monti 2010). Taken together, this is assumed to lead to a more uniform implementation of EU's policies. In this chapter, however, we concentrate on the first point. We show in this chapter that the way in which the Norwegian administration functions in practice under the EEA Agreement does not appear to be essentially different from the way in which the member states' administrations function in the implementation phase. Thus, Norwegian 'administrative sovereignty' is under pressure.

In the next section, our aim is to theorise the national administration's role in the implementation of EU policies. After that, we shall empirically clarify administrative capacity building at the EU level, or what we also call the development of a new centre of executive power in Europe. In the next section we deal with the extent to which national agencies operate at arm's length from the ministries, where it is assumed that this plays a role in determining how close the connection to various EU authorities can become. This kind of connection becomes difficult if the ministry collaborates closely with the subordinate agency. Thereafter, we analyse the ways in which EU executive authorities, that is the European Commission and EU agencies, deal with the Norwegian central administration, that is ministries and agencies, when EU regulations are to be applied in Norway. Before we conclude this chapter, we also raise the question of how the EU affects the room for manoeuvre in national administrative policy. Which constraints does EU legislation impose on the Norwegian government's possibility of organising one's own administrative apparatus; for example, for moving the tasks of agencies (back) to the ministries if it becomes desirable to enhance the possibility of political control?

## Theoretical discussion of multilevel administration

International (governmental) organisations adopt regulations; for example, for handling cross-border trade, transport or environmental challenges. Nevertheless, it is up to the member states to decide whether they want to incorporate these regulations into their own legislation and, if they choose such an incorporation, to administer the application of the regulations in specific cases. Voluntary incorporation expresses formal state sovereignty, whereas *national control over the application of the regulations* expresses administrative sovereignty. When implementation of international regulations is left to the member states themselves, as described earlier, we call this 'indirect implementation'. Historically, the EU also initially adopted this form of implementation as its main form but with one important exception: the incorporation is not voluntary. The member states themselves, including the EEA countries, administer the ways in which the EU's directives are to be written into the texts of national laws, and national authorities are basically the ones who are supposed to administer the legislation in practice.

An important point in this chapter is that even though international organisations and the EU are basically parts of the indirect form of implementation, it is features of the EU's institutional structure that draw the practical implementation over to more 'direct implementation', that is that the EU's executive (the European Commission and the EU agencies) get involved in the member states' (and the EEA countries') application of the Union legislation and thereby challenge their administrative sovereignty. First, most international organisations only have one legislative function. The organisations' secretariats are installed to support this function. Thus, there is usually not any administrative capacity for executive functions, such as monitoring the implementation of international regulations at the national level. The EU is different. Here we find functional specialisation, which means that there are not just institutions for legislation (the European Parliament and the Council of the European Union), but also for executive power (such as the European Commission) and for judicial power (the Court of Justice of the European Union). The existence of executive bodies, such as the European Commission and the EU agencies, entails that there are bodies that specifically have the monitoring of implementation at the national level as one of their tasks, and compared with international organisations, they have the capacity in the form of staff to do so (Egeberg 2006; Trondal 2010).

Second, international organisations are mainly organised according to a territorial principle. This means that their governing structure reflects a political order based on geographical units, in this case nation-states. This is supported by the fact that, as a rule, it is representatives of the member governments who have seats in the most important bodies, often called councils of ministers. Thus, the political leadership in international organisations has its primary institutional affiliation at the national level, and this is assumed to mean that the representatives' loyalty will first and foremost be devoted to the latter and only thereafter to the respective international organisations as such (Egeberg 2012a). Thus, given the way in which international organisations are structured, there is little reason to assume that they will challenge the intergovernmental (international) system in any profound way. It is different with the EU's executive power. The European Commission's structure, organised from the top down by sector and function, does not give the member states as such an equivalently privileged access to the decision-making processes (Trondal et al. 2010). In addition, the political leadership in the European Commission, the commissioners, have their primary institutional connection to the European Commission. All in all, this means that they often base their decisions on supranational considerations (Egeberg 2012a). Therefore, in its interaction with national authorities, the European Commission may act with its own agenda to a different extent than may international organisations, whose agenda is to a much greater extent under the control of the member states themselves. In this way, the national administrative sovereignty is also challenged.

When the European Commission and the EU agencies are to carry out their tasks related to monitoring implementation at the national level, it is expected that they may seek cooperation with the bodies of those national authorities that administer the application of EU law. At the national level, this will often be agencies rather than ministries. During the last two decades, there has been a major outsourcing of tasks, including implementation tasks, from ministries to agencies. This wave of reform, often associated with New Public Management (NPM), has occurred to a greater or lesser extent in most western countries and has often been related to administrative policy initiatives from the Organisation for Economic Co-operation and Development or the EU (Christensen and Lægreid 2006). However, for a long time, a number of countries, including the Nordic countries, have had agencies outside of the ministries, relatively independent of NPM (Lægreid and Pedersen 1999; Verhoest et al. 2010). Since these administrative bodies work at arm's length from the ministries, not just formally but also in practice, for example by being less exposed to political control (Egeberg 2012b), it will hardly come as a surprise if the European Commission and the EU agencies are particularly oriented to deal with these bodies. Such bodies may appear to be particularly attractive collaborative partners. Thus, we can imagine that national agencies may seem to be wearing 'two hats': one for the ministry in charge and one for the EU executive (Egeberg 2006). Because the EU authorities are directly involved in the application of EU law at the national level, at the same time as they may have their own agenda, this puts the national administrative sovereignty under pressure. Centrifugal forces are introduced, not only within the member country (as claimed by the multilevel governance perspective, arguing that sub-national regions would connect themselves directly to the supranational level [Marks et al. 1996]), but also within the central administration of national governments. Therefore, the question is whether we see a tendency for national agencies to become parts of two administrations, both a national administration and an EU administration. In general, however, we know that two factors can enhance a ministry's control over a subordinate agency and thereby counteract co-optation from outside. First, this seems to be the case if the ministry includes units that overlap to some extent with the underling body's portfolio ('organisational duplication'). Second, this occurs through politicisation (measured by increased disagreement and conflict) in the policy area (Egeberg and Trondal 2009a).

## Empirical observations

This section discusses two necessary conditions that must be meet or challenged – capacity building in the EU's executive (section 1) and the relatively large amount of vertical specialization and autonomy national agencies have (section 2) – as well as administrative sovereignty (section 3).

### *1 Capacity building in the EU's executive*

The EU's executive consists of what we can call the administrative centre, which is composed of the European Commission and the new foreign affairs administration, the EEAS (European External Action Service). In addition, the EU's executive is extended EU agencies (Egeberg and Trondal 2011a).

### *Growth in the European Commission*

The administrative capacity of the European Commission, measured by number of employees, has gradually increased over a period of 60 years. As shown in Figure 10.1, the administrative capacity building in the European Commission has never been reduced at any point in time during this period. Despite public criticism of the Brussels bureaucracy – especially perhaps after the fall of the Santer Commission in 1999 – the European Commission's administration has grown continuously. Already in December 1958, the European Commission consisted of more than 1,000 civil servants (Bitsch 2007: 58; Dumoulin 2007: 219). Officially, the staffing of the European Commission was completed in 1961, but the growth in personnel reached 2,892 in 1967, and in 1972, the European Commission had a total staff of 5,778 (Dumoulin 2007: 220). Whereas the European Commission (the High Authority) in 1953 was dominated by national experts who had relatively short-term contracts, the staff of the European Commission has subsequently become dominated by civil servants with permanent employment and prospects of a lifelong career. Data shows, for example, that in 2000, 19 out of 22 directors general had more than 10 years' seniority in the European Commission (Georgakakis and Lassalle 2007: 12).

There are several reasons for the growth in the European Commission's administration. The increase in the number of member states in the EU is an important explanation. Since the last expansion, several thousand new civil servants have been recruited from the new member states (Kurpas et al. 2008: 46). Another reason has been the growth in the number of policy areas in which the EU has been involved. The increase in the EU's legislative and executive tasks has heightened the demand for increased administrative capacities in the European Commission for policy development and implementation. The European Commission has focused increasingly on the implementation of legislation.

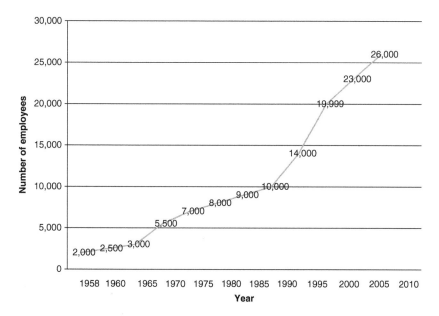

**FIGURE 10.1** Number of employees in the European Commission
*Sources*: Dumoulin (2007: 220); Stevens and Stevens (2001: 15).

In addition to internal administrative capacity building in the European Commission and in EEAS, the administrative capacity has also grown to an increasing extent outside of the European Commission. This capacity consists mainly of EU agencies, but in practice also national agencies. As we show in Section 3, Norwegian agencies have been granted a role that to some extent entails being 'direct' implementing authorities of EU legislation.

## *The growth of EU agencies*

The establishment of agencies at the EU level, so-called EU agencies, has mainly taken place during the last 20 years. The establishment of EU agencies may be regarded as a compromise between functional needs for more regulatory capacity at the European level, on one hand, and the member states' reluctance to transfer more power to the European Commission, on the other (Kelemen 2002). However, this growth – with regard to administrative capacity at the EU level – has not occurred at the expense of administrative capacity building inside the European Commission; during the same period, the European Commission has also undergone a considerable increase in the number of employees (see Figure 10.1). The size of the staff can tell us something about relative administrative capacity in these bodies. Whereas the European Commission has about 26,000 permanently employed civil servants (depending somewhat on which categories are counted), the EU agencies currently have about 5,000 civil servants. Thus, the agencies have gradually developed a substantial administrative capacity, though still not nearly as large as that of the European Commission. We also see a steady increase in the number of EU agencies, that new agencies that are established are delegated greater formal decision-making power (in individual cases) compared to older EU agencies, and that such bodies are established in relatively important policy areas. Since 2008, the growth in the number of EU agencies has accelerated. This growth is visualised in Figure 10.2.

Certain features of the agencies' organisation reflect some of the scepticism against a further enhancement of executive power at the European level. First, their mandate is often limited to tasks related to information processing and documentation, as well as facilitation of network activities among national regulatory authorities within the same policy area. Second, the agencies as a rule have a management board in which the composition is dominated by representatives for national authorities. As regards the first point, however, a questionnaire survey of the EU agencies' top officials indicates that as many as half of them spend much of their working hours on (quasi-)regulatory tasks such as making individual decisions, preparing individual decisions for the European Commission, issuing guidelines for the ways in which EU law shall be applied at the national level, being involved in national authorities' processing of individual cases and preparing new EU legislation (Egeberg and Trondal 2011a).

As regards the second point, the management boards' actual control over the agencies' activities should not be exaggerated either. Studies have indicated that both the substantial size of the boards and the relatively low frequency of their

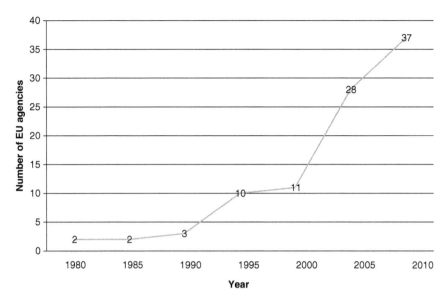

**FIGURE 10.2** Number of EU agencies
*Source*: Europa.eu/agencies/regulatory_agencies_bodies/policy_agencies/index_en.htm.

meetings limit their capacity to govern. There also appears to be a tendency for national representatives on the boards to be poorly prepared and that they are relatively little involved in the discussions (Busuioc and Groenleer 2012; Groenleer 2009). As a rule, the national representatives are the heads of the national agencies who work within the respective EU agencies' policy fields. Therefore, the board membership comes in addition to an otherwise demanding role. Compared with the ministry officials, agency officials are more shielded from signals from the political leadership (see the next section). Therefore, national delegates are not solely government representatives (Buess 2015). It is documented that the European Commission (which is also represented on the board) is the agencies' most important partner in their daily work. National ministries and the Council strengthen their influence when matters are politicised or given a clearer regulatory nature, but also under these conditions the European Commission remains the most important interlocutor for the agencies (Egeberg and Trondal 2011a). All in all, we interpret the role of EU agencies as constituting a supplement to the European Commission and thereby the development of executive power at the European level.

## 2 National agencies with a certain amount of independence from ministries

In contrast to national government, the European Commission and EU agencies do not have their own bodies at lower levels of governance. However, studies show that national implementing authorities, such as agencies, work so closely together with the previously mentioned EU bodies that national agencies are well on their way in practice to functioning as *direct* implementing authorities for EU legislation. In practice, this role challenges national administrative sovereignty more fundamentally than in the cases where the role of a national agency is primarily to function as an indirect implementing authority.

In addition to the assumption that an enhanced executive authority at the EU level is a necessary condition for the development of direct implementation (see the earlier discussion), it is also a necessary condition that national agencies are relatively independent in practice from national political leadership. Based on questionnaire surveys in the Norwegian central administration at three points in time (1986, 1996 and 2006),[1] we have studied how civil servants in the central administration perceive their relative independence from ministers (Egeberg and Trondal 2009a). This study reveals a considerable difference between civil servants in the ministries and those in agencies. Agency personnel appear less exposed to signals from the political leadership than ministry personnel. Professional considerations and expert concerns are regarded as important by a great majority at both administrative levels at all three points in time. User and client interests are also emphasised relatively strongly, especially among agency officials.

## 3 National administrative sovereignty under pressure

The findings so far (Sections 1 and 2) suggest that key conditions are present in order for national agencies to function in practice as 'direct' implementing bodies with regard to EU legislation. They are more autonomous from the national political leadership than the ministerial departments and there is considerable administrative capacity at the EU level for monitoring national implementation in practice. Based on the study of the Norwegian central administration from 2006, we show that among Norwegian agency personnel who are affected in any way by the EU, 61 per cent respond that the agency applies EU legislation in the employees own policy area. This application is not uncontroversial: 45 per cent of the ministry staff who have agencies that apply EU legislation in their own issue area report that the government has disagreed with the way it is applied (Egeberg and Trondal 2009b). Table 10.1 shows Norwegian civil servants' assessment of the *importance* of various bodies when it comes to influencing their own agency's application of EU legislation.

Employees of Norwegian ministries and agencies agree fairly much when it comes to assessing which bodies are important, thus strengthening the data's credibility. Both groups attach importance to the role played by agencies in applying EU legislation. Only the ministry in charge is regarded as somewhat more important. More than half of the respondents also regard the European Commission and ESA (combined) as important when it comes to exerting influence on the agencies' application of EU law. A higher percentage of the ministry employees regard ESA as important, and this may be related to the fact that ESA primarily contacts the ministry if there is any suspicion about insufficient follow-up of EU legislation.

**TABLE 10.1** Percentage of Norwegian civil servants who say that the following bodies are important when it comes to influencing the agency's application of EU legislation[a,b]

| Employed in | Ministry | Agency |
|---|---|---|
| Own ministry | 70 | 67 |
| Own agency | 64 | 66 |
| European Commission | 47 | 43 |
| EFTA Surveillance Authority (ESA)[c] | 58 | 36 |
| European Commission and ESA (combined) | 64 | 51 |
| 'Sister agencies' in other countries | 19 | 32 |
| EU agencies | 19 | 23 |
| Mean $N$ | 538 | 572 |

*Source:* The central administration survey 2006 (see note 1).

[a] The table includes the civil servants who report that their own agency applies laws and regulations that have their origin in EU decisions ('hard law') within their own issue area.

[b] The table combines values 1 and 2 on the following original value scale: very important (value 1), quite important (value 2), somewhat (value 3), quite insignificant (value 4), very insignificant (value 5), and don't know/irrelevant (value 6).

[c] ESA has the task of monitoring the implementation of EU legislation in the EEA countries: Iceland, Norway and Lichtenstein.

'Sister agencies' in other countries and EU agencies score considerably lower, but are not insignificant. Finally, there is a tendency for the same persons to assess different bodies as important *concurrently*; for example, those who assess the ministry as important also assess the European Commission as important (see Egeberg and Trondal 2009b). Thus, conflicting expectations may arise with regard to agency officials' application of EU legislation.

Nevertheless, if there is considerable conflict within a policy area, or if the ministry in question has organisational units that overlap with the agency's portfolio ('organisational duplication'), the percentage that characterise the ministry as important with regard to influencing the agency's application of EU law increases (Table 2). Whereas 62 per cent of the agency staff who experience little public debate and little duplication regard the ministry as important, the same is true of 90 per cent of those who experience both conflict and duplication. Table 10.2 reports how the application of EU legislation among civil servants in Norwegian agencies is determined by these factors.

Finally, Table 10.3 shows how the top leaders in Norwegian agencies perceive the content of the relations that their entities have with the European Commission and EU agencies and to the network of 'sister agencies' in other countries. Almost all of them think that there is an exchange of information, for example, about 'best practice', but a great majority of the agency heads also think that all three relations concern the formulation and discussion of guidelines and standards for the application of EU law, as well as the formulation and discussion of individual cases in connection with the application of EU legislation and programmes. The fact that this also seems to be the case with regard to EU agencies confirms what we reported in

**TABLE 10.2** Percentage of Norwegian agency officials who say that the ministry is important when it comes to influencing the agency's application of EU legislation,[a] controlled for the degree of public debate in its own policy area[b]

| Degree of public debate | Large degree | | Somewhat/little degree | |
|---|---|---|---|---|
| Organisational duplication[c] | Much | Little | Much | Little |
| The ministry is important | 90 | 84 | 77 | 62 |
| Mean N | (87) | (19) | (168) | (55) |

Source: The central administration survey 2006 (see note 1).

[a] This variable combines values 1 and 2 on the following original value scale: very important (value 1), quite important (value 2), somewhat (value 3), quite insignificant (value 4), very insignificant (value 5).
[b] This variable combines values 1 and 2 on the following original value scale: to a very large degree (value 1), to a fairly large degree (value 2) (*large degree of public debate*). This variable also combines values 3, 4 and 5: somewhat (value 3), to a fairly small degree (value 4), to a very small degree (value 5) (*moderate/little degree of public debate*).
[c] This variable combines values 1 and 2 in the following original value scale: yes, (overlapping department in the ministry in charge (value 1), yes, (overlapping) section in the ministry in charge (value 2) (*Much duplication*). This variable also combines values 3 and 4: yes, earmarked position(s) in the ministry in charge (value 3); no, no (overlapping) units and/or positions in the ministry in charge (value 4) (*Little duplication*).

**TABLE 10.3** Percentage of top leaders in Norwegian agencies who report about the relations that their own agency has with EU agencies, the European Commission and 'sister agencies' in other countries[a]

| | European Commission | EU agencies | Network of 'sister agencies' |
|---|---|---|---|
| Formulation and/or discussion of guidelines, standards, etc. when EU legislation and/or programmes are implemented | 93 | 77 | 89 |
| Formulation and/or discussion of individual cases when EU legislation and/or programmes are implemented | 71 | 69 | 82 |
| Formulation of new EU legislation and/or programmes | 82 | 50 | 67 |
| Exchange of information, 'best practice' | 97 | 94 | 100 |
| Mean N | 38 | 17 | 28 |

Source: Questionnaire survey of top leaders in agencies, 2008.[b]

[a] Percentage who report 'yes'.
[b] The survey was conducted among all top leaders of Norwegian agencies in 2008 in cooperation with the Norwegian Agency for Public Management and eGovernment (Difi). In total, 48 top leaders were asked to take part in the survey, 40 of whom responded (response percentage = 83 per cent).

the previous section about the task expansion in the direction of (quasi-)regulatory tasks in these agencies. In addition, formulation of new rules and measures constitutes part of the content of the contacts, though to a somewhat lesser extent with regard to the EU agencies.

A number of case studies that include Norwegian agencies confirm that there are relatively close, direct connections between them and the European Commission, EU agencies and 'sister agencies' in other countries, often through transnational networks linked to the particular policy field. The areas that have been studied so far are postal services and telecommunications (Myhre 2005), competition (Danielsen 2012; Solstad 2009; Stenby 2009; Støle 2006), food safety (Ugland and Veggeland 2006), environment (Martens 2006, 2008a; 2008b), chemicals (Gudbrandson 2011), statistics (Sverdrup 2006), pharmaceuticals (Vestlund 2009), railways (Stene 2010), shipping (Gulbrandsen 2011), aviation (Johannessen 2012), health (Søetorp 2012), data storage and privacy (Løkken 2011) and finance (Isaksen 2012). The fact that national agencies do not just deal with their own ministry when it comes to applying EU law but also to the European Commission, EU agencies and 'sister agencies' in other countries, increases the likelihood that national agencies may have to defend decisions that are in conflict with the wishes of their own government. To illustrate, while the Swedish government actively lobbied in Brussels to support a merger of Scania and Volvo, the Swedish Competition Authority, in close cooperation with the European Commission, opposed this kind of merger (Støle 2006: 98–99). The case studies show that the respective ministries are usually informed about the underlying agencies' network activities, including their relationship to the European Commission. The ministries usually forgo any attempts to control the networking activities, for example, by formulating instructions, and this suggests that there appears to be a relationship of mutual trust between Norwegian ministries and agencies. However, national agencies' room for manoeuvring to deal directly with the EU authorities when it comes to understanding how EU legislation is to be applied are limited by how controversial the matters are. Likewise, for the questionnaire surveys that were discussed earlier, case studies also show that politicisation tends to mobilise the ministry in charge (Isaksen 2012; Søetorp 2012). Even though Norwegian civil servants who participate in EU networks primarily perceive themselves as representatives of their agency, as experts in their field and as national representatives, we also see a tendency for them to express a certain amount of loyalty to a common European administration in their policy area (Myhre 2005; Vestlund 2009). For example, one of the respondents in the Norwegian Medicines Agency stated, 'I see that very much of the Norwegian Medicines Agency has become a part of the EU. Here in our department, we feel like a European department, the jargon is European technical terminology, and all of the professional work takes place in English [. . .] yes indeed, we feel pretty European. This is probably most true of the departments that have the most contact with the EU' (Vestlund 2009: 71).

## Administrative sovereignty in administrative policy

One question that arises is which implications the interweaving of national agencies with the EU's administration and networks might have for administrative sovereignty in national administrative policy. How free are national authorities to organise their own administrative apparatus? Can Norwegian politicians dismantle agencies, for example, if they should wish to do so? Since the middle of the nineteenth century, outsourcing a department from a ministry and transforming it into an agency outside of the ministry, as well as returning this kind of body back into the ministry, has been a key administrative policy instrument (Christensen et al. 2010: 56). In the cases where placing an agency within the ministry has been motivated by desires to increase the possibility of political control, there has also been a knowledge base for this kind of approach (see section 2 in this chapter). There is reason to assume that the interweaving of agencies with the EU's administration and networks will impose constraints on the use of this administrative policy instrument. For instance, the EU may have formalised requirements that there shall be an agency in an administrative area that is organised at arm's length from the ministry in question. We find this, for example, in the transport sector (Official Norwegian Report [NOU] 2012:2: 600) and in the finance sector, where only national supervisory authorities, such as the Financial Supervisory Authority of Norway and thus not the Ministry of Finance, have the right to attend meetings under the new EU agencies in the area of finance (Isaksen 2012: 5). In addition to formal rules, patterns of behaviour that have developed over time within EU networks will probably impose constraints on the room for manoeuvre for administrative reorganisation of the kind that is mentioned here.

In the last Norwegian Report to the Storting (the Norwegian parliament) on administrative policy (Parliament White Paper no. 19 2012–2013), the government emphasises its perception that there are both general and more specific administrative policy constraints from the EU. The constraints experienced in administrative policy are particularly related to the EU's request that member states (including Norway) shall have sufficient administrative capacity to enforce Union legislation. The more specific administrative policy constraints include administrative changes that will presumably have to be implemented in order to enforce particular EU laws (Parliament White Paper no. 19 2012–2013: 26).

## Conclusion

In many ways, the main model for implementation of EU law has been inherited from usual international organisations. In both cases, it is the national authorities that shall administer the implementation of international law, so-called indirect implementation. This has given national authorities a certain room for manoeuvre to adapt the 'downloaded' rules and their application to national and local conditions (see 'administrative sovereignty'). In this chapter, we have discussed how this model is challenged when it comes to the application of EU legislation. The indirect implementation is challenged in that (1) the EU is directly involved in the ways in which the Union law shall be applied nationally; (2) regulations are issued more often, and this gives national authorities less discretion in the application phase; and (3) application of Union law occurs in the European Commission itself or in EU agencies. In this chapter, we have focused on the first case.

We have proposed two necessary institutional conditions for the EU's direct involvement in the ways in which national authorities apply EU legislation.

The first condition is that the EU has administrative capacity at its disposal that makes it possible to monitor national implementation in practice. The second condition is that the national government institutions that administer the application of EU laws operate at arm's length from national political authorities, that is the ministries. We have shown empirically that both of these institutional conditions have been met in Norway. In contrast to international organisations, the EU has its own executive bodies (see the European Commission and EU agencies). During the last two decades, the EU's executive capacity has been substantially enhanced through the growth in the Commission as well as of EU agencies, which seem to be delegated more distinctly regulatory tasks. The EU agencies seem to have the European Commission and national agencies as their closest partners rather than national ministries. At the same time, we have shown that Norwegian agencies are somewhat shielded from their respective ministries, even though this shielding diminishes if policies are controversial. We have argued that the relative shielding allows these national agencies to enter more easily into a form of 'partnership' with the European Commission, EU agencies and 'sister agencies' in other countries.

Consequently, we have shown that the two assumed necessary institutional conditions for more 'direct implementation' have been met. We have also shown that there are in fact tendencies toward more direct involvement of EU authorities in the phase where national agencies apply Union law. The quantitative surveys reveal that national agencies can be described as 'two-hatted' in the sense that both their own ministry *and* the EU authorities are involved in the formulation of guidelines for exercising discretion and resolving individual cases. However, the ministry constitutes the most important hat and tend to strengthen its position in the triangle when matters are politicised. The many qualitative studies share this main observation. In addition, they show that Norwegian administrative staff can also feel like participants in two administrations: both a national and a European one. Finally, we have pointed out that the room for manoeuvre in national administrative policy – especially as regards the organisation of the relationship between ministry and agency – may have been substantially restricted due to the indicated development. What we have not discussed is how the actual sovereignty is not just the result of influence 'from above', but also of the possibility to exert influence on 'those above' (with regard to this last point, see Egeberg and Trondal 2011b; Official Norwegian Report [NOU] 2012:2: 164–197; Parliament White Paper no. 5 2012–2013).

In this chapter, we have concentrated on the ways in which the development in the EU's administrative system challenges administrative sovereignty at the national level. When it comes to determining how EU law shall be applied, the parliamentary chain of command (Parliament–government–ministry–agency) does not have absolute authority (see Olsen 1978). The European Commission, EU agencies and EU-administered network of 'sister agencies' are directly involved in this phase. We have not regarded it as our task here to assess whether or not less room for national adaptation is desirable. This kind of assessment would also have to take into consideration that more uniform implementation of Union law across international borders goes hand in hand with a reduction in national autonomy. It has also been shown that the participation of Norwegian officials in the EU's administrative system improves their competence (e.g. Søetorp 2012). Finally, it is noted that the cooperation may give more availability of resources and better resource utilisation.

## Note

1 The central administration surveys include questionnaire surveys of civil servants in all Norwegian ministries and agencies in 1986, 1996 and 2006. On each of these dates, all of the administrators in the ministries and one out of three administrators in the agencies were sent a questionnaire. Only civil servants at the executive officer level and higher positions were included in the surveys. For a more detailed presentation of the data, see Egeberg and Trondal (2009a).

## References

Bitsch, M.-T. (2007) 'The Hallstein Commission 1958–1967', in M. Dumoulin (ed) *The European Commission, 1958–72: History and Memories*, Brussel: European Commission.

Brandsma, G.J. (2013) 'Seeing the Forest for the Trees: Three Myths about the Number of European Union Legislative and Executive Acts', paper presented at the EGPA conference, Edinburgh, 11–13 September.

Buess, M. (2015) 'European Union Agencies and Their Management Boards: An Assessment of Accountability and Demoi-Cratic Legitimacy', *Journal of European Public Policy*, 22(1): 94–111.

Busuioc, M. and M. Groenleer (2012) 'Wielders of Supranational Power? The Administrative Behaviour of the Heads of European Union Agencies', in M. Busuioc, M. Groenleer and J. Trondal (ed) *The Agency Phenomenon in the European Union: Emergence, Institutionalisation and Everyday Decision-Making*, Manchester: Manchester University Press.

Christensen, T., Egeberg, M., Larsen, H.O., Lægreid, P. and Roness, P.G. (2010) *Forvaltning og politikk*, 3rd Edition, Oslo: Universitetsforlaget.

Christensen, T. and Lægreid, P. (2006) 'Agencification and Regulatory Reform', in T. Christensen and P. Lægreid (eds) *Autonomy and Regulation: Coping with Agencies in the Modern State*, Cheltenham: Edward Elgar.

Danielsen, O.A. (2012) 'The Composite Legitimization of Transnational Competition Governance: A Comparative Empirical Assessment', paper presented at the EGPA conference in Bergen, Norway, 5–8 September.

Dumoulin, M. (ed) (2007) *The European Commission, 1958–72: History and Memories*, Brussels: European Commission.

Egeberg, M. (ed) (2006) *Multilevel Union Administration: The Transformation of Executive Politics in Europe*, Houndmills: Palgrave Macmillan.

——— (2012a) 'Experiments in Supranational Institution-Building: The European Commission as a Laboratory', *Journal of European Public Policy*, 19(6): 939–950.

——— (2012b) 'How Bureaucratic Structure Matters: An Organizational Perspective', in B.G. Peters and J. Pierre (eds) *The Sage Handbook of Public Administration*, 2nd Edition, London: Sage.

Egeberg, M. and Trondal, J. (2009a) 'Political Leadership and Bureaucratic Autonomy: Effects of Agencification', *Governance*, 22(4): 673–688.

——— (2009b) 'National Agencies in the European Administrative Space: Government Driven, Commission Driven, or Networked?', *Public Administration*, 87(4): 779–790.

——— (2011a) 'EU-Level Agencies: New Executive Centre Formation or Vehicles for National Control?', *Journal of European Public Policy*, 18(6): 868–887.

―――― (2011b) Forvaltningsmessige konsekvenser av EØS/EU – Sentraladministrasjonen norsk og europeisk, Report to the EEA Review Committee no. 1, Oslo. Available at http://www.europautredningen.no/wp-content/uploads/2011/04/Rap1-forvaltning1.pdf, last accessed 18 December 2014.

Georgakakis, D. and de Lassalle, M. (2007) 'Who are the Directors-General? European Construction and Administrative Careers in the Commission', paper presented at EU-Consent workshop, Paris, 21–22 June.

Groenleer, M. (2009) *The Autonomy of European Union Agencies*, Ph.D. thesis, Amsterdam: Eburon.

Gudbrandson, S.S. (2011) *Reach: The Climate and Pollution Agency in a European Context*, Master's thesis, Institute of Social Sciences, University of Oslo.

Gulbrandsen, C. (2011) 'Europeanization of Sea-Level Bureaucrats: The Case of Ship Inspectors Training', *Journal of European Public Policy*, 18(7): 1034–1051.

Isaksen, H. (2012) *Finanstilsynet – utenfor og innenfor. En studie av Finanstilsynets arbeid med EU-regelverk*, Master's thesis, Institute of Social Sciences, University of Oslo.

Johannessen, M. (2012) 'When Global and European Regimes Meet: The Case of a National Civil Aviation Authority', paper, Department of Political Science, University of Oslo.

Kelemen, R.D. (2002) 'The Politics of "Eurocratic" Structure and the New European Agencies', *West European Politics*, 25(4): 93–118.

Kurpas, S., Grøn, C. and Kacsynski, P.M. (2008) *The European Commission after Enlargement: Does More Add up to Less?* Brussels: CEPS Special Report.

Lægreid, P. and Pedersen, O.K. (eds) *Fra opbygning til ombygning i staten. Organisationsforandringer i tre nordiske lande*, Copenhagen: Jurist- og Økonomforbundets Forlag.

Løkken, E. (2011) *Fristilt i Norge og integrert i Europa? En studie av Datatilsynets europeiske arbeid*, Master's thesis, Institute of Social Sciences, University of Oslo.

Marks, G., Hooghe, L. and Blank, K. (1996) 'European Integration since the 1980s: State-Centric versus Multi-Level Governance', *Journal of Common Market Studies*, 34(3): 341–378.

Martens, M. (2006) 'National Regulators between Union and Governments: A Study of the EU's Environmental Policy Network IMPEL', in M. Egeberg (ed) *Multilevel Union Administration: The Transformation of Executive Politics in Europe*, Houndmills: Palgrave Macmillan.

―――― (2008a) 'Administrative Integration through the Back Door? The Role and Influence of the European Commission in Transgovernmental Networks within the Environmental Policy Field', *Journal of European Integration*, 30(5): 635–651.

―――― (2008b) 'Runaway Bureaucracy? Exploring the Role of Nordic Regulatory Agencies in the European Union', *Scandinavian Political Studies*, 31(1): 27–43.

Monti, M. (2010) 'A New Strategy for the Single Market: At the Service of Europe's Economy and Society', report to the president of the European Commission José Manuel Barroso, Milano: Università Commerciale L. Bocconi.

Myhre, C. (2005) 'Nettverksadministrative systemer i EU? En studie av det norske Post- og teletilsynet'. ARENA Report 05/9, Oslo: ARENA.

Official Norwegian Report (NOU) (2012:2) 'Outside and Inside: Norway's Agreements with the European Union', delivered to the Norwegian Ministry of Foreign Affairs, 17 January.

Olsen, J.P. (1978) 'Folkestyre, byråkrati og korporativisme', in J.P. Olsen (ed) *Politisk organisering*, Bergen: Universitetsforlaget.

Parliament White Paper no. 5 (2012–2013) The EEA Agreement and Norway's Other Agreements with the EU [Meld. St. 5 (2012–2013) EØS-avtalen og Norges øvrige avtaler med EU], Oslo: Ministry of Foreign Affairs.

Parliament White Paper no. 19 (2012–2013) A Public Administration Promoting Democracy and Community [Meld. St. 19 (2008–09) Ei forvaltning for demokrati og fellesskap], Oslo: Ministry of Government Administration, Reform and Church Affairs.

Søetorp, Ø. (2012) *Påvirkning gjennom medvirkning? En studie av Helsedirektoratets arbeid med EUs politick*, Master's thesis, Institute of Social Sciences, University of Oslo.

Solstad, S.G. (2009) 'Konkurransetilsynet – et sted mellom Norge og EU?' ARENA Report 5/09. Oslo: ARENA.

Stenby, O.C. (2009) *Europeisering av Konkurransetilsynet. En studie av Konkurransetilsynets deltakelse i transnasjonale nettverk*, Master's thesis, Institute of Administration and Organisational Studies, University of Bergen.

Stene, J. (2010) *Mot en europeisk fellesadministrasjon? En studie av Statens jernbanetilsyns arbeid med EUs politick*, Master's thesis, Institute of Social Sciences, University of Oslo.

Stevens, A. and Stevens, H. (2001) *Brussel Bureaucrats? The Administration of the European Union*, Basingstoke: Palgrave Macmillian.

Støle, Ø. (2006) 'Towards a Multilevel Union Administration? The Decentralization of EU Competition Policy', in M. Egeberg (ed) *Multilevel Union Administration: The Transformation of Executive Politics in Europe*, Houndmills: Palgrave Macmillan.

Sverdrup, U. (2006) 'Administering Information: Eurostat and Statistical Integration', in M. Egeberg (ed) *Multilevel Union Administration: The Transformation of Executive Politics in Europe*, Houndmills: Palgrave Macmillan.

Trondal, J. (2010) *An Emergent European Executive Order*, Oxford: Oxford University Press.

Trondal, J., Marcussen, M., Larsson, T. and Veggeland, F. (2010) *Unpacking International Organisations: The Dynamics of Compound Bureaucracies*, Manchester: Manchester University Press.

Ugland, T. and Veggeland, F. (2006) 'The European Commission and the Integration of Food Safety Policies Across Levels', in M. Egeberg (ed) *Multilevel Union Administration: The Transformation of Executive Politics in Europe*, Houndmills: Palgrave Macmillan.

Verhoest, K., Roness, P.G., Verschuere, B., Rubecksen, K. and MacCarthaigh, M. (2010) *Autonomy and Control of State Agencies: Comparing States and Agencies*, Houndmills: Palgrave Macmillan.

Vestlund, N. (2009) 'En integrert europeisk administrasjon? Statens legemiddelverk i en ny kontekst'. ARENA Report 4/09, Oslo: ARENA.

# 11

# REINFORCING EXECUTIVE DOMINANCE

Norway and the EU's foreign and security policy

*Helene Sjursen*

When Norwegian citizens voted 'no' to EU membership, the idea that it would be possible to conduct a foreign policy that was different from that of the European great powers if the country remained outside the Union was important.[1] Nevertheless, Norway has entered into a set of separate agreements with the EU in the domain of foreign and security policy. In this chapter I discuss the nature and extent of these agreements, and assess their implications for sovereignty and self-rule.[2] Is Norway's affiliation to the EU in this domain problematic from a democratic perspective? And if so, why?

The implications of Norway's affiliation to the EU in the domain of foreign and security policy are assessed with reference to the two democratic principles of autonomy and accountability, as outlined in the introductory chapter (Eriksen and Fossum). The requirement of autonomy pertains to the ability of those affected by laws also to be their authors. As for the principle of accountability, it pertains to the possibility of citizens to hold those in power responsible for what they do (see Eriksen in Chapter 5). These principles, which are linked to the concept of popular sovereignty, might be considered to yield unrealistic expectations of citizen influence in foreign and security policy. The main objective here is usually considered to be the protection of state sovereignty, which presumes the executive's capacity to act. Nevertheless, in a constitutional democracy we assume that also foreign and security policy is democratically legitimate. The particularity of foreign and security policy does not justify a neglect of the question of democracy. Rather, this particularity makes it all the more important to discuss and scrutinise how the principles of autonomy and accountability are understood and realised in this specific context.

In the first part of the chapter, I briefly identify the constitutional arrangements and procedures that actually apply to Norwegian foreign and security policy. Focus is directed specifically to how the principles of autonomy and accountability are balanced against the need for action capacity. In the second part I examine the main features of Norway's policy towards the EU in this domain. I find that in the making of this policy the balance has tipped even more in favour of action capacity and executive dominance. In the third part, I discuss to what extent it is possible to find acceptable reasons for the prioritisation of action capacity from the perspective of democracy. And in the fourth and final part I suggest that although it may be difficult to justify this prioritisation from a principled perspective, it is easily explained.

## Autonomy and accountability in Norwegian foreign and security policy

Art. 25 and 26 of the Norwegian constitution make foreign, security, and defence policy an executive prerogative. As Andenæs writes, executive prerogatives are remnants of a system of separation of powers which otherwise abandoned with the transition to a parliamentary system (Andenæs, was cited in Stavang 2002: 98). The transition to parliamentarism in itself does not, however, require these competences to be exercised by the legislative assembly. And the executive's right to govern is indeed still the overriding principle in Norwegian foreign and security policy. The executive signs treaties and declares war 'for the defence of the country'. Pursuant to the constitution, the government also has so-called command authority and therefore decides how Norwegian armed forces will be used.

Norwegian constitutional experts are ambivalent in their reading of the constitution in matters of foreign and security policy. The prevailing opinion is that parliament, given the constitutional prerogatives, may most likely not give the government binding orders regarding the formulation of foreign policy (Andenæs and Fliflet 2008: 301). Parliament must confine itself to parliamentary leverage or possibly bring a no-confidence motion against the government. At the same time, constitutional experts argue that parliament's influence is stronger than what the constitution's text indicates. The standard understanding seems to be that 'according to the constitution, it is the government that decides the country's foreign policy – naturally not against the will of parliament and naturally in accordance with parliament's position on the main dimensions of the country's foreign policy' (e.g. see Castberg, cited in Stavang 2002: 102). Also, legal analyses emphasise that '[p]arliament's position [will] appear politically binding for the government' (Stavang 2002: 301), despite the fact that the parliament's powers are formally limited.

In the following I suggest that the opposite is the case: parliament has taken a passive role in foreign and security policy. It is rather the government's position that appears binding on parliament. Decision-making processes in Norwegian foreign and security policy rest on a series of consensus-making mechanisms designed to facilitate efficient decision-making and thereby strengthen the executive's capacity to ensure state sovereignty. Few mechanisms secure free and open critical debate, which is a condition for citizens' ability to make informed choices and form an opinion regarding the best course of action. This makes it difficult to establish whether policy is in accordance with the will of the people (see the principle of autonomy). It also means that the possibilities of controlling the executive and holding it to account are more limited than in domestic politics.

Parliament's Committee on Foreign Affairs and Defence is responsible for budgetary matters. It is also charged with preparing cases for plenary discussion. International treaties or agreements regarded as being 'of major importance' must, according to Art. 26, be ratified by parliament. All treaties must be presented for review. However, treaty making is only a small part of foreign and security policy. Consequently, a large part of what the executive does in this policy area escapes parliament. By comparison, the Danish constitution has more wide-ranging requirements for parliamentary involvement (Holmøyvik 2014). According to Art. 19 of the Danish constitution, the government cannot undertake any 'action [. . .] of major importance' without the consent of the Danish Parliament, and the executive is obliged to confer with 'the foreign policy committee (den utenrigspolitiske nævn) [. . .] prior to any decision with wide-ranging implications'.

The formal limitations on parliament's opportunity to influence the whole spectrum of foreign policy are somewhat compensated for in that the government informs parliament of its activities in various ways. Parliament receives written reports, amongst other things on Norway's relationship with international organisations such as the North American Treaty Organization (NATO), the Council of Europe and the Nordic Council of Ministers. Moreover, the minister of foreign affairs presents semi-annual reports to parliament. These reports may highlight changes in focus or emphasise new and emerging issues that are considered to be of relevance to Norway. Thus, they are important sources of information regarding the direction and priorities of Norwegian foreign policy. But these reports seldom raise controversial issues or present new information. They are merely taken note of and rarely the subject of much debate in parliament. Most important, however, there is a significant difference between issuing routine reports on general issues and presenting and discussing concrete (and potentially controversial) questions. Thus, these exchanges of information do little to change parliament's generally limited role in foreign and security policy.

The Enlarged Committee on Foreign Affairs and Defence (DUUFK) was established in 1923, to facilitate more general discussions between the executive and legislative branches.[3] The purpose of establishing this committee was to give parliament a role in formulating and controlling foreign policy, something the parliament did not have prior to 1923. Thus, the committee considers 'important questions concerning foreign policy, trade policy, security policy' (Section 16 of Parliament's order of business, Parliament 2012). But the establishment of DUUFK does not really strengthen the possibilities for free and open critical debate regarding foreign and security policy. The executive's dominant position remains. The committee, which consists of the ordinary members of the Foreign Affairs Committee and the Defence Committee, the parliament's president and the leaders of all party groups, is merely consultative. It does not make decisions, nor does it control the executive. Furthermore, discussions within the committee are secret. Minutes of the meetings are recorded but do not become publicly available until 30 years have passed, and the members of the committee sign a declaration of confidentiality. As for the agenda for the meeting, it is (in principle) publicly available, but it may be kept secret.

A minority of six DUUFK members may request the release of cases for debate in an open session of parliament, but this rarely happens. When it does happen it is difficult to understand why the debate was assigned to DUUFK in the first place. A well-known example from recent times concerns the decision regarding Norwegian participation in military operations in Afghanistan in 2001. The debate was moved to an open parliamentary session on the initiative of the Socialist Left Party and the Progress Party.[4] The Labour Party's Thorbjørn Jagland and the Conservative Party's Jan Petersen opposed this move (Sølhusvik 2012: 378–379).[5]

Given the secrecy, there are very few analyses of the committee's role. There is little publicly available knowledge on what is discussed, how it is discussed, whether there is disagreement among the committee members or between the committee and the government, and how these disagreements are resolved. Based on the little that we do know it seems that the committee is subordinate to the executive. Usually, meetings open with a statement by the minister of foreign affairs. It is followed by contributions from the political parties in a sequence agreed upon prior to the meeting: 'The form is more like a delivery of positions' (Sjaastad 2006: 31). The few analyses that do exist of the internal processes in DUUFK point out that the committee is hierarchically organised and that there is little critical debate (Løvold 2002, 2004; Sjaastad 2006). There are seldom any preparatory case papers. At the end of the meeting, agreement is reached on what may be said publicly.

Based on this knowledge, however limited, it is difficult to regard DUUFK as a decisive factor in the parliamentarisation of foreign and security policy. Rather, DUUFK ensures a continuous cooperation between the government and parliament (Colban 1961: 31–48). It is both a 'parliamentary body' and a 'governmental body' (Sjaastad 2006: 45, note 21). The role of DUUFK in limiting rather than encouraging critical debate is also indirectly confirmed by scholars of constitutional law: 'That the consultations [in DUUFK] lessen the potential for parliamentary control and criticism, and contribute to increased political consensus and compromise in foreign policy, however, can hardly be called negative' (Sejersted 2002: 591).

Thus, it is only in the Committee on Foreign Affairs and Defence that open, public exchange of arguments regarding the government's choice may potentially take place. But the challenge is not only that the constitution to a limited extent opens for parliament's influence. Parliament itself has established a practice that differs from that in the other committees. There is inter alia a close cooperation between the chair of the Committee on Foreign Affairs and Defence and the Minister of Foreign Affairs, also when the chair belongs to the opposition. As a result of this cooperation, the basis for debate is often cleared away before a case reaches the committee: 'the normally close and confidential relationship between the Minister of Foreign Affairs and the chair of the Foreign Affairs Committee, who often comes from the opposition, means that the government may sort out tricky issues informally' (Sjaastad 2006: 28).

In addition, a large number of decisions are made outside both DUUFK and the Committee on Foreign Affairs and Defence. As Olav Fagerlund Knudsen (1995: 73) writes, '[o]ne does not convene DUUFK without good reason. In Norway this arrangement is therefore supplemented by an informal practice, whereby the MFA consults the parliamentary leaders on matters that are not important enough to warrant formal procedures such as convening DUUFK'. Limited access to information and debate in the legislative also has ripple effects for the broader public sphere. According to Fagerlund Knudsen, it is thus that 'much of what captures people's attention in foreign policy [can] in reality be window dressing. The really significant matters – seen from Norwegian interests – do not necessarily receive the equivalent public attention' (Fagerlund Knudsen 1995: 65).

As long as parliamentarism is the main principle of the Norwegian political system, one may perhaps assert that '[e]ven though foreign policy is still the King's (the government) prerogative, the government is just as dependent on parliament in this policy area as in other areas' (Andenæs and Fliflet 2008: 308). But this general principle is not necessarily reflected in day-to-day policymaking. To assess parliament's real influence, it is necessary to look at the practice of policymaking. To the extent that there is social scientific research on this topic, it appears that a range of mechanisms ensures that the government receives the support it needs from parliament without much discussion or opposition (Fagerlund Knudsen 1995; Løvold 2002; Sjaastad 2006). Although *in principle* the government depends on parliamentary support, *in practice* it may be quite certain that it will get the support that it requires.

The executive's freedom of action is often legitimated by the claim that there is a consensus on major issues in Norwegian foreign policy.[6] However, with regard to Norway's relations with the EU, we know that there is no such consensus. Does that mean there is more consultation and that all possibilities for debate and critique are used when Norway affiliates itself with the EU's foreign and security policy?

## Norway and EU foreign and security policy

Norway participates in much of what the EU does in foreign and security policy. When, in the early 1990s, it was expected that the EU's security and defence policy would be handled by the Western European Union (WEU), Norway became an associate member of this European military alliance.[7] Norway routinely aligns with the EU's foreign policy declarations and common positions. Norwegian authorities usually accept the EU's invitations to contribute to or participate in crisis management operations. It tops the list of third countries that participate in the EU's operations. Furthermore, Norway is part of one of the EU's so-called battle groups. Consequently, Norwegian troops have been on standby for the EU three times, in 2008, 2011, and 2015. Moreover, Norway also participates in a number of the projects of the European Defence Agency (EDA).

Norway's participation in the EU's foreign, security, and defence activities is regulated by international agreements of various designation. Adherence to the EU's foreign policy statements, interventions in international organisations, for example, as well as alignment with the EU's restrictive measures (sanctions) is regulated through a declaration on political dialogue and is included as an appendix to the EEA Agreement. Cooperation with the EDA is regulated through a so-called administrative agreement between the Norwegian Ministry of Defence and the EU.[8] Norway's contributions to the EU's crisis management operations are regulated through a framework agreement.[9] A chronological overview of Norway's agreements with the EU in the domain of foreign and security policy is provided in Table 11.1.

An international agreement is generally regarded as a contract that does not affect citizens directly and that has limited influence on national legislation and national decision-making processes. It is therefore not common for agreements to affect the democratic chain of government. With one exception, namely the 2005 agreement on participation in the EU's battle groups, this is also true for the agreements between Norway and the EU in the domain of foreign and security policy.

Nevertheless, as conveyed in the first part of the chapter, such international agreements require the consent of the parliament if they are 'of particular importance' (Art. 26). Prior to the parliamentary vote there must be a written proposition and a recommendation from the relevant parliamentary committee. The question of which procedure to apply is not a mere legal formality. An issue will be subject to far more thorough consideration through the procedure contained in Art. 26 than if it is discussed, for example, in connection with a more general foreign policy report. The use of Art. 26 is therefore also in line with the autonomy principle. The problem is that there is no precise definition of 'particular importance'. It is therefore left to parliament itself to identify those agreements that, in their view, necessitate the use of procedures in Art. 26 of the constitution (assuming the executive does not choose to present the agreement in accordance with this procedure). Given the

**TABLE 11.1** Norway's agreements with the EU in the domain of foreign and security policy

1988 – informal consultation arrangement between Norway and the Presidency
1992 – associate member of the Western European Union
1994 – declaration on political dialogue as part of the EEA Agreement
2000 – dialogue on security and defence policy
2001 – agreement between Norway and the EU regarding the establishment of the EU's satellite centre
2002 – agreement on Norwegian participation in the EU's police operation in Bosnia
2003 – agreement on Norwegian participation in the EU's military operation in Macedonia
2004 – agreement between Norway and the European Union on security procedures when exchanging classified information
2004 – agreement on Norwegian participation in the EU's police operation in Macedonia
2004 – framework agreement on Norwegian participation in the EU's crisis management operations
2005 – agreement on Norwegian participation in an EU battle group
2006 – cooperation agreement between Norway and the European Defence Agency

increase in the number of international legal agreements, it is a challenge not only for the Norwegian parliament but also for many other national parliaments to keep track.

The evaluation of whether or not the government must or should request parliamentary consent is based just as much on political considerations as on legal or constitutional considerations. This is so as parliament has usually been considered as responsible for determining the precise meaning of 'particular importance'. This makes the evaluation emphatically political.[10] What status should then be given to Norway's agreements with the EU in the domain of foreign and security policy? Can they be understood as particularly important? If so, on what grounds? And what procedures have been applied when Norway has entered into these agreements?

## *Insignificant legal agreements of particular political importance?*

When the EU's efforts to form its security policy gained momentum in the middle of the 1990s, Norwegian authorities openly expressed concern about the consequences for Norway (Sjursen 1999). Norway already had some bilateral agreements with the EU in this domain, but entered into several new ones in the wake of the new changes.

The agreement on associate membership in the WEU, which had been signed in 1992, was perceived as especially decisive to Norwegian interests. This was so because as an associate member, Norway received the same access as full members to discussions regarding the future organisation of the EU's security policy. Norwegian authorities emphasised their wish to utilise the associate membership 'to the maximum'.[11] At the same time there was a concern that something might upset the agreement:

> If the WEU was to be fully integrated in the EU, as is now proposed, a range of difficult questions would be raised inter alia for the countries – such as Norway – that do not participate in the EU co-operation, but that participate in the WEU. It will lead to a more closed co-operation instead of laying the basis for a broad European security co-operation. But if the EU becomes the governing organ of the WEU, it will be necessary to develop suitable association arrangements for the countries that are members of NATO, but not members of the EU.
> (Bjerke 1995)

Likewise, the other agreements with the EU, such as the declaration on political dialogue, have been described as decisive for Norwegian interests. These agreements do not place obligations on the EU. They have no consequences for the substance of EU policy, or for the EU's internal decision-making processes. The agreement on political dialogue, for example, only promises routine meetings where Norway (and a number of other states) is informed of EU developments. Still, from the Norwegian perspective they are considered *politically* important:

> The opportunity to join or associate with EU initiatives, declarations, and statements regarding foreign policy questions of common interest, is of great

value. We have already used this opportunity on several occasions and evaluate on a continuous basis how and in which manner we can participate.

(Bjerke 1995)

The *legal/constitutional* implications of the agreements are fairly limited also for Norway. Norwegian authorities decide for themselves whether they will accept the EU's invitations to participate in, align itself with, or contribute to policy. At the same time, these agreements are the only formal tools available to the executive when relating to the EU in the domain of foreign and security policy. This is why the agreements are described as politically important:

> The Government places [...] great emphasis on developing the tightest and closest possible connections with the EU on all matters, including the domain of foreign and security policy.
>
> (Bjerke 1995)[12]

The fact that the agreements have limited constitutional implications helps explain why they have not been presented to parliament under the provision contained in Art. 26 of the constitution. Yet, as the interpretation of Art. 26 requires discretionary evaluations, and the executive describes the agreements as politically important, it would not be unreasonable to expect that at least the more extensive agreements were presented to parliament through procedures in Art. 26.

The agreement on Norwegian participation in the EDA is one example of such an extensive agreement. Previously, European cooperation on defence materials was organised under the auspices of NATO, and thereafter the WEU. When it was transferred to the EU in 2004, Norway went from being a full member to non-membership. This was described as dramatic for Norwegian interests:

> From the Norwegian perspective it is serious that we can be in a situation where we on a strategic level have no access to any co-operation organisations on defence materials in Europe.
>
> (Parliament Proposition no. 42 2003–2004: 41)

Norway's diplomatic efforts to achieve an agreement with EDA were massive and the failure to achieve full membership in the agency was a disappointment.[13] The agreement that was finally reached sets clear limits to Norwegian participation. Parliament was informed of the government's efforts to establish such an agreement with the EU (Parliament Proposition no. 1 2004–2005: 54; Parliament Proposition no. 1 2005–2006: 67).[14] However, the agreement is not listed in the Ministry of Foreign Affairs' treaty register, nor has it been discussed as a separate case in parliament. It must therefore be assumed that it has not been subject to parliamentary approval in accordance with Art. 26.

The framework agreement on Norway's contribution to the EU's crisis managements tasks were also not presented to parliament in accordance with Art. 26. The minister of defence, Kristin Krohn Devold, did report to Parliament on the agreement in 2004, but it was not followed by much debate.[15] Every time Norway decides to participate in an EU operation, a specific agreement is also made. It has not been possible to find evidence of any of these agreements having been presented to parliament in accordance with Art. 26. Nevertheless, the contributions to EU-led operations are described as politically important, and Norway accepts as many invitations to participate as possible. Indeed, between 2002 and 2012, Norway contributed to 10 EU-led operations (of a total of 24).[16]

Norway's associate membership in the WEU is a third agreement that cannot easily be rejected as insignificant. The question of Norway's relation to the WEU was discussed in parliament on various occasions (see the Budget – Parliamentary Recommendation no. 7 1992–1993). In 1991, representatives from the Conservative Party suggested that Norway should apply for full membership in the WEU.[17] Only the Conservative Party and the Progress Party were in favour. The idea of applying for associate membership, on the other hand, gained the support also of the Labour Party. The Socialist Party and Centre Party were opposed, while the Christian People's Party would only support this if it gave Norway the possibility, but not the obligation, to participate in WEU operations.[18] The Labour Party's official justification for going against full membership was that there was considerable confusion regarding the direction of developments within NATO, the European Economic Community (EEC) and the WEU. Surprisingly, when associate membership was debated this argument was not perceived as relevant although the future of WEU-EEC-NATO relations remained unsettled. According to historian Rolf Tamnes, the 'real' reason for the Labour Party's rejection of the idea of full membership in the WEU was that it wanted the question of membership in the EC (EU) to be resolved before any public debate regarding the WEU. (Tamnes 1997: 238).

An 'association document' was signed at the WEU's ministerial meeting in Rome on 20 November 1992, and parliament was informed in the spring of 1993. It was emphasised that the agreement 'is a political document that does not entail binding international obligations for Norway' (Parliament White Paper no. 47 1992–1993: 29). It was not considered as a separate matter by parliament, and because it is not considered binding in accordance with international law, it has not been possible to trace the agreement in the Ministry of Foreign Affairs' treaty register.

In sum, the most important mechanisms for ensuring scrutiny and debate on matters of foreign and security policy have not been used to discuss Norway's agreements with the EU in this domain. This is not unusual. Norwegian participation in military actions in Libya in 2011 was, for example, decided on by mobile phone. After deciding that there was agreement in government, the parliamentary leaders for the opposition parties were consulted (by telephone). The DUUFK only met to discuss the matter three days after the decision to despatch fighter aircrafts to Libya had been made (Sølhusvik 2012: 378–379).

The executive usually makes foreign and security policy without much interference from parliament. Relations with the EU in this domain are no exception. In one particular case, however, parliament has gone even further than it usually does in giving the executive freedom to act. This raises questions for both popular sovereignty and state sovereignty.

## *Adverse effects on state sovereignty?*

The agreement on participation in the EU's battle groups, which was signed in 2005, has been the subject of more debate and attention in parliament and the media than the other agreements. The reason is that it was unclear whether or not this agreement entails an obligation on Norway to participate in EU operations. Thus, this agreement raises more complex constitutional questions than the other agreements. Together with Sweden, Finland and Estonia, Norway is part of a so-called Nordic Battle Group. This force participates in a rotating arrangement with the EU's other battle groups. As the battle groups are integrated forces, each participant country contributes with a specialised part.

The Norwegian government had not planned for an open parliamentary debate on this agreement but wished to discuss it in DUUFK. However, the opposition required the matter to be taken out of DUUFK and put to an open debate. The government presented its intentions to parliament in 2004, and votes were made regarding a motion put forward by the Socialist Left Party to reject participation. The motion was defeated.[19] After concluding the agreement, the minister of defence returned to parliament and reported on the specifics of its content. It was accepted by a majority of the votes.[20] However, while parliament debated the matter thoroughly, Art. 26 was not used.[21] Thus, the procedure was less extensive.

Formally speaking, the agreement does not challenge Norway's sovereignty (Holmøyvik 2012). As emphasised by government officials, a decision on participation in a concrete operation shall be made nationally. However, because the battle groups are integrated forces, they depend on the participation of all parties. A 'no' from Norway would thus bring the entire operation to a halt. The potential political pressure on Norway's involvement would most likely be strong also because of the fact that only two forces are on standby at a time. In reality then, this agreement obliges Norway to deploy military forces when and where the EU wants it to.

In his contribution during the 3 June 2005 parliamentary debate, Labour Party Representative Thorbjørn Jagland confirmed his full awareness of the difficulties involved in refusing participation in an operation:

> We must admit that we become interwoven in a military co-operation that naturally binds us more than has been the case with other international operations.[22]

Jan Petersen from the Conservative Party also accepted this premise, as is evident in the exchange of views with a Progress Party representative in a parliamentary debate on 20 November 2007:[23]

> Per Ove Width: Thank you for the report. It was good and clear. Even if one does not need to be in agreement with everything, I understood what was said. I also understand that before things begin to escalate, the minister of Defence will return to parliament and present further details [. . .].

Jan Petersen: I think that many of the bridges that Representative Width believes he will cross, he has in fact already crossed by accepting this agreement. Therefore, what we would probably evaluate, if it gets that far, is considerably more limited than what he implies. It is also important to emphasise that when Norway has said yes to participating in the Nordic Battle Group in a larger European context, it is clear that one does not start at point zero when the clearly defined operation comes before parliament.

## *Prioritising action capacity*

Norwegian citizens had their say regarding Norway's relation to the EU in the referendum in 1994. Afterwards, the executive has been left to manage relations with the Union without much interference. If it had been up to Norwegian authorities alone, the relationship with the EU would have been even more extensive. We see this, for example, from the Parliament White Paper no. 12 (2000–2001), where it was stated that

> [i]n the government's opinion the consultation arrangements, dialogue, and assistance in defined crisis management operations can only to a limited degree compensate for Norway not being part of the continuous consultations [within ESDP].

Similar viewpoints came to light, inter alia in connection with a follow-up of the decisions contained in the Maastricht Treaty (1992):

> As the Minister of Defence, I can nevertheless not omit to note that the EU's intergovernmental conference in 1996 can be of great significance to our interests. Our lack of participation in this conference is therefore a paradox and part of the price we pay daily for the fact that we are outside the EU.
> (Kosmo 1996)

Paradoxically, it is not the citizens' elected representatives that have prevented the executive from entering into more extensive agreements. The EU sets limitations by maintaining a clear division between the Union's members and non-members. Sjaastad's (2006: 19) observations regarding parliament's view of its role in foreign policy in general thus also applies to the relation to EU in this domain: 'Parliament's main task does not consist [therefore] in exercising constitutional control over the government, but in supporting the government's policy'.

As the agreements are not perceived as significant from a purely legal perspective parliament's role can be limited. Yet, because Art. 26 rests on a discretionary evaluation of what is particularly important, parliament could also have chosen to be more active. In line with the executive's own descriptions of several of these agreements, parliament could have considered them so important that they required parliamentary consent in accordance with Art. 26. But parliament may have had good reasons not to insist on a more thorough scrutiny. Three possible reasons must be considered.

## In line with tradition?

### A continuation of alliance policy?

Norway's affiliation to the EU in the domain of foreign and security policy is often described as a mere continuation of its alliance policy. If this is what it is, perhaps there is no particular need to scrutinise it?

In the post-war period, Norwegian foreign and security policy became closely interwoven in various co-operative relationships on a regional and global level. Membership in NATO was central (Berg 2008). Together with Nordic cooperation, NATO remains the key reference for Norwegian security and defence policy. Moreover, Norway cultivates close bilateral ties, especially with the United States, Germany, and the UK.

Thus, the agreements made with the EU in the domain of foreign and security policy may indeed be seen as a maintaining bilateral and multilateral ties, in particular to the member states of NATO. After all, Norway's Nordic allies are now all members of the EU. With the exception of Turkey, Albania and Iceland, all of Norway's European NATO allies are also EU members. The informal European co-operation that previously took place within NATO, such as within the Eurogroup and the Independent European Programme Group has now been moved to the EU.[24] Thus, one could argue that by entering into these various agreements with the EU, Norway simply maintains existing cooperation with its NATO allies.

However, there are several problems with this understanding of Norwegian policy. First, the EU is a separate political entity and not merely the European branch of NATO. Although most of the EU's member states are also NATO members, the EU's foreign and security policy is something other than NATO's policy. The policy is formulated and justified with reference to the EU's interests and values. With the Treaty of Lisbon (2007) the EU also achieved legal personality, which gives the Union an independent status in international law.

The EU's foreign and security policy is also something more than the sum of the policies of individual member countries. As a result of their EU membership, Norway's allies are bound together in a community that alters their policies as well as their relations to other states. This is so even though the EU's foreign and security policy is formally intergovernmental. Participation in the Common Foreign Security Policy (CFSP) binds member states to common principles that are based on the EU's interests and values (Hillion 2014; Sjursen 2011; Wessel 2014). There is a continuous, daily exchange of information where ideas and positions wrestle with one another on various levels in the administration and among political decision makers. These processes are different from traditional diplomatic relations, and they entail the formation of common positions beyond the 'national interests' of each state.

Thus, Norway's agreements with the EU in the domain of foreign and security policy are not simply agreements with Norway's NATO-allies. Rather, they are agreements with a separate polity. A concrete expression of this can be seen in the framework agreement for participation in the EDA's projects, which was signed by High Representative Javier Solana and not by the member states. A second problem with seeing Norway's relations with the EU in the domain of foreign and security policy as a mere continuation of its NATO membership is that the conditions for co-operation are fundamentally different. Norway is only included in the EU's activities after the political decisions regarding what to do and how to do it are made. Furthermore, it is not part of the ongoing political discussions that define longer-term priorities. It joins in when the policy line is already established. This also applies to Norway's contribution to the EU's crisis management operations, where strategic deliberations and decisions regarding each operation are undertaken before issuing an invitation for external contributions.[25] The same goes for the agreement with EDA, which does not allow for Norwegian involvement in the 'political' part of the cooperation.[26] The difference in conditions for participation in NATO and in the EU's foreign policy activities is seen most clearly in the contribution to the EU's battle groups. Here, there is an informal understanding that Sweden will represent Norway in the discussions in the European Council on how and when the force is to be used. Apparently no one had thought through how this would work in practice.[27]

Arguably such differences in the conditions for participation are mere formalities. Surely, a small country such as Norway does not have much of a say within NATO, even if it is a full member? This argument only holds if we consider that relations between allied states are governed by size and material power alone. In fact, participation in the decision-making process provides opportunities to influence the outcome by using competence, convincing arguments and to ally with others who share one's interests or values.

Finally, and on a slightly different note, on might argue that Norwegian policy towards the EU in the domain of foreign and security policy actually represents change rather than continuity. Norwegian alliance policy after World War II was chiefly oriented towards the US. Norwegian governments took no interest in the debates about European integration that took place in the 1950s, and there was never any question of Norway supporting a purely European defence plan (Eriksen 2008). On the contrary, Norwegian foreign policymakers often spoke of Norwegian foreign policy in contrast to the policies of Europe's 'belligerent Great Powers'. From this perspective the conscious attempts to achieve a close connection to the EU in the domain of foreign and security policy, especially since the mid-1990s, can be seen as a change in policy. In fact, the element of change is visible in that while Norwegian authorities have been persistent in pursuing close relations with the EU in this domain, they have also been deeply sceptical to the very idea of an autonomous EU foreign and security policy. When EU security policy cooperation gathered speed in the middle of the 1990s, Norwegian authorities used every opportunity to argue against constructing an independent security policy within the EU (Sjursen 1999). While trying to secure access to the process, they also believed that such a common policy would not materialise and hoped that the entire project would fail. The very establishment of a purely European institution dealing with security and defence goes against the Atlantic orientation of Norwegian security and defence policy.

Lately, however, added nuances have appeared to the Norwegian perspective. This is visible in, for example, the parliamentary debate on Norway's contribution to the EU battle groups. Here, members of several political parties described the EU's security policy as important and as a valuable contribution to the UN's agenda for global security (Sjursen 2008). To the extent that such perspectives have become generally accepted, they would represent a considerable change from the idea of the EU as carrier of belligerent 'Great Power Policies'.

But parliament's passivity with regard to this issue might be explained by the fact that there is agreement on what should be done – that there is consensus. In that case, why not just let the executive do its job?

## *Policy based on consensus?*

Because there has been so little questioning of this policy, can't we simply assume that it rests on consensus?

The problem with such an assumption both with regard to Norwegian foreign policy in general, and with regard the particular issues analysed in this chapter, is that a consensus is supposed to be preceded by a free, open and critical debate. Norwegian foreign policy decisions are taken according to procedures that limit criticism and debate. 'Consensus' is created through closing the debate or by co-opting key actors. Thus, it is not possible to know if a qualified consensus exists or, indeed, if we are rather faced with an illusory agreement.[28]

What is more, references to consensus on foreign policy are often ambiguous: they are used to show that the policy has legitimacy. But when, at the same time, it is repeated that consensus is decisive to protect the national interest, it becomes a means for curbing debate. An example of how the consensus requirement is applied to temper critical debate may be found in parliament's discussion of the situation in Iraq in 2002. Here, representatives of the Labour Party and the Conservative Party stressed the importance of national cohesion, in the face of questions asked by the Socialist Left Party (SV). A representative from the Conservative Party stated,

> On the other hand, I feel a certain need to further emphasise what Thorbjørn Jagland opened and closed with, namely the value and significance of having a united parliament as much as possible behind the main lines in the foreign policy carried out by the government.[29]

And the representative further stated,

> Let me first thank Thorbjørn Jagland for his clear answer and clear confirmation that for his part he evaluates it as essential that we are capable of preserving the predictability and stability in Norwegian foreign policy on the part of parliament as well.[30]

Kristin Halvorsen (SV) replied as follows:

> But I cannot fathom and understand why it should, in the Norwegian Parliament, be unheard of and indelicate to discuss the serious developments that are now seen.[31]

In sum, it is difficult to merely assume that consensus exists. In fact, consensus-making mechanisms at work in Norwegian foreign policymaking processes may contribute to cover disagreement on controversial issues. Yet, parliament might have legitimately chosen not to meddle because of a need for rapid decision-making, or to protect the interests of other states?

## A legitimate need to ensure action capacity?

There is naturally a certain legitimacy to prioritising action capacity in foreign and security policy, where secrecy and quick decisions are often needed. There is no time to wait for lengthy parliamentary debates in the midst of an international crisis. Information from allies is also processed, information that is often confidential and cannot be used in a public debate. But it is difficult to see that such considerations are relevant for Norway's relation to the EU in the domain of foreign and security policy.

Limitations on open debate are typically connected to the notion that foreign policy is ultimately about state survival. The executive is regarded as custodian of the national interest in the face of an anarchical international system. In line with such notions, parliament chooses to support rather than oppose the executive:

> Open disagreement is regarded not only as a strategic problem but as a threat to Norway's role in the world. [...] Instead of politicising – through control and critical questions – parliament contributes to de-politicising.
> (Sjaastad 2006: 20)

But the idea of a national interest has always been a fable. This becomes even more evident in today's security context. What should be done is not given, as it is assumed when reference is made to national interests. In foreign policy one can choose to prioritise a range of different interests and values: Industry, environmental organisations, fishermen and fish farmers, for example, will often have different opinions about what the 'national interest' should be. When one is not faced with matters of state survival, but matters requiring complex evaluations and value judgements, then there is a need for open reflection. In reference to Norway's relation to the EU in the domain of foreign and security policy, this is not an issue of state survival. Neither is it possible to see that there were specific needs for secrecy or rapid decision-making in the negotiation of these agreements.

## Paradoxes in foreign policy

When it remained outside the EU, there was an expectation that Norway would develop a distinct foreign and security policy and that non-membership would better ensure both state and popular sovereignty. But the executive has instead sought to ally itself with the EU. Parliament has in no way attempted to prevent, alter or question this strategy. The search for connection points to the EU in foreign and security policy has not resulted in any substantive changes in Norwegian foreign policy. The similarities between Norwegian and EU policies are too important.

However, the policymaking process suffers from democratic weaknesses, and it is difficult to find legitimate grounds for the parliament's decision to take a passive role. Nevertheless, it is not difficult to understand *why* this policy has been developed.

First and foremost, the Norwegian policy signals a perceived need to compensate for a loss in action capacity. Second, it points to a desire for recognition of Norway as part of Europe.

With the development of the EU's foreign and security policy the external context of Norwegian foreign and security policy has been transformed. The executive's access to relevant information regarding developments in European security, as well as regarding the viewpoints of close allies has become more limited. The agenda set by the EU in foreign and security policy inevitably affects Norway. This became particularly evident in the Ukraine crisis of 2014. The Norwegian executive's ability to influence policy is more limited due to the interaction within the EU. Norway aligned itself with EU restrictive measures towards Russia but did not have any influence on the definition of those measures. Norway is excluded from participation in decision-making processes that it was previously part of as a member of NATO. One way of understanding Norwegian policy is thus that it aimed at regaining some control over external conditions. Nevertheless, the effect must be seen as limited and policymakers are well aware of this.

Quite possibly, then, the policy may also be driven by a concern for recognition (Wendt 1999). A state's foreign policy identity is defined through a process of mutual recognition that also provides the basis for solidarity between states. In parallel with the development of the EU's foreign and security policy, new institutional boundaries have been drawn in European security policy. The various associational arrangements and agreements that Norway has entered into with the EU in this domain demonstrate the importance of these boundaries, as they clearly distinguish between members and non-members. The frustration conveyed by Norwegian authorities by finding themselves on the outside of these borders may thus be the result of foreign policymakers' perception of Norway as belonging on the inside. Formally, Norway has gone from being one of 'us' to being one of 'the others' in European security policy. The policy can therefore be understood as a search for recognition of Norway's rightful place inside a European security community. And while the agreements that have been entered into do not always render a large gain in the form of real influence, they do provide a certain recognition of Norway as part of the European 'family'.

Paradoxically, however, the result of the executive's endeavours to increase action capacity (or reduce the effect of lost action capacity) and to secure recognition is that both state sovereignty and popular sovereignty are weakened.

## Conclusion

According to Norwegian authorities, Norway is independent of the EU in foreign and security policy. Insofar as the EEA Agreement does not cover this domain, the claim is formally correct. However, Norwegian governments have sought to establish as close an affiliation as possible with the EU's foreign and security policy. This fact testifies, if not to a de facto dependency, then at least a strong perception of loss of influence and relevance in the European context on the part of Norwegian foreign policymakers. In particular the agreement on Norwegian participation in one of the EU battle groups comes close to establishing precisely the kind of dependence that the majority of Norwegian citizens sought to avoid by voting 'no' to EU membership. This hegemony, which is unintended by the EU, weakens the democratic anchoring of Norwegian foreign and security policy.

Norwegian foreign and security policy is usually defined by the executive. But, with regard to relations with the EU in this domain, the executive has had an even freer hand than what is usual. Parliament has been passive, and the citizens have been sitting on the sidelines. They know little about what assessments are made and on what grounds. Consequently, the basis on which they form their viewpoints on what should be done is skewed.

While the policy-making procedure is problematic from a principled perspective, the policy-choices make are not difficult to explain. Norway remains a European state and this fact inevitably influences the policy options available to the Norwegian executive when developing national foreign and security policy. This becomes particularly evident with the 2014 crisis in Ukraine. The special needs of foreign policy are not sufficient to justify setting aside the democratic principle that citizens have the right to exercise influence over decisions that affect them. This case confirms the need to review the drawing of boundaries for when closed doors and secrecy is needed to develop an effective foreign and security policy and when open reflection is required. It should indeed be possible also in the case that has been examined here to combine the interests of efficiency and the need for a degree of secrecy with greater co-determination.

## Notes

1 This chapter addresses Norway's relationship with the system that governs the traditional arenas of foreign and security policy as well as defence policy, that is the so-called Common Foreign and Security Policy (CFSP).
2 The analysis draws on relevant secondary literature in law, history and politics, as well as propositions to the Parliament and Parliament White Papers during the period from 1991 to 2011 that directly address Norway's relationship to the EU, foreign policy reports by the minister of foreign affairs (1996–2011) and EU/EEA reports (2007–2011), speeches by representatives of the Ministry of Foreign Affairs (MFA) and the Ministry of Defence (MOD) and the MFA's work programmes for CFSP (2006–2011). Furthermore, systematic searches have been made of the MFA's treaty register, the government's and parliament's databases and the media database Atekst. Some interviews have also been carried out with MOD and MFA representatives. Unless otherwise stated, the citations are intended as examples of statements and arguments that have been retrieved systematically from the previously mentioned texts, and not as exceptions to them. I am extremely grateful to Guri Rosén and Johanne Døhlie Saltnes for their assistance in this work.
3 Originally named the Enlarged Committee on Foreign Affairs, it was renamed the Enlarged Committee on Foreign Affairs and Defence.

4 See 'Afghanistan. Possible Norwegian Force Contributions', matter handled on 30 November 2001 in DUUFK and brought before parliament in pursuant of parliament's Rule of Procedure 13, final paragraph on 5 December 2001.
5 See also Eirik Holmøyvik (2012) for a legal evaluation of the requirements made by the Progress Party and Socialist Left Party in this case. According to Holmøyvik, neither the constitution nor constitutional custom suggests that parliamentary approval is required to send Norwegian forces to Afghanistan during Operation Enduring Freedom.
6 See, for example, the final debate at the Ministry of Foreign Affairs' conference entitled 'Norway and the New World Map', Oslo, 22 May 2013 available at http://www.reg jeringen.no/nb/dep/ud/lyd_bilde/nett-tv-2/refleks_verdenskart.html?id=726903, last accessed 27 January 2015.
7 'Document on Associate Membership of WEU of the Republic of Iceland, the Kingdom of Norway and the Republic of Turkey', Rome, 20 November 1992. Sent by e-mail from the Ministry of Foreign Affairs Treaty and Documentation Department, 16 May 2013.
8 'Administrative Arrangement between the Ministry of Defence of the Kingdom of Norway and the European Defence Agency', Innsbruck, 7 March 2006. Ministry of Defence Case no. 0500445–6.
9 'Agreement between Norway and the European Union on the Establishment of a Framework for Norway's Participation in the European Union's Crisis Management Operations', Brussels, 3 December 2004. Available at the Ministry of Foreign Affairs Treaty Register, http://www.lovdata.no/traktater/, 'Ident 03–12–2004 no. 48 Bilateral', last accessed 27 January 2015. Those agreements that are considered binding by international law are published in the treaty register, however, there may be long time lags between the treaty ratification and its appearance in the register. Also, the appearance in the register does not signify that the treaty has been presented to parliament through Art. 26.
10 Thanks to Holmøyvik for clarifying this point. See also Smith (2012: 274).
11 See Minister of Defence Jørgen Kosmo (1995).
12 In addition to these formal channels, Norwegian authorities also seek informal access to the EU's foreign and security policy (Sjursen 1999, 2008).
13 Interview with three different representatives of the Ministry of Defence in Oslo and Brussels in the spring of 2011.
14 Relations with the EDA were addressed in chapter 5 – Informational matters – of propositions to the Norwegian parliament regarding budgetary matters, as one of a series of items, including the description of trends in international cooperation on defence materials.
15 'Statement to the Storting by the Minister of Defence on the Possible Norwegian Participation in the EU's Battle Groups, and Framework Agreement on Norway's Participation in EU Civilian and Military Crisis Management Operations', 30 November 2004.
16 Five of these operations were police operations, two were peacekeeping and three were military operations.
17 The proposal is found in Parliament Recommendation no. 195 (1990–1991).
18 Parliament Recommendation no. 7 (1992–1993: 5–8).
19 Supra note 15 and 'Debate on the Defence Minister's Statement on Norwegian Participation in the EU's Battle Groups and the Framework Agreement on Norway's Participation in EU Civilian and Military Crisis Management Operations', debate in the Storting on 3 December 2004.
20 Debate in the Storting on the defence minister's statement on the EU's battle groups, advanced storage, and further participation in Afghanistan, 3 June 2005.
21 For a more detailed analysis of the reasons for parliament's acceptance of the agreement, see Sjursen (2008).
22 Supra note 20.

23 Statement to the Storting by the minister of defence on the status of Norwegian participation in the Nordic Battle Group, 28 November 2007.
24 The Independent European Programme Group was established in 1976. In 1993 it was connected to the WEU and changed its name to the Western European Armament Group (WEAG). WEAG was abolished with the establishment of the EDA.
25 In cases where Norway has a so-called significant contribution to the EU's operations, Norway will participate in the contributor committee. The committee is responsible for the daily management of the operation. But strategic leadership and political control remains with the Political and Security Committee or the European Council, where Norway is not represented. Likewise, Norway does not have access to the EU's discussions on EU operations that draw on NATO's resources. The 2003 Berlin Plus agreement between the EU and NATO does, however, provide Norway with a right to participate in such operations.
26 Norway does not have access to the meetings of the working groups. It is granted a meeting with the chairs of some of the working groups after they have concluded their internal business.
27 Interviews with representatives of the Ministry of Defence and Ministry of Foreign Affairs in Brussels and Oslo, summer 2011.
28 For a discussion of different types of consensus, see Eriksen and Weigård (2003).
29 Debate in the Storting on the foreign minister's statement on current foreign policy issues, 17 October 2002.
30 Supra note 29: 210.
31 Supra note 29: 213.

## References

Andenæs, J. and Fliflet, A. (2008) *Statsforvaltningen i Norge*, Oslo: Universitetsforlaget.
Berg, R. (ed) (2008) *Selvstendig og beskyttet: Det stormaktsgaranterte Norge fra Krimkrigen til NATO*, Bergen: Fagbokforlaget.
Bjerke, S. (1995) 'EUs Regjeringskonferanse fra et Norsk synspunkt' [The EU's Intergovernmental Conference from a Norwegian Perspective]. Seminar on the EU Intergovernmental Conference 1996, organised by the European Commission Delegation in Norway, on 27–28 September. Available at http://www.regjeringen.no/nb/dokument arkiv/regjeringen-brundtland-iii/ud/Taler-og-artikler-arkivert-individuelt/1995/eus_ regjeringskonferanse_fra_et.html?id=261355, last accessed 16 December 2014.
Colban, E. (1961) *Stortinget og utenrikspolitikken*, Oslo: Universitetsforlaget.
Eriksen, E.O. and Weigård, J. (2003) *Understanding Habermas: Communicative Action and Deliberative Democracy*, London: Continuum Press.
Eriksen, K.E. (2008) 'På vei mot Atlanterhavsalliansen', in R. Berg (ed) *Selvstendig og beskyttet: Det stormaktsgaranterte Norge fra Krimkrigen til NATO*, Bergen: Fagbokforlaget.
Fagerlund Knudsen, O. (1995) 'Beslutningsprosesser i norsk utenrikspolitikk', in G.M. Sørbø, S. Gjerdåker and T.L. Knutsen (eds) *Norges utenrikspolitikk*, Oslo: Cappelen.
Hillion, C. (2014) 'A Powerless Court? The European Court of Justice and the Common Foreign and Security Policy', in M. Cremona and A. Thies (eds) *The ECJ and External Relations: Constitutional Challenges*, Oxford: Hart Publishing.
Holmøyvik, E. (2012) 'Bruk av norske styrkar utanfor Noreg – statsrettslege utfordringar i fortid og notid', *Jussens venner*, 47(3): 184–215.
——— (2014) 'Grunnlova og avtalene med EU: Pragmatismens siger, det konstitusjonelle demokratiets tap', in E.O. Eriksen and J.E. Fossum (eds) *Det norske paradoks: Om Norges forhold til den Europeiske Union*, Oslo: Universitetsforlaget.

Kosmo, J. (1995) 'Norges forsvar – hvor står vi – hvor går vi?' [Norwegian Defence: Where Are We, Where Are We Going?], speech at Oslo Military Society on 9 January. Available at http://www.regjeringen.no/nb/dokumentarkiv/regjeringen-brundtland-iii/fd/Taler-og-artikler-arkivert-individuelt/1995/taler_-norges_forsvar,_hvor_star.html?id=261280, last accessed 16 December 2014.

—— (1996) 'NATOs framtidige rolle i Europa' [NATO's Future Role in Europe], speech at Forsvarets Høyskole on 18 March. Available at http://www.regjeringen.no/nb/dokumentarkiv/regjeringen-brundtland-iii/fd/Taler-og-artikler-arkivert-individuelt/1996/natos_framtidige_rolle_i_europa.html?id=261629, last accessed 16 December 2014.

Løvold, A. (2002) *Innenriks/utenriks. Den utvidete utenrikskomitéen som skaper og opprettholder av utenrikspolitisk konsensus*, Master's thesis, Department of Political Science, University of Oslo.

Parliament (2012) 'Parliament's Order of Business', enacted 7 June, no. 518.

Parliament Proposition no. 42. (2003–2004) 'The Further Development of the Armed Forces during 2005–2008' [St. prp. nr. 42 (2003–2004) Den videre moderniseringen av Forsvaret i perioden 2005–2008], Oslo: Ministry of Defence.

Parliament Proposition no. 1. (2004–2005) 'For the Fiscal Period 2005' [St. prp. nr. 1 (2004–2005) For budsjetterminen 2005], Oslo: Ministry of Defence.

Parliament Proposition no. 1. (2005–2006) 'For the Fiscal Year 2006' [St. prp. nr. 1 (2005–2006) For budsjettåret 2006], Oslo: Ministry of Defence.

Parliament Recommendation no. 195 (1990–1991) 'Recommendation from the Foreign and Constitutional Committee' [Innst. S. nr. 125 (1990–1991) Innstilling frå utenriks- og konstitutsjonskomiteen], Oslo: Stortinget.

Parliament Recommendation no. 7 (1992–1993) 'Recommendation from the Parliamentary Defence Committee' [Innst. S. nr. 7 (1992–1993) Innstilling fra Stortingets forsvarskomité], Oslo: Stortinget.

Parliament White Paper no. 47 (1992–1993) 'On the Collaboration in the North Atlantic Treaty Organisation in 1992' [Meld. St. 47 (1992–1993) Om samarbeidet i Atlanterhavspaktens organisasjon i 1992], Oslo: Ministry of Foreign Affairs.

Parliament White Paper no. 12. (2000–2001) 'Norway and Europe at the Dawn of a New Century' [Meld. St. 12 (2000–2001) Om Norge og Europa ved inngangen til et nytt århundre], Oslo: Ministry of Foreign Affairs.

Sejersted, F. (2002) *Kontroll og konstitusjon: Statsrettslige studier av Stortingets kontrollvirksomhet*, Oslo: Cappelen Akademisk Forlag.

Sjaastad, A.C. (2006) 'Stortinget som utenrikspolitisk organ', in B.K. Fonn, I.B. Neumann and O.J. Sending (eds) *Norsk utenrikspolitikk i praksis – aktører og prosesser*, Oslo: Cappelen Akademisk Forlag.

Sjursen, H. (1999) 'Med ryggen mot Europa? Endring og kontinuitet i norsk sikkerhetspolitikk', in D.H. Claes and B.S. Tranøy (eds) *Utenfor, annerledes og suveren? Norge under EØS-avtalen*, Bergen: Fagbokforlaget.

—— (2008) 'Fra bremsekloss til medløper: Norge i EUs utenriks- og sikkerhetspolitikk', *Nytt Norsk Tidsskrift*, 25(4): 323–332.

—— (2011) 'Not so Intergovernmental After All? On Democracy and Integration in European Foreign and Security Policy', *Journal of European Public Policy*, 18(8): 1078–1095.

Smith, E. (2012) *Konstitusjonelt demokrati*, Bergen: Fagbokforlaget.

Sølhusvik, L. (2012) *Kristin Halvorsen. Gjennomslag*, Oslo: Cappelen Damm.

Stavang, P. (2002) *Parlamentarisme og folkestyre: Utvalde statsrettslege emne*, Bergen: Fagbokforlaget.

Tamnes, R. (1997) *Oljealder. 1965–1995. Norsk utenrikspolitikks historie*, Oslo: Universitetsforlaget.

Wendt, A. (1999) *Social Theory of International Politics*, Cambridge: Cambridge University Press.

Wessel, R.A. (2014) 'The Dynamics of the European Union Legal Order: An Increasingly Coherent Framework of Action and Interpretation', *European Constitutional Law Review*, 5(1): 117–142.

# PART III
# Sovereignty under hegemony

# 12

# THE UNITED KINGDOM, A ONCE AND FUTURE(?) NON-MEMBER STATE

*Christopher Lord*

On 23 January 2013 David Cameron became the first prime minister of a member state to promise his country a referendum on whether it should remain a member of the European Union. Under Cameron's proposal the British government would, in some undefined way, renegotiate the terms of the UK's participation in the European Union (EU) and then hold a referendum on continued membership by 31 December 2017. If a British exit (Brexit) happens, it will test, for the first time, the politics and practicalities of disentangling a state from its membership of the Union. It will no less obviously create an entirely new category of 'ex-member state'. That would be a challenge for both the UK and the Union. The UK would need to decide how to relate to the EU as an ex-member state. The Union would need to decide what relationship it is prepared to allow the UK. Both will face costs and uncertainties of separation. Some on both sides will perceive new opportunities. All will be wary of a new relationship that just perpetuates the troubles of the old one.

Now, it is possible to see Britain's flirtation with exit as one more sign of its historic inability to make up its mind about Europe. But that would be a mistake. There has, in fact, been a remarkable historical continuity in Britain's relationship with European integration since 1950. Even when the UK was 'out' (1950–1973), its governments did not want to be completely 'out'. Ever since the UK has been 'in' (1973– ) it has not, as will be seen, ever been completely 'in'. Moreover, the same themes ran like red threads through both forms of equivocation. Questions of sovereignty, international power, political economy and deep domestic divisions have changed in their content many times over since 1950. Throughout, though, they have formed a quadrilemma – of four factors that are hard to reconcile – in whatever complicated relationship the UK has had at any one time with the process of integration.

Until recently even proposals for Brexit attempted to deal with the quadrilemma within some continuing relationship with the EU. Few argued that the UK should withdraw from the EU without seeking continued access to its single market.

In contrast, many supporters of Brexit now argue that the UK should be prepared to do just that. Rather than accept the sovereignty costs incurred by Norway or Switzerland, many supporters of Brexit now argue that the UK should only seek such access to the single market within the framework of a free trade agreement (fta) of a kind that really would allow the UK to determine its own policies and laws unencumbered.

To evaluate just how far that would depart from previous British policy, this chapter compares the suggestion that the UK should settle for a free trade agreement with decisions taken at previous critical junctures in Britain's relationship with European integration. In the second section, I present the proposal to settle for a free trade agreement as one of four alternative 'futures' for Britain and the EU. In the third and fourth sections, I discuss previous 'in–out' decisions, namely the UK decision to abstain from the European Coal and Steel Communities (1950–1952) and its accession to the European Communities (1970–1975). Then I return to the suggestion that the UK should now substitute a free trade agreement for full membership of the Union in the fifth section. To ensure consistency, I discuss assumptions made in each case about sovereignty, international power, political economy and domestic politics in sections three through five.

Put methodologically the chapter operates as a longitudinal case study. Doubtlessly, other member states have had similar difficulties with European integration. But few have experienced those difficulties in the same combination as the UK, and none perceives them through the prism of the same history. If then we are to understand proposals that the UK should give up full membership of the Union for a free-trade agreement, we can do worse than compare them with previous conversations the British have had with themselves about being 'with but not of Europe', 'of but not with it' or simply 'apart'.

This exercise yields the following conclusions. First, supporters of exit to a free trade agreement differ from those who have shaped Britain's previous relationship with European integration in assuming that the four considerations of sovereignty, international power, political economy and domestic politics are more of an impossible quadrilateral than a quadrilemma. That is, previous UK policy has assumed the four considerations would be difficult – but not impossible – to reconcile within strategies aimed at securing substantial British participation and influence over European integration. That goes for the 1950–1952 period, almost as much as for the 1970–1975 period. In contrast, many supporters of withdrawal to a free trade agreement doubt the four considerations can be reconciled within any continuing attachment to the Union that amounts to more than a relationship that any state in the international system – say, Japan or Canada – could in principle have with the EU. Because this seems a fairly straightforward test of where 'out would be out' it would, if ever adopted, probably be the least ambiguous policy the UK has ever had to European integration. Gone would be the baroque arrangements where – by design or accident – the UK previously sought not to be 'completely out even when out' or struggled to be 'completely in even where in'.

Second, greater understanding of the existing models by which the Union gives non-member states access to its single market – and in particular the Norwegian and Swiss examples – has triggered the turn in the British debate towards a free trade agreement. Yet, it has only done that in combination with the deeper difficulties I identify here of reconciling considerations of sovereignty, international power, political economy and domestic politics. Thus, even though the UK is not (yet) a non-member state, the British debate has made a distinctive contribution to the question of how non-members should relate to the EU.

## Four futures?

Whilst many uncertainties beset Cameron's plan for a renegotiation and a referendum on Britain's continued membership of the Union, it has provoked a debate which has broadly identified the following four ways in which the UK's future relationship with the Union might be structured.

### Completely in

Under this option the UK would not just remain in the EU. It would eventually participate in all its policies, including the euro. Many would dismiss this as improbable. Yet between the Treaty of the European Union (TEU [1992]) and the financial crisis many – not least British governments themselves – assumed it to be the most plausible long-term trajectory of Britain's membership. François Mitterrand's adviser Jacques Attali (1995: 876–877) recalls a conversation between the French president and British prime minister, John Major, during the negotiations of the TEU. In response to Mitterrand's observation that 'Europe has got used to British opposition and to making plans without the UK in the expectation it would join later' Major cautioned against always regarding the UK as a European integration laggard. As he put it, 'Britain didn't just want to join the train. It wanted to be in the driver's cabin'. Above all, Tony Blair always claimed that euro membership was the long-term goal of his 1997–2007 government. Indeed, he told the 2002 Labour Conference that the euro was 'Britain's destiny'. Although, of course, that destiny was forever postponed by economic circumstances, international crises and divisions within the cabinet, Blair was at least determined that absence from the Monetary Union core should be compensated by presence in the security and foreign policy core of the Union. Indeed, promotion of a European Security and Defence Policy was a quiet revolution in British security policy (Liddle 2014: 113). At the time of the 2004–2007 enlargements, the convention and then the negotiations on the constitutional treaty, few would have regarded absence from monetary union as a significant constraint on how far the UK government could shape the membership, competence or decision rules of the Union (Lord 2008).

### In but not completely in

As will be seen, the UK's first detachment from a Community policy predated its accession on 1 January 1973. However, the UK's semi-detachment has become more obvious as prospects of its participation in the Euro have receded, and as the need for it periodically to renew its opt-ins to Justice and Home Affairs have become more politicized. However, the UK's partial membership of the Union could become more explicit. In part, this is because the British problem may be only partly a British problem. Thus, Sergio Fabbrini (forthcoming) argues the Union may have reached the limits to how far it can combine several Unions within a Union. In his view, the Union needs to separate and recompose models of integration that variously assume (a) a limited form of Economic Union, (b) an intergovernmental Union under the shared – but not individual – control of governments and (c) a supranational union of institutions with some powers that are autonomous of member states. Only by making the commitments entailed by these three forms of Union more explicit – and by simultaneously 'separating' member states into those that really are prepared to commit to each kind of Union whilst also 'recomposing' the different unions so that they cohere with one another – can the EU, in Fabbrini's view, ensure public control and equality between its member states. For its part, a recent report of the Foreign Affairs Committee of the House of Commons anticipated a two-tier Union, with the outer tier based on the single market and the Common Foreign and Security Policy and the inner tier on the closer integration of fiscal and monetary policies within the Eurozone (House of Commons 2013: para. 162). Indeed, the crisis may have been a fork-point between closer integration of the Eurozone and an integration gap with the UK that is finally acknowledged as permanent. Even if such a two-tier structure does not come about through a single act of institutional design, the proportion of integration in which the UK is not involved could gradually increase through repeated use of enhanced cooperation within the Treaties or greater use of treaties outside the Union treaties (Piris 2012).

## Out but not completely out

Under this option, the UK would use Art. 50 of the treaty to leave the EU and then negotiate a continuing relationship with it. This would be unlike anything attempted so far. It would, as it were, be a 'falling apart' – rather than a 'coming together' – form of differentiated integration. Indeed, it would strictly speaking be a form of differentiated *dis*integration from full membership, rather than a form of differentiated integration. Yet, as discussed in detail elsewhere in this volume, the EU has established mechanisms that allow for the differential participation of outsiders in its policies. Thus, the debate on Brexit has already given much attention to whether the UK could employ either a 'Norwegian' or a 'Swiss model' to continue to participate in selected Union policies. As Sieglinde Gstöhl explains in Chapter 2 in this volume, the former would use a mechanism like the European Economic Area (EEA) to ensure more or less 'real-time convergence' between British and Union laws in such matters as single market regulation. In areas covered by the agreement, UK commitments would be more or less automatically updated to take account of new Union legislation and Court of Justice of the European Union rulings. In contrast, the Swiss model would involve the negotiation of 'static' bilateral treaties. The formal commitments of the EU and the UK would be just those specified in whatever treaties they chose to conclude. They would not change continuously over time. The Swiss model, however, would not guarantee that British law would be fully convergent at any one time with single market regulation. It thus implies some risk of disintegration from the single market. Moreover, without the automaticity of the EEA, it is likely to be a complex solution. The Swiss, for example, have had to negotiate 105 bilateral treaties, none of which incidentally covers the financial sector, which, of course, would be important to how the UK would want to structure its relationship with the EU as a non-member state.

## Completely out

Until recently the Norwegian and Swiss examples offered comfort to many shades of British opinion that there was life after the EU, possibly even a better life of easy access to the single market without some of the supposed burdens of EU membership. More recently those options have been questioned. Cameron himself appeared to reject both the Norwegian and Swiss options in the very speech he promised a referendum on Britain's membership:

> There are those who suggest we could turn ourselves into Norway or Switzerland. But would that really be in or best interests? While Norway is part of the single market, it has no say at all in setting its rules. The Swiss have to negotiate access to the single market sector by sector. Accepting EU rules – over which they have little say – or else not getting full access to the Single Market.
>
> (Cameron 2013)

Indeed, many of those seeking withdrawal have recently distanced themselves from the Norwegian and Swiss options. Rather, they argue, the UK should be prepared to negotiate no more than a free trade agreement (fta) with the EU. Importantly, a submission along those lines won the Institute of Directors' much-publicised prize for how Britain should exit the EU (Mansfield 2014). Others have argued that, in exiting, the UK should not just seek an fta with the Union itself. It should also aim to outcompete it in concluding fta's with the rest of the world. Whilst, in their view, protectionist minorities of its member states will always constrain the EU in how far it can conclude fta's that are not shot through with exceptions, the UK would be able to conclude ambitious fta's outside the EU. Thus, in noting that the Union does not yet have fta's with China or India, Roger Bootle (2014) has argued that the UK should conclude fta's that would give it early mover advantage in those markets. For good measure, he argues the UK should also apply to join the North American Free Trade Association (NAFTA). Note just how undeterred these arguments are by the observation that the UK would be giving up participation in the Union's collective bargaining power in international trade and that Brexit would, therefore, put non-EU, as well as EU markets, at risk (Centre for European Reform 2014). Moreover, the idea that the UK should proliferate fta's within and beyond

Europe is not just, as we will see, conceived as an alternative to begging for access to the single market on similar terms to Norway or Switzerland. It also excludes the Turkish model of a customs union with the EU.

Yet, it might be objected that even the substitution of an fta for full Union membership would not leave the UK 'completely out'. An fta could even retain much of the UK's trading relationship with the EU. After all, bilateral fta's – as well as the overall multilateral frameworks of the World Trade Organisation – increasingly overlap anyway with much of the content of the EU's single market programme. They do not just cover tariffs 'at borders' but also many 'behind-border' restrictions to open markets. Indeed, it might be further objected that an fta, thus understood, would not really be so different from the Swiss model and that I am, therefore, exaggerating in suggesting that – in embracing an fta – supporters of Brexit have departed so very much from existing ways in which non-member states cooperate with the EU.

Still, it is important to distinguish two things. Whilst, however, the Swiss bilateral treaties are, indeed, governed by international law, they are also embedded in commitments to core principles of integration such as free movement. Because supporters of Brexit would presumably not want to enter into such a commitment – or, indeed, into any relationship substantially regulated by the Union's institutions or principles – I assume that the only kind of bilateral fta they have in mind is one that any state in the international system might seek to conclude with the EU. Exiting the Union to a relationship of a kind any state can have with the Union seems to me to be as good a test as any of where 'out is completely out'. I will come back to all of this. First, however, I ask how much of a break with Britain's previous relationship with European integration would it be for the UK to withdraw to an fta of a kind that any state in the international system might have with the EU? To answer that question I start at the beginning in 1950.

## 1950–1952: With but not of

On what has come to be seen as the European Union's birthday, 9 May 1950, the US secretary of state, Dean Acheson, was in London for a meeting with the British foreign secretary, Ernest Bevin. The meeting was interrupted with a message that the French foreign minister, Robert Schuman, had just proposed a major new initiative. Acheson had to pretend that he knew nothing, lest he reveal that the Americans had been consulted whilst the British had not (Lord 1996: 6). In some ways the problem was simple. British hostility was assumed in advance. After all, the Schuman Plan was supranational, not intergovernmental.

Still, we will never know whether the incompatibility was fundamental or one that could have been managed. For, the Netherlands participated in the European Coal and Steel Community, even though it too had reservations about its supranational features. To add to the ambiguity of the historical record, the British government was as accident-prone in its response to the Schuman Plan, as many of its successors would be in handling other questions of European integration over the next 65 years. Bizarrely, all three of the most senior members of the government – the prime minister (Clement Attlee), the chancellor of the exchequer (Stafford Cripps) and Bevin himself – were in hospital by the time of the crucial cabinet meeting when the decision had to be taken on Britain's participation in the talks on the Schuman Plan.

Yet it would be a mistake to regard the British as stumbling by accident into the long period of its 'self-exclusion' from European integration between 1950 and 1973. First and foremost, excluding themselves from European integration was not what the British governments of the early 1950s believed themselves to be doing. The exact decision in June 1950 was not to participate in the talks on the Schuman Plan but to associate with it none the less. It is worth labouring this point. The British government expected non-membership to be a very substantial status indeed. When the draft treaty for the Coal and Steel Community was published, an interdepartmental working party remained confident that 'even as non-members' the UK's bargaining power and goodwill would be considerable. 'If the General Agreement on Tariffs and Trade (GATT) could be made to function more effectively, some of the advantages of membership would come to us without being a member'.[1] More, however, than gaining access *de facto* to the benefits of membership, some also expected the UK to be able to exercise an informal veto over the further development of any European Community. A meeting of the top officials in the Foreign Office doubted that the European Coal and Steel Community (ECSC) countries would be able to 'put their federal ideas into practice without at least the blessing and probably the active participation of the UK'.[2]

Second, the decision not to participate in the early European Communities was taken by two British governments of both main parties. Not only was the decision not to participate in the ECSC confirmed by the later decision not to take part in the Treaty of Rome (1957), the 1951–1964 Conservative government confirmed the decision of the 1945–1951 Labour government not to join the ECSC. Within weeks of returning as prime minister, Churchill circulated a note to the rest of the government in which he famously argued that the UK should be '"with not of" Europe [...] Our attitude is that we help, we dedicate, we participate, but we do not merge and we do not forfeit our insular or Commonwealth character'.[3] The policy of seeking to participate without being a member could scarcely have been confirmed in clearer terms. To understand both what kept British governments out and what persuaded them that they could and should avoid being completely out we need to understand how they balanced considerations of sovereignty, international power, political economy and domestic politics.

## *Sovereignty*

From his hospital bed, Bevin urged caution on the grounds that the Schuman Plan would prove to be 'a Pandora's box' full of 'Trojan Horses' (Bullock 1983: 659). Somehow the clumsiness of the mixed metaphor only underlined that some of the main believers in what has come to be known as the spillover theory – that, once started, European integration would be cumulative and irreversible – were to be found in the British government. The Foreign Office described the proposed ECSC authority as 'a step towards a federation' and a 'prototype of federal institutions in Europe. It cautioned that Britain's acceptance or non-acceptance would be 'interpreted as an expression of our attitude towards a federal Europe'. Ministers should only participate if they were prepared to continue the federal journey: to be 'hustled along the road to full federation through the creation of supranational authorities controlling a widening range of functions'.[4] Although otherwise quite sympathetic to the Schuman Plan, Cripps told the House of Commons that 'such a scheme would hardly prove workable in democratic communities without full federation'.[5]

## International actor

Shortly before the Schuman declaration, Churchill made a speech claiming that the UK was uniquely at the intersection of the three circles of the 'free world': the British Commonwealth, the United States and United Europe' (Churchill 1948). Although he was still in opposition, Churchill's three circles doctrine shaped British reactions to the formation of the European Communities. One problem was precisely that the Schuman Plan seemed to entail a commitment to a continuing process of European integration. That, the Foreign Office believed, would eventually clash with the UK's determination 'to play a role in all three circles' and its assumption that 'none can claim our exclusive allegiance'.[6] Anthony Eden, as foreign secretary in the incoming 1951 government, confirmed that commitment to European integration would be incompatible with a need for Britain to balance the circles:

> we wish to cultivate the idea of an Atlantic Alliance based on the three pillars of the United States, the United Kingdom (including the Commonwealth) and Europe. In such a community we can reconcile our world-wide commitments with our responsibilities to Europe and the Commonwealth. That could not be done within the confines of a European federation.[7]

Yet, the UK's determination to balance the three circles did not just limit how far it could participate in European integration. It also constrained how far it could cut itself off from any European Community of which it was not a member. Although of the opinion just quoted, Eden also rejected 'the naïve view that the Anglo-American relationship or the Commonwealth provided alternative routes for Britain which would enable it to dispense with a close European association' (Shuckburgh 1986: 17–18). Just how acute was the dilemma was illustrated just two days after the Schuman declaration when the UK presented a paper designed to operationalise its own aspirations for a special relationship with the US. In his biography of Bevin, Alan Bullock (1983: 772) recounts how Acheson insisted that all copies of the paper should be collected and burned: 'with the first initiative to come from the French in his mind, Acheson had to mind the undesirability of allowing the USA's special relationship with Europe to be pre-empted by the UK's claim to a special relationship' with the US. At the very least, Washington expected

British governments to support the process of European integration from outside. As a senior Foreign Office official put it, 'We do not think we should intervene to prevent progress towards a West European Federation [...] we should incur the utmost political odium were we to attempt to do so'.[8]

## Political economy and domestic politics

Alan Milward (1992) has famously described the early stages of European integration as a European rescue of the state. However, the 1945–1951 Labour government and its supporters were much more likely to see the Schuman Plan as a threat than a rescue: as a threat to their own assumptions about political economy and to their own plans to construct a welfare state that guaranteed full employment. Herbert Morrison, who chaired the cabinet meeting that decided not to join the Schuman talks, famously claimed that participation was impossible because the 'Durham Miners would not have it'. His point was that the government had only just nationalized the very industries that would be included in the European Coal and Steel Community. In keeping with assumptions of the time that the coal and steel were the 'commanding heights' of an industrialised economy, the Labour Party's international department argued that participation in the Schuman Plan would constrain government plans to use investment in those industries as instruments in Keynesian demand management aimed at ensuring full employment. Moreover, the politics of France and West Germany were seen at inherently more conservative to those of the UK with the result 'we could not guarantee that full employment, fair shares and social consensus would be the basis of a European Union'. Indeed, the Labour Party's International Department even implied that it would be better to risk alternation with Conservatives within the British political system, rather than join still more conservative West European societies in a common Coal and Steel authority: 'even the Conservative Party recognizes that social consensus in Britain depends on using economic methods closer to the Labour Party than those of the German, French or Italian Governments'.[9] Yet, such was the size of British coal and steel, that both the Conservative and Labour Governments were confident that it would be feasible and much to their advantage to co-ordinate those industries with the ECSC from the outside. 'Out without being completely out' was therefore the UK's preferred position for reasons of political economy, as well as foreign policy.

## When in, not completely in

Just as the 1950–1952 period demonstrated limits to how far British governments wanted to be 'out' when they 'out', the 1970–1975 period showed how difficult it would be for British governments to be 'in' when they were 'in'. Differentiated integration – by which some member states do not participate in all common policies – began for the UK even before its formal accession on 1 January 1973. In barely 40 days in May and June 1972 the UK first joined and then withdrew the pound from the common currency float (the snake).

Although this was an important indicator of subsequent difficulties, it was overshadowed at the time by another uncertainty. When the 1970–1974 Conservative government – led by Edward Heath – opened negotiations in June 1970 it was widely assumed there was bipartisan support for Britain's membership of the European Communities. Both a Conservative and a Labour government had applied for membership in the 1960s. However, in opposition, the Labour Party divided on European Community (EC) membership. To avoid a mandate from its party conference that would have committed a Labour government to withdraw altogether, the Labour leadership promised in 1972 to renegotiate the terms of British accession and then hold a referendum on the UK's continued membership. Far, then, from entering the EC with cross-party support, the UK joined with the real possibility that a future government would seek to reverse its membership. That was a huge uncertainty in a system of alternating one-party government. Edward Heath (1998: 358) later explained the difficulty: 'If the opposition plays party politics on the question it can raise a serious doubt in the minds of our partners as to whether the UK will deliver on its obligations under the treaties, because the opposition of today maybe the government of tomorrow'.

Moreover, the same four factors – sovereignty, international power, political economy and domestic politics – that had once persuaded British governments that they should be 'out but not completely out' now affected adaptation to membership, with the first two easing the transition and the latter two complicating it. The following sub-sections explain.

## Sovereignty

British governments were probably most relaxed about sovereignty between 1966 – when the Luxembourg compromise affirmed that member governments should be allowed to use a veto in matters they considered of fundamental interest – and the reintroduction of qualified majority voting to the Council in 1986. However, contrary to many subsequent claims, the Heath government did not pretend that British membership of the European Community would have few implications for sovereignty. To the contrary, at the very moment that British accession was most at risk – the second reading of the European Communities Bill in February 1972 – Heath bluntly told the House of Commons that majority voting would probably have to be reintroduced within 10 years.[10] Sir Geoffrey Howe, then attorney-general, also told the Commons that the 'Communities' were a 'dynamic organisation' and that many future changes to the Treaties should be expected (ibid.). Moreover, Britain's chief negotiator, Geoffrey Rippon (1971), sang the praises of the 'community system' as a means of 'balancing integration with continuing national consent' (Rippon 1971). Nor was this just window dressing designed to reassure partners that the UK had accepted EC institutions. Even after UK membership had been agreed, Heath discouraged Pompidou's suggestions that Britain and France might align to constrain the powers of the Commission (Lord 1994: 38, 156).

## International power

Sir Con O'Neill, the senior official on Britain's negotiating team argued that the main driving force behind British entry was a 'feeling that' the UK 'was becoming increasingly side-tracked and insignificant'.[11] The three circles doctrine – which had once been used as an argument for not participating in European integration – now became an argument for joining after all. From the first application in 1961, the British government worried that it would – in some undefined way – lose influence over the European circle by staying out of the European Community. If, however, the UK had less influence in Europe, the US and the Commonwealth would also have less interest in the UK. These concerns took a special form in the early 1970s. On one hand, the decision to begin accession talks with the UK was itself part of a three-way deal at The Hague in 1969 to complete, deepen and enlarge the European Communities. Not only did this raise the possibility that the European Community would attempt a monetary union. It also anticipated foreign policy cooperation (European Political Co-operation). The possibility that the EC countries might coordinate foreign policies plainly increased the risks to the UK of diminishing relative influence in foreign policy. On the other hand, shifting power relations seemed to offer the UK the real possibility that – if it did join – it could 'trilateralise' the strong bilateral relationship between France and West Germany. Concern that West Germany's economic strength and its policy towards Eastern Europe would allow it to dominate a Europe of six was the principal reason why the French president, Georges Pompidou, now favoured UK entry.

Just how far the Heath government was prepared to reorient British foreign policy towards Europe is illustrated by two striking examples. First, at the Paris summit in May 1971 which decided British entry to the EC, Heath made a dramatic offer to Pompidou for the UK and France to cooperate in maintaining their nuclear deterrents. Indeed, in a lecture a few years before he had even argued that the UK and France might – in some way – hold their nuclear weapons 'in trust' for other European countries (Heath 1970). Second, in his memoirs, Henry Kissinger (1979) recalls the extent of Heath's commitment to making a go of Britain's newly won membership of the Community. As Kissinger puts it, Heath's recent predecessors had all pretended to a special relationship that US presidents had been reluctant to accord. In contrast Heath was the only British prime minister who was reluctant to accept a special relationship that a US president was prepared to offer. The reason, in Kissinger's view, was simple:

> Heath was determined that Britain should join Europe not reluctantly and calculatingly but with real conviction [. . .] the 'special relationship' was an obstacle to the British vocation in Europe. Heath was content to enjoy no higher status in Washington than any other European leader. Indeed, he came close to insisting on receiving no preferential treatment'.
>
> (Kissinger 1979: 933–934)

## Political economy

One reason why it is so important to mention Heath's determination to demonstrate that 'in really was in' is that even his government failed to achieve that objective right from the start of Britain's membership. The fact that the UK joined and left common currency float in a space of just 40 days in 1972 was no minor detail. Looking forward monetary integration would be precisely the area where the UK would drift ever further apart from many of its new partners over the next 40 years. Looking back, it had been precisely the ability of the UK to participate in monetary integration on which Pompidou had most sought reassurance – and Heath had given it – before lifting the French veto on British accession (Lord 1994). Here there were two underlying problems. First, even a Government as favourable as Heath's to the institutions of the European Community, could find itself confronted with a need to choose between its own domestic political programme and Community policies. When it had to choose between remaining in the snake, and its own domestic policy, it chose the latter. Second, the UK had persistent balance of payments problems in the post-war period. Those then interacted with the collapse of the wider Bretton Woods system of internationally fixed exchange rates after 1971 to make it hard for any British government to commit to any form of currency integration with its new European patterns.

## Domestic politics

The domestic politics of British accession were unusually difficult. Although a vote approving the principle of British entry passed the House of Commons with a majority of 112 in October 1971, the government's majority fell to just 11 on the second reading and to just three on one of the votes on amendments. Indeed, the enabling legislation would have been lost altogether without secret collusion between Conservative and Labour pro-Europeans. Two lasting legacies of these years were parties divided on European integration and a volatile pattern of public support for UK membership. In only 15 parliamentary votes since the war had more than 10 per cent of Conservatives voted against their party and in only 40 had Labour members of Parliament (MPs) done so (Norton 1975). Yet, in the vote on British entry to the EC, more than 10 per cent of MPs from both parties voted against their leaderships, albeit only in the Labour case was that a rebellion against a formal voting instruction. Whilst the parties were divided, public was not so much hostile, as unformed and, therefore, changeable. Support for entry fell from more than 60 per cent in 1967 to just 20 per cent in early 1971, only to return to two-thirds in the referendum on the renegotiated terms of UK membership in June 1975.

Because the strategy of combining a renegotiation and a referendum has obvious parallels with Cameron's, it is worth appraising, in parenthesis, how successfully it was deployed in 1974–1975. It is questionable whether the 1974–1979 government got much of it wanted from the renegotiation. As John Young (2004: 145) notes,

> there was no firm promise of reform to the Common Agricultural Policy (CAP) and the Lomé Convention would probably have been renegotiated regardless of British demands [...] True, there was an improvement of sorts on the financial side, but one that still left Britain as the second largest net contributor with a sum amounting to £800m by 1979.

Nor did the referendum produce full closure. The UK, arguably, continued to renegotiate the terms of its membership until it received a rebate from the budget in 1984 (see also George 1990). Meanwhile, the Labour Party would go into a further election – in 1983 – committed to withdrawal, albeit only after the defection of its more pro-European members in 1981.

## Ways of being a non-member (again)

I suggested earlier that arguments for UK withdrawal from the EU are shaped by the same four considerations – of sovereignty, international power, political economy and domestic politics – that shaped Britain's earlier European policy in the 1950–1952 and 1970–1975 periods. However, a better understanding of relationships between Norway, Switzerland and the EU has recently convinced some Brexiters that it may not be possible for the UK to reconcile the four factors in any continuing relationship with the EU beyond a free trade agreement of a kind that any state in the international system could in principle agree with the Union. I now return to that argument.

### *Sovereignty*

Many Brexiters once believed Norway and Switzerland enjoyed an ideal of access to the Single Market, without participation in the Common Agricultural Policy and the Common Fisheries Policy. More recently, however, they, and others in the UK debate, have become more aware of the sovereignty costs of the Norwegian and Swiss models. Thus, an all-party report of the Foreign Affairs Committee of the House of Commons observed that

> current arrangements for relations with the EU that are maintained by Norway or Switzerland are not appropriate for the UK if it were to leave the EU. In both cases, the non-EU country is obliged to adopt some or all of the body of single market law without the ability to shape it. If it is in the interests of the UK to remain in the single market, the UK should remain in the EU, or launch an effort for radical institutional change in Europe to give decision-making rights in the single market to all its participating states.
> (House of Commons 2013, para. 164)

The joke that Norway is a 'fax democracy' – which applies 75 per cent of the Union's *acquis* even though it does not have full decision-rights in making those laws and only receives notification of some of the laws it is supposed to enforce by fax – has been endlessly repeated in the UK. As the Centre for European Reform (2014) has put it, the EEA entails 'regulation without representation' (Centre for European Reform 2014: 12). Instead of being examples to follow, Norway and Switzerland are more likely to be cited as warnings of how far *de facto* autonomy in the making of laws can be lost even within arrangements that supposedly preserve *de jure* sovereignty. A particularly compelling example was the evidence of Jóhanna Jónsdóttir (2013a) – who has both worked for the EFTA Secretariat and contributed to the academic literature on the EEA – to the Foreign Affairs committee. Jónsdóttir doubted the mechanisms by which the *de jure* sovereignty of Norway, Iceland and Liechtenstein is supposedly safeguarded, namely their right to agree between themselves not to adopt a Union law into the EEA and the right – in the absence of any 'direct effect' – of their national parliaments not to ratify laws proposed for incorporation into the EEA. Yet, she continued, these mechanisms do not confer much 'real veto-power'. Each EEA government and parliament knows that – under A102 of the EEA – the EU can respond to any refusal to incorporate an EEA-relevant Union law by suspending that part of the EEA to which it relates. However, Jónsdóttir notes that 'there is a real fear that the entire EEA Agreement' would collapse were A102 ever to be used. Given that the EFTA countries would then lose their automatic 'access to the internal market', it is 'difficult, if not impossible, for the EFTA countries to say "no"' to Union legislation (Jónsdóttir 2013b: 67).

If, indeed, forms of mutually assured destruction at least have the redeeming feature of being balanced and reciprocal, the EEA, arguably, only works precisely because it an asymmetric relation, held together by a threat of unilaterally assured destruction. Sure, there is an EEA Court to arbitrate disputes. But it is ultimately circumscribed by the priority of the Union's overall system of law (see Haukeland Fredriksen in Chapter 6 in this volume).

At first sight Switzerland retains greater autonomy over its own laws. It has made no commitment – such as the EEA – aimed at automatic convergence of laws. It is only obliged to adopt Union laws it has itself accepted in bilateral treaties with Union. Yet precisely because this does not assure legal and market certainty, Switzerland has adopted a policy of unilateral approximation. This means its *de facto* autonomy is, arguably, even less than Norway. Both Norway and Switzerland are alike in applying a great deal of law made by a legislature – namely the Council of Ministers of the European Union and the European Parliament – in which they are not represented. Yet Norway, in contrast to Switzerland, at least participates in expert committees and comitology which shape much of the detail of legislation that it eventually adopts. Moreover, as seen, the bilateral treaties with Switzerland, no less than the EEA, require free movement of persons, which, of course, many British Eurosceptics consider an unacceptable loss of the UK's sovereign right to 'control its boundaries' or to control who lives on its territory.

Adopting equivalent arrangements to Norway or Switzerland would, then, be incompatible with the procedural and substantive autonomy that many British Eurosceptics hope to regain by leaving the Union in the first place. Indeed, the incoherence of this position is one reason why it is unclear that other actors would make the EEA or the Swiss model available to the UK. The EEA, arguably, only works because much of the legislation proposed by the Union is already close to the preferences of EFTA countries. The EFTA countries easily converge around acceptance of Union legislation that mainly only requires them to regulate even less than they would on their own. But that would obviously be incompatible with any British ambition to exit the Union in order to deregulate. Yet, a clash within an enlarged EEA between UK and existing EFTA countries would be peculiarly destructive, because all EFTA countries must agree to incorporate proposals if there is to be no risk of a part suspension of the EEA Agreement. Given the importance of compromise to the workings of the EEA, and given the importance of the EEA to the delicate compromises on European integration within their own countries, existing EFTA countries would be wary of admitting any partner likely to turn the EEA away from compromise to confrontation.

Nor, is it certain that the Swiss model would be available to the UK, or, indeed, to the Swiss themselves for much longer. For several years the Union has taken the view that the bilateral treaties with Switzerland have reached their limits and cannot be developed further. Thus, the Council has argued that 'participating in parts of the EU internal market is not only engaging in a bilateral relation but participating in a multilateral project'. Without an overarching – multilateral – structure of legislative initiative, administrative surveillance and judicial control provided by credibly 'independent' bodies there are, in the view of Union institutions, real limits to how far the single market can be extended to non-member states without exposing it to risks of regulatory arbitrage, legal uncertainty and unfairness (Council of European Union 2012). In effect then, the EU institutions want the Swiss model to converge on the Norwegian model, which itself converges on full membership to the extent that the EEA is itself a multilateral system of legislation, surveillance of implementation and judicial control.

It is unsurprising, then, that some supporters of Brexit have recently shown less interest in the Norwegian and Swiss models and more in a form of free trade agreement that any other state in the international system might agree with the Union. There would seem little point in leaving the Union for reasons of autonomy, only to reassume similar obligations with fewer decision rights. What, however, do arguments for withdrawal to an fta imply for the remaining elements of the quadrilemma I have discussed here?

## *International power*

Many supporters of Brexit are, to repeat, confident that, in trade matters, the UK will be able to rely well enough on a combination of the rules of the World Trade Organization and its own bargaining power. However, the fact remains that the UK is a country with a large trade deficit that depends on access to the Union's single market for 50 per cent of its exports. Moreover, the terms of UK access would need to be agreed by member states and by the European Parliament. Hence, they would need to satisfy a spread of interests, and not just the Union's overall interest (Centre for European Reform 2014: 28). There would be more veto points against liberal solutions than Eurosceptics allow. Indeed, it seems odd – even contradictory – to suppose that, as long as the UK remains a member of the EU, veto points within the Union will prevent it participating in ambitious free trade agreements with India and China, whilst, supposing, on the other hand, that those same veto points will not also constrain any free trade agreement that the UK attempts to negotiate with the Union.

Moreover, more than trade relations would plainly be involved in substituting a free trade agreement for full membership of the EU. In particular, the UK would need to consider implications for its relations with the US. There is much at stake here. The US gives the UK privileged access to military technology and intelligence. Not least its supposedly independent nuclear deterrent is, of course, dependent on the US. As if eager that the UK's role in the EU should be precisely to confirm De Gaulle's prediction that it would act as a Trojan Horse for Washington, US policymakers have often assumed that the EU – and especially the Common Foreign and Security Policy (CFSP) – is more likely to evolve on terms they can accept with British participation than without it. Supporters of Brexit differ only in the kind of insouciance with which they react to these concerns. One view is that the CFSP is where the UK could follow the Norwegian example, even if the EEA is not. If Norway can opt into CFSP mission wherever it feels itself to be a part of a 'coalition of the willing', then so can the UK. A second view is that the UK should be unafraid about scaling down as an international power. Many Conservative supporters of Brexit also voted to defeat their own government on military intervention in Syria. In any case, the British military has now been reduced to less than 80,000 personnel compared with 300,000 in early Thatcher years.

## *Political economy*

Those who favour substituting a free trade agreement for full membership can hardly be dismissed as Little Englanders who have no conception of globalisation. However, their conception is largely the libertarian one that states should just coordinate on minimal rules needed for globalisation to function as a market-led spontaneous order. To the extent, indeed, that their calculations of potential gains from substituting a network of fta's for membership of the EU largely assume that Britain would not replace Union regulation, they plainly also have a largely libertarian understanding of how the UK's own political economy would operate outside the EU.

## *Domestic politics*

Although proposals for withdrawing to an fta have sought alternatives to the political incoherence of substituting full membership for sovereignty costs comparable to the EEA or Swiss bilateral treaties, those proposals are, of course, technical economic solutions. Yet they need to work within domestic UK politics all the same. Here they have strengths and weaknesses. In contrast to Norway – where it is often remarked that an arrangement such as the EEA is everyone's 'second best' – it may be better for supporters of Brexit to say from the outset that they do not expect the broadest possible post-withdrawal coalition to be found by seeking arrangements comparable to Norway or Switzerland. Such a position may not survive 'trial by public debate' given the incoherence of exiting for reasons of sovereignty only to accept the sovereignty costs of the Norwegian or Swiss models.

Where, however, arguments for withdrawal to an fta run into political difficulty is that any option for how the UK should structure its relations with the EU as a non-member state is likely to have sectorally specific consequences. The problem can be illustrated by the two large examples of the car industry and the City of London, both of which are strategic to the British economy. In the former case it really could make a difference to choose an fta over participation in the EU's Customs Union. The common external tariff on cars is 5 to 10 per cent. Moreover, the car industry is one example of how it may be easier for Norway – rather than the UK – to operate outside the Customs Union. Because Norway is not part of the EU's customs union, its exports to the EU have to be custom checked. This is not too much of a difficulty for a country which exports oil, gas and fish. But in the case of a country such as the UK which exports cars it would involve checking the cars for components made outside the Union (Dixon 2014).

In the case of financial services, the Centre for European Reform (CER) explains what has become a core difficulty. Until the crisis the single market in financial services 'allowed continental banks to concentrate much of their activity in London'. Yet, the CER, continues, large parts of 'continental' opinion considers the crisis to have been in significant part a massive negative externality imposed on the Eurozone by 'Anglo-Saxon' finance. At the very least 'Eurozone authorities' have responded to the crisis by preferring 'that trading and lending between banks be conducted under their watch'. Now this is plainly going to be a major difficulty whether the UK stays in the EU or leaves it. However, the key point is that the options for handling the problem will be fundamentally different depending on whether the UK is in or out. As the CER notes, the British government has taken the European Central Bank (ECB) to the European Court of Justice over its attempt to make trading-houses specialising in euro-denominated trading relocate to the Eurozone: 'If it left the EU, and did not join the EEA, the UK would have little recourse to institutions that police the single market' (Centre for European Reform 2014: 12).

## Conclusion

In the weeks before Britain joined the European Community, the political economist Andrew Shonfield was chosen to give the influential annual Reith Lectures. Shonfield (1973) argued in favour of British membership. But, he warned, it would be a 'journey to an unknown destination'. Until recently those urging British exit have assumed that withdrawal would be a journey to a relatively known destination, as provided by the Norwegian and Swiss models of how the EU provides non-member states with access to its single markets. However, as British Eurosceptic opinion has found out more about the EEA and Switzerland's bilateral treaties with the Union, those models have lost favour as means of reconciling British exit with any sovereignty arguments for leaving in the first place.

## Notes

1 PRO FG WP 51 43 PRO Report of a Working Party of Officials on the Treaty constituting the European Coal and Steel Community, 31 December 1951.
2 PRO ZP 18/1 Minutes of a Meeting of the Permanent Under-Secretaries' Committee, 29 March 1951.
3 PRO C 51 32 'United States of Europe', Memorandum by the Prime Minister to the Cabinet, 29 November 1951.
4 PRO CAB 134/295 'Constitutional problems involved in a supranational authority as proposed by M. Schuman, 16 June 1950. See also PRO ZP 18/20 Memorandum by Permanent Under-Secretary's Committee of the Foreign Office, 9 June 1950.
5 House of Commons Debate, 26 June 1950, Series 5 Vol. 476.
6 PRO WU 10712/32 The Council of Europe 9 November 1951.
7 PRO FO 953/1207 Eden to HM Representatives Overseas 15 December 1951.
8 PRO CE 3353/2141/181 Makings to Strang 28 June 1950.
9 'European Unity' and 'Report on the International Conference on the control of European Basic Industries 16–18 June 1950, Archives of the British Labour Party.
10 House of Commons Debates, 17 February 1972, Series 5 Vol. 831.
11 Interview with Sir Con O'Neill, *The Seventies/4*, Interview transcripts, LSE Archive.

## References

Attali, J. (1995) *Chronique des Années 1988–1991*, Paris: Fayard
Bootle, R. (2014) *The Trouble with Europe*, London: Nicholas Brealey
Bullock, A. (1983) *Ernest Bevin, Foreign Secretary 1945–51*, London: Heinemann.
Cameron, D. (2013) 'The Prime Minister's Speech on the Future of the United Kingdom's Relationship with the EU', Bloomberg's European headquarters, London, 23 January.
Centre for European Reform (2014) 'The Economics Consequences of Leaving the European Union', London: Centre for European Reform. Available at http://www.cer.org, last accessed 8 August 2014.
Churchill, W. (1948) 'Speech to Mass Meeting of the Conservative Party', Llandudno, 9 October 1948.
Council of the European Union (2012) 'Council Conclusion on EU Relations with EFTA Countries', 3213th Transport, Telecommunications and Energy Council Meeting, Brussels, 20 December.
Dixon, H. (2014) *The In/Out Question: Why Britain Should Stay in the EU and Fight to Make it Better*, Kindle Single/Scampstonian.
Fabbrini, S. (forthcoming) *Which European Union? Europe after the Euro Crisis*, Cambridge: Cambridge University Press.

George, S. (1990) *The Awkward Partner: Britain and the European Communities*, Oxford: Oxford University Press.
Heath, E. (1970) *Old World, New Horizons: The Godkin Lectures 1967*, London: Oxford University Press.
—— (1998) *The Course of My Life*, London: Hodder and Stoughton.
House of Commons (2013) 'The Future of the European Union. UK Government Policy', First Report of Session 2013–14, Volume 1, London: House of Commons.
Jónsdóttir, J. (2013a) 'Written Evidence from Jóhanna Jónsdóttir, Policy Officer, European Free Trade Association', London: House of Commons. Available at http://www.publications.parliament.uk/pa/cm201314/cmselect/cmfaff/87/87we02.htm, last accessed 12 December 2014.
—— (2013b) *Europeanisation and the European Economic Area. Iceland's Participating in the EU's Policy Process*, London: Routledge/UACES.
Kissinger, H. (1979) *The White House Years*, London: Weidenfeld and Nicholson.
Liddle, R. (2014) *The Europe Dilemma, Britain and the Drama of European Integration*, London: Tauris/Policy Network.
Lord, C. (1994) *British Entry to the European Community under the Heath Government of 1970–4*. Aldershot: Dartmouth.
—— (1996) *Absent at the Creation: Britain and the Schuman Plan 1950–2*. Aldershot: Dartmouth.
—— (2008) 'Two Constitutionalisms? A Comparison of British and French Government Attempts to Justify the Constitutional Treaty', *Journal of European Public Policy*, 15(7): 1001–1018.
Mansfield, I. (2014) *A Blueprint for Britain: Openness not Isolation*, London: Institute for Economic Affairs.
Milward, A. (1992) *The European Rescue of the Nation State*, Berkeley: University of California Press.
Norton, P. (1975) *Dissension in the House of Commons 1945–1974*, London: Macmillan.
Piris, J.-C. (2012) *The Future of Europe: Towards a Two-Speed Europe*, Cambridge: Cambridge University Press.
Rippon, G. (1971) Speech by Geoffrey Rippon MP, 10 September, RIIA Press Collection.
Shonfield, A. (1973) *Europe: Journey to an Unknown Destination*, London: Pelican.
Shuckburgh, E. (1986) *Descent to Suez: Diaries 1951–6*, London: Weidenfeld & Nicholson.
Young, J (2004) 'Europe', in K. Hickson and A. Seldon (eds) *New Labour, Old Labour: the Wilson and Callaghan Governments 1974–1979*. London: Routledge.

# 13

# HEGEMONY BY ASSOCIATION

*Erik O. Eriksen and John Erik Fossum*

### Differentiated integration and democratic self-rule

Europe has always been a matter of negotiating *unity and diversity*. In the post-war period, the balance has been altered from one of differentiation largely faithful to the precept of state sovereignty, to a more complex governing tapestry, not the least because of European integration. Under this framework states are differently incorporated; thus exhibiting a new and more complex mixture of unity and diversity across Europe.

The key question that this book has addressed was whether democratic self-rule could prevail under such altered conditions of complex structured interdependence. We have analysed this question with specific reference to the constitutional-democratic arrangements of states that are not EU members but have nevertheless entered into binding systems of association with the EU. Given that EU norms and rules effectively apply on these non-members' territories, it is imperative to establish whether these states have retained their status as sovereign democracies. As has been pointed out, democracy requires not only citizens' right to self-determination within a given territory it requires congruence between social and political space and it requires citizens' participation and influence (citizens need capacity to act on their own agenda). For political orders to be legitimate and non-dominant, they must meet the democratic criteria of *autonomy* and *accountability*. With autonomy it is meant that the addressees of the law should also be able to understand themselves as the authors of the law, directly or through elected representatives. Accountability is about holding the decision makers responsible to the citizenry and, in the last resort, *dismissing* incompetent rulers.

In addressing the question of constitutional democratic implications of EU association, the contributions to the book have focused both on formal constitutional democratic arrangements, and on actual practices. It was important to establish differences in formal attachments, which range from narrow *bilateral international agreements* to the broad, *multilateral, dynamic EEA Agreement*. The latter is far more comprehensive than the free trade agreements that the EU has signed with numerous third countries, and it is clearly also more comprehensive than the broad bilateral EU–Swiss agreements. Clarifying the nature of the EU's various agreements with non-members, whether they can be seen as voluntary contracts between sovereign parties or whether they involve substantial inroads into the states' sovereignty has figured centrally in this book for several reasons. One was because it would help to establish whether forms of association varied significantly in terms of their implications for independence. A second was to identify democratic-constitutional implications. A third was to help establish when and under what conditions of asymmetrical interdependence we would encounter hegemonic patterns of *domination*.

It is obvious that this research agenda required paying attention not only to formal arrangements, but also to actual practices. Practice and formality are related but particularly in periods when governing systems undergo comprehensive transformations the *discrepancies* between formally enunciated arrangements and what is happening on the ground can be very considerable. In the EU setting that problem is particularly acute given that the EU ascribes to normative principles but lacks agreement on the kind of polity configuration that the principles are to be embedded in. Nevertheless, as the contributions to the book have shown, there are significant changes in the nature and exercise of sovereignty.

EU membership is optional, and states diverge considerably on the kind and scope of *supranational cooperation* to which they are willing to accede. Such cooperation is an intrinsic part of erecting a European political structure. Even though the EU is quite differentiated, it is a post-national Union in its own right. EU has experimental features, as it claims to have a justified mission and its own legitimacy basis. It has neither a historical predecessor nor a fixed template – and it formulates its own set of legitimacy criteria despite not being a state. And yet, there is no *a priori* assurance that the EU is capable of substituting state-based constitutional democracy with something that is capable of delivering legitimate rule at the European level. To the extent that it is possible to identify an explicit normative justification for the EU, such a justification is anchored in the common constitutional principles embedded in the member states' democratic constitutions. The point is that insofar as EU law is in compliance with the core principles embedded in the member states' constitutions, and the EU abides by certain procedural requirements, the EU is constitutionally authorised and hence validated.

The EU's member states voluntarily pool sovereignty in a set of common European-level institutions whose operations they co-determine (see Chapter 9). The supranational EU institutional arrangement was intended to provide the member states with increased governing capability so as to handle externalities and the many problems and challenges that stem from increased globalisation and *complex interdependence* in post-war Europe. The core idea was that these increases in governing capability through supranational institutions would not undermine the states' abilities to govern themselves in accordance with democratic principles.

The EU system is such structured that the different peoples govern themselves jointly through common institutions they all have direct access to and influence on. These apparently pragmatic adaptations can have systemic implications: when taken sufficiently far the very nature of state and popular sovereignty changes dramatically. Then national self-determination and independence is replaced by co-determination and joint control.

In the multilevel constellation that makes up the EU, popular sovereignty is disentangled from national bonds; it is proceduralised and institutionalised in a complex compound. This conception of constitutional democracy – insofar as it can be anchored in a legitimate EU – stands in marked contrast to constitutional *democratic orthodoxy* as we know it from the long national tradition of constitutional democracy. That tradition highlights congruence between state and popular sovereignty in the sense that the people governs itself through the institutions of the state and that those self-same institutions ensure the continuity and integrity of the democratic people.

We started the book by underlining that constitutional orthodoxy is based on the notion of the constitution as constitutive of the national community; constitutions define nation states, and nation states give rise to and sustain constitutions. Rights protection does not have an autonomous basis but depends on the nation states. In this model of democratic constitutionalism, only *the citizens of political communities* have rights, not *human beings* in general, as was discussed in Chapter 5. The key paradox that informs this book is that even the states that have been the most eager to preserve this national tradition through having declined EU membership – *the sovereign democrats* – find themselves challenged by a dynamic EU that reconfigures the operating premises of state sovereignty and constitutional democracy. The sovereign democrats have found it necessary to collaborate closely with the EU. But because their concern has been to conserve the traditional conception of state-based constitutional sovereignty, and because they are not EU members, they lack the compensatory measures that member states have in place. The upshot is that they face a set of distinctive constitutional democratic problems and challenges.

What these problems and challenges are – across forms of EU association – has been spelled out in this book. In the remainder of this concluding chapter we first briefly summarise the findings from the various chapters and case studies. Based on that in the final section of the chapter we discuss in more detail why the book deserves the strange title *Independence under Hegemony*. The title directs us to the conundrum facing these states: why is it that the effect for states that voluntarily enter into binding cooperation without formally joining the EU is nevertheless one of *hegemonic submission*? We bring the answer together in a concept of hegemony that is 'voluntarily' brought about but which at the same time is undermining nation state democracy and represents a case of dominance.

## Many forms of association amidst strong gravitational pulls

The book was structured in three parts. The first part provided a survey of all forms of association that the EU has developed with its neighbouring states (Chapter 2), as well as two chapters with in-depth assessments of the Swiss case of sectoral bilateralism. Part II was devoted to the assessment of the broader, more formally committing, EEA Agreement, and in-depth studies of the Norwegian and Icelandic cases (Chapters 5 through 11). Part III traced the UK's historically ambiguous EU relationship because the UK might be the first case of a member state to leave the EU (Chapter 12). Part Three ends with this concluding chapter. The book is structured in line with the assumption of progressively more encompassing and binding forms of association, from Part I through Part III. The findings in the book show that this intuitive ranking of associations makes less sense on the ground than is generally thought to be the case.

Part I started with a survey encompassing all the arrangements that the EU has with non-member states (Chapter 2). Here three sets of observations stand out. First is that the EU has developed a broad range of arrangements with non-member states: six in total. The EU is however trying to simplify that because the plethora of external arrangements – instances of horizontal differentiation – can contribute to undermine the EU's core principle of *legal homogeneity* and common operating principles for the internal market. The second observation is that the non-member states that clearly qualify for EU membership are also the states that have the closest relations with the EU. The farther away from fulfilling the EU's entrance requirements, the less likely a state is to be offered an EEA form of affiliation. The third observation is that there are numerous challenges involved in organising EU – non-member-state relations and the challenges figure on both sides of the equation. As Sieglinde Gstöhl has shown in Chapter 2, the main challenge facing the EU is that of ensuring uniformity and coherence, whilst at the same time trying to accommodate non-members. The upshot is that the EU faces obvious coordination and fragmentation challenges. The affiliated states are torn between the need to obtain market access and the threats of exclusion and marginalisation on the other. The general tendency Gstöhl notes is for the EU to try to reduce the number of affiliations, in particular with regard to moving towards the multilateral EEA form and away from the sectoral bilateral Swiss form of affiliation.

## The sovereign democrats

The remaining chapters of the book sought to untangle the paradoxical effects of non-EU membership for the states with the strongest, best-entrenched, democratic traditions: states that are wealthy, well organised, qualify for EU membership, yet have opted not to become members. The in-depth case studies in Chapters 3 through 11 have analysed why and how the citizens in those closely affiliated non-member states – 'the sovereign democrats' – have had their political autonomy undermined through the type of association they have developed with the EU.

In Chapter 3 Sandra Lavenex and René Schwok provided an in-depth assessment of the Swiss case and its form of sectoral bilateral relationship with the EU. Lavenex and Schwok also compared and contrasted Swiss sectoral bilateralism with the multilateral EEA Agreement. Formally speaking, the former is marked by issue specificity, is for most portions static, is based on the notion of *equivalence of legislation* and voluntary adaptation, whereas the EEA Agreement is marked by breadth, dynamism and hierarchy. But, in practice, as they note,

> the main characteristics of 'pragmatic bilateralism' between the EU and Switzerland are the fluid junctions between formal obligations and informal practices and the organisational complexity, highlighting the sectoral diversity of forms of association to EU structures. While at first sight the negotiated issue-specificity of the Bilateral Agreements, their mainly static nature as well as the lack of supranational enforcement mechanisms promise a stronger preservation of Swiss sovereignty vis-à-vis the EU than the more comprehensive, dynamic and hierarchical EEA, in practice the scope for derogations from the dynamically evolving *acquis* is similarly limited, thus reducing the relevance of these formal differences.

The key point is therefore that despite important formal differences, the reality on the ground is quite similar.

This important finding has obvious constitutional-democratic implications: formal differences in mode of association are considerably less important than what might have been assumed. Nevertheless, as Joachim Blatter pointed out in Chapter 4, Swiss democracy is quite distinctive. The question is whether such differences would be associated with less intrusiveness. Blatter examines the constitutional democratic implications for Switzerland with due attention being paid to its distinctive features. He notes that the Swiss case is marked by a strong reliance on classical *republican ideas of popular sovereignty*, weak political liberalism and hence weak judicial review albeit strong economic liberalism. Blatter, drawing on neo-republican theory of democracy, argues that Switzerland's bilateralism

> combines strong resistance against interference from neighbouring states and international organizations with an extreme opportunism towards the demands of multinational corporations. Such a stance undermines the capacities of larger polities like the EU to secure political self-determination against private capital holders and multinational corporations.

These detrimental external effects combine with important internal changes in the Swiss model which are associated with decline in trust, weakened patterns of accountability, and *participatory pathologies* that together result in democratic problems. There is little then to suggest that the distinctive Swiss democratic tradition is any more resilient than its Nordic non-EU counterparts.

Part II focused on the EEA Agreement with detailed case studies of the two main EEA countries, Norway and Iceland (Liechtenstein is the third EEA member but is considerably smaller than the other two and, hence, was left out of this analysis). Part II included chapters that focused on spelling out not only the formal character of the EEA states' association with the EU but also its practical operation and effects, as well as detailed assessments of internal implications for citizens' constitutionally entrenched right to self-rule in the two cases, with particular emphasis on the considerably larger Norwegian case.

It was shown that the EEA Agreement has constitutional implications, for Iceland and Norway. The EEA countries participate in the internal market on an equal footing with the EU member states. Since the EEA Agreement was entered into in 1994, the countries have been brought closer to the EU, and a number of additional parallel agreements have been signed. These include agreements on border controls (the Schengen Agreement), and asylum and police cooperation. Norway even puts troops at the disposal of the EU's battle groups (see Chapter 11). Approximately three-fourths of the Norwegian legislation that applies to the member states also applies to Norway. New agreements have been established over time, and existing agreements have been developed and expanded. Their *cumulative effects* are large and still not well enough comprehended. Chapter 5 notes that the volume of agreements, the way in which Norway is affiliated to the EU through the EEA Agreement and the establishment of new EU authorities and agencies to which Norway renounces sovereignty, have obvious implications for national independence and democracy. Norway's relationship to the EU subverts the democratic chain of rule whereby citizens authorise political power through public debate and elections and hold the decision makers to account through a system of rights and the separation of powers: the legislative, judicial and executive branches (a finding that is further corroborated in all the chapters). Norway has ceded sovereignty in a number of areas; it pays (through the EEA financial contributions) and is subject to EU law on the same basis as EU member states. Norway has surrendered sovereignty without having received anything in return in the form of co-determination that EU membership would have granted. In Norway, the slogan 'no taxation without representation' from the American War of Independence does not apply. On the contrary, Norway obeys and pays but remains without representation in the decision-making bodies. The democratic principle of *no legislation without representation* is breached.

In Chapter 6 Halvard Haukeland Fredriksen examined the legal dimension of the EEA Agreement, with particular emphasis on the relationship between national supreme courts (notably the Norwegian), the EFTA Court and the Court of Justice of the European Union (CJEU). He showed that whereas a judicial dialogue has developed between the CJEU and the EFTA Court, 'the reality of the EEA is that the EFTA states have to play by the rules of the internal market as they are interpreted by the "foreign judges" of the CJEU'. The EFTA states have accepted the hegemony of the EU and the CJEU. Fredriksen suggests that this may be accounted for by the greatly increased asymmetry in strength between the two pillars of the EEA Agreement: the EFTA and the EU. That *structural asymmetry* also manifests itself in economic asymmetry and lack of viable alternatives. Thus, he underlines that

> the survival of the EEA Agreement is hardly due to its judicial architecture being so much better than perceived by those predicting its demise more than twenty years ago, but rather to the fact that the remaining EFTA States

have proven to be far more pragmatic than any commentator back in the early 1990's would have expected them to be. In a way, they have grown accustomed to life under the hegemony of the CJEU, a fact which is demonstrated by their adherence to CJEU case-law even outside the reach of the EEA Agreement.

In Chapter 7, Baldur Thorhallsson conducted an in-depth study of the implications of the EEA Agreement for Iceland. He pointed to the many similarities between Iceland and Norway with regard to the effects of the EEA Agreement and Schengen. He noted that

> [t]he cost of full access to the internal market has created a structure of inbuilt democratic deficit within the EEA and Schengen. Furthermore, the dynamic character of the EEA Agreement means in practice that Iceland becomes drawn ever deeper into this inbuilt decision-making structure characterised by the transfer of autonomy from the EFTA/EEA states to the European Union. Hence, the closer the affiliation of Iceland becomes with the EU – within the EEA and Schengen Agreements – the more vulnerable to hegemony the relationship will be. Public debates in Iceland (or, one could say, debates within its political public sphere) have no influence at all on decision makers within the EU.

Iceland thus experiences clear and discernible detrimental constitutional and democratic effects from its current association with the EU. It has however been able to sustain independence in the few areas that are not included in the agreements; the irony is that these sectors are less able to meet the accountability criterion. Thorhallsson also discusses a range of important differences between Iceland and Norway of relevance to the assessment of constitutional-democratic effects. One important difference pertained to *size*. Iceland's small size and limited administrative capacity has meant that Iceland's EU affiliation has in fact strengthened the public administration, limited political patronage in many sectors and led to somewhat closer cooperation between the government and the labour market organisations. At the same time, he also underlined that Iceland's EU association has not challenged the traditional political culture with its penchant for political patronage in those sectors that have not been much affected by Iceland's EU association.

Eirik Holmøyvik in Chapter 8 focused on the implications of Norway's EU association for the Norwegian constitution. The point of departure is that Norway's ever-closer EU integration increasingly requires Norway to transfer sovereignty – formal and substantive – to both EU and EEA bodies. This gives Norway's affiliation with the EU a constitutional dimension. Holmøyvik focused on the requirements and limits that the Norwegian Constitution imposes on transfers of sovereignty. He noted that the Constitution provides a specific decision-making procedure in Art. 115, which requires a three-quarter majority in the Norwegian parliament, the Storting. The problem he pointed to is that Art. 115 and its requirements are very frequently disregarded, so that during the life of the EEA Agreement, in the last 20 years, it has only been applied once: in 1994 in connection with the EEA Agreement. Instead of the high threshold in Art. 115, the Storting has made decisions about transfers of sovereignty in accordance with the general treaty-making rules in Art. 26 (2), which only requires a simple majority. Thus, Holmøyvik identifies a marked gap between on the one hand what the text of the constitution prescribes and how the Storting upholds this in actual practice, on the other. Careful assessment of the legal reasoning of the choice of constitutional procedure shows that the Storting's interpretation of the constitution is far from judicially sound. The Storting's *pragmatic interpretation* reflects Norway's troubled stance on the EU, and a strong-felt political pressure to keep up with the institutional development in the EU. The Norwegian practice on transfers of sovereignty thus illustrates how difficult it is to integrate Norway into the EU under the EEA Agreement whilst at the same time being faithful to the national model of constitutional sovereignty.

In Chapter 9, John Erik Fossum focused on the effects of Norway's affiliation with the EU on the domestic system of democratic governing, paying particular heed to the nature of Norway's representation in the EU. Norway in its relations with the EU has opted to stay out of the EU because it has sought to preserve the traditional conception of state sovereignty, a decision that has not served as an effective defence of autonomy. Norway's relationship to the EU – its privileged partnership – effectively deprives Norway of joint decision power and challenges Norway's ability to set the terms of self-rule. Norway is represented in the EU, but the lack of political representation makes the structure more akin to Burke's notion of *virtual representation*. Here we have to do with voluntary submission and dominance. Norwegian citizens have no access to a set of institutions that provide them with assurance of influence. The assessment of how this form of affiliation shapes Norway's internal workings showed that the affiliation exacerbates a common EU problem of executive dominance (and technocracy), amplified by a particularly weak system of parliamentary scrutiny and control. The upshot has been for the Norwegian political system to be structurally speaking stacked in favour of *output legitimation*. That in turn leaves political parties in a difficult situation of balancing responsibility and responsiveness in a context of strong international constraints, with great scope for populist politics.

Morten Egeberg and Jarle Trondal in Chapter 10 examined the implications of Norway's EU association for national administrative sovereignty. They note that whereas the EU is a supranational entity, member states implement EU law, and a widely accepted precept has been that member states should enjoy a measure of administrative sovereignty. Egeberg and Trondal argue that this notion of administrative sovereignty is under considerable pressure and that the same also applies to the Norwegian administration. That in practice under the EEA Agreement does not appear to be essentially different from the manner in which the member states' administrations function in the implementation phase. This manifests itself in the manner in which the European Commission, often aided by EU agencies, involves itself directly in the manner in which EU legislation is applied. That takes place through close cooperation with national agencies (directorates and supervisory authorities), and generally without incorporating national ministries to any large extent. Whereas the EU's executive branch has no agencies at the national level, it does nevertheless appear to have established strong ties to already relatively independent national agencies. The latter thus adopt a *two-hatted* role in the sense of being linked-in to their own ministry on the one hand and to the European Commission and the EU agencies on the other. The upshot is for national agencies to become part of two administrations: that of the member state on the one hand and that of a general EU administration on the other. This development also subverts the democratic lines of authorisation and accountability.

In Chapter 11, Helene Sjursen assessed the principled implications of Norway's relations with the Union in the domain of foreign, security and defence policy, with reference to the two democratic principles of autonomy and accountability. Even though a majority of Norwegian citizens voted no to EU membership on two occasions, Norway is closely affiliated to the EU in the domain of foreign and security policy – in fact, it is even member of one of the EU's battle groups. Is this problematic from a democratic perspective, and if so why? She found that while it is common practice to leave the foreign policy-making in the hands of the executive, the tendency of the legislature to take a *hands-off approach* is even stronger on the particular issue of relations with the EU. While it is difficult to find principled reasons that may justify this abdication on the part of the parliament, it is perfectly possible to understand why it has happened.

## Brexit and a new category of ex-member state

The third part of the book is devoted to broader reflections on the implications of non-membership and starts with a chapter by Chris Lord (Chapter 12), which discusses the question of a possible British exit (Brexit) from the EU. That would be a movement in the opposite direction of the general patterns exhibited in Parts I and II and would in effect create an entirely new category of 'ex-member state', an entirely unprecedented situation that would present significant challenges for the UK and the EU alike. Lord underlines that there has been a remarkable *historical continuity* in the UK's relationship to the EU which dates back to the early 1950s. That continuity is marked by attempts to deal with a *quadrilemma* made up of issues of sovereignty, international power, political economy and deep domestic divisions. It is against the continued efforts of seeking to address these issues that we need to consider the present debate. That also marks the manner in which the UK debates possible non-membership models – in particular the Norwegian and Swiss examples. The important difference Lord identifies between the present and past UK debates is that the present is more prone to dismiss any possibility of reconciling the various portions under the quadrilemma. The UK debate is instructive in terms of how it relates to the various forms of non-membership association that have been discussed here; it is also instructive for the added insights it provides in terms of the questions the British have discussed over time.

## Independency under hegemony

The book's main finding is that the states – whether affiliated through sectoral bilateral agreements such as Switzerland or multilateral dynamic agreements such as Iceland and Norway – are increasingly closely associated to a constantly changing and integrating entity over which they have no formal say. They relinquish sovereignty and this is not recompensed through co-determination. In the following, we argue that this entails that the EU's closely associated non-members exist under a form of *self-inflicted hegemony*. The interesting point is that this problem becomes more manifest the closer, more formalised, the association is.

A hegemon wields power over other subordinate states. It dominates by interfering in zones of autonomy and by limiting the subordinates' sovereignty. There is a profound irony in applying this notion to the EU: after all, the integration process was initiated to abolish political rivalry and hegemony in Europe by granting the states equal membership in the fledgling European political order. This book has analysed the effects on *the sovereign democrats*. The EU autocratically rules these associated states neither by intentional obstruction nor by deception or manipulation. As was discussed in Chapter 5, this is *hegemony by default*, viz., by rejecting EU membership they have become subjected to hegemonic dominance. These states have unintentionally turned the EU into a hegemon vis-à-vis themselves. Hegemony is the effect of the manner in which some countries have chosen as close as possible an affiliation without formal membership. Hegemony then pertains to how the affairs with the associated non-members are organised and to the internal implications on the associated states. If then the EU is not in itself structured as a hegemon in relation to its member states, in what sense more specifically is the relationship with the associated states who remain free to abolish their relations a matter of hegemony?

First is that the relationship they have with the EU is a highly lopsided or *asymmetrical power* relationship, where one side is far more dependent on the other than the reverse. This is reflected in enormous differences in size, in population, in patterns of trade, in military prowess and so forth. It is an asymmetric power relationship that breaches the requirements of a fair bargaining process. The *sovereign democrats* have rejected membership but cannot back their claims by credible threats, whereas the EU can unilaterally destroy or disband the entire arrangement with limited perceptible costs. The associated countries are therefore faced with a take-it-or-leave-it option. Dominance occurs because there is no parity of power to render the use of threats or counter-measures credible under international law, nor are there possibilities for participation in systems of joint decision-making to wield influence or to demand justifications under EU law. Dominance occurs when the citizens are subject to others' will, to alien control. There is no assurance that the current representative order tracks the interests, views or wills of the citizens of the non-members (see Chapter 5).

Second, is that hegemony is also in a deeper sense *institutionalised*. One aspect is that the EU reconfigures state sovereignty in terms of placing a stronger accent on *co-determination*. Because that clearly also includes constitutional questions, then lack of access to these bodies, notably the European Council, also entails lack of influence on the processes that determine the associated state's scope and terms of self-determination (Chapter 9). The structure of the association is such that the closer the association, the more the EU determines the conditions for democratic self-rule in the associated non-member stats. Furthermore, given that the CJEU does not understand the EEA countries – in contrast to the member states – as 'sources of EU law' (Chapter 6), the former do not figure, whereas the latter play a central role in the multilevel EU constitutional structure. The irony is that for the associated countries it is the EU's legal structure that increasingly takes on constitutional shape, whereas for the member states the EU constitution is a composite multilevel arrangement where the member states' constitutions play a central role.

Third, the EEA and the Schengen agreements are formally speaking *dynamic arrangements*. They are continually developed and expanded in ways that change the internal workings of the states, without the recipient states being able to wield influence. Even the Swiss relationship is far more dynamic in practice than its formal bilateral arrangements would suggest. Dynamism plays a particular role in the EU context for two reasons. One is because the EU is still a system under construction and has over the last two decades become far more deeply involved in the activities of the member states. The other is that the EU has also undergone a number of so-called enlargements, which in fact amount to instances of *re-constitutionalisation*. Non-members to a much higher degree than members experience such instances as 'shocks' that they for want of access to the EU are far less prepared to handle. These factors add a great measure of uncertainty to the dynamism: the ability to foresee or predict is very low and that is a distinctive problem facing non-members. From the point of view of the associated members barred as they are from co-determining, Enlargements increase asymmetry and arbitrariness.

Fourth, there is a problem of *uncertainty*. That, as noted, is related to dynamism and lack of access; it is also amplified by the nature of the relation. Consider the important Swiss notion of 'autonomer Nachvollzug' (Chapter 3). Consider also how the Norwegian Supreme Court in the rulings Nye Kystlink and Bottolvs (see Chapter 6) voluntarily adapts to EU law, even in issue-areas that are not regulated by the EEA Agreement. This self-initiated and unilateral form of adaptation illustrates the dilemmas facing the legal systems of non-members that are nevertheless subject to *and by dint of association seek to subject themselves to* many of the EU's norms and rules. One aspect is functional asymmetry: associated states' EU agreements never cover the same functional reach as does the EU. That yields different dynamics of rule adoption. In the EU the norms and rules are tied together by strong norms not only of homogeneity but also of contiguity – which spill over on the institutions in the associated states that therefore seek to 'fill the gaps', thus implicitly adopting the same logic or even explicit provisions. All states have agreements with such 'gaps' that institutions seek to fill. A case in point is the Schengen Agreement: for the associated states this is a static, functionally delimited agreement,[1] whereas for the EU it is not. Much of the substance of the initial Schengen Agreement has been transferred to the Community system and is subject to the ordinary legislative procedure. The associated states must therefore involve themselves in an ongoing process to figure out what is Schengen-relevant and what is not in the EU's legislation. That adds a significant measure of uncertainty for the associated states.

The associated states legally commit themselves to incorporate most of the EU's rules and regulations with no possibility of influence or co-determination. This is a case of relinquishment of de facto sovereignty on a grand scale. This situation has often been defended with reference to the fact that the agreement is an international contract that can be terminated. However, the *cost of exit* is high because there is a very high degree of connectivity. The general feeling is that uncertainty is greater without an agreement. The EU reaches into almost all policy fields of the member states and these horizontal dynamics are also important both in the Nordic region and for Switzerland. The EEA arrangement is therefore not merely an international contract regulating a specific area of common interest and there is strong public support for close forms of association with the EU.

The upshot is a very awkward notion of *hegemony by default*. It is initiated by an act of responsibility and *Staatsraison* at the cost of democratic *responsiveness*, clearly in breach with the fundamental democratic norms that the associated states are constitutionally committed to.

Dominance is the case when power-wielding institutions are not authorised or controlled by the subjected parties. It is a kind of injustice that people experience when they are in the power of others, a form of suppression that can in principle be eliminated by those who have installed it or by a political act of those subjected. The associated members can reduce the problem of dominance either by terminating the comprehensive agreements with the EU or by becoming EU members. That would establish a situation of parity, viz., a situation in which one is not controlled in an alien way by others and where one has the obtained the status of an autonomous subject – a co-legislator.

Democratic forms of rule are antithetical to dominance, because they put the citizens on an equal footing and assign the citizens the rights to enforce their will, against the will of the power holders also. Greater interconnectedness and interdependence are not only affecting the sovereignty and autonomy of the states but also the citizens and their ability to govern themselves through institutions they can control. There is a growing need for legitimate decision-making not only within the states but also between them. The normative meaning of democracy does not stop at the borders. When larger orders are needed to deter dominance there is a need to expand the political community and to make it capable of acting. That is to establish the power, resources and competence necessary to protect the freedom and integrity of the political community. Hence, *hierarchy is needed* beyond the nation-state as well. We should therefore dissociate dominance from hierarchy and the presence of power structures. Hierarchies become systems of domination only when those affected are excluded from participating in decisions (decisional exclusion); when they experience the rule or the system as unjust; and when they are subject to forms of rule that are arbitrary, in-transparent and generally inattentive to democracy and legitimacy. As we have shown it is therefore not hierarchy as such that matters for hegemony; it is the manner in which asymmetry carried by hierarchy is at the same time associated with uncertainty, unpredictability, and lack of transparency – that engender hegemony.

What is peculiar with the form of dominance that the associated non-members experience is that it is both structural and at the same time voluntary. It does not involve direct intervention and autocratic submission; it is an arrangement that accidentally inhibits and intimidates the parties. The externalities caused by interdependence and the collective action problems that need to be handled through concerted action are skewed by the European political order in favour of the members. By being excluded from co-decision-making procedures, the citizens of the associated states understand themselves as *second-rate Europeans*.

Precisely the question of second-rate status takes on added importance at a time of crisis-induced transformation in Europe. The crisis leads to more uncertainty and unpredictability; thus increased dominance. How the EU over time grapples with the fallout of the crisis will therefore be fundamentally important also for the associated states.

## Note

1 Bøckman-Finstad, F. (2014) 'Norges tilknytning til EUs justis- og innenrikspolitikk' in E.O. Eriksen and J.E. Fossum (eds) *Det norske paradoks – Om Norges forhold til Den europeiske union*, Oslo: Universitetsforlaget.

# INDEX

accountability, defined 9, 63, 230
Acheson, Dean 216, 218
agencification 141–2
Agency for Air Transport Security 43
Andenæs, J. 190
Andorra 18, 25
Armenia 27
associated non-membership, defined 2
asymmetry and dominance 1–14; dangers of hegemonic dominance 3; democratic constitutionalism 4–10; EEA Agreements 10–11; non-member states, categories of 2; sectorial bilateralism in Switzerland 11–12
Attali, Jacques 213
Austria 17, 61, 84
autonomy, defined 9, 230

banking secrecy laws 60–2, 68, 71*n*12
Belarus 27
Belgium 61
Bevin, Ernest 216, 217
Blair, Tony 213
Blocher, Christoph 64–5, 69
Blockmans, Steven 27–8
Bodin, Jean 82
Body of European Regulators for Electronic Communications 143
Bootle, Roger 215
Brexit *see* United Kingdom and EU
Bulgaria 58

Bullock, Alan 218
Burke, Edmund 156–7

Cameron, David 211, 215, 222
Canada 132
Centre for European Reform (CER) 224, 227
CEPOL (European Police College) 43
Churchill, Winston 217, 218
Common Foreign and Security Policy (CFSP) 200, 213, 226; *see also* Norway and EU Common Foreign and Security Policy (CFSP)y
constitution, use of term 6, 81–2
constitutional democracy 4–10
cosmopolitanisation of nation states, defined 77, 93–6
*Costa v. ENEL* (CJEU) 89
Council of Europe 5
Council of the European Union 21, 22, 23–4, 30, 43–4, 89, 95, 96, 225
Court of Justice of the European Union (CJEU) 22, 24–5, 26, 227; jurisdiction of 41, 47–8, 88–9, 142; Opinion 1/91 29, 103, 114; Opinion 1/92 104; *see also* EEA and CJEU case law
Cremona, Marise 29
*Critique of Practical Reason* (Kant) 83

deep and comprehensive free trade areas (DCFTAs) 26–7
deep integration, defined 18–19

De Gaulle, Charles 226
*de jure* sovereignty *see* sovereignty
Delors, Jacques 17, 18, 38
democracy: and accountability 84, 230; defined 6; requirements of 9–10, 96
democratic autonomy, defined 84
democratic corporatism (Katzenstein) 125
denationalisation 79, 96, 97*n*6
Denmark 126, 132, 165, 191
dominance, defined 3, 83, 241–2
domination, sources of (Pettit) 59
Dublin agreements 23, 39, 40, 41, 43, 57

Eden, Anthony 218
EEA and CJEU case law 102–17; CJEU common rules for internal market 112–14, 116*n*36; debates over Switzerland/UK accession to EFTA 114; EFTA Court approach 106–9; EFTA state national court approach 109–12; independence vs. homogeneity 104–5; origins of judicial structure 102–4; summary conclusion 114–15, 235–6, 240
Energy Community Treaty 27–8
Eriksen Søreide, Ine Marie 158
Estonia 198
Eurasian Economic Union 27
Eurocontrol 44
Eurojust 23, 43
European Agency for the Cooperation of Energy Regulators 44–5, 143
European Aviation Safety Agency (EASA) 44, 98*n*12, 142, 145, 146
European Banking Authority (EBA) 145, 147
European Coal and Steel Community (ECSC) 216, 217, 218, 219
European Commission (EC) 89; on EEA Agreement 22; enforcement powers of 142; and ENP 20–1, 26–7; on EU-EFTA relations 29; growth in 176–8, *177*; Neighbourhood Economic Community (NEC), proposed 27, 28–9; proposes autonomic information exchange 61; rejects Swiss surveillance counterproposals 46–8; on small-sized states 26; and Turkey 24
European Common Aviation Area 28
European Community (EC) 17–18
European Convention on Human Rights (ECHR) 60, 69, 93
European Council 161, 201
European Court of Human Rights (ECtHR) 60, 93, 113

European Defence Agency (EDA) 23, 193–4, 196, 200, 201
European Economic Area (EEA): establishment of 20–1; Joint Committee 21, 22, 24, 40; Parliamentary Committee 155; potential members 21; as regulation without representation 224; as two-pillar model 29–30; *see also* EEA and CJEU case law
European Economic Area (EEA) Act of 1992 89
European Economic Area (EEA) Agreement 2, 10–11; Article 1 85; Article 2 89–90; Article 31 90; Article 102 224; comparison to Swiss sectorial bilateralism 11; establishment of 17; members of 10–11, 12; as treaty *sui generis* 90; as two-pillar model 21–3; *see also individual member states*
European Environmental Agency 43, 44
European External Action Service (EEAS) 26, 41–2, 43, 46–8
European Free Trade Association (EFTA) 10, 17, 23; Court 21, 22, 24–5, 90, 140, 141, 142, 154; Surveillance Authority 21, 24, 85–6, 123, 128, 140, 141, 142, 154, 155; *see also* EEA and CJEU case law
European Insurance and Occupational Pensions Authority (EIOPA) 145, 147
European Neighbourhood Policy (ENP) 18; Eastern Partnership 21, 27; and EC more for more approach 28–9; Euro-Mediterranean Association Agreements 26; Partnership and Cooperation Agreements 26; static hub-and-spoke model 20–1, 26–7, 30
European Organisation for the Safety of Air Navigation 147
European Parliament (EP) 21, 22, 58, 89, 95, 226
European Regulators Group for Electricity and Gas 44–5
European Securities and Markets Authority (ESMA) 145, 147
European Union (EU): Age Discrimination Directive (1000/78/EC) 111; agencification 141–2; Customs Union 227; Directive on employees' rights in transfers of undertakings (77/187/EEC) 109–10; growth of EU agencies 178–9, *179*; as international organisation 1–2; legislative direct effect on members 87; membership in 1; Posted Workers Directive (96/71/EC) 110, 111; Product Liability Directive (85/374/EEC) 110;

status contracts 88; Trademark Directive (89/104/EEC) 107, 110; Trade Policy Committee 25; *see also individual agencies; individual member/non-member states*
Europol 23, 43
Eurozone crisis 9, 12–13, 160, 214, 227

Fabbrini, Sergio 214
Fagerlund Knudsen, Olav 193
Finland 17, 84, 132, 165, 198
Fjellner, Christofer 158
Fleischer, Carl August 143–4, 145
France 219, 220, 221
Franck, Thomas M. 19
free trade agreements (FTAs) 27; *see also* United Kingdom and EU
Frontex 43

Georgia 26
Germany 126, 200
globalisation: cosmopolitanisation of nation states 77, 93–6; world economy 79
Grolimund, Nina 11–12, 42
G20 61
guillotine clause 39, 48

Halvorsen, Kristin 202
Heath, Edward 220, 221–2
hegemony by association 230–42; Brexit and ex-member status 238; differentiated integration and democratic self-rule 230–2; forms of association 232–3; independence under hegemony 239–42; sovereign democrats 232, 233–8; *see also* asymmetry and dominance
Howe, Geoffrey 220

Iceland: as associated non-member 2, 5; and EFTA 10–11; European Common Aviation Area 28; Foreign Service 127; political party viewpoints 132
Iceland and EEA Agreement 21, 22, 87, 118–34; administrative capacity 127–9; and the Athingi (parliament) 120–2; challenges to political patronage 129–31; constitutional implications 119–24; historical background 118–19; legacy of US hegemony 131–3; passive integration 122–4; political party viewpoints 119; as small state 124–7; summary conclusion 133–4, 235, 236; Working Group on Ethics 128–9
input congruence 79
input legitimacy 19
Institute of Directors 215

International Criminal Court (ICC) 93
International Monetary Fund (IMF) 126
international organisation, defined 1
Italy 83

Jackson, Robert 79
Jagland, Thorbjørn 192, 198
Joint Aviation Authorities 44
Jónsdóttir, Jóhanna 224
Justice and Home Affairs (JHA) 43, 86, 213–14

Kant, Immanuel 6, 80–1, 83
Katzenstein, P. 125, 126
Kazakhstan 27
Kissinger, Henry 221
Krohn Devold, Kristin 197
Kux, Stephan 31

Lawrence, Robert Z. 18
Lazowski, Adam 29–30
legitimacy, defined 19
Libya 197
Liechtenstein: as associated non-member 2, 5; and EEA Agreement 21, 22, 87, 124; and EFTA 10
Lisbon Treaty (2007) 22, 200
*L'Oréal* case (EFTA) 106, 107–8, 109, 115n15
Luxembourg 61

Maastricht Treaty 199
Madrid Forum 44
*Maglite* case (EFTA) 107
Mair, Peter 166
Major, John 213
Mansbridge, J. 158
Maurer, Ulrich 65
Menon, Anand 19
Milward, Alan 219
minimal impact doctrine *see* Norway's Constitution, and EEA Agreement
Mitterrand, François 213
Moldova 26, 28
Monaco 25
Morrison, Herbert 219
multinational corporations *see* tax havens

national administrative sovereignty 173–86; in administrative policy 183–4; capacity building in EU's executive 176–9; growth in European Commission 176–8, 177; growth of EU agencies 178–9, 179; multilevel administration 174–6; national agencies with independence from

ministries 179–80; Norway, pressures of 180–3, *181–2*; summary conclusion 184–6, 237–8
Neighbourhood Economic Community (NEC), proposed 27, 28, 29–30
neighbourhood models 17–33; challenges of 28–30; customs union model 18, 24–5; and economic integration 18–19, 20–1; EEA as two-pillar model 21–3; Energy Community Treaty as sectoral multilateralism 27–8; ENP as static hub-and-spoke model 26–7; and internal market 17–20; sectoral bilateralism 17–18, 23–4; static absorption model 25–6; summary conclusion 30–2, 233
Netherlands 216
New Public Management (NPM) 175–6
*no demos* thesis 7
Nordic Battle Group 198–9
Nordic Council 126
North American Free Trade Association (NAFTA) 215
North Atlantic Treaty Organization (NATO) 91, 126, 131–2, 196, 200–1, 204, 207n25
Norway 12–13; as associated non-member 2, 5, 17; and CJEU case law 109–10; and EFTA 10–11; European Common Aviation Area 28; Ministry of Foreign Affairs 77; political party viewpoints 170n18, 197, 198–9, 202; relations with Iceland 132; Supreme Court decisions 109–12; *see also* national administrative sovereignty
Norway and EU Common Foreign and Security Policy (CFSP) 77, 189–207; Article 25 (Constitution) 190; Article 26 (Constitution) 190, 191, 194–7, 199; autonomy and accountability in Norwegian policy 190–3; continuance of alliance policy 200–2, 207n25; Enlarged Committee on Foreign Affairs and Defence (DUUFK) 191–3, 197, 198; impact on state sovereignty 198–9; listing of agreements *194*; paradoxes in foreign policy 203–4; Parliament Committee on Foreign Affairs and Defence 191, 192–3; participation level 193–5; political importance of legal agreements 195–7; prioritising action capacity 199, 202–3; role of consensus 202–3; summary conclusion 204–5, 238
Norway and representation in EU 153–71; Article 76 (Constitution) 154; executive dominance 163–4; Foreign Ministry white paper on 164; *Outside and Inside: Norway's Agreements with the European Union* (EEA) 156; parliamentary oversight 165, 170n17; political parties and elections 166–8, 170n18; representation and presence in EU 154–9; sovereignty and constitutional implications 159–62, 170n9, 170nn12–13; summary conclusion 168–9, 237, 239–40; as surrogate representation 157–9; as virtual representation 156–7
Norway's Constitution, and EEA Agreement 21–2, 77, 137–50, 155; Agreement, Article 2 89–90; Agreement, Article 102 139; Article 26 (Constitution) 137–48; Article 49 (Constitution) 139; Article 75 (Constitution) 139; Article 88 (Constitution) 139; Article 115 (Constitution) 98n13, 137–48, 149n18; Article 121 (Constitution) 140; constitutional impacts 146–8; and court rulings 93; current practice in transfers of sovereignty 140–6, 149n19; *The EEA Agreement and Norway's Other Agreements with the EU* (Legislative Department) 144; formal/substantive transfers of sovereignty 138–40; history of 84–7; incorporation of EU law into national legislation 87–9; legal supremacy of EEA law 89–91, 94–6; and promise of sovereignty 137–8; reservation right 90–1, 139; Standing Committee on Foreign Affairs 144; summary conclusion 235, 236–7
Norway's democracy, EU affiliation impact on 77–99; citizens' self-rule 78–80; greater system effectiveness 84–7; hegemony by default 89–91, 239, 241; homogeneity and dynamics 87–8; indigent contract 88–9; juridical supranationalism 93–4; law and democracy 80–2; right to co-determination 94–6; rule without justification 91–2; state vs. popular sovereignty 80–4; summary conclusion 96–7, 235

O'Neill, Con 221
Organisation for Economic Co-operation and Development (OECD) 60, 61
O'Sullivan, David 47
output congruence 79–80
output legitimacy 19

*Outside and Inside: Norway's Agreements with the European Union* (EEA) 156

patronage *see* Iceland and EEA Agreement
Petersen, Jan 192, 198–9
Pettit, Philip 59, 71*n*8
Pompidou, Georges 220, 221
pooling of sovereignty concept 8–9, 160, 163–4
popular sovereignty *see* sovereignty
*Prigge* case (CJEU) 111
Prodi, Romano 18, 20

Rehfeld, Andrew 71*n*14
'A Republican Law of Peoples' (Pettit) 59
reservation right 90–1, 139
*Restamark* case (EFTA) 106
*Reversion* case (EFTA) 106
Rippon, Geoffrey 220
Romania 58
Rossier, Yves 47
Rousseau 6, 58
Russia 27, 204

Saglie, Jo 167
*Sánchez* case (CJEU) 110
San Marino 18, 25–6
Schengen Agreement 11, 12–13, 23; as dynamic arrangement 240–1; and Iceland 118–19, 120, 122, 130; and Norway 77, 86, 87, 154, 155, 162; and Switzerland 39, 40, 41, 43, 44, 57
Schuman, Robert 216
*Sebago* case (EFTA) 107
Serbia 21
shared sovereignty 95
Shonfield, Andrew 227–8
*Silhouette* case (EFTA) 107
Singapore 60
Single European Act (1986) 37–8
Sjaastad, A.C. 199
small states and EU 124–6; *see also individual states*
Solana, Javier 200
South Eastern Europe 28
sovereignty: defined 78–9, 97*nn*4–5; *de jure* 49, 79, 84, 86, 112, 224; external 82; formal 138–40, 160, 236–7; internal 161; loss of 77; pooling of sovereignty concept 8–9, 160, 163–4; popular sovereignty 5, 52, 60, 80–4, 92, 189, 203–4, 234; shared sovereignty 95; sovereign statehood 22; state sovereignty 4, 5, 13, 37, 80–4, 94, 96, 154, 159–63, 169, 174, 189–90, 198–9, 204, 230, 232, 237, 239–40; substantive 138–40, 161, 236–7; *see also* national administrative sovereignty; *individual states*
spillover theory 217–18
state sovereignty *see* sovereignty; *individual states*
surrogate representation, defined 157–8
Sverdrup, Ulf 30, 31
Sweden 17, 84, 126, 132, 165, 198, 201
Switzerland 36–72; as associated non-member 5, 17; *autonomer Nachvollzug* doctrine 11, 40; Bundesrat and political accountability in 64–6, 71*n*14; deliberative accountability within popular democracy 66–9; and EEA 21, 56; and EFTA 56; Federal Council 23–4, 38, 39, 40, 46; Federal Department of Justice 44; Federal Office for the Environment 44; Free Movement of Persons 38; FTA with EC (1972) 17–18, 23, 37; and future of pragmatic bilateralism 45–8; legal scope of bilateralism with EU 38–41; and model of democracy 53–5; neo-republican theory of democracy 58–9; organisational scope of bilateralism with EU 41–3; origins of bilateralism with EU 37–8; political accountability between republicanism and regional integration 63; political design vs. bottom-up functionalism 37, 43–5; political party viewpoints 47–8, 64–5, 69; political republicanism and economic liberalism 55–8; restrictions on immigrants in 48, 68; sectoral bilateralism 2, 11–12, 23–4, 214–15, 224–5; selective stance toward domination 59–63; as signatory of ECHR 60, 69; summary conclusion 48–9, 70, 233–4; surveillance counterproposals 46–7; UN membership of 60
Syria 226

Tamnes, Rolf 197
tax havens 60–2, 68
three circles doctrine (Churchill) 218, 221
Tovias, Alfred 11
Transport Community Treaty 28
Treaty of Rome (1957) 217
Treaty of the European Union (TEU) 7–8, 25, 213, 214
Turkey 18, 21, 24–5

Ukraine 26, 28, 204
United Kingdom and EU 13, 132, 200, 211–28; during 1950–1952 216–19;

differentiated integration option 214–15, 219–23; and domestic politics 219, 222–3, 226–7; EC autonomic information exchange 61; and EEA 21; full participation option 213; and international power 218–19, 221, 225–6; non-member option 215–16, 223–7; partial membership option 213–14; and political economy 219, 222, 226; Schuman Plan 216–19; and sovereignty 217–18, 220, 223–5; summary conclusion 227–8, 238
United Nations (UN) 60, 79, 93
United States (US): and Churchill's three circles doctrine 218–19, 221; pressures Switzerland on bank secrecy 61; relations with Iceland 131–3; relations with Norway 200
Urbinati, Nadia 163

Vahl, Marius 11–12, 42
Van Vooren, Bart 27–8
Vital, David 126

Weatherill, Stephen 19
Western European Union (WEU) 193, 195–7
West Germany, former 219, 221
World Trade Organization 26–7, 93, 216, 225

Young, John 223

CPSIA information can be obtained
at www.ICGtesting.com
Printed in the USA
JSHW011319201219
3107JS00002B/27